ACPL ITEM
DISCARDED

D1604240

DO NOT REMOVE
CARDS FROM POCKET

*This work is dedicated
to the men and women who,
for the past three and a half centuries,
have informed and enlightened
the American people in peace and in war
through all forms of communication;
especially to those of the late twentieth century
whom we have enjoyed reading,
listening to, and watching
while they covered a world
in turmoil and in growth.*

JOURNALISTS OF THE UNITED STATES

Biographical Sketches of
Print and Broadcast News Shapers
from the Late 17th Century
to the Present

by

Robert B. Downs *and* Jane B. Downs

McFarland & Company, Inc., Publishers
Jefferson, North Carolina, and London

British Library Cataloguing-in-Publication data are available

Library of Congress Cataloguing-in-Publication Data

Downs, Robert Bingham, 1903–
    Journalists of the United States : biographical sketches of print
and broadcast news shapers from the late 17th century to the present
/ by Robert B. Downs and Jane B. Downs.
      p. cm.
    Includes bibliographical references and index.
    ISBN 0-89950-549-X (lib. bdg. : 50# alk. paper) ∞
    1. Journalists—United States—Biography. I. Downs, Jane B.
II. Title.
PN4871.D68 1991
070′.92′273—dc20
[B]   91-52634
                                             CIP

Manufactured in the United States of America

McFarland & Company, Inc., Publishers
  Box 611, Jefferson, North Carolina 28640

TABLE OF CONTENTS

ACKNOWLEDGMENTS

Expressions of appreciation are due William David Downs, Jr., and John T. Flanagan for suggestions for journalists to include; to John T. Flanagan for permission to republish biographies by him of William Randolph Hearst, William Allen White, and Walt Whitman; to Julia Allen, Rebecca Van Meter, and Kim Trumbull, for typing the manuscript; to Pat Stenstrom for her kind help with research; to Eleanor Blum for her critical review of the manuscript; to Teresa Lynne Smith for general encouragement and help.

Especial appreciation is offered Clara Downs Keller for her excellent Index.

INTRODUCTION

This present reference work is not intended to serve also as a general history of American journalism. That purpose is adequately served by such standard works as Frank Luther Mott's *American Journalism: A History; 1690–1960;* James Melvin Lee's *History of American Journalism;* George Henry Payne's *History of Journalism in the United States;* and Robert A. Rutland's *Newsmongers: Journalism in the Life of the Nation, 1690–1972.* The purpose of this volume is to gather in a convenient alphabetical format the hundreds of men and women who have shaped the news world in America from the late seventeenth century to the present, and to bring out something of their personalities. In short, the concern is biographical.

Obviously, certain names stand out in the course of these centuries: James Gordon Bennett, William Lloyd Garrison, Horace Greeley, William Randolph Hearst, Henry Luce, Samuel McClure, Robert McCormick, Benjamin Franklin, Joseph Pulitzer, Edward Murrow. But there are many lesser-known figures who have contributed in important measure to informing the public of unfolding events.

While this volume is not a comprehensive history there are certain aspects of journalism's past which will be briefly considered. Biographical sketches of newsmakers of all periods will then be presented.

CENSORSHIP

Official censorship has been a fact of life in the newspaper world from the outset. The first American newspaper was attempted in 1690 by Benjamin Harris, who issued, in Boston, *Publick Occurrences Both Foreign and Domestick.* It was summarily suppressed after only one number and the governor and council declared that no publication could be issued without a license. The passages in Harris's paper to which particular objections were taken dealt with gossip about the immoralities of the French king and the French and Indian War.

1

Fourteen years passed before the next venture in newspaper publishing. John Campbell, Boston postmaster, founded the *Boston Newsletter* in 1704. It was the first continuously published American newspaper.

The printing press was generally recognized as a dangerous force by the early colonial authorities. Their attitude was expressed in a famous statement by Sir William Berkeley, governor of Virginia for thirty-eight years. He wrote to his home government in 1671: "But I thank God, we have *no free schools nor printing;* and I hope we shall not have these for the next hundred years. For *learning* has brought disobedience and heresy sects into the world; and *printing* has divulged them and libels against the government. God keep us from both!"

Freedom of expression was not especially cherished in colonial American society. The most severe suppression of expression came not from royal judges or governors appointed by the Crown, but from the popularly elected assemblies. During the eighteenth century especially, the law of seditious libel was enforced in America chiefly by the provincial legislatures. The assemblies considered themselves immune from criticism and issued warrants of arrest for, interrogated, fined, and imprisoned those accused of libeling its members, or the body as a whole, by written, spoken, or printed words.

A more celebrated event than the Harris case was the trial of John Peter Zenger, that contributed greatly to establishing the principle of a free press in British North America. Zenger's newpaper, the *New York Weekly Journal,* had printed satirical ballads, reflecting on William Cosby, the highly unpopular governor, and his council. The charge against Zenger and his paper was that the issues discussed "tended to raise seditions and tumults among the people of this province, and to fill their minds with contempt for his majesty's government." At Zenger's trial in 1735, the defense was conducted by Andrew Hamilton, a Quaker lawyer from Philadelphia who was also speaker of the Pennsylvania Assembly. The court was packed against Zenger, but he was acquitted after Hamilton convinced the jury that it should judge on the basis of the law and the facts.

A major challenge to freedom of speech and the press occurred in 1798, when Congress enacted a series of alien and sedition laws. One law, for example, made it a crime to publish any "false, scandalous, and malicious" writing against the government, Congress, or President. These laws were a prime issue in the 1800 presidential campaign. When Jefferson became president, he pardoned all those who had been convicted under the 1798 laws. The Alien and Sedition Act expired in 1801.

The slavery controversy prior to the Civil War often led to violent attacks on newspapers and attempts to silence unpopular views. A celebrated case was the murder of Elijah Lovejoy, who in 1833 established a religious weekly, the *Observer,* with antislavery sentiments. His press was moved across the river to Alton, Illinois, for protection from mobs in Lovejoy's crusade against the slave system. His press was destroyed and thrown into the river by mobs, three times in one year. When a fourth press was being set up, a pitched battle took place, during which Lovejoy was shot and killed, thereby becoming one of the martyrs of the antislavery cause.

At its first session, Congress adopted a Bill of Rights. The First Amendment states that "Congress shall make no law . . . abridging the freedom of speech, or of the press." A number of blatant attacks on the principles contained in the First Amendment have occurred in this century. Raids were conducted under the direction of Woodrow Wilson's attorney general in 1920; several thousand alien workers were jailed by FBI agents looking for Communists to deport. Another instance was "McCarthyism" in the early 1950s, which led to the burning of books accused of being communist propaganda and the closing of a number of U.S. information libraries abroad.

The various wars in which the United States has engaged have brought censorship problems: the War of 1812, the Civil War, the Spanish-American War, the two World Wars, and the Korean War. Despite handicaps imposed by the military and governments, however, the media were generally able to reveal and publish essential information. By different agreements, a *modus vivendi* was generally arranged to protect military secrets without suppressing the news or its purveyors.

MUCKRAKING

The term "muckraking" was coined by Theodore Roosevelt. The term came from the man with the muck-rake in *Pilgrim's Progress,* who would not look up from the filth on the floor even when a celestial crown was offered to him.

During the decade from 1902 to 1912 a number of reform crusades were begun by several weekly and monthly magazines. The leaders were *Collier's, Cosmopolitan, McClure's, Everybody's,* and the *Arena.* Among the most famous articles were Ida M. Tarbell's "History of the Standard Oil Company," Lincoln Steffens's "Shame of the Cities," David Graham Phillips's "Treason of the Senate," Thomas W. Lamson's "Frenzied Finance," and Samuel Hopkins Adams's "Great American Fraud." Most celebrated of all was Upton Sinclair's book *The Jungle* (1906), which exposed unsanitary conditions in the Chicago stockyards.

The muckrakers charged that wholesale corruption permeated the nation's life, and their stories were documented with accounts of stolen franchises, payroll padding, fraudulent contracts, alliances of police with vice, foul slum dwellings, poverty in the cities, worthless stock schemes, dishonest insurance companies, and thieving monopolies.

The writings of the muckrakers, baring social, economic, and political evils, aroused public indignation and led to important reform legislation, such as the Food and Drug Act in 1906 and the Federal Reserve Act in 1913.

An early contribution to the muckraking movement was an article on political corruption by Mark Sullivan entitled "The Ills of Pennsylvania." It appeared (anonymously) in the October 1901 *Atlantic Monthly*. The article attracted the attention of Edward Bok, editor of the *Ladies' Home Journal,* who invited Sullivan to investigate patent medicines for his magazine. Samuel Hopkins Adams also crusaded against patent medicines and medical quackery in the early 1900s and influenced the enactment of the Food and Drug Act, using *Collier's* and *McClure's Magazine* as forums.

A spectacular success was achieved by *McClure's Magazine* in a series of muckraking articles, starting with the January 1903 issue, which presented contributions by three of the principal muckrakers: Lincoln Steffens's sensational article "The Shame of Minneapolis," an installment of Ida Tarbell's history of the Standard Oil Company, and Ray Stannard Baker's "Right to Work." Having discovered this rich vein, McClure continued to mine it. Issue after issue of the magazine exposed scandals. Other periodicals followed its lead. Over the next several years the reading public learned about corruption in local, state, and national governments, industrial management, race relations, railroads, insurance, patent medicines, liquor and white slave traffic, slum housing, food and drugs, child labor, stock and money markets, poverty, unemployment, the judicial system, and the press. By 1900, *McClure's Magazine* had four hundred thousand subscribers.

Popular writers of the period included Finley Peter Dunne, who spoke through "Mr. Dooley." "Mr. Dooley," writing for *Collier's American Magazine* and Chicago newspapers, was full of prejudices. He was a blue-collar stalwart who disapproved of high society, the packinghouse gentry, political corruption, social pretensions, the Republican party, and almost every race except the Irish.

Lincoln Steffens's *Shame of the Cities* was an exposé of bribery and graft in six of the nation's largest cities (St. Louis, Minneapolis, Pittsburgh, Philadelphia, Chicago, and New York). His series of articles in *McClure's* was influential in cleaning up many abuses in city governments.

Ida Tarbell's *History of the Standard Oil Company,* serialized in *McClure's,* was one of the first and best-known contributions by the muckrakers. Although written in an objective style, her articles caused a sensation because they revealed corrupt methods that the company had used to gain a monopoly in the petroleum industry.

Perhaps best-known of the muckrakers was Upton Sinclair, author of *The Jungle.* The novel was written primarily as an attack on unfair labor conditions, but it had an immediate effect on legislation, leading to the passing of meat-inspection and pure-food laws in 1906. Sinclair's savage indictment of labor and sanitary conditions in the Chicago stockyards first appeared serially in *The Appeal to Reason,* a socialist weekly.

A different type of muckraking was undertaken by Carl Bernstein and Robert Woodward, two *Washington Post* reporters, who were primarily responsible for revealing the Watergate scandal in 1974, a tale of political misbehavior in the national administration, leading in the end to the resignation of President Richard Nixon.

ILLUSTRATIONS

Before the first practical photographic process was invented by Louis Daguerre in the 1830s, there were practical limitations on the use of illustrations in newspapers and magazines. So omnipresent is photography in modern life, it is difficult to realize that the process dates back only a century and a half. Present-day books, periodicals, and newspapers would seem barren without the products of highly sophisticated cameras, and large corporations and industries have been built around the demand for pictorial material.

Prior to photography, woodcuts were used for illustrations. Maps of war operations were printed in various papers. The *Albany Evening Journal* filled a page with a large spread eagle to celebrate the Whig victories of 1838 and 1840. The *Philadelphia Inquirer* printed woodcut portraits of generals and forts. The *New York Herald* created a sensation in 1845 with a full-page engraving of the Andrew Jackson funeral procession. The following year the *Herald* issued a Christmas special containing woodcuts of the Mexican War and a variety of other subjects. But wood engraving was expensive and too slow for timely news illustrations.

The first daily paper to use cartoons regularly was Bennett's *New York Evening Telegram,* although the *Telegraph* of Washington in 1832 had run cartoons in campaigning against Jackson.

The first great pictorial weekly was Gleason's *Pictorial Drawing Room Companion* (1851–59) in Boston, a sixteen-page paper copiously illustrated with woodcuts, modeled after the *Illustrated London News. Graham's Magazine* in Philadelphia in the 1840s was lavishly illustrated by engravings on copper and steel. Later, illustration became common in the weeklies and monthlies. *Harper's Magazine* and *Scribner's Monthly* were filled with woodcuts. *Harper's Weekly* and Frank Leslie's magazines were richly illustrated. Steel plates adorned the women's magazines. Political cartoons regularly appeared in *Harper's Weekly, Leslie's Illustrated Newspaper,* and the weekly *Day Book.*

The first American illustrated weekly, with Nathaniel P. Willis as editor, was *Brother Jonathan,* founded by Benjamin Henry Day in 1838.

Leslie's Illustrated Newspaper was first issued in 1855. It presented current news events in both pictures and text. After the outbreak of the Civil War, correspondents and artists were employed to illustrate battles, sieges, marches, and other war incidents.

Perhaps the first to take advantage of the new invention of daguerreotype photography for journalistic purposes was Henry Hunt Snelling, who has been called the father of photographic journalism. While librarian of the New York Lyceum, Snelling met Edward Anthony, who awakened his interest in photography. Anthony started manufacturing and selling "daguerrean" supplies in 1843, at which time Snelling became his general sales manager. In 1849, Snelling published *The History and Practice of the Art of Photography,* the first book on the subject published in America. In 1851, Snelling began publishing the *Photographic Art Journal* (later the *Photographic and Fine Arts Journal*), meant to provide artistic and technical instruction to photographers. As late as 1889–90, he published an article entitled "Photographic Entertainments" in *Wilson's Photographic Magazine.*

The celebrated Civil War photographer Matthew Brady opened a portrait studio in New York City at age twenty. He won a first prize at the 1851 World's Fair in London and learned there about the new wet-plate process in photography. In the years following he photographed hundreds of prominent persons, including nineteen presidents (starting with John Quincy Adams), Mary Todd Lincoln, Walt Whitman, Ulysses S. Grant, Washington Irving, P. T. Barnum, Brigham Young, and James Fenimore Cooper. The Lincoln picture on the five-dollar bill is from a Brady photograph.

Shortly after the beginning of the Civil War, Brady received permission to accompany the Union Army to make a pictorial record of camp and battle scenes. Carrying a cumbersome tent that served as a darkroom, fragile glass plates, and bulky cameras, Brady created a record of more than seven thousand stark pictures of the war in all its grim reality. Brady spent $100,000 of his own money on the project, only to find himself financially ruined at the end of the war. About two thousand of his photographs were purchased by the federal government for $25,000 in 1875. After the war, Brady resumed photographic portraiture in Washington, D.C.

Most famous of the early cartoonists was Thomas Nast, whose first published sketches appeared in *Leslie's Illustrated Newspaper* and later in *Harper's Weekly* and *New York Illustrated News.* Nast's reputation as a political cartoonist was established by his Civil War drawings and subsequently by his attacks on the Tweed Ring and Tammany Hall. Nast created the elephant and the donkey as symbols of the Republican and Democratic parties.

A cartoonist belonging to a later era was Jay Darling, known as

"Ding," whose drawings won Pulitzer prizes and were widely syndicated from about 1911 to 1949.

Another politically oriented cartoonist is Herbert Block ("Herblock"), who has been drawing for the *Washington Post* since 1946. Eric Sevareid described Herblock as "the most powerful and effective political commentator in the United States."

R. F. Outcault pioneered in creating the newspaper colored comic supplement and the cartoon strip. His "Origin of a New Species," featuring an anaconda and a yellow dog in color in the *New York World* in 1894, started the "funny paper." That series was followed by "Hogan's Alley," which was developed into "The Yellow Kid," the first comic strip. Later, when Outcault transferred his strip to the *New York Journal,* a controversy arose, described as "yellow journalism." Outcault began his "Buster Brown" drawings for the *Herald* in 1902. According to one critic, it inflicted upon small boys Buster Brown suits, collars, and haircuts.

Pictures were used as weapons for sociological reform by Jacob Riis, who campaigned to clean up slum conditions in New York City late in the nineteenth century. To document his stories, Riis used photographs of the crowded tenement districts.

Noteworthy American photographers whose work was widely published were Margaret Bourke-White and Edward Steichen. Bourke-White specialized as an industrial photographer, taking pictures for *Fortune* magazine and *Life* from 1929 to 1971. She was an accredited war correspondent and photographer in World War II and the Korean War. Edward Steichen's technique helped to make photography a fine art. Steichen was Carl Sandburg's brother-in-law.

HUMORISTS

Wit and humor have long been featured in American journalism. The most famous example is Samuel L. Clemens, better known as Mark Twain. His humorous accounts of his foreign travels led to publication of *Innocents Abroad,* a book that established his name as a humorist.

An early humorist was James Montgomery Bailey, who began by writing amusing sketches of army life during the Civil War. Bailey had an exceptional talent for seeing humor in ordinary events or inventing ridiculous situations.

Irvin S. Cobb was a regular contributor to the *Saturday Evening Post,* writing humorous articles.

Finley Peter Dunne was the greatest American humorist of his day. He invented the character of "Mr. Dooley," whose wit, skepticism, and keen perceptions, mainly political and expressed in an Irish brogue, delighted a multitude of readers in Chicago, New York, and elsewhere.

Eugene Field's celebrated "Sharps and Flats" column was first published in the *Chicago Morning News* in 1883. Its combination of whimsical humor, satirical, farcical, and pathetic stories, and verse became nationally famous. His writings were noted for keen satire, genuine wit, and bright literary touches.

David Ross Locke became known under his pen name of Petroleum V. Nasby. Nasby was depicted as an illiterate, hypocritical, cowardly, loafing dissolute country preacher, used by Locke to ridicule ideas with which he disagreed.

A contemporary was John Armoy Knox who belonged to a breed of American humorists popular in the nineteenth century. His column, entitled "Siftings," was filled with humorous anecdotes and proverbs.

Charles Henry Smith was popularly known as "Bill Arp." Bill Arp was an uneducated character, a wise, humorous rustic philosopher, using the illiterate dialect favored by many early American humorists.

Opie Read was said to have made country humor into a national institution. His writing was done principally for a weekly paper, the *Arkansas Traveler*. Its sketches of back-country scenes and characters attracted a wide circle of readers throughout the country.

Philip Henry Welch devoted himself to journalistic humor from 1882 until 1889, through a column called "The Present Hour" in a Rochester (New York) paper. He also contributed humorous material to *Puck, Life, Judge,* and other periodicals.

Among later writers, Ring Lardner's writings are noted as of permanent literary importance. Lardner was known for his use of American vernacular slang, his familiarity with colorful American characters, and his mastery of the American vernacular speech.

James Thurber's writings continue to be popular with readers. In a long association with the *New Yorker,* Thurber established his reputation as a leading American humorist and cartoonist.

H. Allen Smith always thought of himself as more of a humorist than a journalist. He was the author of a number of humorous anecdotal books, including *Low Man on a Totem Pole.*

Frank Sullivan gained a reputation as a brilliant satirist of the American life of his time. His satiric wit was applied to a variety of subjects.

Don Marquis is rated by most critics as one of the most important American humorists. As a member of the *New York Sun* staff, Marquis became known for his humorous column "The Sun Dial" and later, after he transferred to the *New York Herald Tribune,* "The Lantern."

Another popular columnist was Franklin P. Adams, author of "The Conning Tower," filled with humorous wit, verse, and satire. Dorothy Parker and Ring Lardner contributed to the column.

Noteworthy among present-day humorists are Art Buchwald, widely recognized as a leading political humorist and satirist, and Russell Baker, whose writings relieve the generally pontifical tone of the *New York Times.*

Another American humorist fascinated by politics was Will Rogers, a homespun philosopher and political debunker. Rogers was a successful syndicated newspaper columnist and radio commentator.

A different medium was used by Charles M. Schulz who invented the comic strip "Peanuts," syndicated by the United Feature Syndicate since 1950. Featured are child characters who talk and think like adults.

The large crop of humorous writers in newspapers, beginning with such names as Mark Twain, Artemus Ward, David Locke, and Bill Arp, and later Will Rogers, Art Buchwald, and others, served to enliven the news with wit, to examine less serious aspects of current events, and to keep politicians from taking themselves too seriously.

WOMEN JOURNALISTS

Women have been reporters since colonial days. They began moving into important posts during World War II. A majority of undergraduates studying to become journalists today are women. A recent study shows that 37 percent of newspaper staffs and 36 percent of general news reporters are women.

Newspapers today devote space to a variety of subjects, formerly neglected or taboo, because of feminine connotations, such as child care, women in politics, rape, battered women, and health. Nevertheless, three-fourths of the nation's daily newspapers have no women among their senior editors. Editorial policies and major decisions in general are determined by all-male chiefs. Exceptions are Janet Chusmir, executive editor of the *Miami Herald,* and Katherine Fanning, editor of the *Christian Science Monitor* and the first woman president of the American Society of Newspaper Editors. Eight women are editors of papers of considerable importance, including the *New York Post* and the *Fresno* (California) *Bee.*

Criticisms aside, women have achieved distinction in a variety of journalistic fields, principally in the twentieth century.

The first periodical for women in the United States was *Godey's Lady's Book,* started in 1820. The coeditor from 1836 to 1877 was Sara Josepha Hale. The magazine was largely devoted to women's interests, manners, morals, and fashions. Another writer on fashion was Jane Cunningham Croly, who has been called the first American newspaper woman. She wrote, under the pen name of "Jennie Jane," about parties, clothes, and beauty, probably the first of the women's pages in later newspapers. Croly was also an early leader of the feminist movement. A later magazine devoted to women's affairs was the *Ladies' Home Journal,* founded by Edward Bok in 1889.

Elizabeth Meriwether Gilmer, who wrote under the name of "Dorothy Dix," gave popular advice to the lovelorn. As a writer for *Good Housekeeping* and *Cosmopolitan,* she carried on an extensive correspondence with readers writing for advice on a variety of problems. Dorothy Dix was widely syndicated and after 1910, she became an active suffragist.

Another early advisor on personal problems was Marie Manning, whose pen name was "Beatrice Fairfax" and whose writings preceded Dorothy Dix's by nineteen years. The column was reputed to attract 1,400 letters daily and was syndicated to about 200 newspapers.

The most popular and widely read advice columns currently published are by two sisters, Abigail Van Buren, known as "Dear Abby," and Esther Lederer, who writes under the name of "Ann Landers."

After Eleanor Patterson became editor-publisher of the *Washington Herald* in 1930, she filled the paper with gossip, as a device for increasing circulation.

Two columnists who built their reputations on Hollywood gossip were Hedda Hopper and Louella Parsons. Somewhat related are "sob sisters," such as Winifred Sweet Black, known as "Annie Laurie," who wrote sensational and sentimental stories for the *Denver Post,* and Adela Rogers St. Johns, called the veteran sob sister of American journalism, who wrote about movie stars and other topics for Hearst papers.

As editor for thirty-seven years of the *Herald Tribune Book Review,* Irita Van Doren was an important influence on American literature. Another outstanding editor was Harriet Monroe, who founded and edited *Poetry: A Magazine of Verse* from 1912 to 1930, and published the early works of many leading American and English poets.

Elizabeth Cochrane, who wrote under the name "Nellie Bly," was a crusader for cleaning up city slums, prisons, and insane asylums. Hazel Brannon Smith, owner and editor of four weekly newspapers in rural Mississippi, has been exposing political and social injustice in Mississippi. Jane Grey Swisshelm fought for the abolition of slavery and women's rights.

Women who wrote principally about politics for the press, radio, or television include Dorothy Thompson, Doris Fleeson, and Elizabeth Drew. Anne McCormick won fame as a European correspondent.

The versatility of women in the business world was demonstrated by several successful women publishers, among them Anne Royall, described as the pioneer woman publicist; Helen Reid, who became president of the New York Herald Tribune Corporation; Katharine Meyer Graham, owner of the *Washington Post* and *Newsweek;* Eleanor Medill Patterson, owner of the *Washington Times Herald;* and Alicia Patterson, who made the *Long Island Newsday* a major newspaper.

Women who became experts in special areas include Helen Delich Bentley (maritime affairs), Margaret Bourke-White (photography); and Sylvia Porter and Jane Bryant Quinn (financial advice).

The coming of radio and later television brought opportunities for a number of women in broadcasting news: Diane Sawyer, a fixture on the CBS "60 Minutes" show; Susan Spencer, with the "CBS Evening News"; Lesley Stahl, correspondent for CBS News in Washington; Jessica Savitch, NBC anchorwoman; Charlayne Hunter-Gault, with the "MacNeil/Lehrer News Hour"; Connie Chung, with "NBC Nightly News"; Georgia Anne Geyer, world traveler, concerned with international affairs; Barbara Walters on "ABC World News Tonight"; and Judy Woodruff on the "MacNeil/Lehrer News Hour."

Columnists who wrote about a variety of matters included Eleanor Roosevelt and Sara Payson Parton, who wrote under the pen name of "Fanny Fern."

ETIQUETTE

Related to the interest in social behavior and muckraking among the American people was a concern for good manners. Since colonial days, Americans have been concerned with matters of social behavior. Breaches of proper conduct — cursing, lying, scandalmongering, name-calling, flirting, and drinking to excess — might be punished by ducking, flogging, being placed in the stocks, or other unpleasant chastisement. Foreign critics, such as Frances Trollope in her *Domestic Manners of the Americans,* made people self-conscious and sensitive to criticism. As a result, there was a ready market for a large homegrown literature, self-improvement books, and newspaper columns. Most of such writings, which began to flourish in the nineteenth and early twentieth centuries, were dreadful.

Over a period of decades, the name of Emily Post became synonymous with good manners in America. Her *Etiquette: The Blue Book of Social Usage* first appeared in 1922 and thereafter went through at least a dozen revisions and scores of printings with sales amounting to more than a million copies.

The phenomenal success of Emily Post naturally encouraged the rise of competitors and emulators. A chief rival in the early years was Lillian Eichler's *Book of Etiquette.* More recently, Amy Vanderbilt's *Complete Book of Social Etiquette,* first published in 1952, has had a great vogue. Some young moderns consider Amy Vanderbilt more in tune with current mores than Emily Post. Syndicated columns in magazines and newspapers were indicative of the subject's continued fascination.

A comparative newcomer to the ranks of dispensers of advice on love and other personal problems is Judith Martin. Under the nom de plume of "Miss Manners," Martin began in 1978 to write a column on etiquette for the *Washington Post.* The column appears in over 250 newspapers internationally and answers questions on a wide range of subjects, drawing on the author's Washington experience and social observation.

BLACK JOURNALISTS

Black Americans (or "African Americans," a term currently preferred by some of the race's leaders), have produced a number of noteworthy journalists. One of the earliest was Frederick Douglass, a former slave, who spent fifty-seven years fighting the institution of slavery. Douglass's *North Star* was one of the most successful black newspapers in the United States.

Another son of former slaves was Robert S. Abbott, who began publishing a newspaper, the *Chicago Defender,* in 1905. The paper's aim was to serve the nation's blacks and it covered a variety of relevant news. The *Defender* continued after Abbott's death in 1940. A less successful publication started by Abbott in 1929, and continued until 1933, was *Abbott's Monthly,* designed as a medium for black writers and artists.

W. E. B. Du Bois was one of a trio of great black leaders, the other being Douglass and Booker T. Washington. Du Bois is best known as editor (1910–34) of a militant monthly periodical *The Crisis,* the official organ of the National Association for the Advancement of Colored People.

One of the longest-lived and most important of newspapers founded by blacks in the United States was T. Thomas Fortune's *New York Age,* beginning in 1879. The title was later changed to the *Freeman.* Later, Fortune worked on a black weekly, the *People's Advocate,* and in 1923, he became editor of Marcus Garvey's *Negro World* in New York.

John Harold Johnson became a leading American publisher of books and magazines aimed at black readers. His magazines included *Ebony,* a monthly picture and news journal; *Jet,* a weekly news magazine; *Tan,* a monthly women's magazine; and *Black World,* a monthly literary magazine.

George S. Schuyler was assistant manager of the *Messenger,* journal of the Friends of Negro Freedom, columnist for the *Pittsburgh Courier,* which had a large circulation among black readers, business manager of *Crisis,* the NAACP magazine, and associate editor of the *African,* a monthly magazine.

Robert Lee Vann's career was also spent in part with the *Pittsburgh Courier* as editor. In 1920, he launched an illustrated monthly magazine, the *Competitor,* but it was too expensive for potential black readers and was short-lived. In 1939, Vann founded the Interstate United Newspaper Company, the first black-owned newspaper advertising agency.

Ida Bell Wells-Barnett, born to slave parents, had her *Memphis Free Speech* printing office mobbed and destroyed in 1892 because of editorials denouncing lynching. She served as a staff writer for the *New York Age,* married a black lawyer in Chicago, was founder and editor of the *Chicago Conservator,* founded the first black women's suffrage organization, and worked with Jane Addams in a successful campaign to prevent separate schools for black children in Chicago.

Black journalists who have become prominent in recent times include Robert Maynard, owner of the *Oakland* (California) *Tribune;* Charlayne Hunter-Gault, announcer on the "MacNeil/Lehrer News Hour"; Carl Thomas Rowan, a columnist who enjoyed a long career with the *Minneapolis Tribune;* Max Robinson, the first black network anchor for ABC; and Ed Bradley, a fixture on CBS's "60 Minutes" show.

The first black newspapers were established primarily to combat slavery. Later they espoused many causes significant for blacks, such as voting rights, employment opportunities, legal protection, and proper housing.

Sports Reporters

Reporting on sports was a common assignment for many journalists early in their careers. It was the central concern of a number of names well-known to journalism.

W. O. McGeehan has been called the greatest sportswriter who ever lived. Nearly his entire career was spent reporting baseball, boxing, and other sporting events. He wrote about boxing for Hearst's *Evening Journal* and later for the *New York Tribune* and the *New York Herald.*

William Trotter Porter was particularly devoted to horses and horse racing, although he also covered field and water sports. In 1831, he started a weekly sporting paper, the *Spirit of the Times and Life in New York.* The popularity of the paper was increased by adding color prints of famous race horses.

Grantland Rice's widely syndicated column "The Sportlight" made him America's favorite sportswriter. Rice witnessed thousands of sporting events and wrote about football, baseball, racing, golf, tennis, hunting, polo, rowing, race and track, and yachting.

Damon Runyon wrote sports columns for the Hearst syndicate after military service in World War I. His sports column, "Both Barrels," was carried in the *New York American.*

Sports reporting by the late nineteenth century had enjoyed remarkable success, reflected in special pages, pictures, and newswriting.

Sportswriters created a special style and vocabulary and became individually famous. Their writing did much to promote national interest in football, basketball, baseball, and other sports.

WAR CORRESPONDENTS

Among the earliest war correspondents were Henry Crabb Robinson, representing the *London Times,* who accompanied a British force to Spain in 1808, and George Wilkins Kendall of the *New Orleans Picayune,* who wrote dispatches from Mexico in 1848, fought with the cavalry, and served on the staff of General William J. Worth.

During the Civil War, more than 250 war correspondents reported the war's progress — from the fall of Fort Sumter to Appomattox. The *New York Herald* alone had from thirty to forty writers in the field with Union forces during the last year of the war. *Harper's Weekly* and *Leslie's Illustrated Newspaper* had as many as a dozen artists in the field drawing pictures for reproduction by woodcuts.

On occasion the editors of Northern papers covered the war in person. Examples are Henry Raymond of the *New York Times,* Whitelaw Reid of the *New York Tribune,* Joseph Medill of the *Chicago Tribune,* Murat Halstead of the *Cincinnati Commercial,* John Russell Young for the *Philadelphia Press,* Henry Villard from the *New York Herald,* and Charles Carleton Coffin for the *Boston Journal.* One of the most famous of the Civil War correspondents was George W. Smalley of the *New York Tribune,* whose six-column first-hand report on the battle of Antietam is rated as one of the greatest battle stories to come out of the war. The most famous naval correspondent of the war was B. S. Osbon, first of the *New York World,* and later of the *Herald.*

Civil War correspondents operated under handicaps. Some Union generals and the secretary of war regarded correspondents as intruders, hampering military operations and possibly leaking key information to the enemy.

There were few battles in the short Spanish-American War. Most news stories dealt with malaria in the camps and tainted beef supplies. The leading reporters included Stephen Crane and Richard Harding Davis.

In early twentieth-century conflicts, Jack London was a star of the Russo-Japanese War, and Frederick Palmer of the Balkan Wars.

When World War I erupted, newsmen were barred from fighting areas by British, French, and German military leaders. In 1915, a small group of correspondents was accredited to the front lines. Restrictions imposed by General Pershing when the United States entered the war caused problems for newsmen at first, but were eventually resolved. War reporting became more complex because of new instruments of war — airplanes, Zepplins, tanks, long-range guns, and poison gas. Among the top reporters on the American side were Richard Harding Davis, Irwin S. Cobb, William G. Shepherd, Frederick Palmer, Paul Scott Mowrer, Floyd Gibbons, and Fred S. Ferguson.

With the coming of World War II, there was much more tolerance of news correspondents and their work was even facilitated in many ways. During the five years of fighting, more than two thousand correspondents were accredited to the American forces, including several hundred radio reporters and commentators and a small group of women. Among the outstanding correspondents were Ernie Pyle, John Hersey, Homer Bigart, A. J. Liebling, cartoonist Bill Mauldin, and photographers Carl Mydans and Joseph Rosenthal. More than twenty correspondents were killed in the line of duty.

POLITICAL REPORTERS

Probably a majority of the individuals included in this volume dabbled in politics at one time or another, sometimes full time and sometimes occasionally. Horace Greeley even ran for president!

SPECIAL FIELDS

Responses to the demands of special interests were met by a number of magazines and newspapers. In agriculture, Thomas Green Fesserden in 1822 established and edited the *New England Farmer.* Much later, Edwin Thomas Meredith in 1902 founded *Successful Farming* and in 1924, *Better Homes and Gardens.* Related was Harvey L. Goodall's *Drover's Journal,* a livestock market paper, the first paper ever published in its field, started in 1873.

The first labor paper, the *Journeyman Mechanics' Advocate,* was published in Philadelphia in 1827. The second, and most important, was the *Working Man's Advocate,* edited by George H. Evans, a famous leader in the early labor movement in New York.

Medicine was a prime area requiring periodical coverage. The *Richmond Medical Journal* was established by Edwin Samuel Gaillard at the Medical College of Virginia in 1865.

George Putnam Upton was music critic of the *Chicago Tribune* for many years. His musical criticisms were published under the name of "Peregrine Pickle," and influenced Chicago's cultural life.

Special fields naturally created opportunities for reporters in such areas as law, medicine, music, theater, and labor. These fields required different qualifications from general news reporting. The writings of specialists are naturally slanted toward their field of interest. They make important contributions to popular culture and public understanding.

JOURNALISM EDUCATION

Formal preparation for a career in journalism was a late development. The beginning in the United States dates from 1869, when General Robert E. Lee, president of Washington College at Lexington, Virginia, proposed a plan that combined work in the printing trade with the college's classical curriculum. The courses were discontinued, however, after Lee's death in 1870.

For its first two centuries, journalism in America was not recognized as a profession. Its practitioners had frequently begun in another field, such as law, or worked their way up to editorial or managerial positions from lowly printing office jobs such as typesetters. That attitude began to change as newspaper work attracted an increasing number of college-educated reporters and editors.

Prior to Lee's experiment at Washington College, Cornell University offered a Certificate of Journalism for the completion of a prescribed liberal arts curriculum plus some work in the university printing department, but it had no special journalistic courses. The Wharton School of Business in the University of Pennsylvania offered the first curriculum in journalism in 1893, and the first four-year curriculum was offered by the University of Illinois in 1904. The first regularly organized school of journalism was established at the University of Missouri under Dean Walter Williams in 1908.

Joseph Pulitzer recognized that journalists should be trained as well and as thoroughly as individuals who entered other professions. Like most outstanding leaders in the field, Pulitzer had been forced to educate himself. He was convinced that there should be a better system. He proposed setting up a school of journalism at Columbia University. Pulitzer agreed to provide an endowment of $2 million for a graduate school of journalism at Columbia, but the program did not open until 1912.

Of the hundreds of schools and colleges presently offering courses in journalism, the work is generally concentrated in the last two years of a four-year program, with technical courses scheduled in the junior and senior years. The remainder of the time is devoted to the study of the arts and sciences. The curriculum covers such areas as news, advertising, magazine, and radio and television journalism. Emphasis is increasingly on the liberal arts, to assure the broad educational background required by modern journalists. Typically only about one-third of the courses are journalism subjects.

THE ELECTRONIC AGE

Radio and television revolutionized the gathering and distribution of news. Many modern journalists achieved fame through these media.

Before television was fully developed, radio transmission was bringing news of World War II to millions of listeners through broadcasts by Edward R. Murrow and Fred Friendly. Other stars of the radio era were Gabriel Heater and H. V. Kaltenborn. Edward Murrow made an easy transition from radio to television after his return to the United States.

Every major news network has developed familiar personalities since television broadcasting became common. Of particular note are Walter Cronkite, who was top performer for CBS from 1962 to 1981, and who was succeeded by Dan Rather, supported by Robert Schieffer, Connie Chung, Lesley Stahl, and others. The chief voices for NBC include Tom Brokaw and John Chancellor. ABC is led by Peter Jennings, whose team includes Sam Donaldson, David Brinkley, and Ted Koppel. Robert MacNeil, Jim Lehrer, Charlayne Hunter-Gault, and Judy Woodruff make up the regular staff for the "MacNeil/Lehrer News Hour." CBS's popular "60 Minutes" is staffed by Morley Safer, Mike Wallace, Ed Bradley and others. Bill Moyers is one of the leading figures on the Public Broadcasting Service network; and of importance is Daniel Schorr, who is now with National Public Radio, and Hodding Carter, who is often seen on David Brinkley's show.

SOURCES OF INFORMATION

There are many bibliographical sources for the history of journalism. A valuable reference is the *Dictionary of Literary Biography,* specifically, the four volumes entitled "American Newspaper Journalists," edited by Perry T. Ashley. The volumes cover American journalism from 1690 to 1950.

Among general histories of journalism, the most important is Frank L. Mott's *American Journalism* (New York: Macmillan, 1962). Also useful are James Lee's *History of American Journalism* (Boston: Houghton Mifflin, 1923); George H. Payne's *History of Journalism in the United States* (New York: Appleton, 1920); Edwin H. Ford's *History of Journalism in the United States* (Minneapolis: Burgess, 1938); Robert Allen Rutland's *Newsmongers: Journalism in the Life of the Nation* (New York: Dial, 1973); Alfred M. Lee's *Daily Newspaper in America: The Evolution of a Social Instrument* (New York: Macmillan, 1937); and Michael Schudson's *Discovering the News: A Social History of American Newspapers* (New York: Basic, 1978).

A pioneer early work in the field is Isaiah Thomas's two-volume *History of Printing in America* (Worcester: Worcester Press, 1810).

Two general biographical dictionaries are recommended: the *Dictionary of American Biography* and the *National Cyclopedia of American Biography*. Modern names are covered by *Current Biography* (New York: H. W. Wilson, 1941–   ); *Contemporary Authors* (Detroit: Gale, 1962–   ); *Who's Who in America* (Chicago: Marquis, ongoing); and *Who Was Who* (Chicago: Marquis, ongoing).

More specialized or covering shorter periods are the following:

Bailyn, Bernard. *The Press and the Revolution.* Worcester: American Antiquarian Society, 1980.

Boorstin, Daniel J. *The Americans: The Colonial Experience.* New York: Random House, 1958.

Brown, Charles H. *The Correspondents: Journalists in the Spanish American War.* New York: Scribner, 1967.

Crozier, Emmet. *Yankee Reporters, 1861–65.* New York: Oxford, 1956.

Fang, Irving E. *Those Radio Commentators.* Ames: Iowa State University Press, 1977.

Fisher, Charles. *The Columnists.* New York: Howell, 1944.

James, Edward T. *Notable American Women, 1607–1950.* 3 vols. Cambridge: Harvard University Press, 1971.

Kobre, Sidney. *The Development of the Colonial Newspaper.* New York, 1944.

Lewis, Jerry D. *The Great Columnists.* New York: Collier, 1965.

Paneth, Donald. *The Encyclopedia of American Journalism.* New York: Facts on File, 1983.

Regier, C. C. *The Era of the Muckrakers.* Chapel Hill: University of North Carolina Press, 1932.

Sanders, Marlene, and Marcia Rock. *Waiting for Prime Time: The Women of Television News.* Urbana: University of Illinois Press, 1988.

Saturday Evening Post. *More Post Biographies.* Athens: University of Georgia Press, 1947.

Schmidt, Jo Ann. *Fighting Editors.* San Antonio: Naylor, 1958.

Sicherman, Barbara, et al., eds. *Notable American Women.* Cambridge: Harvard University Press, 1980.

Taft, William H. *Encyclopedia of Twentieth-century Journalists.* New York: Garland, 1986.

Weiner, Richard. *Syndicated Columnists.* 3d ed. New York, 1979.

Discerning comments on prominent twentieth-century journalists may be found in David Brinkley's *Washington Goes to War* (New York: Knopf, 1988), especially chapter 7 on "Press Lords and Reporters."

Of the general encyclopedias, the most complete are the *Britannica* and *Americana.* An older work sometimes useful is the *Encyclopedia International.* Smaller titles that are reliable are the *American Peoples, New Standard, Academic American, World Book,* and *Compton's.*

Current affairs in the journalistic world are covered by the *Washington Journalism Review,* which began publication in 1977. Regular features include the business of journalism, biographical sketches of persons concerned with journalism, legal issues, and book reviews. An older standard title is the *Journalism Quarterly,* founded in 1924.

THE BIOGRAPHIES

WILLIS J. ABBOT
1863–1934

Willis J. Abbot began his long career in journalism as a cub reporter for the *New Orleans Times-Democrat*. There he enjoyed the friendship of Lafcadio Hearn, who frequently contributed literary columns to the paper. Abbot's first major assignment was to interview Jefferson Davis for the *New York World*. A year later he was reporting for the *New York Tribune*.

With several partners, Abbot in 1886 attempted to establish the *Evening News* in Kansas City to compete with the *Star*. The venture was a failure, and in 1889 Abbot began a five-year stay in Chicago, writing editorials for the *Chicago Evening Mail*. He was promoted to managing editor in 1892. When the *Evening Mail*'s owner, the mayor of Chicago, was assassinated in 1893, the paper was purchased by Abbot and his brother-in-law, and merged with the *Herald*. A series of mergers combined to produce the *Chicago Times-Herald, Record and Inter-Ocean*.

In 1895, William Randolph Hearst appointed Abbot editor-in-chief of the *New York Journal* (renamed the *American* in 1897). It was a frustrating experience for Abbot, who compared his stay with the paper to living in a "lunatic asylum."

During the 1890s, Abbot was a prolific contributor to the *Review of Reviews, Literary Digest, New Republic, Outlook, Collier's Forum, Munsey's, Harper's Weekly,* and other periodicals, writing about public affairs, travel, and distinguished personalities. He covered the 1896 Democratic convention in Chicago, and in 1897 chaired the New York mayoral campaign of Henry Georgy. Abbot managed the Democratic national press bureau during the 1900 presidential campaign. He also ran the Democratic party press activities in the 1908 campaign. In both instances, his candidate,

William Jennings Bryan, lost. For the next four years, Abbot traveled in Europe, wrote syndicated political analyses, wrote editorials for the *New York Sun,* and was author of a syndicated column for *Collier's Weekly* and the *Times* of London.

The last and most distinguished phase of Abbot's career began in 1921, when he became editor of the *Christian Science Monitor.* He rebuilt the *Monitor,* which was at low ebb when he took over. He was active on the editorial board until his death, writing editorials and a signed cartoon, "Watching the World Go By," traveling and lecturing extensively, and promoting world peace.

ROBERT S. ABBOTT
1868–1940

Robert Abbott was the son of former slaves. He began his career as a newspaperman as a child, when he worked on one of Savannah's oldest newspapers, the *Echo.* After a period as a student in Claflin College, Orangeburg, South Carolina, Abbott assisted his stepfather in publishing a new newspaper, the *Woodville Times.* He entered Hampton Institute in Virginia to learn the printer's trade, and then went on to Chicago, where he received a bachelor of law degree from Kent College of Law in 1899.

Unable to find other work, Abbott accepted a job in Chicago as a piecework printer setting railroad timetables. Long anxious to start a newspaper, he began publishing the *Chicago Defender* in 1905. It was largely a one-man operation, although many of Abbott's friends aided in writing, printing, and distributing the paper. The *Defender*'s aim was to serve the nation's blacks. It reported accomplishments, social gatherings, and other activities. The news was treated sensationally and with banner headlines, sometimes printed in red ink. Departments covering sports, editorials, women's news, and state news were set up. Like other Chicago newspapers, the *Defender* treated the 1919 race riots sensationally, although Abbott urged blacks to restore order.

The *Defender*'s policies varied on some issues. It promoted the mass migration of blacks from the South to Chicago. Its stand on racial integration was firm. The paper wavered about labor unions, but finally came out defending them.

The *Defender*'s financial services enabled it to install a full-fledged printing shop in 1919, instead of depending on job printing. There were financial problems, however; several employees, including the business manager, were stealing from the paper. The Depression years caused circulation to drop from two hundred thousand in 1925 to sixty thousand in 1935.

In 1929, Abbott published the first issue of a magazine, *Abbott's Monthly*, providing a medium for talented black writers and artists. Here again the Depression proved too much of a problem and the magazine ceased publication in 1933.

Abbott's achievements in breaking down racial discrimination were substantial, and the campaign has continued to be carried on by the *Defender* since his death in 1940.

ARUNAH ABELL

1806–1888

Arunah Abell began his journalistic career as a printer's apprentice at the *Providence Patriot* at age sixteen. Five years later he moved to Boston, to serve as foreman of a large print shop. Heeding the demand for master printers in New York, he began work for the *Mercantile Advertiser* in 1828. There he met Benjamin Day, who in 1833 pioneered a one-cent, reader-oriented paper, the *New York Sun,* filled with human interest stories of crime, pathos, and humor.

Emulating Day's example, Abell started a successful penny paper in Philadelphia, the *Public Ledger,* in 1836. A year later, the *Baltimore Sun,* patterned after the *New York Sun,* under Abell's direction, began publishing and won quick popularity. The paper covered local events in detail and followed a policy of editorial independence. Abell and his partner William Swain became wealthy from their publishing empire.

Abell introduced a number of innovative practices in newspaper publishing. His *Sun* was the first large newspaper to install the newly invented rotary presses that were destined to transform newspaper printing. Still more revolutionary was Abell's devices for speeding up the gathering and printing of news, first by setting up a pony express system between Washington, Baltimore, and Boston; second, by use of the telegraph immediately after Morse's invention in 1844; and, finally, by establishing a network of wire, railroads, steamboats, stagecoaches, and fast horses to expedite the collecting and dissemination of news.

In 1887, on the *Baltimore Sun's* fiftieth anniversary, Abell turned over control of the paper to his three sons. He died a year later. In the course of his long tenure as publisher, he had established the paper's reputation for trustworthiness and as an opponent of political corruption.

FRANKLIN PIERCE ADAMS
1881–1960

FPA, as he was popularly known, was born in Chicago. He was for many years a leading newspaper columnist. In 1903 he began to write a daily feature for the *Chicago Journal*. Later he transferred to New York City, where he wrote a column "Always in a Good Humor" for the *Evening Mail*. There followed a stint (1913–22) with the *New York Tribune* as author of "The Conning Tower." From 1922 to 1931 the column appeared in the *World,* from 1931 to 1937 in the *Herald-Tribune*, and from 1938 to 1931 in the *Evening Post*. "The Conning Tower" was filled with humorous wit, verse and prose, satire, autobiographical sketches, and miscellaneous comment. Dorothy Parker and Ring Lardner were among the contributors to the column.

Adams's popularity was enhanced further by appearing as a regular panel member of the "Information Please" radio quiz program. There his quick wit, familiarity with American and English literature, and knowledge of music and dramatic history contributed much to the program's high ratings.

Adams was a prolific author. In 1935, his columns for the preceding twenty-four years were brought together in a two-volume work, *The Diary of Our Own Samuel Pepys*. Another best-seller was *Toboganning on Parnassus* (1910).

SAMUEL ADAMS
1722–1803

Samuel Adams, born in Boston, Massachusetts, is remembered more as an American patriot, political agitator, and statesman than as a journalist. Nevertheless, his inclinations toward journalistic activity were demonstrated early, when at age twenty-six, he and some of his friends established a newspaper, the *Independent Advertiser*, in 1748 to promote their views on public affairs. Later, Adams became the most voluminous political writer of his time in America.

Adams, Revolutionary War leader and second cousin of President John Adams, was a failure in his every undertaking except as a political figure. Adams discovered his true forte: local politics and protest against Britain's colonial policies. The disputes with Great Britain gave him a perfect opportunity to exercise his talents as a radical speaker and writer.

In Boston he was the leader of the opposition to arbitrary measures of the British government and to the exclusive, wealthy, conservative class typified by Governor Thomas Hutchinson. Indeed, Adams, more than any other man, prepared the way for the American Revolution. Adams took a prominent part in protests against the Sugar Act of 1764 and the Stamp Act of 1765. He helped form the Sons of Liberty, a secret revolutionary society. While serving in the Massachusetts legislature (1765–74) and as clerk of the House (1766–74), he led the radicals in stirring up opposition to the 1767 Townsend Acts (taxing glass, lead, paint, paper, and tea imported into the colonies), and was an organizer of the Non-Importation Association in 1768.

He was unsurpassed as a political writer. He kept discontent alive by writing numerous inflammatory newspaper articles. As clerk of the House, he drafted most of the official papers of that body. He also wrote many letters to prominent persons in England and America, aiming to gain their support. He contributed some forty articles to Boston newspapers in which he elaborated on the colonists' grievances.

Adams drafted the Boston Declaration of Rights in 1772. This document, that stressed natural rights and asserted America's legislative independence of Parliament, aroused the wrath of Governor Hutchinson, who attempted to respond to it himself in a series of newspaper articles. Naturally, Adams inspired the bitter enmity of the royal authorities in Massachusetts, who regarded him as the chief source of trouble. It was partly to capture him that the 1775 expedition that ended in the battle of Lexington was sent out from Boston. Adams and John Hancock were specifically excluded in the Proclamation of Pardon issued by Governor Gage later that year.

Inspired by the Boston Tea Party and other events, Adams concluded that a congress representing all the colonies was an "absolute necessity." He was chosen by the Massachusetts General Court as one of five delegates to attend the First Continental Congress meeting in Philadelphia in 1774, and later chosen to attend the Second Continental Congress in 1775. At Philadelphia, Adams exercised a powerful influence in the debates, favored immediate independence, proposed a confederation of the colonies, supported the resolution for the formation of state governments, and voted for and signed the Declaration of Independence.

During the Revolutionary War, Adams served as Massachusetts secretary of state, took an important part in drafting the first state constitution (1779–80), and in 1781 was president of the state senate. He served in Congress until 1781 and was a member of the committee to draft the Articles of Confederation. John Adams's speech nominating George Washington as commander in chief of the army was seconded by him. At first opposed to the U.S. Constitution, fearing too much power was concentrated in a central government, Adams eventually supported its ratification.

Adams received belated recognition from Massachusetts voters when he was elected lieutenant governor (1789–94) and governor (1794–97). After parties were formed, he joined the Democratic-Republicans rather than John Adams's Federalists.

SAMUEL HOPKINS ADAMS
1871–1958

As a journalist, Samuel Hopkins Adams served on the staffs of the *New York Sun* (1891–1900) and *McClure's Magazine* (1903–5). His muckraking articles on public health and medicine, printed in *McClure's* and *Collier's,* helped to inspire the Pure Food and Drug Act of 1906. His accounts of the scandal-ridden Harding administration, *Revelry* (1926), and *Incredible Era* (1939) were also widely read. In 1955, at age eighty-four, Adams published *Grandfather Stories,* reminiscences about the early days of the Erie Canal.

GEORGE ADE
1866–1944

After graduation from Purdue University in 1887, George Ade, destined to win fame as a journalist, humorist, and playwright, spent three years as reporter and telegraph editor on the *Lafayette* (Indiana) *Evening Call.* In 1890 he became a reporter on the *Chicago Record* (later the *Record-Herald*). There he soon attracted attention as author of a daily feature, "Stories of the Streets and the Town." In those sketches he invented the character Artie Blanchard and began his celebrated slang fables. The immediate popularity of this serio-comic series was shown by its syndication in a number of Sunday newspapers.

In his column, Ade presented a realistic portrayal of city dwellers of the period, and introduced the slangy wise-cracking characters who became familiar to his readers. *Fables in Slang,* his most successful work, adopted the form of *Aesop's Fables,* full of wit and ending with a flip moral. Ade's fables are often cited as the most accurate literary treatment of common American speech. An example of the flippant morals is one ending "Early to bed and early to rise, and you'll meet very few prominent people." Rural characters were treated sympathetically. One critic noted that "many Americans were then leaving the farms for lives in the city and could be identified with Ade's Yokels-turned-city-slickers." Altogether Ade wrote twelve books of slang.

Ade was also a highly successful playwright. Three of his plays ran simultaneously in New York. *The Sultan of Sulu* began a long run on Broadway in 1902, followed by such popular comedies as *The County Chairman* (1903), and *The College Widow* (1904). Ade also wrote many motion-picture scenarios.

FELIX AGNUS
1839–1925

Felix Agnus was born in France. He came to America near the outset of the Civil War and was a veteran of that war. Soon afterward he became business manager and publisher of the *American*. Under his direction the paper was long a power in Baltimore and throughout Maryland. In 1908 Agnus established an evening paper, the *Star*. Both papers were sold to Frank A. Munsey in 1920, when Agnus retired.

WILLIAM LIVINGSTON ALDEN
1837–1908

William Alden practiced law from 1860 to 1865, and then gave up that profession for journalism. He was employed for a short time as assistant editor on the *New York Citizen* under Charles G. Halpine, and then went on to become a writer for the *Times, World, Graphic,* and other papers. His reputation as a clever writer was established by his humorous skits. While living abroad, he wrote for the Paris edition of the *Herald*. From London, Alden wrote humorous stories over a period of fifteen years for a variety of magazines and acted as literary correspondent for the *New York Times.*

FREDERICK LEWIS ALLEN
1890–1954

Frederick Lewis Allen was born in Boston. He graduated from Harvard University, where he then taught English two years. He became widely known for his books on the American scene, such as *Only Yesterday* and *Since Yesterday,* and as a magazine editor. Allen began his editing career with the *Atlantic Monthly* in 1914. He became managing editor of *Century* two years later. At *Harper's* magazine, he progressed from assistant editor in 1923, to associate editor in 1931, to editor from 1941 to 1953.

ROBERT ALLEN

1900–

Robert Allen preceded Jack Anderson as Drew Pearson's associate on the highly popular radio program "Washington Merry-Go-Round." The secret of the team's success was its diligence in unearthing exclusive stories missed by other journalists. In their tireless efforts they obtained information from every possible source: cabinet members, senators, other newspapermen, clerks, and often the president himself. The two columnists divided the task of assembling news stories. Pearson covered the State Department, Treasury, Department of Justice, Army, Navy, and diplomatic corps, while Allen concentrated on Congress, the Supreme Court, labor, and agriculture.

Allen had begun reporting local events while still in grade school. When he and Pearson first met, Allen was head of the Washington bureau of the *Christian Science Monitor*. Previously, he had worked for a time for the United Press Association in New York. He covered the 1928 and 1932 presidential campaigns, went with Herbert Hoover on his good-will tour of Latin America, and wrote a series of articles on the political situation in various European countries.

Allen's and Pearson's first collaboration was in an anonymous publication, *Washington Merry-Go-Round* (1931), full of gossip gathered by the two men, which their newspapers had been unwilling to print. Their employers fired them because of the book, but the authors proceeded to write *More Merry-Go-Round* (1932). Both books were best-sellers, with sales estimated at 190,000 copies. United Features contracted with Pearson and Allen to write a newspaper column under the same name. The column was slow to catch on, but eventually won phenomenal success. By 1940, "Washington Merry-Go-Around" was being carried in a larger number of papers than any other syndicated political offering.

While still engaged in producing their column, Allen and Pearson coauthored *Nine Old Men* (1936), aimed at debunking the Supreme Court.

JOSEPH ALSOP AND STEWART ALSOP

1910–   1914–1978

The Alsop brothers were noted for their analyses of national and international affairs. The older of the two, Joseph, joined the staff of the *New York Herald Tribune* in 1932, after graduation from Harvard. With Robert E. Kintner he wrote a Washington political column, "The Capitol Parade," for the North American Newspaper Alliance. Stewart, a graduate of Yale, began his career in the publishing business as an editor for Doubleday Doran. Following military service in World War II, the brothers teamed up, from 1945 to 1958, to write a syndicated column, "Matter of Fact," for the Herald Tribune Syndicate. After 1958, Joseph continued to do the column alone, while Stewart became a contributing editor of the *Saturday Evening Post* and a columnist for *Newsweek* (1968-74).

MARY E. CLEMMER AMES
1831-1884

Mary Clemmer, journalist and author, came from a large family in Utica, New York. Because of an improvident father, the Clemmer family was always in financial straits. Under financial pressure and after a failed marriage, Clemmer began contributing letters to the *Utica Morning Herald* and the *Springfield Republican*. Later, while residing in Washington, she chose a serious literary career as author of a regular "Woman's Letter from Washington" for the New York religious weekly, the *Independent,* starting in 1866.

The Clemmer letters were devoted to informal but pointed comments on the political issues of the day. In gathering her material, she spent long hours in the ladies' gallery of the Senate and House. The letters were highly critical of any lapses in ethics on the part of political leaders.

For three years (1869-73) Clemmer wrote a daily column of book reviews for the *Brooklyn Daily Union,* in which she commented on public men and events and other matters. Her salary reached $5,000 a year, reportedly the largest ever paid to an American newspaperwoman up to that time.

Other writing also occupied Clemmer's time, including three novels and two volumes drawn from the newspaper writings. She favored women's suffrage, but never took an active part in the feminist movement.

JACKSON ANDERSON
1922-

Jack Anderson first came into prominence in 1947 as an associate of Drew Pearson, riding "The Washington Merry-Go-Round." After Pearson's death in 1969, Anderson continued the column, which reportedly had forty-five million daily readers and was carried in 746 newspapers. One biographer characterized Anderson as "an investigative reporter, an advocacy journalist and a crusader who in his hard-hitting column, along with his radio and TV broadcasts, has exposed scandal and corruption in high places with greater regularity and impact than any other newsman in the country."

Anderson grew up in Cottonwood, a small town near Salt Lake City. Early on, at age twelve, he wrote the Boy Scout page of the *Deseret News,* a church-owned newspaper, progressing to a seven-dollar-a-week job with the *Murray Eagle,* and at age eighteen joining the staff of the *Salt Lake City Tribune.* For two years he served as a Mormon missionary, preaching in several Southern states. At the end of that stint, he went to China as a foreign correspondent for the *Deseret News.* After World War II he served in the Quartermaster Corps until 1947. On his discharge from the Army, he proceeded to Washington, where Drew Pearson hired him as a reporter.

Among the scandals Anderson uncovered working for Pearson were the gift of a vicuna coat to Sherman Adams, Eisenhower's assistant; the "five percenters" of the Truman administration; the excesses of Congressman Adam Clayton Powell, Jr.; the personal use of campaign contributions by Senator Thomas J. Dodd; the Nixon administration's anti-India bias in the war between India and Pakistan; and disclosure that the Justice Department had settled an antitrust suit against ITT after the International Telephone and Telegraph Company contributed $400,000 to the Republican national convention in San Diego.

Since 1968 Anderson has been bureau chief of *Parade* magazine, stationed in Washington. As a practicing Mormon, Anderson abstains from alcohol, coffee, and smoking.

PAUL Y. ANDERSON
1893–1938

Paul Y. Anderson was born in Knoxville, Tennessee. His first newspaper job was as a reporter for the *Knoxville Journal* at age eighteen. He moved to St. Louis in 1912 for a job with the *St. Louis Times* and then transferred in 1914 to the *St. Louis Post-Dispatch,* where he remained for twenty-three years. With the *Post-Dispatch,* he won a reputation as a great investigative reporter, carrying on crusades exposing race riots, miscarriages of justice, judicial corruption, and the Teapot Dome scandal. As a columnist for the *Nation* (1929–34), Anderson's hard-hitting critiques of government were even more outspoken than his newspaper columns.

In January 1938, Anderson was removed from his *Post-Dispatch* job because of prolonged absences from his work, but he was promptly hired by the *St. Louis Star-Times* for its Washington bureau. He committed suicide in December 1938, leaving a note stating that his "usefulness was at an end."

SHERWOOD ANDERSON
1876–1941

Sherwood Anderson, famous as the author of short stories, especially for his volume *Winesburg, Ohio* (1919), and novels about life in the Midwest, had a short career as a journalist. In 1924, he moved to a farm near Marion, Virginia. There he bought and edited two Marion newspapers, one Democratic and the other Republican. Anderson expressed his hope that female leaders might rescue American culture from mechanization in a nonfiction work *Perhaps Women* (1931).

SIDNEY ANDREWS
1835–1880

Sidney Andrews, a native of Massachusetts, started writing for the press at age thirteen. After leaving college he was assistant editor and later editor of the *Daily Courier* in Alton, Illinois. From 1864 to 1869, Andrews was special correspondent for the *Chicago Tribune* and the *Boston Advertiser,* writing under the pseudonym "Dixon." While traveling through the South after the Civil War, he wrote a series of letters on his observations, which were published in Chicago and Boston. For a few months in 1871, Andrews was on the staff of *Every Saturday.*

HENRY BOWEN ANTHONY
1815–1884

Henry Bowen Anthony, a Rhode Island native, became a journalist by chance. In 1838, at age twenty-three, he was invited to take the editorship of the *Providence Journal* on a temporary appointment. He showed such aptitude for editorial work that the appointment was made permanent. Anthony was in charge of the paper, the most influential journal in the state, during a critical period, at the time of the Dorr Rebellion. The *Journal* came to exercise political power and was admired for its excellent literary style. Anthony was elected governor of Rhode Island in 1849 and became a U.S. senator in 1858, a position that he held until his death in 1884.

BENJAMIN PARKE AVERY
1828-1875

Benjamin Avery was born in New York City. Tempted by reports of the gold strike, he went to California in 1849 to seek the fortune that always eluded him. With money saved from working as a druggist and storekeeper, in 1856 he started a weekly newspaper, the *Hydraulic Press,* at North San Juan, Nevada County. The paper's editorial policies were unpopular, and Avery moved to Marysville. In 1860 he established the *Appeal,* the first daily newspaper in the state outside San Francisco. After being elected state printer for a two-year term, Avery moved to San Francisco and for the next ten years was editor of the *Bulletin.* His final journalistic assignment was the editorship of the *Overland Monthly.* He died in China while on a diplomatic mission.

BENJAMIN FRANKLIN BACHE
1769-1798

Benjamin Franklin Bache, grandson of Benjamin Franklin, was publisher of the leading Democratic-Republican organ, the *Philadelphia General Advertiser,* known later as the *Aurora.* At age seven, Bache accompanied his grandfather, newly appointed ambassador to France, to Paris. He was enrolled in a French boarding school. There he began to form the strongly pro–French views that influenced him for the remainder of his life. In Paris, he learned the basics of the printing trade.

Bache's career as an American journalist started in 1790, when he founded the *Aurora.* When Philip Freneau's *United States Gazette* suspended publication, the *Aurora* became the mouthpiece of the Republican party. Features of the paper, under Bache's direction, were extended accounts of European affairs and reports on the proceedings of Congress. Its most notorious feature, however, was virulent personal abuse, for which that period of journalism was famous. A main target was George Washington, who was charged with various crimes and misdemeanors. Later John Adams came under severe attack.

The end of Bache's career came with the passage of the Sedition Statute in 1798. Bache was arrested, charged with "libeling the President and the Executive Government in a manner tending to excite tradition, and opposition to the laws." He was released on bond, but before his case came to trial, Bache succumbed to yellow fever in Philadelphia on November 17, 1798.

The *Aurora* suspended publication for a short time after Bache's death, but then resumed with Bache's widow Margaret as publisher and William Duane as editor.

Perhaps Bache's major contributions to the progress of journalism were to reveal the inner workings of Congress and the federal government generally to public view, and to stage one of the early battles for freedom of the press.

EDWIN MUNROE BACON
1844–1916

Edwin Bacon, born in Rhode Island, began his journalistic career as a reporter on the *Boston Daily Advertiser*. He gained further experience working for a year with the *Illustrated Chicago News* and with the *New York Times* as assistant night editor and news editor (1868–72). In 1873 Bacon was appointed editor of the *Boston Globe*. That position he resigned in 1878, to return to the *Daily Advertiser,* of which he became chief editor in 1883. His final undertaking as a journalist was to assume editorial control of the *Boston Post,* a position that he held until 1891. Thereafter, Bacon devoted his time to writing and publishing books about Boston and New England.

FRANCIS BAILEY
1735–1815

Francis Bailey, a native of Lancaster County, Pennsylvania, learned the printing art from Peter Miller, the Dunkard printer at Ephrata. He used this skill for a quarter-century to publish the *Lancaster Almanac* and several books. In 1779, Bailey joined Hugh Henry Brackenridge in publishing the *United States Magazine* in Philadelphia. During the same period, he became official printer for Congress and the State of Pennsylvania.

In 1781, Bailey began to edit *The Freeman's Journal or the North American Intelligencer,* a weekly announced to be "open to all parties but influenced by none." The paper was successful and attracted a number of prominent contributors. Gradually Bailey withdrew from the printing business in favor of his son Robert.

GAMALIEL BAILEY
1807-1859

Gamaliel Bailey, son of a New Jersey minister, went as a youth on a trading vessel to China. After returning to America, he became editor in Baltimore of a short-lived journal, the *Methodist Protestant.* An interlude of various adventures followed. Bailey then associated himself with J. G. Birney in editing the *Cincinnati Philanthropist,* the first antislavery organ in the West. The printing press was destroyed by mobs. Undeterred, Bailey launched a daily, the *Herald,* in 1843. Four years later the American and Foreign Anti-Slavery Society chose him to be editor-in-chief of a new national antislavery periodical in Washington. This journal, the *National Era,* usually weekly, sometimes daily, was edited by Bailey for twelve years, starting in 1847. Among its distinguished contributors were Whittier, Theodore Parker, Mrs. Southworth, and Harriet Beecher Stowe.

JAMES MONTGOMERY BAILEY
1841-1894

James Montgomery Bailey was an early Art Buchwald. Bailey introduced a new feature in journalism: humor. His first published writing was done while a prisoner of war in the Civil War. As a soldier he wrote humorous sketches of army life for a Danbury, Connecticut, journal.

Following the war, Bailey and a fellow soldier, Timothy Donovan, purchased the *Danbury Times,* consolidated it with the *Jeffersonian,* and initiated the *Danbury News.* Therein Bailey assumed the name "The Danbury News Man." By 1873, the paper had thirty thousand subscribers—a tribute to the appeal of Bailey's humorous writing. In 1878 Donovan withdrew from the partnership, leaving Bailey as sole editor of the *News.* A daily, the *Danbury Evening News,* was added in 1883.

Bailey had an exceptional talent for injecting humor into ordinary events or inventing ridiculous situations. He visited California in 1873 and Europe in 1874, always seeing the humorous side of everything. A critic noted that his humor was always "natural and kindly." His writings not only increased the circulation of his papers but also created a number of best-selling books.

HUGH BAILLIE
1890-1966

Hugh Baillie, born in Brooklyn, New York, came from a newspaper family. His father had been a reporter or wrote for newspapers in Dumfries, Scotland, and Birmingham, England, before emigrating to New York to work for the *New York Tribune, New York World,* and *New York Press,* and later for the *Los Angeles Herald.* One of his grandfathers was a political writer for the *New York Tribune.*

Young Baillie's first job was with the *Los Angeles Record,* serving as a sportswriter and then police reporter. One critic noted that Baillie always had a special affinity for stories about crime and violence.

In 1912, Baillie began an association with the United Press that was to last for the rest of his career. He started in Los Angeles, went on to Portland, Oregon, moved to UP's Chicago bureau, and then for two years served on the New York City bureau. A major break for Baillie came in 1919, when he was made business manager of the UP Washington bureau. In 1920, he returned to New York as manager of the New York bureau, was promoted to assistant general news manager, then became UP's general news manager. In 1924, Baillie was transferred to the business department to gain broader experience. His success in adding new clients for UP, especially in the South, led to his promotion to UP sales manager.

By 1927 Baillie had become a UP vice president and general business manager. Another promotion in 1931 raised him to the position of executive vice president and general manager. The final step came in 1935, when the UP board named Baillie the company's fifth president and general manager, succeeding Karl A. Bickel. Baillie held the position for twenty years until 1955, the longest of anyone in that office.

Baillie took advantage of his opportunities to undertake first-hand reporting on major news stories, such as interviews with Adolf Hitler, Benito Mussolini, and Russian officials, the Spanish Civil War, the Simpson affair, various stages of World War II, and later interviews with Eisenhower, Bradley, Montgomery, Chiang Kai-Shek, Emperor Hirohito, and Douglas MacArthur. Baillie did reports on the Korean War.

JAMES HEATON BAKER
1829-1913

James H. Baker, born in Lebanon, Ohio, had a fairly short career as a journalist. He entered the field by purchasing the *Scioto Gazette* of Chillicothe, Ohio, and gained influence with the Republican party by advocating the party's cause. Another foray into journalism was made in 1879, when Baker purchased two newspapers in Mankato, Minnesota, and consolidated them into the *Mankato Free Press,* which he published for two years.

RAY STANNARD BAKER
1870–1946

Ray Stannard Baker is known as a historian rather than as a journalist. His eight-volume *Woodrow Wilson: Life and Letters* is a standard work on its subject and won the 1940 Pulitzer Prize for history. He was a close friend of Woodrow Wilson and was his authorized biographer. At the end of World War I, Baker was director of the press bureau for the U.S. commission to negotiate peace in Paris.

Baker's journalistic experience primarily came early in his career. He was a newspaper reporter on the *Chicago Record* (1892–97) and worked on the staffs of *McClure's Magazine* (1899–1905) and *American Magazine* (1906–15).

RUSSELL BAKER
1925–

The *New York Times* is popularly regarded as a staid and sober journal, somewhat pontifical in tone. Since the early 1950s, however, it has had a resident wit to lighten its tone.

After graduating from Johns Hopkins in 1947, Baker was employed by the *Baltimore Sun* to cover police news from 6:00 P.M. to 2:00 A.M. For the next two years his beats were police stations and hospitals, "hanging out with raffish characters all night" as he described the experience, "and sleeping till one or two in the afternoon." A promotion followed, when Baker was assigned to London as bureau chief for the *Sun.* His dispatches took the form of a weekly "Window on Fleet Street" feature, in which he reported political, social, and cultural affairs in London. From London, Baker came to Washington to be the *Sun's* White House correspondent, a job that he found boring and filled with humdrum routine.

The escape for Baker was to accept an offer from James Reston, Washington bureau chief of the *New York Times,* to join the Washington bureau staff of the *Times.* His first beat was the State Department, which he found dull. Capitol Hill was more exciting and his accounts of congressional wheeling and dealing were enjoyed by his readers. But Baker was tired of the life of a reporter. To hold him, the *Times* publisher arranged for him to write a thrice-weekly column, entitled "Topics," to appear on the editorial page. Baker wanted his column to be "an antidote to the heavy tone of the news." His ironic essays were directed especially toward politicians and bureaucrats, but his targets included many of the problems of contemporary life.

After two decades in Washington, Baker moved to New York City in 1974. There he became preoccupied with the trials of urban living, the problem of inflation, and the plight of elderly persons trying to make ends meet on fixed incomes. He tried his hand at children's fiction with a book entitled *The Upside-Down Man*. His script for a musical comedy based on some of Baker's columns never reached Broadway.

JOHN DENISON BALDWIN
1809-1883

John Denison Baldwin graduated from Yale Divinity School in 1834. He served a term in the Connecticut state legislature, where he sponsored a law establishing the state's first normal school. Baldwin abandoned the ministry in 1849, believing that he could perform more usefully as a journalist. In that year he became owner and editor of the *Charter Oak,* a Free Soil party organ at Hartford. Three years later, he moved to Boston to become editor of the daily and weekly *Commonwealth*. In 1859, he and his sons bought the *Worcester Spy* and made it one of the state's leading newspapers. Baldwin wrote and published a number of books, but his influence was exerted mainly through the *Spy*. The paper's political leanings caused it to be known by the Republicans as the "Worcester County Bible," and by the Democrats as the "Lying Spy." After Baldwin's retirement from active editorial work, the *Spy* was carried on by his two sons.

MATURIN MURRAY BALLOU
1820-1895

Maturin Murray Ballou's journalistic career began in a minor way when employed as a clerk in the Boston post office. He wrote for a small paper known as the *Olive Branch*. Later he gained distinction as founder and editor of *Gleason's Pictorial,* subsequently called *Ballou's Pictorial,* one of the earliest of American illustrated papers. Ballou was the first editor and manager of the *Boston Daily Globe* from 1872 to 1874.

Another area in which Ballou gained fame was as a world traveler. He circled the globe in 1882 and took part in numerous tours, sending back for periodical publication descriptions of countries and people. He died on one such expedition in Cairo, Egypt, in 1895.

MOSES YALE BEACH
1800–1868

Moses Yale Beach had New England ancestry dating back to about 1635 in the New Haven colony. Beach was inventive and mechanically inclined. That talent was put to use about 1834 when he went to New York City to join his wife's brother, Benjamin H. Day, owner of the *New York Sun,* as manager of the mechanical department of that newspaper.

The *Sun* was the first among "penny papers," but had strong competition in James Gordon Bennett's *New York Herald.* Beach set up a ship news service, sending his sailing vessels out to meet steamships coming from Europe to obtain the freshest European news. To bring important news from Albany, horse expresses were used. Special trains were run from Baltimore to New York with news of the Democratic national convention of 1844. A huge pigeon house was built for the birds that brought news from Sandy Hook, Albany, and as far away as Washington. Edgar Allan Poe satirized the passion for speed with his "Balloon Hoax" published in the *Sun* on April 13, 1844.

One of Beach's important contributions was to persuade the *Herald, Tribune, Courier and Enquirer, Express,* and *Journal of Commerce* to join the *Sun* in founding the New York Associated Press, to reduce the expense of gathering news. The conference also formed the Harbor Association to maintain one fleet of news-boats instead of the half-dozen previously employed.

Beach is credited with inventing the syndicated newspaper article; he was the first American publisher to issue a European edition, the *American Sun* (1848). He also established the *Weekly Sun,* circulated among farmers at one dollar a year. Another venture was the *Illustrated Sun* and *Monthly Literary Journal,* freely illustrated with woodcuts.

A ruthless rival of Beach and the *Sun* was Horace Greeley's *Tribune.* Nonetheless, the *Sun's* circulation rose to 38,000. It became the country's most popular newspaper, employing a large staff of editors, reporters, compositors, pressmen, and carriers. In 1848, Beach turned the paper over to his sons, Moses Sperry and Alfred Ely, and retired.

HENRY WARD BEECHER
1813-1887

Of the thirteen children sired by the fire-and-brimstone preacher Lyman Beecher, only Harriet achieved greater fame than Henry Ward, her brother. This remarkable family was involved in practically every issue of the day—feminism, abolition of slavery, civil rights, education, spiritualism, and a variety of other moral, political, and religious concerns.

Beecher was born in Litchfield, Connecticut, in 1813. His early education included periods spent in a seminary managed by his sister Catherine in Hartford (where he was the only boy among forty girls) and at the Boston Latin School. At age seventeen, he entered Amherst College. It appears that he achieved no special distinction as a student, but through careful training became a fluent extemporaneous speaker. While still an undergraduate, Beecher was a popular lecturer on temperance and phrenology. Given the family's strong religious orientation, it was inevitable that he should enter the ministry. In preparation, he studied at Lane Theological Seminary in Cincinnati, of which his father was president. Possibly influenced by Calvin Stowe, Harriet's husband and a member of the Lane faculty, Beecher was already moving away from the stern fundamentalist theology of his father.

Beecher's first opportunity in his chosen field came in 1837, when he received a subsidy from the Home Missionary Society to go to Lawrenceburg, Indiana, a little river town where he served as both sexton and preacher for a church with only twenty members. Two years later, he accepted a call to a new church in Indianapolis. His national fame began in 1844 with publication of *Seven Lectures to Young Men,* in which, according to one commentator, "he treated the commonest vices with realistic description and with youthful and exuberant rhetoric." This display of literary talent, combined with active participation in the State Horticultural Society, led to his appointment as editor of the *Western Farmer and Gardener,* further enhancing his reputation, locally and nationally.

A third move was made by Beecher in 1847, when he went on to the pastorate of the newly established Plymouth Congregational Church in Brooklyn, New York, where he spent the remainder of his career. In that position, he began to build a reputation that for conspicuousness and influence exceeded that of any clergyman in American history. Among the qualities that attracted large congregations to hear him were his stalwart figure, liberality of thought, eloquence of language, wit and humor, dramatic ability, sympathetic understanding of human problems, and innate friendliness. His weekly audience grew until it averaged about 2,500 persons. His sermons were printed in pamphlet form and widely circulated.

Other contributions appeared in *The Independent,* for which he served as editor (1861–63), and later in the *Christian Union,* a weekly, undenominational paper, of which he was founder and editor from 1870 to 1881.

Much of Beecher's reputation was based on his activities as a reformer. He became a recognized leader of the antislavery forces, although unsympathetic to extreme abolitionists. He believed that slavery would be overthrown under the Constitution, trusting the national conscience and enlightened self-interest. From the beginning, Beecher used his church as a platform to discuss public, often controversial, questions and to advocate reforms. Among other issues, he urged disobedience of the Fugitive Slave Law, and supported Lincoln in the 1860 election. In 1863, he visited England and delivered a series of speeches to influence English opinion to support the Northern cause. Following the war, he advocated prompt readmission of the seceding states to the Union—a stand that exposed him to much criticism and abuse.

Beecher was not a deeply intellectual person, but appears to have been swayed principally by his emotions and inner feelings. Thus, the condition of the slaves stirred his sympathies because he was a lover of freedom. He supported women's suffrage because he felt that the franchise was a natural right. In his later years, he strongly endorsed the theory of evolution because it fitted his optimistic belief that man is ever ascending.

Beecher's popularity continued in the postwar years. He may have been tempted to run for president, but he continued to preach, lecture, and write prolifically. He not only contributed to the *Independent* but also began writing for the *New York Ledger,* a mass circulation paper published by Robert Bonner.

Beecher's last years were darkened by charges of immorality. A parishioner and former associate, Theodore Tilton, filed a formal complaint against Beecher, charging that he had committed adultery with Mrs. Tilton, and demanding damages of $100,000. The trial lasted for six months, ending in a hung jury, the final vote being nine to three in favor of the defendant. The remainder of Beecher's career was tarnished by the scandal, although his popularity remained undiminished. He conducted his usual services in Plymouth Church on February 27, 1887; a few days later he died of a cerebral hemorrhage. Some forty thousand people came to view his body before burial in Greenwood Cemetery.

ALFRED HORATIO BELO

1839–1901

Alfred Horatio Belo was a native North Carolinian and a veteran of the Civil War. After the war, he rode horseback from North Carolina to

Texas and joined the *Galveston News* in 1865 as bookkeeper. In 1875 he bought an interest in the publishing firm. With his associates Belo contracted with the Galveston, Houston and Henderson Railroad to run a daily train to carry papers around the state. This is reported to be the first daily newspaper service of its kind in the world. Another innovation was to build the first modern exclusive newspaper plant in the United States. The *Galveston News* was duplicated simultaneously at Dallas to facilitate early delivery in all sections of Texas. The *Dallas News,* started in 1885, was the third major American paper to own its own home devoted exclusively to the publication of a newspaper.

Belo showed his forward-looking vision by becoming one of the incorporators of the Associated Press and serving two terms as its vice president.

JAMES GORDON BENNETT
1795–1872

James Gordon Bennett, a Scotsman who emigrated to the United States in 1819, was founder of the *New York Herald*. Under his guidance, the paper became the most powerful voice in American journalism in its day.

Bennett's climb to the top met with difficulties. In the beginning, he worked as a proofreader and book salesman in Boston, then performed minor newspaper jobs in New York City and Charleston, South Carolina. In 1827, he became Washington correspondent for the *New York Enquirer.* Over the next four years he reported congressional proceedings and wrote comments on American politics.

Bennett was eager to establish a newspaper of his own, but lacked capital and equipment. With $500 he had saved in 1835, he launched his penny daily, the *New York Herald*. Without staff, except for two printers, Bennett served as editor, proofreader, ad-taker, folder, and cashier. His innovations quickly made a place for his paper in the competitive newspaper world. The *Herald* was the first to print accounts of stock market transactions. Single-handedly, Bennett wrote a detailed description of the great fire of December 1835 in New York City. Patent medicine advertising provided financial security; national crises were covered in the news with skill and imagination. For example, during the 1846 Mexican War, overland express service was arranged to carry the war news to New York City. To speed news from Europe, fast dispatch boats were maintained to meet incoming ships fifty to one hundred miles at sea to bring fresh news for the *Herald*. During the Civil War sixty-three war correspondents were employed to report war news. Bennett was also the first editor to employ European correspondents, the first publisher to sell papers through newsboys, and the first to use illustrations for news stories. The *Herald* also pioneered regular use of the telegraph to gather news. A society column was introduced, religious news was reported, political speeches were published in full, and with the Helen Jewett case, the *Herald* was the first in U.S. journalism to publish an account of a love-nest murder.

JAMES GORDON BENNETT, JR.
1841-1918

James Gordon Bennett, Jr., inherited the management of the *Herald* from his father and was faithful to traditions established by the senior Bennett. His editorial taste, like his father's, inclined toward the sensational. Some of his exploits made journalistic history. Reporters were assigned to all minor European and Middle Eastern wars; relief kitchens were opened in New York during the 1873 depression; the paper covered the search for the Northwest Passage in 1875; the George DeLong arctic expedition was equipped in 1879; Irish relief was organized in 1882; a cable monopoly was broken by laying a second transatlantic line in 1883; and a Paris edition of the *Herald* began publication in 1887. A widely publicized event was sending Henry Stanley in 1871 to Africa in a successful search for David Livingston, a story fully covered by the *Herald.*

After the outbreak of the Civil War, Bennett enlisted in the U.S. Navy and was commissioned as lieutenant. Thereafter, he maintained a lifelong interest in nautical affairs, causing the *Herald* to devote much space to ship, naval, and military news. He was especially interested in yachting and sailed in two races across the Atlantic in 1886 and 1870. As further evidence of his infatuation with sports, Bennett offered yachting, automobile, balloon, and airplane racing cups in his father's honor. In Paris, he figured prominently as a promoter of sports.

Because of the younger Bennett's involvement in a duel in New York in 1877, he moved to Paris and directed his editors by cable thereafter. In addition to the *New York Herald* and the *Paris Herald,* his newspaper empire included the *New York Evening Telegram,* established in 1867.

Bennett had an irascible, erratic temperament and was unwilling to delegate authority. The *Herald* declined in importance under his absentee ownership and because of the competition of yellow journalism.

Allan Nevins in the *Dictionary of American Biography* notes Bennett's "personal peculiarities": his lavish trips, hatred of Jay Gould and William Randolph Hearst, love for owls, fondness for dogs, and "strange mixture of canniness and naivete."

HELEN DELICH BENTLEY
1923–

Helen Delich Bentley, who later attained fame as a foremost expert on maritime affairs, began her career in journalism as a part-time reporter on the *Ely* (Nevada) *Record,* while still a high school student. She gained experience in politics in the campaign in two Nevada counties of Jones G. Scrughan, a successful candidate for the U.S. Senate in 1942. Afterwards, she went to Washington to serve as Senator Scrughan's secretary. Her college education was completed in 1944, with a bachelor of journalism degree from the University of Missouri, where she worked on the university paper, the *Columbian Missouri.*

For several months after college, Bentley was a reporter and bureau manager for the United Press in Fort Wayne, Indiana, followed by a brief spell as telegraph editor for the *Lewiston* (Idaho) *Tribune.* In 1945 she was hired as a reporter by the *Baltimore Sun.* In 1948, she began to concentrate on labor news.

Bentley's education in labor affairs started when she covered an American Federation of Labor convention in San Francisco in 1947. In 1948 she was assigned by the *Sun* to report news from the Baltimore port. She familiarized herself with problems of the nation's shipping by investigating waterfront events, and talking to dockhands, industrial leaders, and government officials. In 1952, she was promoted to the position of maritime editor of the *Sun.* Thereafter she traveled around the world for her paper, wrote national and international stories on labor and transportation, and reported on maritime developments. Her column "Around the Waterfront" was syndicated in fifteen newspapers. Another program to educate the public was a television show aired on a Baltimore station, "The Port That Built a City and State," written and produced by Bentley (married in 1959 to William Roy Bentley).

She achieved national prominence in 1969 when President Nixon appointed her as chairman of the Federal Maritime Commission, a post previously dominated by men. In her influential position she fought hard to upgrade the deteriorating U.S. merchant marine.

JOEL BENTON
1832–1911

Joel Benton was a local rather than a national figure in the world of journalism. At age nineteen he was placed in charge of the *Amenia* (New York) *Times,* which continued to be published later under the title *Harlem*

Valley Times. Apparently bored with the job, he followed other occupations for the next fifteen years, then returned as editor in 1872 to promote the candidacy of Horace Greeley for president. Benton spent two years in Minnesota during the 1880s, where he wrote for papers in Chicago and St. Paul. As a professional writer, he produced magazine articles and much verse, some of which was republished in anthologies.

MEYER BERGER
1898–1959

Meyer Berger was born on New York's lower east side, one of eleven children raised in a slum. He began selling newspapers at age eight and at age eleven was a night messenger for the *New York World,* promoted afterward to be head office boy. Employment with the *World* continued until 1917, when Berger enlisted in the Army. In World War II he won several awards for bravery in action.

After the war, Berger became a police reporter for the *World* in Brooklyn and then rewrite man and general reporter. For the remainder of his career, starting in 1928, Berger was on the staff of the *New York Times.* An exception was a year with the *New Yorker* magazine in 1937–38, before returning to the *Times* (1938–59). During those eventful years Berger became a star reporter and columnist, and most admired member of the *Times* staff.

CARL BERNSTEIN
1944–

Two *Washington Post* reporters, Carl Bernstein and Robert Woodward, were primarily responsible for revealing the Watergate scandal in 1974, a tale of political shenanigans that brought on a constitutional crisis.

Bernstein's initiation into the newspaper world began at age sixteen as a copy boy at the *Washington Star.* Shortly he was advanced to city desk clerk and then to telephone dictationist. In the latter position, his job was to type up stories called in by reporters, write obituaries from information supplied by relatives and funeral parlors, and to write short articles based on press releases. His experience was broadened by covering fires and crimes at night and evening as a summer replacement on the *Star's* reporting staff. He left the *Star* to accept a reporter's job with the *Elizabeth* (New Jersey) *Daily Journal.* Soon bored with his assignments there, he landed a place on the metropolitan staff of the *Washington Post* in 1966. His beats included the police department, the courts, city hall, and the Virginia state legislature. The scope of the job was extended on Bernstein's own initiative, when he was inspired to write about ethnic neighborhoods, slum landlords, police corruption, drug traffic, and fraudulent trade schools.

The big break for Bernstein came when he was assigned to a team to investigate the break-in of the Democratic National Committee headquarters in the Watergate complex on June 17, 1972. At first, Bernstein and Woodward worked independently, but soon combined to share their sources and efforts. By late September 1972, they knew most of the links in the chain, leading up to President Nixon himself. *All the President's Men,* published in 1974, traces the steps from the Watergate break-in to the beginning of the Senate hearings eleven months later. The book was, of course, an immediate best-seller, in hardback and paperback editions. A moving-picture version based on the book was also phenomenally successful.

As a follow-up for *All the President's Men,* Bernstein and Woodward published in 1976 *The Final Days,* a detailed account of Nixon's last fifteen months in office. A 15,000-word excerpt appeared in *Newsweek.* The book was denounced by Nixon associates and conservative columnists, but again was on the best-seller list for many months. Bernstein's latest book is *Loyalties, a Son's Memoir* (1988).

JOHN NICHOLS BERRY III
1933–

John Nichols Berry III was a graduate of Boston University and Simmons College. He served in the U.S. Army (1955–57). He began his professional career as reference librarian of Simmons (1960–62) and assistant librarian of Simmons (1962–64). He was editor of the *Bay State Librarian* (1962–64), assistant editor of the *Library Journal* (1964–66), managing editor of R. R. Bowker New Book Project (1966–69), and editor-in-chief of the *Library Journal* from 1969.

AMBROSE BIERCE
1842–1914?

Ambrose Bierce, journalist and short-story writer, was born in a log cabin on Horse Cave Creek, Meigs County, Ohio. He was twice wounded severely in the Civil War and promoted to major for bravery. Following the war, he went to San Francisco, where he wrote for the *Argonaut, Overland Monthly,* and the *News Letter* (of which he became editor in 1868). He soon became known for his caustic wit, a characteristic that caused him to be called "Bitter Bierce." After a stay in London (1872–76), he returned to San Francisco to edit *The Wasp* (1880–86), and to contribute a column entitled "Prattle" to the *Argonaut.*

Bierce's macabre short stories on death, horror, and the supernatural have often been compared to Poe's.

In 1896, Bierce moved to Washington, D.C. Employed by William Randolph Hearst, he continued newspaper and magazine writing, serving as Washington correspondent for the Hearst papers. He also contributed to the *New York Journal,* the *San Francisco Examiner,* and *Cosmopolitan* magazine. Among the books published during his Washington stay was *The Devil's Dictionary,* originally entitled *The Cynics Word Book,* a collection of numerous pessimistic, cynical definitions. As a newspaper columnist, Bierce's favorite targets were amateur poets, clergymen, bores, dishonest politicians, and all sorts of frauds.

Late in 1913, Bierce retired from writing, toured the Civil War battlefields, and then went to Mexico where he was attached as an observer to Pancho Villa's army. He was last heard from in December 1913. It is assumed that he died shortly thereafter. His end is a mystery, but the general belief is that he was killed in the siege of Ojinaga in January 1914.

ROBERT WORTH BINGHAM
1871–1937

Robert Worth Bingham, a native of North Carolina and son of the headmaster of a boys' preparatory school in Asheville, North Carolina, started his career as an attorney in Louisville, Kentucky. He became a county judge and for a brief time was mayor of Louisville.

Bingham changed direction when he inherited $5 million from his second wife. This bequest enabled him to buy control of two nationally known newspapers, the *Louisville Courier-Journal* and the *Louisville Times.* Under his management, the papers prospered in both business and reputation.

Bingham was a personal friend and supporter of Franklin D. Roosevelt, who in 1933 appointed him ambassador to Great Britain. While still holding that office, he died in Baltimore in 1937. His son Barry Bingham succeeded him as publisher and editor of the Louisville papers.

JOHN BINNS
1772-1860

John Binns was an Irish-born journalist, politician, and author, who emigrated to the United States in 1802. From 1802 to 1807 he published the *Northcumberland* (Pennsylvania) *Republican Argus.* His next stop was Philadelphia, where he established the *Democratic Press,* published from 1807 to 1829. The paper's main intent was opposition to Andrew Jackson. Binns's home was attacked by a mob and financial difficulties forced him to discontinue his paper.

WINIFRED SWEET BLACK
1863-1936

Winifred Sweet Black, known also as "Annie Laurie," originally planned a stage career. When that was unsuccessful, she accepted a job as a reporter on William Randolph Hearst's *San Francisco Examiner.* She was married in 1892 to a fellow journalist, Orlow Black, while continuing newspaper work. As a pseudonym, she adopted the name "Annie Laurie," from her mother's favorite lullaby. In the course of promoting charitable projects, Annie Laurie was an ardent do-gooder, helping, for example, to bring about needed hospital reforms.

Further steps in Annie Laurie's lively career were divorce from Black and marriage to the brother of Frederick Bonfils, publisher of the *Denver Post.* She was given a job at the *Post,* already notorious in the field of yellow journalism. Her ties with Hearst, however, were maintained and as a Hearst feature writer, she traveled throughout America and Europe reporting on political campaigns, natural disasters (such as the storm and tidal wave that killed seven thousand persons in Galveston, Texas, in 1900, and the San Francisco earthquake in 1906), sporting events (the first woman to report a prize fight), and sensational trials. Her sentimental treatment of the evidence in the case of the trial of Harry Thaw for the murder of Stanford White caused a cynical male reporter to describe her as a "sob sister." In fact, she became known as "the greatest sob sister of them all."

Major assignments for Annie Laurie's later career were traveling to Europe to report on the war and the Versailles Peace Conference, to Washington for the naval disarmament conference in 1921-22, and to Geneva in 1931 for an international conference on narcotics. She was mainly occupied, however, with the writing of a regular column for the *San Francisco Examiner.* Her biographer, Walton Bean, comments that while

Black was "not the first woman to win success in the era of sensational journalism, she was unquestionably one of the best known and most colorful."

FRANCIS PRESTON BLAIR
1791–1876

Francis Preston Blair's fame rests mainly on his role as confidant of Andrew Jackson. As a member of Jackson's "kitchen cabinet," Blair met with the president almost daily and even vacationed with him. Subsequently, Blair became an elder statesman of American politics, founder of the Republican party, and a close friend of Abraham Lincoln.

Journalistically, Blair was invited by Andrew Jackson to establish a Democratic newspaper in Washington. This party organ, the *Washington Globe,* was owned and edited by Blair from 1830 to 1845. He was also publisher of the *Congressional Globe,* and contributed to the *Argus of Western America,* published in Frankfort, Kentucky.

Although Blair himself was a slaveholder, he opposed the extension of slavery and in 1848 supported the Free Soil presidential candidate, Martin Van Buren. He assisted nationally in Abraham Lincoln's nomination in 1860 and became an influential adviser in Lincoln's administration. At the end of the Civil War, he supported Andrew Jackson's Reconstruction measures, opposed the harsh proposals of the Radical Republicans, and rejoined the Democratic party. In 1868, the Democrats nominated Blair for vice president, but his vigorous opposition to the Reconstruction Acts led to the ticket's defeat. Two years later, however, the Liberal Republicans in Missouri joined with the Democrats to elect Blair to the U.S. Senate.

As a newspaper editor, Blair argued against the United States Bank, nullification, and abolitionism, and campaigned for elimination of imprisonment for debt, legislative control over judicial decisions, cheap land for settlers, and direct election of the president — some of the issues reflecting Andrew Jackson's views.

HERBERT BLOCK
1909–

"Herblock," as he is familiarly known to millions of his admiring fans, has been drawing politically oriented cartoons for the *Washington Post* since 1946. He is widely known for his syndicated humorous, hard-hitting drawings, reflecting a politically liberal point of view.

Block adopted the pen name "Herblock" at his father's suggestion. His first journalistic experience was with the *Chicago Daily News* (1929–33). His humorous cartoons appeared daily on the editorial page of the *News* for four years. He spent ten years with the Newspaper Enterprise Association (1933–43), before he joined the *Washington Post*. He soon became, in Eric Sevareid's words, "the most powerful and effective political commentator in the United States."

Herblock has been the winner of many awards, notably a Pulitzer Prize in 1942 and 1954 and the Heywood Brown Award in 1947 and 1950. His drawings were exhibited in the Corcoran Gallery in Washington and at the Associated American Artists Gallery in New York. Several hundred have been republished in book form.

Herblock's likes and dislikes are revealed in his cartoons. Favorite targets at one time were Senators Joseph McCarthy and Pat McCarran, expressing Herblock's dislike of hearsay reports and vigilante tactics. Over the years, he has produced many powerful anticommunist cartoons. He is often called a liberal, an appellation that he questions as meaningless. His intention, he states, is to try to present "the right thing, effectively." His philosophy he declares, is summed up as follows: "First be right, then be effective, then be a good artist."

EDWARD BOK
1863–1930

Edward Bok was six years of age when his Dutch emigrant parents brought him to the United States. He entered public school in Brooklyn without knowing a word of English.

Bok's genius as an entrepreneur was exhibited at a tender age, beginning with window cleaning for a baker at fifty cents a week, delivering papers, and working at odd jobs. His first journalistic venture was reporting children's parties (being certain that the name of every person present was included) for the *Brooklyn Daily Eagle*. At thirteen, Bok quit school to become an office boy for the Western Union Telegraph Company, where his father was employed as a translator. He developed money-making schemes on the side, including a profitable one writing or editing one hundred-word biographical sketches of well-known actors and actresses and famous Americans to be printed on the backs of pictures enclosed in cigarette packages.

Now thoroughly bitten by the journalistic bug, Bok proceeded to report public speeches for the local paper, edit a church paper entitled the *Brooklyn Magazine,* write theater news for the *Daily Eagle,* publish theater programs (which he designed), and serve successively as stenographer in two publishing firms, Henry Holt and Charles Scribner.

Bok soon observed that few women read newspapers and the concomitant fact that the papers of the time paid slight attention to women's interests. Thus was born an embryo idea that was to lead to the young journalist's greatest success. He began to gather material designed to appeal to women and to influence their reading habits. Ella Wheeler Wilcox and others were engaged to write on women's topics, and shortly, through his syndicate, Bok was supplying newspapers with a full page of women's features.

Another void to be filled, in Bok's view, was news about books and authors. This led to a feature known as "Bok's Literary Leaves," and soon had a following of readers in more than forty newspapers. In 1887 Bok was placed in charge of advertising for the newly established *Scribner's Magazine,* and in that capacity a year later helped to make famous Edward Bellamy's utopian novel, *Looking Backward.*

In April 1889, Cyrus H. K. Curtis, who had been impressed by Bok's book reviews in the *Philadelphia Times,* invited him, at the age of twenty-six, to become editor of the *Ladies' Home Journal,* then a six-year-old magazine. He accepted the post. Thus began the career that was to make him an internationally known figure. Under his guidance, the *Ladies' Home Journal* became a national institution to a degree which no other magazine had ever achieved. By the time Bok retired, after thirty years as editor, two records had been set: the magazine's circulation had reached two million, and each issue carried advertising in excess of a million dollars.

For a mere man, furthermore an unmarried one, to undertake editorship of a women's magazine exposed Bok to a great deal of jocular comment and even ridicule. As a first step to compensate for his own want of intimate knowledge of the gentler sex, Bok offered prizes for the best suggestions for improving the contents of the magazine. Thousands of answers poured in, and combining them with his own ideas Bok proceeded to establish departments to inform young mothers about prenatal and postnatal care, and a less savory subject: venereal diseases. His magazine lost many thousand readers upon the publication of the first article on this subject. When the matter became acceptable to public discussion, understanding and education grew.

Guided by high principles in editing a magazine for women, Bok inaugurated a series of crusades, using the *Ladies' Home Journal* as a forum and pulpit. Some campaigns ended in splendid victories, others in ignominious defeats. The *Journal* stopped accepting patent medicine advertisements, a chief source of revenue for magazines and newspapers. Bok was disillusioned by the reliance of American women on Paris fashions, the lack of support for his campaign to stop the killing of egrets, and the shallow nature of women's clubs' activities. More successful were his campaigns to improve the architecture of the small American home, to upgrade the interior appearances of homes, and to promote interest in music.

FREDERICK GILMAN BONFILS
1860–1933

Frederick Bonfils set new high or low levels, depending upon the point of view, for sensational presentation of news.

With the opening of the Oklahoma Territory Bonfils made a small fortune overnight in the real estate boom. Using his profits, and employing several aliases, he operated the "Little Louisiana Lottery" in Kansas City, Kansas. Persistent attacks by the *Kansas City Star* under William Rockhill Nelson finally drove him out of town.

Bonfils's next venture was a newspaper partnership with Harry Heye Tammen, a bartender in Denver. Tammen persuaded Bonfils to invest $12,500 in the purchase of the *Denver Post,* a paper established in 1892. All the devices of sensational journalism were used to increase the newspaper's circulation: screaming headlines, often in red ink, scary captions, and constant attacks upon public officials. The stories of two "sob sisters," Polly Pry (Leone Campbell) and Winifred Black, had avid followers. There were reports of strong-arm methods in obtaining advertisers. Emphasis was on local news, for the partners agreed that "a dog fight in a Denver street was more important than a war in Europe." Denver's mayor, the utilities, officials, preachers, and leaders in general were victims. There were libel suits, shootings, and street fights, but the *Post* rolled on. There was a long and often violent feud with the *Rocky Mountain News.* On one occasion, when the paper opposed a street-car strike, a crowd sympathetic with the strikers sacked the newspaper's offices.

The *Post's* sensationalism paid off. From a circulation of 4,000 in 1895, its circulation had grown to 83,000 by 1907, and during Bonfils's lifetime it reached a daily circulation of 150,000 and 300,000 on Sunday. The *Post's* weekly rate of ten cents attracted subscribers. In the 1920s the paper was making over a million dollars a year and Bonfils and Tammen were paying themselves a thousand dollars a week each.

Some of the issues raised by the *Post* were in the public interest. It exposed the Teapot Dome scandal, supported such progressive causes as prison and child labor reform, fought official corruption, served as a club over monopolies, and forced down the price of coal. An editorial in the *Christian Century* concluded that the work of Bonfils and Tammen had "many constructive aspects." For these reasons, judgments differ about the

Post. L. C. Paddock, publisher of the *Boulder Daily Camera,* called it "a cancerous plague eating at the vitals of the business and public life of Colorado." Frank Luther Mott, in his history of American journalism, characterizes Bonfils and Tammen as "paternalistic pirates of journalism."

From 1909 to 1922, Bonfils published the *Kansas City Post,* using tactics similar to those found effective in Denver, but Kansas City did not approve of these methods and the paper was sold in 1922.

MARGARET BOURKE-WHITE
1906–1971

Margaret Bourke-White recorded on film many of the important events of the first half of the twentieth century. Her professional name is a combination of her surname, White, and her mother's maiden name, Bourke.

For *Fortune* magazine, Bourke-White did a report on the Soviet Union's five-year plan in 1931. For *Life,* with which she became associated in 1936, she did studies of most of the European countries, India, the Soviet Union, Africa, Korea, and the Arctic. During World War II, she had assignments in Russia, Germany, and Italy. Bourke-White was the first accredited woman war correspondent to go overseas during the war. She survived a ship torpedoing and flew on combat missions. When *Life* magazine was founded in 1936, she became one of four staff photographers.

Bourke-White wrote and illustrated several books, including *Eyes on Russia* (1931), *Shooting the Russian War* (1942), *Halfway to Freedom, a Study of the New India* (1949), and with her husband, Erskine Caldwell, *You Have Seen Their Faces* (1937). She specialized in industrial photography and became associate editor of *Fortune* magazine.

The Bourke-White photographs have been shown in the Library of Congress, the Cleveland Museum of Art, the Museum of Modern Art, and other art centers.

CHARLES ADDISON BOUTELEE
1839–1901

Charles Boutelee, a native of Maine, was a U.S. naval officer during the Civil War. From boyhood, he had been interested in journalism and in 1870, he became managing editor of an old and influential paper, the *Whig and Courier* of Bangor, Maine. Most of his active career, however, was spent as a Republican congressman, where he fought for high tariffs, legal rights of blacks, and a tough Reconstruction policy.

OLIVER K. BOVARD
1872–1945

Oliver K. Bovard, born in St. Louis, came naturally to the newspaper profession. His father had been a printer and editor for several newspapers, including the *Post-Dispatch*. Furthermore, unlike most well-known journalists of his time who moved around from city to city and paper to paper, practically the whole of Bovard's career was spent with the St. Louis *Post-Dispatch*.

Bovard was hired as a reporter by the *St. Louis Star* in 1896. In addition to general assignments he reported on the cycling craze then sweeping the country. An ardent devotee of the sport, he bicycled from St. Louis to Mexico City.

Bovard's long association with the *Post-Dispatch* began in 1898 after he wrote a report exposing a bribery scandal involving the local street railway's franchise. Within two years he was promoted to city editor in charge of the local reporting staff. In a short time the *Post-Dispatch* developed the strongest group of reporters in the city. Pulitzer transferred Bovard for a few months to New York to gain additional experience working for the *New York World* and then returned him to St. Louis to be the *Post-Dispatch's* managing editor. In that position, he expanded the paper's national and international coverage, sent correspondents overseas, and set up a Washington bureau. He was ruthless in dealing with incompetent reporters.

In 1938, after policy disagreements with Joseph Pulitzer, Jr., who had taken over after his father's death, Bovard resigned his position with the *Post-Dispatch,* and disassociated himself thereafter from journalism.

CLAUD G. BOWERS
1878–1958

The newspaper career of Claud Bowers, journalist, historian, and diplomat, began in 1901 with the *Indianapolis Sentinel* and continued with other Indiana papers. He moved to New York City in 1923 to become chief editorial writer for the *New York World* and later political columnist for the *New York Journal.*

Bowers was an active, liberal Democrat, serving as chairman and keynote speaker for the party's 1928 presidential nominating convention in Houston. After Franklin Roosevelt was elected, Bowers was appointed ambassador to Spain in 1933. The Spanish Civil War was going on during his term. A similar post was filled in Chile, where Bowers served as ambassador for fourteen years.

Bowers was author of a number of noteworthy biographical and historical books, including *Jefferson and Hamilton* (1925), *The Tragic Era* (1929), and *Mission to Spain* (1954).

SAMUEL BOWLES III
1826–1878

In 1856 Horace Greeley declared the *Springfield* (Massachusetts) *Republican* to be "the best and ablest country journal ever published on the continent." The *Republican* was the first Massachusetts daily outside of Boston. It had been started as a weekly by Samuel Bowles in 1824, primarily as an organ of the National Republicans. Daily publication began about twenty years later, in 1844. Even before the Civil War, it had become one of the most influential of provincial press papers.

Samuel Bowles III began work on his father's paper at age seventeen and eight years later, following his father's death, he assumed control of the *Republican*. Young Bowles announced that his aim was to create a paper "that should stand firmly in the possession of powers of its own; that should be concerned with the passing and not with the past; that should perfectly reflect its age, and yet should be itself no mere reflection."

Under Bowles's direction, the *Republican* was shaped to reflect his views, such as emphasis on local news and local interests, straightforward and concise style (contrary to the current wordy literary fashion), and independence from party politics. The *Republican* was among the first newspapers to advocate universal suffrage without regard to race or color, and was among the first to advocate women's suffrage. A rival newspaper, the *Springfield Gazette,* was started in 1846, but two years later it was absorbed by the *Republican*. The success of Bowles's efforts was demonstrated by his paper attaining a daily circulation of more than five thousand and a national circulation of over ten thousand for a weekly edition.

Bowles crusaded against slavery and called for the formation of an antislavery party. He was prominent in building the Republican party in New England and consistently supported Abraham Lincoln. After the war, he denounced the carpetbag system and postwar corruption. The *Repub-*

lican exposed many political and financial scandals. In one case the stock market speculator James Fisk sued Bowles for libel.

The Bowles dynasty was continued by Samuel Bowles IV, who assumed control after his father's death in 1878. His most notable change was the *Sunday Republican,* starting on September 15, 1878.

The historian Allan Nevins characterizes Greeley, Bryant, and Bowles as "masters of controversial journalism," adding, "Greeley excelled in forcible hard hitting prose such as Cobbett wrote, Bryant in swelling eloquence and Bowles in logical power and slashing wit."

ANDREW BRADFORD
1686–1742

The Bradford family was prominent in early American printing and publishing for an amazing 140 years. The founder of the hierarchy in the New World was William Bradford, who arrived in Philadelphia in 1685. There Andrew, the first of two sons, born in 1686, became printer to the Commonwealth of Pennsylvania from 1712 to 1730, in 1719 founded the first newspaper, the *American Weekly Mercury,* outside Boston, and in 1741 started publication of the first magazine in America, the *American Magazine.* The *Mercury* lasted until 1746, but the *American Magazine* survived for only three issues.

Like other colonial printers, Andrew Bradford had difficulties with the civic authorities. An article in the *Mercury* expressed "great expectations" that the General Assembly would do something for the province's finances and credit was considered critical of the provincial council. Bradford was reprimanded by the governor, and ordered not to print anything else about government affairs without express permission. Some years later, the council was alarmed again when Bradford published an essay on liberty and hereditary power. The publisher was arrested, but the matter was dropped for lack of evidence.

Bradford held a monopoly on printing in Philadelphia during his first ten years. From 1713 to 1723 he is known to have published about seventy-five items. A regular feature on his list was almanacs, always a mainstay of eighteenth-century printers.

During much of the time that Bradford was publishing the *Mercury,* he was postmaster of Philadelphia, advantageous for him in obtaining news. His printing house sold pamphlets, school books, and stationery, and operated a book bindery.

After Bradford's death in 1742, his widow, Cornelia, continued publication of the *Mercury* until 1747, thereby becoming one of the first woman newspaper editors in America.

JOHN BRADFORD
1749–1830

John Bradford, Kentucky's first printer, was apparently not related to the famous line of early American printers. His place in the history of journalism is based on his establishment of the *Kentucky Gazette,* the first newspaper in Kentucky and the second west of the Allegheny Mountains.

Bradford was not a trained printer. Kentucky at the time was a part of Virginia and a strong movement existed for separation and setting up an independent state. A printing press was regarded as a political necessity and Bradford was asked to establish a press. Fielding Bradford, John's brother, was sent to Pittsburgh to learn printing, equipment was procured in Philadelphia, and the press was transported by flatboat down the Ohio River to Lexington. Some type was cut out of dogwood, and on August 17, 1787, the *Kentucky Gazette* was issued. Bradford, a Virginia surveyor and planter, served as its founder and editor until 1802.

A second newspaper, the *Kentucky Herald,* began publication in Lexington a year later. Bradford acquired the *Herald* in 1802 and merged it with the *Gazette.* In the same year he turned over editorship of the *Gazette* to his son Daniel. In 1821, Bradford became editor of the *Lexington Public Advertiser* until it ceased publication in 1825. In his late seventies, he returned to the *Gazette* for two years as editor (1825–27).

In addition to being a newspaper founder and editor, Bradford produced a major work, *Notes on Kentucky,* recording events relating to early Kentucky history. Bradford's other publishing activities included the first *Kentucky Almanac* in 1788, continued annually, a number of literary works, the Kentucky Constitution, annual acts of the state legislature, and *Laws of Kentucky.*

All of Bradford's five sons became printers and three established and edited newspapers in other states. Bradford also organized a press association of Western printers and booksellers.

WILLIAM BRADFORD
1663–1752

William Bradford, founding father of several generations of early American printers and journalists, was born in Leicestershire, England. He learned the art of printing in London and in 1682 came with William Penn to the Quaker Colony of Pennsylvania. There he established the first printing press outside of New England. In 1690, Bradford and others established the first paper mill in America.

Bradford brought with him from London letters of introduction stating that he was coming to be a printer of Quaker books, guaranteed not to contain hearsay. The first book known to have been issued from his press was an almanac for the year 1686. This publication brought on an immediate clash with the government because it referred to Penn as "Lord Penn." The printer was ordered to blot out those words and forbidden to print anything without license from the council.

Bradford's problems with the censors continued. The governor and the people became involved in a dispute about their rights. Bradford was persuaded to print the colony's charter. He maintained that he had the right to print the laws, especially since the charter had been printed in England. In any case, Bradford went on trial for printing a seditious pamphlet. He conducted his own defense and began by objecting to two of the jurors on the grounds that they had already formed an opinion.

Bradford was permitted to go free because the jury was unable to reach a verdict. By now, however, he was sick of the colony and of the Quakers. Providentially, in 1693, the council of New York City passed a resolution stating that if a printer would come and settle in the city of New York for the printing of the Acts of Assembly and public papers they would give him forty pounds for his salary and allow him to carry on his printing business. Bradford promptly accepted, after eight years as a printer in Philadelphia.

Bradford held the position of royal printer for the New York colony for more than fifty years. On November 8, 1725, he issued the first number of the *New York Gazette,* the first paper established in New York and until 1733 the only paper in the colony. The *Gazette* continued publication until 1744.

WILLIAM BRADFORD
1722–1791

William Bradford, grandson of the first William and nephew of Andrew, founded the *Pennsylvania Journal, or Weekly Advertiser* in 1742, and made it into a powerful anti–British organ in the years before the Revolution. The paper remained under his and his son's control for sixty years. In 1774–75, the journal bore the oft-reproduced logo of a divided serpent with the motto "Unite or Die." Earlier, when the British imposed their stamp tax on the press in 1765, Bradford issued the *Journal* with an imprint of skull and crossbones across the top and the borders in black to signify the death of freedom of the press. The *Journal* also published Thomas Paine's Revolutionary War essay *Crisis.* Bradford served in the War of Independence, rising to the rank of colonel. His son Thomas became sole publisher of the *Journal* in 1778 and carried it on until 1793. Thomas founded the *Merchants' Daily Advertiser* in 1797. When he sold that paper in 1813, the Bradford era in Philadelphia publishing ended.

BENJAMIN P. BRADLEE
1921–

Before he became vice president and executive editor of the *Washington Post* in 1968, Benjamin Bradlee had more than twenty years of experience as a police reporter, State Department official, foreign correspondent, and national political reporter.

Following his graduation from Harvard College in 1942, Bradlee enlisted in the U.S. Navy to serve as a combat communications officer on a destroyer in the South Pacific. Postwar, he worked in the American Civil Liberties office in New York. With several friends he moved to Manchester, New Hampshire, in 1946 to start the *New Hampshire Sunday News.* After a period as police and federal courts reporter for the *Washington Post,* Bradlee resigned in 1951 to work as a press attaché at the U.S. Embassy in Paris.

An important break for Bradlee came in 1953 when *Newsweek* appointed him as its chief European correspondent. Four years later, he came back to Washington, where his assignments covered the 1960 presidential election and Richard Nixon's 1962 gubernatorial campaign. Bradlee's *Conversations with Kennedy,* a record of informal talks with the president from 1959 to 1963, quickly became a best-selling book.

In 1965, Bradlee became deputy managing editor for foreign and national affairs for the *Washington Post* and a few months later, he succeeded Alfred Friendly as managing editor. In 1968, Bradlee was named vice president and executive editor of the *Post.*

Major space was devoted by the *Post* to the Watergate story and the relentless investigation by two of its reporters, Bob Woodward and Carl Bernstein, leading eventually to President Nixon's resignation. The *Post* was accused of using stories based on hearsay and Bradlee was attacked by a number of administration hatchet men. Bradlee's only comment was that the attacks "led me to the conclusion that we were right."

EDWARD BRADLEY
1941-

Ed Bradley, who has long been a fixture on "60 Minutes," had an inauspicious beginning when he did unpaid news spots for a Philadelphia radio station. He became a hero years later. As a correspondent for the television documentary "CBS Reports," he dived into the South China Sea off Malaysia to help pull a boatload of Vietnamese refugees to shore.

In 1967, Bradley began a stretch of three-and-a-half years with WCBS radio in New York broadcasting news. Becoming dissatisfied, he quit the job and moved to Paris. CBS persuaded him to go to Southeast Asia as a television correspondent for the next eighteen months. In 1974, he went back to the Far East to cover the fall of the Vietnamese and Cambodian capitals to communist forces.

After returning to the United States, Bradley reported on the presidential campaign first of Senator Birch Bayh, and then of Jimmy Carter. Following Carter's victory, Bradley became one of three CBS White House correspondents. At the same time, he was named anchorman of the "CBS Sunday Night News." Finding the White House job somewhat tame, he again became restless and returned to the Far East, where his principal assignment was to report on the plight of the "boat people," the thousands of Vietnamese refugees stranded in small boats along the Malaysian coast and Southeast Asian peninsula.

Bradley accompanied a CBS news team covering the Boston Symphony Orchestra in its 1979 tour of China. In the same year a much publicized documentary "Blacks in America with All Deliberate Speed," produced by Bradley, dealt with the progress made by black Americans. Other programs directed by him dealt with inflation, the CIA's covert actions, American relations with Saudi Arabia, and the U.S. foreign service.

Since 1968, CBS television news magazine "60 Minutes" has been one of the most watched and highly rated programs on the air. As a member of the regular panel, Bradley traveled one hundred thousand miles in his first year, visited fifty cities, and conducted numerous interviews with celebrities searching for information.

JAMES BRADY
1941-

James Brady was appointed press secretary for President Ronald Reagan in 1981 after previously serving as assistant to John Connally and other prominent politicians. Brady was seriously wounded in the assassination attempt on Reagan later that year. Although he was still given the title of press secretary, the work was actually left to others because of his disability. At the end of the Reagan administration he resigned his more or less honorary press secretary position. He became a freelance writer, and with his wife Sarah, has become a strong proponent of handgun control.

MATHEW B. BRADY
1823-1896

Mathew Brady was born about 1823 in Warren County, New York, the son of a poor Irish family. The extent of his formal education is unknown, but he seems to have been mostly self-educated. He showed some talent as an artist and at age sixteen was sent by a friend to the Samuel F. B. Morse Academy of design for training. Morse had learned about Daguerre's process on one of his trips to Europe and had set up a studio in New York in conjunction with his art and telegraphy research. Young Brady was so impressed with the artistic and commercial possibilities of the daguerreotype that he set up his own studio (1844), the "Brady's Daguerrian Miniature Gallery."

Brady conceived the idea of producing a "Gallery of Illustrious Americans," one of the most fortunate decisions of the decade of the 1840s. It made available to future generations the true image of some of America's most notable people. The following incomplete list indicates the extent of Brady's contact with the leading people of the time: Lincoln (including the picture on the five-dollar bill), Daniel Webster, Andrew Jackson, John Calhoun, Henry Clay, Brigham Young, John Tyler, Thomas Benton, Stephen Douglas, Edgar Allan Poe, James Polk, James Fenimore Cooper, Jenny Lind, Phineas Barnum, John J. Audubon, Winfield Scott, the Prince of Wales (Edward), John Fremont, Millard Filmore, Walt Whitman, Samuel Morse, John Quincy Adams, Rutherford Hayes, Robert E. Lee, Ulysses S. Grant, Andrew Carnegie, Mrs. Benjamin (Caroline Scott) Harrison, and Mary Todd Lincoln. Brady published his "Gallery" in 1850, but it was an expensive item and not a financial success. It sold for $20 per copy or $1 per plate. Nevertheless, Brady had met so many people from Washington, D.C., that he decided to open a studio there in 1849. He made a photograph of President James Knox Polk, the first president to sit for a daguerreotype. In the course of time, he photographed all presidents from John Quincy Adams to William McKinley, with the exception of William Henry Harrison, who died before Brady set up his first gallery.

Brady photographed Lincoln first in February 1860. He took several other portraits of Lincoln. Brady had no trouble getting permission from General McDowell to take his camera to the battlefield. Thus, when the war began Brady was ready to accompany the army to Bull Run and record the first defeat. The newspapers declared that: "Brady has fixed the cowards beyond a doubt."

When General McClellan replaced McDowell as the new commander and a major war was in the offing, Brady needed War Department approval. Lincoln sent him to Secretary Stanton, who grudgingly gave him permission but informed Brady that he would have to pay his own expenses because the proposal was without merit in Stanton's eyes. Brady believed he could sell enough war pictures to make a profit. At least ten assistants were engaged who were familiar with his methods; most were from his own studios. Different sized cameras and supplies, including chemicals, tripods, plate holders, and negative boxes, were carried in a specially designed wagon that was soon named the "Whatizzit Wagon" by the soldiers.

Brady accompanied McClellan's army down the Potomac to the battlefront in the spring of 1862. His mission to photograph the Civil War had begun. One of his first pictures at Fortress Monroe was of McClellan and his staff of ten. Brady arranged the eleven men in different poses, McClellan looking like Napoleon with his hand inside his coat. For the remainder of the war Brady and his crews moved with the army. They took more than 3,500 photos, depicting everything from grisly death scenes and firing of cannon during combat to field conferences between Lincoln and his generals. Brady and his men worked under trying circumstances involving not only danger but also the limitations imposed upon them by the art of photography of that day. Nevertheless, they acquired an unsurpassed pictorial record of the war that became a heritage for future generations.

In 1870 Brady published *Brady's National Photographic Collection of War Views and Portraits of Representative Men.* The government purchased in 1875 about two thousand of the photographs for the War College at a cost of $25,000. After the war, Brady continued to operate his Washington gallery but on a modest scale. In September 1877 he photographed Spotted Tail and Red Cloud and their twenty-two chiefs who had come to Washington for a conference with President Rutherford B. Hayes.

Brady's last few years were spent in poverty, but he busied himself with lecturing and showing pictures (there were 135 pictures in his lecture book) with the stereopticon. Brady will be long remembered as the man who recorded American history with his beloved camera.

CHARLES FREDERICK BRIGGS
1804-1877

Charles Frederick Briggs, a native of Nantucket, Massachusetts, spent much of his youth on sailing voyages to Europe and South America. In 1844, he founded the *Broadway Journal,* with Edgar Allan Poe as associate editor. Briggs stayed with the *Journal* only a year. In 1853 he became one of the editors of *Putnam's Magazine.* After that magazine suspended publication, Briggs was an editor of the *New York Times* under Henry J. Raymond. He was given editorial charge of the paper during Raymond's absence in Europe.

In 1870, Briggs was appointed financial editor of the *Brooklyn Union.* He left that post after three years to join the editorial staff of the *Independent,* with which he stayed for the remainder of his life.

DAVID BRINKLEY
1920-

David Brinkley, a native of Wilmington, North Carolina, attended the University of North Carolina and Vanderbilt University. His career as a disseminator and interpreter of the news began as a high school student, when he wrote for the *Wilmington Morning Star.* Following army service in World War II, he was employed by the United Press and then became White House correspondent for NBC News. A fortunate break came for Brinkley when he and Chet Huntley teamed up in 1956 to inaugurate "The Huntley–Brinkley Report." During the next fourteen years, the program became tremendously popular, winning every major broadcasting award. The partnership continued until 1970, when Huntley retired.

In addition to the "Huntley–Brinkley Report," Brinkley produced "David Brinkley's Journal," a weekly NBC public affairs program (1961–63), and was a commentator on "NBC Nightly News" for five years. From 1976 to 1979, he was coanchor with John Chancellor of the "NBC Nightly News."

In 1981, Brinkley changed bases. He resigned from NBC and signed a contract with ABC to produce a weekly news and discussion show, serve as political commentator for "World News Tonight," and cover the 1982 and 1984 elections. One outcome was the popular Sunday morning show "This Week with David Brinkley," first aired in 1981. Featured were interviews with distinguished guests and round-table discussions participated in by Sam Donaldson and George Will. Within about a year "This Week with

David Brinkley" outstripped two long-standing programs of a similar nature, "Meet the Press" and "Face the Nation."

Brinkley has been the recipient of ten Emmy awards and three George Foster Peabody Awards, the most recent of which, in 1987, was for his current program. The prevailing opinion of Brinkley is summed up by Roger Mudd, who observes that Brinkley "brought a level of political sophistication and literary craftsmanship and a lively sense of humor that television had never known before and that hasn't been equaled since."

In 1988, Brinkley published a best-selling book, *Washington Goes to War,* dealing with the Capital during World War II, presenting his memories of many memorable personalities and events from that historic period.

ARTHUR BRISBANE
1864–1936

Arthur Brisbane was born in Buffalo, New York. At the height of his career, he was the most widely read of any journalist of his time and probably of any age. His "Today" editorial, written in large print and simple language, usually appearing on the front page, revolutionized the style of the American newspaper editorial. From 1917 to 1936 it was being syndicated in about two hundred dailies and 1,200 weeklies, with a circulation of twenty million.

Brisbane's writings were highly influential. As a proponent of yellow journalism, he stirred up popular opinion against Spain, often slanting the news, and created sentiment for the Spanish-American War. He was the master of the sensational headline and the atrocity story.

Brisbane began his newspaper career in 1883 as a reporter on the *New York Sun.* Three years later he became the *Sun's* London correspondent. When the *Evening Sun* was established in 1887, he was appointed managing editor. The next step in his upward climb in 1890 was as managing editor of the *New York World,* where he remained until 1897. From that position he was induced by William Randolph Hearst to take the editorship of the *New York Evening Journal.* The "Today" column was printed daily in all Hearst papers, along with a column entitled "This Week" and a weekly Sunday page. The Brisbane contributions dealt with an amazing variety of subjects, written in a style easily understood by his multitude of readers.

Brisbane branched out by buying the *Washington* (D.C.) *Times* in 1917 and the *Evening Wisconsin* of Milwaukee in 1918, but subsequently sold both papers to Hearst. From 1918 to 1936, he was editor of the *Chicago Herald Examiner.*

An innovation introduced by Brisbane, first in the *World,* was the first colored pictures ever attempted on a fast newspaper press. Comic strips in color were instantly popular. Hearst took over the idea for his *Sunday Journal* and the war of the comics was on. Such comics as the "Yellow Kid," printed in bright yellow, led to the term "yellow journalism."

Brisbane made his papers more attractive in appearance and readable by using large type, very wide columns, boxed side-heads, and large pictures.

In evaluating Brisbane's journalistic career the *New Republic* concluded that he "used some sound principles in preparing his articles and editorial campaigns: simple words, sentences, and paragraphs; large readable type, color, and pictures. But he mixed facts with false stories to achieve his aim — a strong form of yellow journalism."

DAVID S. BRODER
1929–

David Broder was born in Chicago Heights, Illinois, and won two degrees from the University of Chicago. He was a reporter for the Bloomington (Illinois) *Pantagraph* (1953–55); reporter for the *Congressional Quarterly,* Washington, D.C. (1955–60); reporter for the *Washington Star* (1960–65); reporter for the *New York Times* in Washington (1965–66); and a reporter, columnist, and associate editor of the *Washington Post,* starting in 1966. Broder was in the U.S. Army (1951–53). He has won various honors, including a Pulitzer Prize in 1973, three awards from the American Newspaper Guild, and is widely syndicated.

TOM BROKAW
1940–

Tom Brokaw, born in South Dakota, has been a television news broadcaster for more than twenty years. From 1973 to 1976, Brokaw worked as a reporter and anchorman for NBC affiliate stations in Nebraska, Georgia, and California and as the network's White House correspondent.

Brokaw's interest in broadcast news was stimulated by his admiration for the "Huntley–Brinkley Report" in the 1950s and 1960s. At the age of fifteen he found a job as an announcer at KYNT, a Yorkton, South Dakota radio station. After graduating from the University of South Dakota, he worked as a roving reporter for several radio stations in the university area. Later affiliations were with KMTV in Omaha, Nebraska, as newscaster and morning news editor, and in 1965 with WSB-TV in Atlanta as editor and anchorman of the nightly news broadcast. The following year Brokaw moved to the West Coast to cover the late night broadcasts to KNBC-TV in Los Angeles. During his stay there, he reported the assassination of Robert Kennedy, the 1971 earthquake, and the gubernatorial campaigns of Ronald Reagan and Edmund G. Brown.

Brokaw served fifteen months as White House correspondent. According to one critic he was the most dynamic reporter on the White House beat during that period. The Watergate scandal news was still breaking. Brokaw preferred a job with wider scope than the White House, however, and changed pace by covering gubernatorial elections, anchoring the Saturday evening edition of the "NBC Nightly News," and reported the 1976 Republican and Democratic national conventions.

In May 1976, Brokaw agreed to take over as host of NBC's "Today Show," with a five-year contract. The primary purpose of the program, as Brokaw saw it, was to provide information, not entertainment. To that end, he dealt with most of the major issues facing the American people and interviewed a wide variety of newsworthy persons. Since 1982 he has been an anchorman for "NBC Nightly News."

ISAAC HILL BROMLEY
1833-1898

Isaac Hill Bromley began life as a member of a large family in Norwich, Connecticut. He was admitted to the bar in 1854, but concluded that newspaper work was more exciting. His first venture in the journalistic field was with the *Norwich Bulletin* in 1858, a daily that Bromley enlivened with his wit and satire. The next stop was in Hartford, where he was editor of the *Evening Post* from 1868 to 1872. A connection with the *New York Tribune* began in 1873 and continued for ten years.

While serving as a government director of the Union Pacific Railroad, a position to which he was appointed by President Arthur in 1882, Bromley had short editorial engagements with the *Commercial Advertiser and Evening Telegram* of New York and the *Post Express* of Rochester. His editorial connection with the *New York Tribune* resumed in 1891 and lasted until a few months before his death.

ERASTUS BROOKS
1815-1886

Erastus Brooks was given a taste of printing by being apprenticed at a very early age to a compositor. While a student at Brown University, he supported himself by working in a printing office. He left college to start a paper, the *Yankee,* in Wiscasset, Maine. The next move was to become editor and owner of the *Haverhill* (Massachusetts) *Gazette,* and then to serve as a reporter on the *Portland Advertiser.* Still in his twenties, Brooks went on to Washington to write correspondence for a group of papers: the *New York Daily Advertiser,* the *Boston Transcript,* the *Portland Advertiser,* the *Baltimore American,* the *St. Louis Republican,* and the *New York Express.* Five years later, he returned to Portland to edit the *Advertiser.* Time out was taken in 1843 for a tour to Moscow, fully reported in his group of papers. Finally, Brooks joined his brother James in managing the *New York Gazette,* later taking over full control. Altogether, Brooks had an editorial career spanning thirty-four years. He remained with the *Express* until 1877.

NOAH BROOKS
1830–1903

Noah Brooks showed a natural talent for writing. By age twenty-one, he was contributing short sketches, essays, and humorous stories to magazines and newspapers and serving on the staff of the *Atlas,* a Boston daily. On a trip to California, Brooks joined Benjamin P. Avery in publishing the *Marysville* (California) *Daily Appeal.* Brooks was also a regular contributor to the *Overland Monthly,* then edited by Bret Harte. After returning East he served as Washington correspondent of the *Sacramento Union.* Going back to California in 1866, Brooks became managing editor of the *Alta California* in San Francisco. His last positions before retiring from journalism in 1892 were five years on the staff of the *New York Tribune,* eight years as an editor of the *New York Times,* and finally editor of the *New York Daily Advertiser.*

WILLIAM BROSS
1813–1890

William Bross, a New Jersey native, had his first journalistic experience helping to start a religious newspaper, the *Chicago Prairie Herald* in 1849, a paper that met with only moderate success for the two years of its existence. Another paper, the *Democratic Press,* was established in 1852. A popular new feature, a review of Chicago business at the beginning of each year, was introduced. During the 1857 panic, the *Democratic Press* was merged with the *Tribune* under the title of *Press Tribune.* Two years later, the paper became simply the *Tribune.* Bross left the newspaper field to enter politics.

HEYWOOD BROUN
1888–1939

Heywood Broun, born in Brooklyn, New York, was the son of a printer. As a student at Horace Mann School, he edited the school paper and was active in athletics. Four years were spent at Harvard, where he showed exceptional writing ability. A taste for newspaper work was formed by a summer spent with the *New York Morning Telegraph* in 1908. He joined the *Telegraph* in 1910, but was discharged two years later when he asked for a pay increase. There followed a tour of China and Japan in 1912.

Broun's next job was with the *New York Tribune,* writing feature stories and reporting baseball and, later, serving as drama and literary critic. Broun married Ruth Hale, president of the Lucy Stone League, in 1917; they were incompatible, lived apart for the last five years of their married life, and were divorced in 1933. Broun and his wife went to France in 1917, he as war correspondent for the *Tribune* and she for the overseas edition of the *Chicago Tribune.*

Broun's literary columns for the *Tribune,* started in 1919, were immensely popular. In 1921, he moved to the *New York World,* where his column "It Seems to Me" was outstandingly successful, based on highly personal reactions to the world around him, especially liberal causes. When the *World* refused to print his controversial columns about the Sacco–Vanzetto case, Broun attacked the paper for timidity and he was fired for "disloyalty." At the invitation of Roy W. Howard, he moved over to the *New York Telegram.* Three years later, the *World* was sold to the *Telegram,* and the *World-Telegram* remained Broun's home base for the remainder of his career.

Broun's column was syndicated nationwide and it was estimated that he had a million readers daily. In addition, he began publication of the *Connecticut Nutmeg,* a literary and humorous magazine, a title changed later to *Broun's Nutmeg.* A weekly column, "Shoot the Works," first appeared in the *Nation* and later in the *New Republic.*

A further distinction for Broun was to found the American Newspaper Guild in 1933, a union for newspaper employees. He served as first president of the organization.

MARY EDWARDS BRYAN
1842–1913

Mary Edwards Bryan was born in Florida, but grew up in Georgia. Her first experience in journalism was as literary editor of the *Literary Crusader* in Atlanta in 1862. She was also a regular correspondent of *Southern Field and Fireside*. She was editor of the *Natchitoches* (Louisiana) *Tri-weekly,* starting in 1866, and associate editor of the *Sunny South* from 1874 to 1884. She contributed sketches, poems, stories, and political articles.

In 1885, Bryan went to New York to superintend publication of her novels and while there she became assistant editor of the *New York Fashion Bazaar and the Fireside Companion.* After returning to Georgia in 1895, she continued to work on the *Sunny South,* later merged with *Uncle Remus' Magazine.* She was also an editor of the *Half Hour Magazine.*

WILLIAM CULLEN BRYANT
1794–1878

William Cullen Bryant has been called the first important nature poet in America and "the American Wordsworth." His reputation as a poet has tended to overshadow the fact that his distinguished career as a journalist extended over more than half a century.

Bryant showed early evidence of a brilliant mind. He entered the community school at age four and began composing poetry at age nine. In 1808 there was published *The Embargo; or Sketches of the Times: A Satire; By a Youth of Thirteen,* attacking President Jefferson on a current issue. Lack of funds forced Bryant to give up plans to enter Yale. Instead, he began to study law and after about a year was admitted to practice for about nine years in Great Barrington, Massachusetts. Gradually he became disillusioned with the legal profession and determined on a literary career.

A collection of Bryant's poems was published in 1821. Previously he had contributed poems and reviews to the *North American Review* and other periodicals. His best known poem, "Thanatopsis," was published by the *Review* in 1917. In mid-1825, he moved to New York and became coeditor of a new periodical *New York Review and Atheneum Magazine.* Then followed a fortunate happening for him. The editor of the *New York Evening Post,* William Coleman, was injured in an accident, needed help, and hired Bryant as an editorial assistant.

For a short period, Bryant divided his time between the *New York Review* and the *Post.* In 1828, he bought an eighth interest in the newspaper and Coleman promoted him to joint editor. When Coleman died the following year, Bryant became editor-in-chief, a position that he held for the next forty-nine years.

Bryant showed a talent for dealing with political and social issues. He and his paper aligned with the Democrats and supported Andrew Jackson for president. Formidable competition faced him in winning first place for the *Post* in the New York press field. Among the obstacles were the "penny-press revolution," and the rivalry with James Gordon Bennett's *Herald,* Horace Greeley's *Tribune,* and Henry J. Raymond's *Times.*

As an editor, Bryant took strong stands on many controversial issues. He supported free speech and the rights of organized labor. In the late 1840s, he became an outspoken opponent of slavery; he left the Democrats and joined the Republican party because the Republicans opposed slavery. His main concern was the threat of dissolution of the Union, however, rather than slavery.

Bryant became a civic leader in New York. He helped to establish Central Park and the Metropolitan Museum of Art. Bryant Park, adjoining the New York Public Library, is named for him.

PATRICK BUCHANAN
1938–

Patrick Buchanan was reared in a conservative Catholic tradition and he has always remained faithful to his early training. Conservatives were therefore delighted at the announcement, in 1985, that Buchanan had been appointed director of communications in the Reagan White House, reversing what some conceived as a liberalizing trend in the administration.

After graduating from Georgetown University in 1961, Buchanan completed a master's degree at Columbia University School of Journalism. He tried unsuccessfully to gain a job with *National Review* or *Washington Post,* but joined the *St. Louis Globe-Democrat,* first as a reporter, then editorial writer, and finally assistant editorial editor.

By 1965, Buchanan was ready for a change. In January 1966, he went with Richard Nixon's law firm as executive assistant, factotum, and researcher. John Ehrlichman and H. R. Haldeman resigned after Nixon's victory, but Buchanan stayed on as special assistant. In that position his main responsibility was to prepare the "President's Daily Briefing Book," summarizing the media's reaction to the Nixon administration. Buchanan is believed to have drafted some of the hard-hitting speeches delivered by Nixon. In any event, he remained steadfastly loyal, and was one of the most effective witnesses to appear before Senator Erwin's committee investigating the Watergate affair. When the president resigned in 1974, Buchanan remained to serve his successor, Gerald Ford. At the same time, he began writing a three-times-a-week commentary on political and social affairs, carried first by *Special Features,* a subsidiary of the New York Times Company, and then by the *Chicago Tribune*–New York News Syndicate. At last report the column was being run by 138 papers.

The Buchanan saga came to at least a temporary halt in 1987 when Donald Regan, White House chief of staff, who had nominated Buchanan for the position of special assistant, resigned. Buchanan quit at the same time. He can now be seen as cohost with Michael Kinsley on CNN's "Crossfire."

ART BUCHWALD
1925–

Art Buchwald, widely recognized as a leading political humorist and satirist, started life in the Westchester County suburb of Mount Vernon, New York. He joined the U.S. Marines, attended the University of Southern California, and lived as an expatriate in Paris. Along the way, he picked up some journalistic experience: editing his Marine Corps magazine; becoming managing editor of the campus humor magazine, the *Wampus,* while at Southern California; and conducting a column for the college newspaper, the *Daily Trojan.*

While in Paris, Buchwald served as correspondent for *Variety.* The European edition of the *New York Herald Tribune* then added him to its editorial staff to write a column "Paris after Dark," about Parisian night life. In 1952, the same column and a comparison piece, "Mostly about People," began to be published in U.S. papers.

To gather raw material for his columns, Buchwald is reported to have marched in a May Day parade in East Berlin, chased goats in the Yugoslav mountains, made a three-week trip behind the Iron Curtain in a limousine driven by a uniformed chauffeur, and traveled to Turkey to get a first-hand impression of a Turkish bath.

After fourteen years in Paris and elsewhere in Europe, Buchwald moved to Washington, D.C., in 1962. His column, at last report, was being syndicated to 380 newspapers. Many of his columns have been reprinted in book form. The popular view of Buchwald is summed up by one critic who called him "an amazing zany literate commentator on the passing scene."

WILLIAM F. BUCKLEY, JR.

1925-

William Buckley has come to be accepted as a leading spokesman for conservative causes in America—a highly articulate and literate defender of economic individualism and opponent of big government. His influence has been exerted as a newspaper columnist, editor of *National Review,* host of television's "Firing Line," and author of a number of best-selling books. Buckley has been characterized as a laissez-faire capitalist, an anticommunist, an elitist, and a moral traditionalist.

Buckley began life in Stamford, Connecticut, one of ten children, reared in a devoutly Catholic family. His early childhood was spent in France and England. From 1944 to 1946 he served in the U.S. Army. His first noteworthy contribution to the conservative cause was *God and Man at Yale: The Superstitions of Academic Freedom* (1951), written after his graduation from Yale, where he majored in economics, political science, and history. The book was a polemic indictment of liberal education in general, and a criticism of what Buckley viewed as an antireligious and collectivist Yale curriculum.

Another shot in Buckley's war against liberalism was the publication of a book defending Senator Joseph R. McCarthy, *McCarthy and His Enemies.* While acknowledging the excesses of McCarthyism, Buckley asserted that "it is a movement around which men of good will and stern morality can close ranks."

A further step to "revitalize the conservative position" was taken by Buckley in 1955 when he established *National Review,* a biweekly journal whose circulation grew to one hundred thousand and that came to be regarded as the most important publication for the American political right wing.

Buckley's readership was also greatly expanded through a syndicated newspaper column "On the Right" begun in 1962. By the 1980s, the column was being carried by more than three hundred newspapers and has been republished in book form. Another forum was provided by a weekly television program, "Firing Line," marked by lively exchanges among its participants.

JONAS MILLS BUNDY

1835-1891

Jonas Mills Bundy, born in New Hampshire, was educated for the legal profession, but instead became a reporter on the *Milwaukee Daily*

Wisconsin. A feature created by him for the paper was a department of market reports. Later he joined the staff of the *Milwaukee Sentinel.* After military service during the Civil War, Bundy was made dramatic, musical, and literary critic of the *Evening Post* under William Cullen Bryant. Three years later he was one of the founders and became editor-in-chief of the *New York Evening Mail.* The *Mail* was owned by Cyrus W. Field, who bought the *New York Evening Express,* and consolidated the two papers under the title *Mail and Express.* Bundy continued as editor-in-chief, both under Field and Elliott F. Sheppard.

WILLIAM HENRY BURLEIGH
1812–1871

William Henry Burleigh, born in Woodstock, Connecticut, was apprenticed as a youth to a printer. In 1830 he became a journeyman on the *Stonington Phenix,* where he began to set up his own articles. Two years later he was printer and contributor to the Schenectady (New York) *Cabinet* and in 1833 assisted his brother in editing the *Unionist* in Brooklyn, Connecticut. About 1836 he became editor of the *Literary Journal* in Schenectady, but a year later moved on to be editor of the *Christian Witness* and afterward the *Temperance Banner* in Pittsburgh. In 1843, the Connecticut Anti-Slavery Society at Hartford arranged for Burleigh to edit its journal, the *Christian Freeman,* a title changed later to the *Charter Oak.* His last journalistic assignment was as editor of the *Prohibitionist* (1849–55) for the New York State Temperance Society in Albany and Syracuse.

HERB CAEN
1916–

Herb Caen is a native Californian, born in Sacramento, and a columnist for newspapers in that state since 1938. He has been called "the longest running columnist in America."

From 1938 to 1950, Caen worked for the *San Francisco Chronicle.* For eight years, until 1958, he was a columnist for the *Examiner.* In 1958 Caen returned to the *Chronicle,* with which he has since remained a fixture. He is widely read and quoted. Caen has also published a number of books concerned with San Francisco and the Bay area.

ABRAHAM CAHAN
1860–1951

Abraham Cahan, Russian-American newspaper editor and writer, was born in Lithuania and emigrated to New York in 1882. He helped to organize the first Jewish labor union and in 1886 began editing *Neu Zeit (New Era),* which existed for only a few months. At the same time, he was a frequent contributor to the *Workman's Advocate,* organ of the Socialist Labor party. In 1890 various labor groups cooperated in setting up a Yiddish-language labor newspaper, *Arbeiter Zeitung.* The following year, Cahan became editor. Two years later he also edited *Die Zukunft,* Yiddish organ of the Socialist Worker's party of America. Another new paper was started in 1897, the *Jewish Daily Forward,* again with Cahan as editor for a short time. From 1897 to 1901 Cahan worked for the *New York Commercial Advertiser,* an English-language, Republican-oriented newspaper.

In 1902, Cahan returned to the *Forward,* which was to occupy him for nearly fifty years, until his death in 1951. During this long period the *Jewish Daily Forward* became the voice of Jews around the world. Oswald Garrison Villard described the *Forward* as "the most vital, the most interesting, the most democratic of New York's daily journals."

BARTLEY CAMPBELL
1843–1888

Bartley Campbell was born in Pittsburgh. His first newspaper experience was with the *Pittsburgh Post.* Afterward, he was editor and part-owner of the *Pittsburgh Leader.* In 1869, he founded and edited the *Southern Monthly Magazine* in New Orleans. In 1871, Campbell retired from journalism for a career as a playwright.

JOHN CAMPBELL
1653–1728

John Campbell was of Scottish ancestry. He arrived in Boston about 1692. He succeeded his brother Duncan as postmaster of Boston.

The ruthless suppression of Benjamin Harris's *Publick Occurrences* after a single issue intimidated for fourteen years other attempts to establish a newspaper in Boston. During the interim, Campbell wrote manuscript newsletters to other postmasters and public men, based on news reports from captains of ships arriving in Boston harbor and other sources. When copying by hand became too laborious, Campbell obtained permission from government authorities to print his newsletter. The first number of the weekly *Boston News-Letter* appeared on April 24, 1704. It was an unimposing little sheet. About two-thirds of the space was filled with items taken from London journals, dealing with English politics, the royal court, and European wars. The rest contained brief items about ship arrivals, deaths, sermons, political appointments, storms, Indian uprisings, pirates, fires, counterfeiting, accidents, and court actions. There were few advertisements. Foreign news was dated.

Campbell left his postmastership in 1718, but continued his paper for five more years. He then turned it over to Bartholomew Green. Ten years later, Green's son-in-law, John Draper, inherited the *News-Letter,* which was then passed on in 1762 to Draper's son Richard. The *News-Letter* ceased publication early in the Revolution, because of its Tory policies, having survived seventy-two years, one of the longest-lived American newspapers of the eighteenth century.

HENRY SEIDEL CANBY
1878–1961

Henry Seidel Canby was born in Wilmington, Delaware. For more than twenty years, he was a faculty member at Yale University. In 1920, Canby became editor of the literary review section of the *New York Evening Post.* A more ambitious undertaking was the founding of the *Saturday Review of Literature* in 1924, for which Canby served as editor until 1936. Under his direction, the magazine became the leading literary weekly in the United States. Canby was also chairman from 1926 to 1958 of the Book of the Month's board of judges.

DABNEY SMITH CARR
1802–1854

Dabney Smith Carr was born in Virginia. His keen interest in writing and politics induced him to found a newspaper in 1827, the *Baltimore Republican and Commercial Advertiser.* His strong support for Andrew Jackson won him an appointment as naval officer for the Port of Baltimore. Carr sold his paper in 1829 to begin his new work.

HODDING CARTER III
1935-

Hodding Carter III was born in New Orleans, son of a famous newsman of the same name. The younger Carter first became well known to the general public in the television evening news as the spokesman for the U.S. State Department during the Iranian hostage crisis in 1979 and 1980. Later he became the anchorman of "Inside Story," the Public Broadcasting Service television series. He served two years in the U.S. Marine Corps.

After graduating from Princeton in 1957, Carter returned to Greenville, Mississippi, to assist his father in publication of the *Delta Democrat-Times,* writing editorials and later becoming managing editor, editor, and associate publisher.

Carter was a political activist from 1956 on, a leader among Democrats working to reform convention rules, for racial desegregation, and in support of a strong biracial party. When Jimmy Carter became president, he named Carter as Secretary of State for Public Affairs in 1977. He resigned his State Department job in 1980 after the departure of Secretary of State Cyrus Vance. Since then his time has been filled with lectures and news broadcasts.

In 1972, Carter won a Pulitzer Prize for editorials against racial intolerance. In his writings he denounced demagogues, racists, and racketeering, for which he became known as the "conscience of the South." He is a frequent guest on the "This Week with David Brinkley."

WILBUR JOSEPH CASH
1900-1941

Wilbur Cash was born in Gaffney, South Carolina. He was a freelance writer and newspaperman for an extended period. In 1923, he was on the staff of the *Charlotte* (North Carolina) *Observer.* For a brief time in 1924 he joined the *Chicago Post,* but returned to North Carolina to become associate editor of the *Charlotte News.* He was a frequent contributor to periodicals, the *American Mercury,* the *Nation,* and others.

Cash is best known for his book, *The Mind of the South,* an attempt to penetrate the Southern mentality and to explain the psychological factors that have shaped the thinking and attitudes of Southerners.

Cash took his own life in 1941 while writing a novel about Mexico.

WILLIAM CASSIDY
1815-1873

William Cassidy, born in Albany, New York, began contributing articles to two newspapers at age twenty-five, the *Plain Dealer* and *Rough Hewer,* the latter an Albany paper. Through political influence, he was appointed state librarian, after which he and Henry Van Dike became joint editors of the *Albany Atlas.* In 1856, the *Atlas* and *Argus* were united to fight the Republican party. During the Civil War the *Atlas and Argus* was classed as a copperhead sheet and barred from the mails.

TURNER CATLEDGE
1901-1983

Turner Catledge was born near New Prospect in Mississippi. As a teenager he wrote some local stories and rewrites for the *Neshoba Democrat,* a weekly. In college he was assistant to Mississippi State University's agricultural editor and wrote and edited agricultural bulletins for distribution to Mississippi farmers. After graduation he served as editor of the *Tunica* (Mississippi) *Times,* but the newspaper plant was destroyed for publishing a series of anti–Ku Klux Klan articles. The following year Catledge moved to Tupelo, Mississippi, to take over as managing editor of a biweekly *Journal.* In 1924, he joined the staff of the Memphis (Tennessee) *Press,* a Scripps–Howard daily, but quickly transferred to the *Commercial Appeal,* a rival newspaper.

Another change came in 1927 when Catledge signed with the *Baltimore Sun* as a feature writer and later as a Washington-based political correspondent.

The most important move for Catledge came in 1929, when, on Herbert Hoover's recommendation, he joined the *New York Times.* There he covered the Depression era, the New Deal administration, and other political developments that caused the *Times* to name Catledge its chief Washington correspondent in 1936.

For a period (1941–43), Catledge withdrew from the *Times* to serve as editor of the *Chicago Sun,* but in 1943 he returned to the *Times* as its national correspondent. Four months were spent in the European, North African, and Southeast Asian war zones and later he and Arthur Hays Sulzberger traveled through the Pacific war areas. Following his return, Catledge was appointed the *Times's* managing editor and in 1951 the position of executive managing editor was created for him. The paper's national and foreign news coverage was expanded to cover areas previously slighted and more emphasis was placed on local news, especially society and women's news and art.

Catledge opposed government censorship and published such widely publicized stories as the CIA's foreign operations, the planned invasion of Cuba in 1961, and Harrison Salisbury's dispatches from Hanoi.

In 1968 Catledge was appointed vice president and director of the *New York Times*. He resigned in 1970.

JAMES MCKEEN CATTELL
1860-1944

James M. Cattell was born in Easton, Pennsylvania. As a psychologist, he became noted for his pioneering activities in the field of intelligence testing and was first president of the American Psychological Association in 1895. He was best known as a science editor of the *Psychological Review, Scientific Monthly, Science, The American Naturalist,* and *American Men of Science.* In addition, he taught psychology at the University of Pennsylvania, Cambridge University, and Columbia University.

BRUCE CATTON
1899-1978

Bruce Catton was born in Petoskey, Michigan. He is most celebrated as a historian of the Civil War and winner of a Pulitzer Prize and National Book Award. He was also active as an editor, in particular for *American Heritage* magazine, starting in 1954, and as Washington correspondent and special writer for the Newspaper Enterprise Association. Catton was a journalist until World War II and served as a government information officer during the war. Afterward he wrote for the *Nation,* but the Civil War was always his primary interest as was evidenced by his numerous books on the subject.

HENRY RICHARDSON CHAMBERLAIN
1859-1911

Henry Richardson Chamberlain, born in Peoria, Illinois, showed a precocious interest in news gathering before he had any formal connection with a newspaper. He searched for news on his own while living in Boston, and turned over lively items to the *Boston Journal*. By age eighteen he had become a regular reporter on that paper. In 1888 Chamberlain went on to New York City as managing editor of the *Press*. There was an interval of travel in Europe, after which he was employed by the *New York Sun,* a connection that continued until 1891, when Chamberlain returned to Boston to be managing editor of the *Journal*. A year later he was appointed London correspondent for the *Sun*. His European news service, for which he became celebrated, was syndicated to many U.S. newspapers. Although he died several years before the outbreak of World War I, he displayed remarkable foresight in observing the gathering war clouds, and predicting the coming of war.

SAMUEL S. CHAMBERLAIN
1815–1916

Samuel S. Chamberlain, born in New York City, had a journalistic career of more than thirty years, mainly associated with William Randolph Hearst. His father at one time was an editorial writer for *New York World,* before Pulitzer, and his son, William Henry Chamberlain, became a distinguished newspaper man.

From 1884 to 1886, Chamberlain was the founder and editor of the *Paris Le Matin,* later one of the most successful Parisian papers. For two years, he was secretary to James Gordon Bennett, Jr. He helped Bennett to start the *Paris Herald*. Previously, he had worked as a reporter and editor for the *Newark Advertiser,* the *Herald,* the *World,* and the *Evening Telegram*. Chamberlain first met Hearst in 1888, and he was hired by Hearst the following year to become managing editor of the *San Francisco Examiner*. One of the outstanding reporters Chamberlain managed was Winifred Sweet (later Black), a San Francisco chorus girl who became famous as the first "sob sister," writing under the pen name of "Annie Laurie."

After his success with the *Examiner,* Hearst sent Chamberlain to New York to revitalize his newly acquired *Morning Journal*. Hearst's *Journal* and Pulitzer's *World* were soon engaged in a war for circulation. Chamberlain was addicted to big screaming headlines, four or five inches high, and other devices to make news reports sensational. He also was instrumental in the *Journal's* reports, leading up to and during the Spanish-American War, designed to stir up war sentiment and to appeal to American patriotism.

In 1907–8, Chamberlain was editor of *Cosmopolitan* magazine, which

Hearst bought in 1905. That journal, too, adopted sensational features similar to those that had worked so well on newspapers. At the time of his death in 1916, Chamberlain was publisher of the *Boston American,* also owned by Hearst.

WILLIAM HENRY CHAMBERLIN
1897–1969

William Henry Chamberlin was born in Brooklyn, New York, the son of a newspaper man and the grandson of the head, for a number of years, of the Associated Press Bureau in Cincinnati, Ohio. In his own words, Chamberlin "drifted into newspaper work." In 1917 he became a cub reporter on the *Philadelphia Public Ledger* staff and a year later he joined the *Philadelphia Press* as assistant editor of the weekly magazine section. He was drafted for military service in World War I, but the war ended before he was sent abroad.

After the war, Chamberlin obtained a job with the *New York Tribune,* where he became assistant book editor under Heywood Broun. Using a pseudonym he contributed pieces for the *New York Call,* a socialist daily paper, and *Soviet Russia* magazine. The *Tribune* discharged him in 1921. By luck, the *Christian Science Monitor* commissioned him to contribute articles and Chamberlin and his wife used their savings to go to Russia. During his years in the Soviet Union, Chamberlin became thoroughly disillusioned with the Bolshevik Revolution.

Chamberlin's next foreign mission was to Japan, followed by trips to China, Malaya, the Philippines, and French Indochina. The Chamberlins returned to the United States in 1939, and he produced numerous articles for magazines based on his foreign observations and experiences. A trip to France in April 1939 was made immediately prior to the outbreak of World War II. When the Chamberlins returned home, they settled in Cambridge, Massachusetts. He served as a book reviewer and editorial correspondent for the *Wall Street Journal* and was a contributing editor of the *New Leader.* Subsequently, Chamberlin wrote many articles on European affairs and American current events for general magazines in the United States.

JAMES JULIUS CHAMBERS
1850–1920

At age eleven, James J. Chambers decided that he wanted to become a newspaperman and spent his spare time around the office of a Bellefontaine, Ohio, paper in his hometown. After graduating from Cornell, he was a reporter for the *New York Tribune* under Horace Greeley. Taking time out to explore the headquarters of the Mississippi River, he returned to the *Tribune* in August 1872. With the connivance of the city editor, Chambers was committed to the Bloomingdale Asylum for the insane. Following his release he wrote a series of articles for the *Tribune* that resulted in important reforms.

In 1873 Chambers joined the staff of the *New York Herald,* where under James Bennett he served as correspondent in various parts of the world, as city editor for a time, and helped to establish the *Paris Herald.*

Another move was made in 1889, when Chambers received and accepted an offer from Joseph Pulitzer to be managing editor of the *New York World,* a position that he retained until 1891. His final journalistic undertaking began in 1904 when he wrote a column in the *Brooklyn Eagle* called "Walks and Talks," continued until his death in 1920.

JOHN CHANCELLOR
1927–

John Chancellor was born in Chicago and has always been closely identified with that city. He joined the staff of the *Chicago Sun-Times* in 1948 and moved up to become a reporter, rewrite man, and feature writer. In 1960 he joined NBC station WNBC to track down exciting stories. Helpful for this purpose was his early experience covering gangland shootings in Chicago, racial violence in Little Rock, and political developments in Moscow.

In 1958 NBC assigned Chancellor to its Vienna bureau. While overseas he covered events in Paris, Rome, and Tunis, the Algerian revolt, the civil war in Lebanon, and the abortive summit conference in Paris. In 1960 Chancellor was assigned to Moscow. He covered the 1961 meeting in Vienna between President Kennedy and Khrushchev. After he returned to New York, NBC executives named him as host and moderator of NBC-TV's "Today Show," succeeding Dave Galloway. From 1970 to 1982, he was anchorman for "NBC Nightly News." Since 1982 Chancellor has been NBC News commentator.

HARRY CHANDLER
1864–1944

Harry Chandler, born in Landaff, New Hampshire, was founder of the family dynasty that has dominated Southern California journalism for about a century.

In 1885, Chandler was employed as a clerk in the circulation department of the *Los Angeles Times*. He soon went into business for himself, operating delivery routes not only for the *Times* but also for the *Herald* and the *Express*. To stimulate Los Angeles economic and general development, special issues of the *Times* were printed for distribution in the Midwest. The *Times* was strongly anti–labor union, described by *Time* magazine as "the most rabid labor-baiting, red-baiting paper in the United States." In 1894, Chandler married the daughter of Harrison Gray Otis, owner of the *Times,* and became the paper's business manager.

Chandler succeeded Otis as publisher of the *Times* in 1917, by which time he had already established himself as the paper's highly successful manager and one of California's most powerful business leaders. The *Times* expanded by adding a pictorial section, Sunday magazine, and a farm and garden supplement. In politics, the *Times* was fiercely and undeviatingly Republican, and was highly hostile to Franklin Roosevelt and the New Deal.

Chandler began withdrawing from management of the *Times* in the 1940s, but remained as chairman of the board until his death in 1944. He left an estate estimated in value at half a billion dollars. His son Norman succeeded him as president and publisher in 1941.

JOSEPH RIPLEY CHANDLER
1792–1880

Joseph Chandler, born in Kingston, Massachusetts, began editorial writing in 1822 on the *Gazette of the United States,* established more than forty years earlier by John Fenno. With two partners, Chandler bought the paper, later merged it with the *North American,* and continued as editor until 1847. Another journalistic venture, from 1843 to 1849, was editing *Graham's American Monthly Magazine of Literature, Art and Fashion.* Among Chandler's other achievements were the presidency of Girard College's board of directors, election to Congress on the Whig ticket, minister to the Two Sicilies, and leader in prison reform.

OTIS CHANDLER
1927–

Otis Chandler was born in Los Angeles, a member of the dynasty that rules what is reported to be the third largest publishing empire in the United States. When Chandler became publisher of the *Los Angeles Times* in 1960, the paper was described as "stodgily provincial and predictably reactionary with a conservative Republican bias." Chandler determined to make radical changes, despite the fact that the paper was the sixth largest and one of the nation's most profitable. He aimed first at political balance. Talented writers and editors were added to the staff, correspondents were appointed to cover key regions of the country, twelve foreign bureaus were set up, several new departments expanded the Sunday *Times,* and many syndicated columnists and cartoonists began to be featured. In cooperation with the *Washington Post,* the Times-Post News Service was inaugurated to send out news stories to subscribing newspapers around the world. A large percentage of the *Times's* daily circulation is home-delivered and to serve its middle-class clientele seven suburban editions are published. Under Chandler, the *Times* became one of the most influential newspapers not only in the West, but nationwide with a huge staff and a daily circulation of about one million.

WILLIAM EATON CHANDLER
1835–1917

William Eaton Chandler was born in Concord, New Hampshire. As a journalist on the *Concord Monitor and Statesman,* he was called the "stormy petrel" of state politics. Chandler held a number of political offices, including speaker of the New Hampshire house of representatives, a U.S. senator, appointments under Abraham Lincoln and Andrew Johnson, director of several presidential campaigns, and secretary of the navy under Chester A. Arthur.

JAMES CHEETHAM
1772–1810

James Cheetham was English-born. He came to the United States about 1798 and bought a half-interest in Greenleaf's *Argus,* which he began publishing as a daily paper under the name of the *American Citizen.* A weekly paper, the *American Watchman,* was also issued, both promoting Republican policies. Two leaders with whom he came into violent disagreement were Aaron Burr and Thomas Paine. Eventually, as he lost political influence, Cheetham's paper was replaced by the *Columbian.*

DAVID LEE CHILD
1794-1874

David Lee Child, born in West Boylston, Massachusetts, engaged in various ventures before his start as a journalist. While a member of the Massachusetts legislature in 1829, he edited the *Massachusetts Journal,* a leading Adams paper. In 1843-44, he assisted his wife, Lydia Maria Francis, who was prominent in the antislavery movement, in editing the *National Anti-Slavery Standard* in New York.

GEORGE WILLIAM CHILDS
1829-1894

George W. Childs was born in Baltimore. He engaged in a variety of occupations in the early years such as book-selling and book publishing. In 1863 he founded the *American Publisher's Circular and Literary Gazette.* His greatest success came when he bought the *Philadelphia Public Ledger* in 1864. Through his skillful management, the *Ledger's* circulation increased enormously, to reach ninety thousand copies a day in 1876. At the same time, Child's own reputation as publisher and editor spread in the newspaper world.

MARQUIS CHILDS
1903-

Marquis Childs was born in Clinton, Iowa. After working for the United Press in Chicago, Detroit, New York, and St. Louis, Childs became a staff member of the *St. Louis Post-Dispatch* in 1926. There he remained, usually as Washington correspondent, until 1944. For ten years, Childs was a columnist for the United Feature syndicate, writing from Washington and Europe. During that period he spent several months touring battlefields in World War II. In 1954, he returned to the *Post-Dispatch,* becoming chief of the newspaper's Washington bureau in 1962, a position that he held for six years.

Childs was awarded the first Pulitzer Prize for commentary in 1969. Sigma Delta Chi named him the best Washington correspondent in 1944. Sweden and Germany have also decorated him. He has been president of both overseas writers' and the Gridiron clubs.

Childs was author of a number of published books, of which the most popular were a history of the Mississippi River and a work on the Swedish economy.

CONSTANCE CHUNG
1946–

Connie Chung was born in Washington, D.C., while her father, a diplomat in Chiang Kai-Shek's government, was stationed there. The family remained after the Maoist victory in 1949. There were ten children in the family, five of whom died in China.

Chung started as a television news reporter on WTTG-TV in Washington in 1969. She joined CBS there in 1971, and in 1976 became the news anchor at CBS station WNXT-TC in Los Angeles, a position that she held from 1976 to 1983, when she left for an NBC spot. She went to China in 1987 to trace her family roots and reported her experiences in a moving series for "NBC Nightly News." In 1986 she and Roger Mudd attempted to produce a "Magazine" show to compete with CBS's "60 Minutes." That program failed and since then Chung has done two successful prime-time specials, one on obesity and the other on American attitudes toward sex. Beginning in 1987, Chung presented Saturday news specials for NBC, until she went to CBS in 1991.

WILLIAM CONANT CHURCH
1836–1917

William Conant Church was born in Rochester, New York. From 1855 to 1860 he helped his father, a Baptist clergyman, publish the *New York Chronicle,* a religious daily newspaper. In 1863 he and a brother established the *Army and Navy Journal,* still the official publication of the United States Armed Forces.

WILLIAM WARLAND CLAPP
1826-1891

William Clapp, a native of Boston, spent much of his youth about the office of the *Saturday Evening Gazette,* one of his father's papers. At age twenty-one, he was placed in charge of the paper and owned and operated it from 1847 to 1865. At that point, Clapp assumed the editorship of the *Boston Journal,* a position that he held until the end of his career. Clapp's success as executive and editor may be judged by the fact that the *Journal* for many years was regarded as the standard newspaper in the Boston area and throughout New England.

RAYMOND CLAPPER
1892-1944

Raymond Clapper was born in LaPygne, Kansas. After attending the University of Kansas, he worked for a few months on the *Kansas City Star* and then joined the United Press. From Chicago he went to Milwaukee and St. Paul, ending up in 1921 in Washington. Some of his big stories out of the national capital were the 1920 Republican party convention, the Scopes trial in Tennessee, and the international conference of naval powers in London. Clapper became manager of the United Press capital staff in 1929, but he left the UP in 1933 to join the *Washington Post* staff, as head of its national bureau and to write a column of political commentary. When his contract with the *Post* expired in 1936, Clapper moved over to the Scripps–Howard papers to write a daily column. The next year the column was taken over by the United Feature Syndicate, where Clapper became the nation's most widely syndicated newspaper writer. At the time of his death, in an airplane accident during the invasion of the Marshall Islands in 1944, the Clapper column was appearing in 180 newspapers throughout the country. In addition to writing for newspapers, Clapper was a radio commentator, a contributor to magazines, and a popular lecturer.

JOSEPH IGNATIUS CONSTANTINE CLARKE
1846-1925

Joseph Clarke, a native of Ireland, came to America in 1868. After landing in New York, he found work with the *Irish Republic,* a weekly paper. Later, he began writing at space rates for the *New York Herald,* and was appointed to its staff, where he remained until 1883. Clarke was sent to the Pacific coast in 1871 to report on a murder trial and to interview Brigham Young. His position on the *Herald* required versatility; he served as night, dramatic, literary, musical, and sporting editor.

After leaving the *Herald,* Clarke was managing editor of Albert Pulitzer's *Morning Journal* (1883–95), editor of the *Criterion,* a literary and social weekly (1898–1900), Sunday editor of the *Herald* (1903–6), and publicity director of the Standard Oil Company (1906–13). He also had a successful career as a playwright.

CASSIUS MARCELLUS CLAY
1810–1903

Cassius Clay, a Kentuckian, was the son of a large slaveholding family. His journalistic career was brief and stormy. Duels and street encounters marked his days as an editor. In 1846, Clay established an antislavery paper, the *True American,* in Lexington, Kentucky. For protection, he usually went about armed with two pistols and a bowie knife, while his office was fortified with two cannons and an armory of Mexican lances and rifles. Clay had apparently been inspired, while a student at Yale, by William Lloyd Garrison, the fiery editor who had dedicated his life to the emancipation of the American black.

The *True American* had been going only two months, when a group of proslavery men got possession of the printing plant, boxed it up, and sent it north to Cincinnati. Clay sued the Committee of Sixty and collected $2,500 in damages. The judgment had symbolic importance in reaffirming the right to publish in Kentucky.

Meanwhile, Clay continued to edit his paper in Lexington and publish it in Cincinnati, until he went off to fight in the Mexican War, followed by a long and picturesque career in politics, war, and diplomacy.

SAMUEL LANGHORNE CLEMENS
1835–1910

Samuel L. Clemens, better known as Mark Twain, was born in Florida, Missouri. Shortly thereafter the family moved to Hannibal. In 1847 Clemens became a printer's apprentice and learned to set type. Between 1853 and 1857 he worked as a journeyman printer in the composing room of the *St. Louis Exchange News.* In New York City he worked as a composer for a printshop; he was a typesetter for the *Philadelphia Inquirer;* in Washington, D.C., he wrote letters to his brother's newspaper in Muscatine, Iowa; he returned to the *St. Louis Evening News;* and he was employed by a newspaper in Keokuk, Iowa. Starting in 1856, there was a period of travel on the Mississippi River, during which Clemens earned a pilot's license.

After Clemens's brother Orion was appointed secretary of the Nevada Territory, Clemens traveled overland to Carson City, Nevada. There he became a reporter on the *Virginia City Territorial Enterprise,* beginning in 1862. In 1863, he used the pseudonym "Mark Twain" for the first time. Proceeding to San Francisco in 1864, he worked for several newspapers, including the *Morning Call.* The next year there was a trip to the Sandwich Islands (Hawaii), from where Clemens contributed a series of humorous travel letters to the *Sacramento Union.* In 1866 he became a traveling correspondent for the *Alta California,* which included a trip to the Holy Land and led to publication of *Innocents Abroad,* a book that established his name as a humorist.

While in Washington, Clemens became correspondent for the *New York Tribune* and contributed to the *New York Herald.* His writings were also picked up by a variety of newspapers in the Midwest and West.

In 1869, Clemens became part-owner of the *Buffalo Express* and contributor of a column to the *Galaxy* magazine. Soon his connections with the newspaper and magazine were terminated and he moved to Hartford, Connecticut. Thereafter, he devoted his time to writing and lecturing.

Clemens was a humorist and novelist rather than a journalist, but he was associated with newspapers for at least twenty years and spent about ten years as a full-time editor and reporter.

Nineteenth-century printers dreamed of a machine that would relieve them of the tedious task of setting type by hand. Clemens thought that the problem had been solved by the invention of the Paige machine, which he said could do everything except drink, swear, and go on strike. When the Paige was tested by the *Chicago Times-Herald* in 1894, it was a failure. Clemens had invested $190,000 in the invention and was forced into bankruptcy by the failure.

EDWARD HENRY CLEMENT
1843–1920

Edward Henry Clement was born in Chelsea, Massachusetts. He had a profound interest in the future of the black race after the Civil War. To procure first-hand information, he was employed by the *Savannah Morning*

News in 1865. The atmosphere was unfriendly for a Bostonian, however, and Clement returned North. There followed a number of journalistic assignments: with the *New York Tribune* (1867); with the *Newark Daily Advertiser* (1869); and the *Elizabeth Daily Journal* (1873). In 1875, Clement returned to Boston, first as associate editor and then editor-in-chief of the *Transcript.* He was a playwright and poet of some distinction.

FRANK IRVING COBB
1869–1923

Frank Irving Cobb, Kansas-born, began his newspaper career in Grand Rapids, Michigan, in 1896, with the *Detroit Evening News,* as a political correspondent and editorial writer. In 1900, he transferred to the *Detroit Free Press* as chief editorial writer. In 1904, Cobb became confidential advisor to Joseph Pulitzer, who had been impressed with his editorials, and soon was given control of the *New York World's* editorial page. After Pulitzer's death in 1911, Cobb became the newspaper's editor-in-chief. When Woodrow Wilson was elected president in 1912, Cobb was offered a place in his cabinet, but declined.

IRVIN SHREWSBURY COBB
1876–1944

Irvin S. Cobb was born in Paducah, Kentucky, the locale for his most popular stories. He left school early to work for local newspapers. At age nineteen he became managing editor of the *Paducah Daily News,* and later reported for the *Louisville Evening Post.* His ambitions took him to New York City in 1904 to become a staff writer for the *Evening World* and *Sunday World,* where he reportedly was the highest-paid reporter in the country.

Cobb became a regular contributor of humorous articles to the *Saturday Evening Post* and was a member of the magazine's staff from 1911 to 1922. Another ten years were spent as a staff writer for *Cosmopolitan* magazine.

Cobb became celebrated for his tales of a kindly old Confederate veteran, Judge Priest. He was a prolific writer, publishing more than sixty books, and was a popular lecturer and after-dinner speaker throughout the country.

WILLIAM COBBETT
1763–1835

William Cobbett, English-born, was the most controversial journalist
and political figure of his generation. Before coming to America he served
with his regiment in Nova Scotia and New Brunswick. Afterward he attempted to have his officers court-martialed for corruption, but was afraid
to appear as a witness against them for fear of reprisal. Instead, he went
to Paris to study French. As a journalist in America from 1792 to 1800, he
wrote against the ideas of the French Revolution, attacked Thomas Paine,
and upheld Tory ideals. In 1800 he returned to England and began publication of *Cobbett's Weekly Political Register,* which he edited from 1802 to
his death. Still fighting for reforms in the British government, he attacked
flogging in the Army, was tried for sedition, found guilty, fined a thousand
pounds (paid by his followers), and sent to Newgate prison for two years.
Realizing that the government was engaged in a campaign of repression,
Cobbett fled in 1817 to the United States, and settled on a farm on Long
Island. Copy for the *Political Register* was sent regularly to his agents in
England, who continued to produce the paper.

Another legal problem, which led to Cobbett's bankruptcy, was his ac-
cusation against Benjamin Rush, famous Philadelphia physician, of being
a killer because of his practice of blood-letting. Rush sued for libel, won,
and Cobbett was fined $5,000.

After the Reform Act of 1832, Cobbett was elected to Parliament.
Earlier he had begun an unofficial record of parliamentary debates, continued until his death and then taken over by the printing firm of Hansard,
to become the official record of Parliament.

Cobbett's nickname was "Peter Porcupine," derived from his journal
Porcupine's Gazette and Daily Advertiser, published briefly in Philadelphia
(1797–1800).

ELIZABETH (NELLIE BLY) COCHRANE
1867–1922

Elizabeth Cochrane (Seaman), born in Cochrane's Mill, Pennsylvania,
came into a world dominated by male journalists and she had difficulty
breaking into it. A letter to the managing editor of the *Pittsburgh Dispatch,*
which she signed "E. Cochrane," led to a job offer. She was the first woman
on the *Dispatch.* Her pen name "Nellie Bly" appears to have been derived
from the popular Stephen Foster song by that title.

Cochrane's first article was on divorce, followed by a series of articles on working girls living in Pittsburgh's slums. The articles dealt with such sordid subjects as starvation, filth, and despair and brought demands for reform. The factory owners and community leaders put pressure on the paper to silence her. For a time they succeeded, but then she exposed conditions in Western Penitentiary, wrote again about the factories, and spent six months in 1887 in Mexico describing contrasts between the rich and the masses who slept hungry in the streets. These articles were published in the *Dispatch.* In the course of her travels she was with the Hoosier poet Joaquin Miller, another investigator.

In 1888 "Nelly Bly" Cochrane left Pittsburgh for New York, looking for a position with one of the city's newspapers. Again, there was prejudice against a woman journalist, but she was finally hired by Joseph Pulitzer to write an investigative piece about the treatment of patients in the Blackwell's Island asylum. She was admitted as a patient under the name "Nellie Brown." After her release, she wrote an account of conditions that led to a grand jury investigation. Cochrane was given a regular reporting job on the *New York World.* Other crusades initiated by her included exposures of shady practices used by employment agencies, graft by public officials, and dishonest street beggars.

Cochrane's last big adventure, approved by Pulitzer, was a trip around the world, aimed at bettering Jules Verne's fictional eighty days in *Around the World in Eighty Days.* After a series of exciting events navigating the globe, she set a new record of seventy-two days, six hours, ten minutes, and eleven seconds. She was now a celebrity and Arthur Brisbane gave her a job with the *Evening Journal* in 1919. By then, women in newspaper work were becoming common. A biographer states that her "short but lively career makes her one of the more vivid figures in the annals of American journalists."

JOHN A. COCKERILL
1845-1896

John A. Cockerill was born in Locust Grove, Ohio. Early on, he was fascinated by a visit to the nearby newspaper office of the *West Union Scion.* The editor, Sam Burwell, gave young Cockerill a job as a printer's devil. In 1868 he spent a few months as an editor for the *Dayton Daily Ledger.* Shortly thereafter, he joined the *Cincinnati Enquirer,* first as a reporter, then as city editor and managing editor. One of the contributors encouraged by Cockerill was Lafcadio Hearn, just beginning his literary career. The *Enquirer's* circulation quadrupled during Cockerill's editorship. John McLean, the publisher, perhaps envious of the managing editor's success, sent Cockerill abroad to cover the Russian-Turkish War for the *Enquirer*. When he returned, McLean had established himself as managing editor.

Cockerill's next stop was Washington, where he helped to start the *Washington Post*. Several months were spent as editor of the *Baltimore Gazette,* and then he was recruited by Joseph Pulitzer to be managing editor of the *St. Louis Post-Dispatch*. His stay there was marred by the shooting of a St. Louis lawyer, Alonzo Slayback, for which Cockerill was blamed. In any case, he was transferred by Pulitzer to New York to manage his newly acquired *New York World*. Again circulation climbed rapidly, from twenty thousand to one hundred thousand, boosted by such sensational stories as the opening of the Brooklyn Bridge, and star reporter "Nellie Bly" beating Jules Verne's eighty days on a globe-circling trip. Eventually, the *World* attained a circulation of 250,000, claimed to be the largest ever reached by an American newspaper up to that time. Differences between Cockerill and Pulitzer led the former to resign from the *World* in 1891. For four years Cockerill worked to strengthen two New York papers, the *Commercial Advertiser* and the *Continent,* and met with limited success. Early in 1895, he joined the staff of the *New York Herald* and was sent to the Far East as a special correspondent in China and Japan. On his way home, he was stricken with apoplexy and died in Cairo, Egypt, in 1896. A biographer, Jo Anne Smith, termed "John A. Cockerill perhaps the finest editor to come out of Joseph Pulitzer's talent hunts."

CHARLES CARLETON COFFIN
1823-1896

Charles C. Coffin, a native of New Hampshire, wrote under the pen name of "Carleton." He began newspaper work as assistant editor of the *Boston Argus* (1856-57), and as correspondent for the *Boston Journal* in the Midwest in 1854 and again in 1857 and 1860.

Coffin's fame derives mainly, however, from his Civil War dispatches. He wrote a first-hand account of the battle of Bull Run at the outbreak and reported on all the major engagements until the end of the war, from the Wilderness to the fall of Richmond. Following the war, he exploited his war experiences in a number of published books.

WILLIAM TURNER COGGESHALL
1824-1867

William T. Coggeshall was born in Lewistown, Pennsylvania, but moved to Ohio in 1842 to become an editor and part-owner of a temperance paper (1844–46) in Akron. A short time later he went on to Cincinnati to work with a monthly publication, *Genius of the West* (1853–56). From 1856 to 1862, Coggeshall was librarian of the Ohio State Library at Columbus and editor of the *Ohio Educational Monthly* (1858–59). Two other journalistic positions were owner and editor of the Springfield, Ohio, *Republic* (1862–65), and editor of the *Ohio State Journal,* in Columbus, toward the end of 1865.

In 1866, Coggeshall was appointed American minister to Ecuador, a fatal mission for him and his daughter, both of whom died before returning to the United States.

WILLIAM COLEMAN
1766–1829

William Coleman, born in Boston, was called the most effective Federalist journalist during Alexander Hamilton's time. He established the *Impartial Intelligencer* and contributed frequently to it in 1795 and 1796. In 1800 Coleman was made editor and proprietor of the *Evening Post,* established for political purposes by Hamilton and his friends. A semiweekly edition, the *New York Herald,* gained a national circulation.

HENRY DAVID COOKE
1825–1881

Henry David Cooke began life in Sandusky, Ohio, and originally planned a legal career, for which he had little interest. After a visit to Chile and a stay in California, he returned east in 1849 to become financial editor of the *United States Gazette* in Philadelphia. The next stops were back in Sandusky to edit the *Register,* which he and his brother Jay Cooke had bought, and in 1856 to edit the politically powerful *Ohio State Journal.* After the Civil War began, Cooke moved to Washington, abandoned the newspaper field, and became involved in business and politics.

KENT COOPER
1880–1965

Kent Cooper was born in Columbus, Indiana. He was given an early taste of the newspaper world by delivering the *Columbus Republican* and later setting type and reporting for Columbus newspapers. In 1899 the *Indianapolis Press* hired him as a reporter. When the *Press* folded after eighteen months, Cooper went to the *Indianapolis Sun,* as a police reporter. In 1901 he became Scripps–McRae's Indianapolis correspondent and then manager of the Indianapolis bureau, supplying news to a network of small Indiana newspapers.

When United Press took over Scripps–McRae and two other regional organizations to form a national news service, Cooper was transferred to UP's New York City headquarters. In 1910, he was offered a position as the Associated Press's first traveling inspector. Under a cost-cutting scheme devised by Cooper, the AP created a traffic department in 1912 and he became its first chief.

By 1920, Cooper had moved up to be assistant general manager of AP, and in 1925, the AP board approved Cooper's appointment as general manager. In this key position he set about revitalizing the organization that, according to one commentator, had become "dull and stagnant." Cooper introduced regular staff bylines, news pictures, lively writing style, emphasis on human interest, a photo service, and full coverage of foreign news.

In 1943, Cooper's title was changed to "executive director" of the AP, to add to his authority. In a biographical sketch, Leonard A. Schwarzlose declares: "It was under Cooper's tutelage that AP started its journey to becoming the far-flung, hierarchical, and powerful journalistic enterprise it is today."

LOUIS RICHARD CORTAMBERT
1808–1881

Louis Cortambert was born in Paris and emigrated to the United States as a youth. He first settled in St. Louis and there edited *La Revue de L'Ouest,* a weekly French newspaper (1855–58). Later, in New York City, Cortambert edited a French daily newspaper *Le Messager Franco-Americain* (1864–81). He was also the author of several historical works and was widely regarded as the most distinguished writer in French in the United States.

NORMAN COUSINS
1915–

Norman Cousins was born in Union City, New Jersey. Early in his career he was an editor for the *New York Evening Post* (1934–35) and managing editor of *Current History* (1935-40). In 1940 he joined the *Saturday Review of Literature* magazine, established in 1924. During Cousin's thirty-five-year tenure as editor, a struggling literary magazine with a circulation of 26,000 became a weekly forum for books, provocative ideas, the arts, and world affairs, with 600,000 subscribers. Except for a brief period during the 1970s, when Cousins took time out to found *World* magazine, he continued as editor of the *Saturday Review* until 1977. The *World* later merged with the *Saturday Review.*

Cousins was a leader in the world government movement. For several years he was president of United World Federalists, a group dedicated to global government, and later served as international president of the World Association of World Federalists.

Cousins was a prolific author with hundreds of editorials and essays and more than a dozen books to his credit.

EDWIN COWLES
1825-1890

Edwin Cowles was born in Austinburg, Ohio. He entered a printer's office at age fourteen and in 1844 he and T. H. Smead became partners in the printing business. Another partnership was formed in 1853 with Joseph Medill and John C. Vaughn. The new organization published the *Forest Hill Democrat,* a Free-Soil Whig newspaper, later changed to the *Cleveland Leader.* In a short time, Cowles became owner and editor and he began to publish both a morning and an evening daily newspaper.

Cowles was one of the founders of the Republican party. In 1861, Lincoln appointed him postmaster in Cleveland, an office that he held for five years. Later he was a delegate to the 1876 and 1884 Republican national conventions, and he remained a political power in northern Ohio for a generation.

GARDNER COWLES
1861-1946

Gardner Cowles was born in Algona, Iowa. His father, a banker, bought the *Des Moines Register and Leader* and thus Cowles grew up in a newspaper atmosphere. In 1908, the *Register* bought the *Tribune,* changing the title to *Register and Tribune.* In 1926, a year after graduating from Harvard, Cowles became news editor, the next year associate managing editor, and within a few months managing editor of the *Register and Tribune.* This arrangement continued until 1931, when he became executive editor. The competition was too much for other Des Moines papers; the Scripps–Howard *News* was bought in 1924 and in 1927 the *Capital.* In 1935 the *Minneapolis Star,* a key to controlling Minneapolis newspapers, was added. The *Star* was merged with the *Minneapolis Journal* in 1939, and in 1941 the *Minneapolis Tribune* was purchased. A chain of radio stations covering all the northern Midwestern states was established by the Cowles family.

A new field was entered by Cowles in 1935 with *Look,* a weekly picture magazine that quickly reached a million in circulation.

Another innovation by Cowles was to start George Gallup on his career of polling public opinion, a technique that has grown steadily in news value and influence.

In the summer of 1942, Cowles joined the Office of War Information as deputy director in charge of its domestic division, similar to the Creel Committee in World War I. Cowles resigned from the post in 1943 when he became president of the *Des Moines Register and Tribune,* and chairman of the board and editor-in-chief of Cowles Magazines and Broadcasting.

JAMES MIDDLETON COX
1870–1957

James M. Cox was born in a log cabin farmhouse near Jacksonburg, Ohio. He left school at age sixteen to become a country schoolteacher for a few years before working in a printer's office. Later he was a reporter on the *Cincinnati Enquirer.* He began to build up a chain of newspapers in 1898 when he bought the *Dayton News.* Subsequently the *Dayton Journal Herald, Miami* (Florida) *News, Springfield* (Ohio) *News, Springfield* (Ohio) *Sun, Atlanta* (Georgia) *Journal,* and in 1950, the *Atlanta Constitution* were added to the Cox empire. Besides newspapers, Cox owned radio and television stations.

Cox was long a political power in Ohio: U.S. congressman (1909–13) and governor of Ohio (1913–15, 1917–21), earning a reputation as a liberal, friend of labor, opponent of Prohibition, and supporter of Woodrow Wilson and the League of Nations. He was nominated by the Democrats for president in 1920, but was decisively defeated by Warren G. Harding in the November election.

Cox won a Pulitzer Prize in 1927 for crusading against corruption in city government. His last public service was as vice chairman of the world economic conference in London in 1933, on appointment by President Roosevelt.

DANIEL H. CRAIG
1811–1895

Daniel H. Craig, born in New Hampshire, is credited with developing the Associated Press as a national news monopoly starting in 1851. Halifax was the North American port nearest England and therefore, the point at which news was first obtained from English vessels. For that purpose, Craig established a private news agency, employing carrier pigeons. The *New York Sun* had been using pigeons for three or four years. Craig also used them successfully to bring the news from Halifax to Washington. His chief client was the *New York Herald,* which paid him bonuses for being first with news items. After the coming of the telegraph, Craig arranged to have boats meet English vessels at sea, several days before they docked in New York harbor. The "hot" news was published as an extra by the *Boston Daily Mail* and Bennett's *New York Herald.*

In 1851, Craig moved to New York to take charge of the New York Associated Press, in which the city's six leading morning papers were partners: *Journal of Commerce, Courier and Enquirer, Sun, Herald, Express,* and *Tribune.* The *New York Times* became the seventh partner late in 1851. At the time, there were five other local or regional APs, but the New York organization controlled most foreign, Washington, and domestic news, because of its location and telegraphic network.

Craig ruled over an Associated Press news monopoly during the rest of his tenure as general agent, which lasted until 1866. The news gathered by the New York Associated Press was sold to other cities, the scope of the news was broadened, and soon correspondence was established at all important points. A major principle, emphasizing from the beginning, was nonpartisan, nonpolitical reporting of the news.

STEPHEN CRANE
1871–1900

Stephen Crane is most celebrated as a novelist, especially for his Civil War classic, *The Red Badge of Courage,* in which he portrayed realistically the terror of battle. His listening to many old veterans recall the War between the States enabled him to give vivid, accurate accounts. He was born in Newark, New Jersey, and was a student at Lafayette College and Syracuse University. He went to New York in 1892, where he worked as a newspaper reporter. In 1897, he was a news correspondent in the Greco-Turkish War, and in 1898, in the Spanish American War. Crane lived in England near the end of his life and died of tuberculosis in a German sanitarium. Two years before *The Red Badge of Courage,* Crane wrote *Maggie: A Girl of the Streets* which showed the influence of the French Naturalist writers upon him. In turn, his bare impressionistic style suggested the technique to be exhibited in Hemingway and Farrell. "The Open Boat," the story of four survivors of a shipwreck, is considered his best short story.

GEORGE CREEL
1876-1953

George Creel was born in Lafayette County, Missouri. After a brief stint with the *Kansas City World,* he left for New York and searched in vain for a newspaper or magazine job. He finally sold four items to Hearst's *Evening Journal* and then caught on with *Puck, Judge,* and other periodicals. He was lured back to Kansas City in 1899 to assist in starting a new journal, the *Independent.* This weekly was edited and published by Creel until 1909. Its contents included editorials, the arts, sports, social news, and politics.

In 1909, Creel went West to become editorial writer for the *Denver Post,* continuing until 1911, followed by a year (1911-12) with the *Rocky Mountain News.* Time was also spent in New York in 1911 writing for Hearst's *Cosmopolitan* magazine. During a period of freelancing, Creel did muckraking articles for *Harper's Weekly, Everybody's,* and other periodicals. He was also active in Woodrow Wilson's 1916 reelection campaign.

The opportunity that made Creel known came in April 1917, when President Wilson made him chairman of the Committee on Public Information, the United States' information agency in World War I. Creel assembled a large staff and made the office a powerful weapon for the American cause. His committee promoted voluntary newspaper censorship of confidential war information. The committee was primarily a propaganda bureau and not a censorship organization. The committee's work ended with high praise from Wilson and from critics who had been skeptical about Creel's appointment in the beginning.

Creel never returned to full-time newspaper work, although he served for a time as *Collier's* Washington correspondent. He was chairman in 1935 of an advisory committee of the Works Progress Administration and was U.S. commissioner of the Golden Gate International Exposition in 1939.

JAMES CREELMAN
1859–1915

James Creelman, born in Montreal, Canada, came to New York at age twelve. He learned the printer's trade working in the printing plant of the Protestant Episcopal Church's newspaper, followed by brief and irregular work for the *Brooklyn Eagle*. At age eighteen he was hired as a cub reporter by the *New York Herald*.

Probably no newspaper man ever had a more adventurous life than did Creelman: taking part in dare-devil stunts; covering the Hatfield–McCoy feud in Kentucky, where he was shot at by one of the Hatfields; covering the Sino-Japanese War; accompanying the Japanese army on its invasion of Manchuria; and leading an assault on a Spanish post in Cuba where a Mauser bullet smashed an arm and tore a hole in his back.

Colorful personalities interviewed by Creelman for his paper included Sitting Bull, Pope Leo XIII, Count Leo Tolstoy, Henry Stanley, the king of Korea, and King George of Greece.

Creelman's newspaper assignments included serving as editor of Bennett's *New York Evening Telegram* in 1892; associate editor of the *Illustrated American;* and manager of the London edition of *Cosmopolitan* magazine. In 1894, he joined Joseph Pulitzer's *New York World,* where he was sent on various foreign missions. Back home, a routine assignment was to travel with William Jennings Bryan in the 1896 campaign.

William Randolph Hearst, competing with Pulitzer, hired Creelman for the *New York Journal,* and in 1897 sent him to visit the European capitals. In 1898 he joined Hearst's army of correspondents covering the war in Cuba. Later in the year, after recovering from wounds received there, he went to the Philippines to cover the battles of American forces and Filipino rebels. In 1900 Creelman rejoined the *New York World* as special correspondent and editorial writer. His final positions were the associate editorship of the *New York Evening Mail* in 1913, and being sent by Hearst and the *New York American* to Berlin in 1915 to report on the European War. He died shortly after his arrival in Germany.

DAVID GOODMAN CROLY
1829–1889

David Croly was born in Ireland, came to America when a small boy, and grew up in New York City. In 1855 he became a reporter on the *New York Evening Post*. Afterward he was in charge of the *Herald's* intelligence department, a position he held until 1857. There was an interlude of three years in Rockford, Illinois, as editor of the *Daily News*. In 1860, he and his wife Jane Cunningham Croly, another journalist, moved back to new York. Croly was first city editor and then managing editor of the *World* until 1872. In 1868, Croly and C. W. Sweet founded the *Real Estate Record and Builder's Guide*. The next step for Croly was to become editor of the *Daily Graphic,* a new illustrated paper, a post that he resigned in 1878 in a dispute over editorial management.

Croly's final fling was to start a new quarterly magazine, the *Modern Thinker,* designed to promote the editor's philosophical theories. It survived for three issues.

HERBERT DAVID CROLY
1869–1930

Herbert Croly, born in New York City, was the son of two famous journalists, David and Jane Croly, and it was almost inevitable that he should follow the same profession. Croly was a political theorist whose views influenced Theodore Roosevelt's "Bull Moose" Progressive campaign in 1912.

Croly's most lasting achievement was the founding in 1914, and editing of the *New Republic,* which he aimed to make the mouthpiece of the Progressive movement. At first a supporter of Woodrow Wilson, the *New Republic,* under Croly, broke with Wilson over the Treaty of Versailles. As Croly conceived it, the magazine was aimed at intellectuals, rather than the "masses." He enlisted contributors like Walter Lippmann and Randolph Bourne. Croly approved of Woodrow Wilson's reform programs and advocated a League of Nations after World War I. As editor of the *New Republic* until his death in 1930, Croly continued to exert influence on political leaders and social scientists through the 1920s.

JANE CUNNINGHAM CROLY
1829–1901

Jane Croly was born in England and brought to the United States by her father when she was twelve years old. The records appear to show that she was the first American newspaperwoman.

Croly's first experience in journalism was with the *New York Tribune,* of which Charles A. Dana was managing editor. She adopted the pen name of "Jennie Jane" and began writing on topics of interest to women—

parties, clothes, and beauty. It was the start of the women's pages in later newspapers. As the popularity of the Croly column spread, she wrote for the *New York Times* and *Noah's Sunday Times,* as well as for the *Tribune.*

Croly's husband, David, became editor of the *Rockford* (Illinois) *Register,* and Croly assisted her husband in the editorial management of the paper. In 1860 the family returned to New York, where David became editor of the *New York World.* Jennie Jane was the paper's fashion editor. By 1872 her articles were being syndicated by the *Chicago Times,* the *New Orleans Democrat,* the *Richmond Whig,* and New York papers. She was editor of *Demorest's Quarterly Mirror of Fashion* and of its successor *Demorest's Illustrated Monthly,* a position that she held until 1887. For fifteen years, she was a New York correspondent for the *New Orleans Picayune,* the *Baltimore American,* and other newspapers. She was also connected with *Godey's* and with the *Homemaker.*

Croly's main topic as a journalist was fashion, but her interests were diverse. She gave young women advice on proper public behavior, criticized women for applying lipstick in public, advocated sex education, gave hints on planning parties, published tested recipes, ridiculed long skirts, hoops, and crinolines, wrote instructions on knitting, sewing, and crocheting, and advised on shopping.

Croly was an early leader of the feminist movement. She called the first women's congress in 1856; founded, in 1868, Sorosis, the first important women's club, which later led to the formation of the General Federation of Women's Clubs; and in 1889 organized the Women's Press Club.

Late in her career, Croly started, in 1889, a new magazine, the *Woman's Cycle,* as an organ for the General Federation. This was merged with the *HomeMaker* and then the *New Cycle,* which she edited for the three years that it lasted.

WALTER CRONKITE
1916–

Walter Cronkite was born in St. Joseph, Missouri. As a youth his ambition was to become a foreign correspondent. In preparation, he worked on school publications and studied journalism at the University of Texas. At the same time he served as campus correspondent for the *Houston Post.* He also did sports announcing and reporting for the Scripps–Howard Houston bureau. After dropping out of college to become a full-time newspaperman, Cronkite worked as a reporter for the United Press in Houston, Kansas City, Dallas, Austin, and El Paso.

Cronkite's opportunity for foreign experience came during World War

II when, from 1942 to 1945, he was a war correspondent for United Press. In that capacity, he covered the major battles of the war. He remained in Europe after the war as one of UP's European correspondents. From 1946 to 1948 he was manager of UP's Moscow bureau. He also was UP's chief correspondent for the Nuremberg war crimes trial.

After returning to the United States, Cronkite became Washington news correspondent for the Columbia Broadcasting System and then moved to the CBS News in time to cover the 1952 presidential campaign. His evening show began on April 16, 1962, and he continued in that post until March 1981, when he was succeeded by Dan Rather. Cronkite's report on his 1968 trip to Vietnam had an important influence on American public opinion, helping to create a strong sentiment against the war. In 1981 he was awarded the Medal of Freedom by President Carter. Also having a great impact were Cronkite's hard-hitting reports on the Watergate scandal in 1972.

EDWIN CROSWELL
1797–1871

Edwin Croswell was born in Catskill, New York, the son of Mackay Croswell, editor of the *Catskill Packet,* founded in 1792, and of its three successors. Croswell spent much of his boyhood in his father's newspaper office, along with his friend Thurlow Weed. At age fourteen he was hired by the *Catskill Recorder,* of which he soon became assistant editor. Another move occurred in 1823, when Croswell was called to be editor of the *Albany Argus.* The following year he was elected state printer, an office he filled until 1847, except for one interruption (1840–44), when Thurlow Weed held the job.

As an editor, Croswell was a strong partisan of the Democratic party. The party was split on a number of issues, including disputes in which Croswell was involved. He retired from the *Argus* in 1854 to enter business.

AMOS JAY CUMMINGS
1841–1902

Amos Jay Cummings was born in Conkling, New York, a son of the editor of the *Christian Herald* and *Christian Palladium.* At age twelve he was apprenticed to the printer in whose shop the papers were produced. At fifteen he ran away and was a tramp printer and compositor in various

Eastern towns. In New York he worked as a typesetter on the *Tribune* until the start of the Civil War. Military service followed, leaving Cummings with impaired health. He returned to the *Tribune,* but lost his job because of a strike. There was an interim with the *Law Transcript* in Yonkers, but again he was employed by the *Tribune* as night editor, by Horace Greeley. A change occurred in 1864 when Cummings went to the *Sun* as night editor and later as managing editor. He resigned in 1872 for health reasons and spent four years traveling through the South and West. His observations and experiences were reported in a series of letters to the *Sun.*

In 1876 Cummings edited for a time the *Evening Express,* wrote feature articles for the *Sun* on political affairs, and reported several famous murder trials. He was elected to Congress in 1886, but declined renomination, preferring his career in journalism. The evening *Sun* was started under his editorship. Mott called Cummings "one of the best newspaper men of the period."

CYRUS CURTIS
1850–1933

Cyrus Curtis, a native of Maine, was probably the most successful magazine publisher in journalistic history. As a twelve-year-old newsboy, he started his first publication, *Young America.* Later he moved to Boston and in 1872 founded a magazine called the *People's Ledger.* Moving on to Philadelphia, Curtis started another magazine, the *Tribune and Farmer.* Showing a touch of genius in 1883, the *Ladies' Home Journal,* previously a supplement to the *Tribune and Farmer,* began separate publication. Under Edward Bok's editorship, the *Ladies' Home Journal* reached a circulation of a million within ten years. Another important step was taken in 1897 when Curtis bought the *Saturday Evening Post* for $1,000. With George Horace Lorimer as editor, the *Post* attained a circulation of over 2.7 million subscribers by 1933. Still another popular addition was the *Country Gentleman,* acquired by Curtis in 1911.

Perhaps encouraged by the phenomenal growth of his magazines, Curtis later branched into the newspaper field, buying the *Philadelphia Public Ledger* in 1913, the *Philadelphia Press* in 1920, the *New York Evening Post* in 1924, and the *Philadelphia Inquirer* in 1920. The entry into the newspaper field, however, was a failure, and Curtis disposed of his papers later at a considerable loss.

Curtis was the first magazine publisher to recognize the potential of advertising. The generous arrangements made by his publications boosted the growth of the advertising industry.

GEORGE WILLIAM CURTIS
1824–1892

George William Curtis, born in Providence, Rhode Island, spent time in Concord, Massachusetts, doing farm work and associating with such literary lights as Emerson, Thoreau, Hawthorne, and Alcott. Curtis assisted Thoreau in building his cabin at Walden Pond. In 1846, Curtis and his brother took the "grand tour" of Europe and the Near East. The tour was the start of a journalistic career for Curtis, who acted as a correspondent of the *New York Tribune* and became a staff member on his return to America in 1851. From 1852 to 1857, Curtis served as associate editor of the short-lived *Putnam's Monthly.*

A much longer connection was made with *Harper's Monthly.* From October 1853 and for nearly forty years, Curtis wrote the "Easy Chair" columns for *Harper's,* discussing an endless variety of subjects.

As political editor of *Harper's Weekly* from 1863 to 1892, Curtis had substantial influence on American public affairs. He championed women's suffrage and is credited with bringing about civil service reform. Curtis enjoyed his writing for *Harper's* and declined other attractive offers, such as the editorship of the *New York Times.*

WILLIAM ELEROY CURTIS
1850–1911

William E. Curtis was born in Akron, Ohio. His primary interest was in travel; he attempted to visit as many foreign countries as possible. After graduation from Western Reserve College, his first newspaper job was as a reporter on the staff of the *Chicago Inter-Ocean.* A more exciting job for him was the position of Washington correspondent for the *Chicago Record* in 1887. Even more to his liking was an appointment as a special commissioner from the United States to the Republics of Central and South America, giving Curtis an opportunity to visit those countries. When the Bureau of the American Republics (later the Pan American Union) was established Curtis became its first director in 1889, continuing until 1893.

During his subsequent career, Curtis was a traveling correspondent, writing a daily column on affairs of the day, describing important events and picturing foreign countries for publication in the *Chicago Record.* He also wrote many books, among them important travel and handbooks describing Latin American countries for the Pan American Union.

CHARLES A. DANA
1819–1897

Charles A. Dana was born in Hinsdale, New Hampshire. After dropping out of Harvard because of poor eyesight, he taught for five years at Brook Farm, where he wrote for the *Harbinger,* the Brook Farm organ. He was employed by the *Boston Chronotype* in 1846. The following year Dana became city editor of Horace Greeley's *New York Tribune* and remained there for sixteen years. During an interim in 1848 he was in Europe reporting on the revolutionary movements of that year. Because of wide temperamental differences with Greeley, he resigned from the *Tribune* in 1862. From 1863 to 1865, Dana was assistant secretary of war and reported on the progress of the Civil War directly from the front.

A major step in Dana's career occurred in 1867, when he became editor and part-owner of the *New York Sun,* of which he remained in control until his death. Under his guidance, the *Sun's* circulation increased from 43,000 in 1868 to 150,000 in the early 1880s. It became one of the most important newspapers of its time. The paper's format underwent radical changes to make it more attractive and readable. Emphasis was on large headlines, human interest and crime stories, and a lively writing style. Dana's vigorous editorials, expressing his own likes and dislikes, were widely read.

The *Sun* became actively involved in the political campaigns and controversies of the period, but it was often inconsistent, varying from quasi-liberal to conservative. Government corruption was denounced, but the paper was also opposed to civil service reform and labor unions.

According to Mott, other editors generally admired the *Sun*. It was called "the newspaperman newspaper." An important contribution, as Dana had promised, was to report the news in a lively, amusing style. The price was also an asset — two cents when other papers were generally charging six cents.

E. CLIFTON DANIEL
1912–

Clifton Daniel was born in Zebulon, North Carolina. While still in high school he wrote news items for his hometown paper, the *Zebulon Record*. For three years he worked for the *Raleigh* (North Carolina) *News and Observer*. Thereafter, he joined the Associated Press in New York and had assignments in Switzerland and England. In 1944 he switched to the *New York Times* as a London correspondent. During World War II, Daniel covered the Allies' advance into Germany and later reported from the

Middle East and Russia. The Overseas Press Club gave him its award for the best reporting from abroad on the basis of his work in Moscow.

When Daniel returned to America he was appointed in 1957 assistant to the managing editor of the *New York Times,* Turner Catledge. Later he became managing editor in charge of the news department.

In 1956, Daniel married Margaret Truman, daughter of President Harry Truman.

JOHN M. DANIEL
1825-1865

John M. Daniel, a Virginian, was an unreconstructed Confederate all his life — a zealous defender of slavery, a strong believer in Southern rights, and convinced of the rightness of sovereignty for the Confederate states. He was also a severe critic of Jefferson Davis.

Daniel, who founded the *Richmond Examiner* in 1847, was famous for participating in nine pistol duels, most of which were reactions to his editorial policies. The last issue of the *Examiner* was published on the eve of the evacuation of Richmond and carried the news of Daniel's death.

As an editor, Daniel's approach was highly personal. Nothing appeared in his paper, not even advertisements, without his approval. Regardless of its blemishes, the *Examiner* came to be regarded as the most influential newspaper in the South. Among its admirers were Edgar Allan Poe and President Franklin Pierce. Daniel was appointed by Pierce to be chargé d'affaires to the court of Victor Emmanuel II, king of Sardinia, and spent time in Turin.

JONATHAN DANIELS
1902-1981

Jonathan Daniels, born in Raleigh, North Carolina, was the son of Josephus Daniels. After his college years, he became Washington correspondent for his father's paper, the *Raleigh News and Observer*. While his father was ambassador to Mexico, Daniels served as editor-in-chief of the *News and Observer* and officially succeeded to the position when his father died in 1948.

In earlier positions, Daniels had been a reporter with the *Louisville Times* and from 1930 to 1932 had worked on the editorial staff of *Fortune* magazine. From 1940 to 1942, he contributed a regular weekly page to the *Nation,* entitled "A Nation at Large," dealing with a variety of affairs.

Outside his journalistic career, Daniels was administrative assistant and then press secretary to President Franklin D. Roosevelt (1943–45), and political advisor to President Harry Truman in 1948. He was the author of several books concerned with politics, the New Deal, and the South.

JOSEPHUS DANIELS
1862–1948

Josephus Daniels, editor and publisher of the *Raleigh News and Observer* for fifty-four years, was born in Washington, North Carolina. His interest in journalism began at age sixteen, when he and his brother Charles published an amateur newspaper, the *Cornucopia.* In 1880, Daniels became editor of the *Wilson Advance,* a small rural weekly. Five years later, in 1885, he took over a weekly paper in the state capital, the *Raleigh State Chronicle,* a paper near failure that he revived. Daniels's efforts to turn the *Chronicle* into a daily, however, were unsuccessful, and he sold it in 1892. The next venture was to start another weekly, the *North Carolinian.* When one of Raleigh's dailies, the *News and Observer,* went bankrupt, Daniels purchased it, with backing from friends. He remained associated with that paper for the rest of his life.

Throughout his career, Daniels was active in Democratic politics, supporting William Jennings Bryan, Woodrow Wilson, and Franklin D. Roosevelt. He also became a leader in movements for railroad and utility regulation, Prohibition, labor legislation, and women's suffrage.

Daniels was appointed secretary of the navy by Woodrow Wilson in 1913 and brought the U.S. Navy to a high state of efficiency during World War I. He chose Franklin D. Roosevelt to be assistant secretary of the navy, an appointment that was reciprocated in 1933 when Roosevelt appointed Daniels to be ambassador to Mexico. In that country he won Mexican friendship, while protecting U.S. property rights.

Daniels returned to his Raleigh newspaper in 1941. He remained prominent in state and national politics, fought the Ku Klux Klan, and supported the League of Nations and World Court. His son Jonathan succeeded him as editor of the *News and Observer.*

JAY NORWOOD DARLING
1876–1962

Jay Darling, known around the world as "Ding," was born in Norwood, Michigan, but spent much of his life in Des Moines, Iowa. As a youth he explored the Missouri River country, inspiring his long dedication to the conservation of natural resources.

Ding's first published efforts at cartooning, the art that made him famous, appeared in the 1898 Beloit College yearbook, lampooning the dignified faculty as a line of chorus girls. Before graduating from college in 1900 he was briefly a reporter on the *Sioux City Tribune* and then for the *Sioux City Journal*. For six years, Ding combined drawing with reporting. A major step toward his future career came in 1906, when he accepted an offer to be a cartoonist for the *Des Moines Register and Leader*. From 1911 to 1913 he was in New York working for the *New York Globe* syndicate but then returned to his Des Moines home. His national fame was established in 1917, when the New York Tribune Syndicate began to distribute Darling's work to 130 newspapers nationally. He also drew for *Collier's Weekly*.

Darling won two Pulitzer Prizes, the first in 1923 and the second in 1943. His most celebrated cartoons marked the death of Buffalo Bill Cody, an Iowa native, and the death of his friend Theodore Roosevelt.

The *Register* placed no restrictions on Darling's work, although the cartoons were often at odds with the paper's editorial policies.

Among highlights in Darling's later career were a trip to the Soviet Union in 1931, at Joseph Stalin's invitation; and a term (1934–35) as chief of the U.S. Bureau of Biological Survey in the Department of Agriculture. In the latter position, he was an active conservationist, promoting his strong beliefs in protecting natural resources and preserving wildlife. For his work in this field, Darling was elected president of the National Wildlife Federation.

After two years Darling returned to Des Moines, where he published cartoons regularly in the *Register* until his retirement in 1949.

ELMER HOLMES DAVIS
1890–1958

Elmer Davis became nationally and internationally famous during World War II as director of the Office of War Information (1942–45). Davis was a native of Aurora, Indiana, a Rhodes scholar to Oxford in 1910, and received a B.A. Degree in 1912.

Davis's journalistic career began with a year on the editorial staff of

Adventure. As a boy he had been printer's devil on the *Aurora Bulletin.* After the Oxford experience, he became a cub reporter on the *New York Times.* In ten years he advanced to serving as feature man on American politics and editorial writer. By World War II Davis had become widely known and respected as a skillful analyst of contemporary politics and events.

The OWI under Davis had two functions: propaganda and accurate news reports on the progress of the war. Davis performed both functions with skill and distinction.

Before becoming director of war information, Davis had been a news commentator for the Columbia Broadcasting System in 1939. His articles on various topics had appeared in *Harper's, Forum, Saturday Review of Literature,* and other periodicals. When the war ended, Davis returned to radio news analysis in 1945 with the American Broadcasting Company. He retired in 1953.

MATTHEW LIVINGSTON DAVIS
1773-1850

Matthew Davis, it is assumed, was born in New York. He started as a printer, and edited the short-lived *Evening Post* in 1794. Later he collaborated with Philip Freneau on the *Time Piece and Literary Companion* (1797-98). For forty years, Davis was a close friend and associate of Aaron Burr, and was present at the Burr–Hamilton duel in which Alexander Hamilton was fatally wounded. Subsequently he went to jail for refusing to testify against his friend, Burr.

RICHARD HARDING DAVIS
1864-1916

During the course of his thirty-year journalistic career, Richard Harding Davis became the symbol of an adventurous, swashbuckling war correspondent. He convinced generations of college youths that the journalist's life was the most picturesque and exciting of all careers, full of glamour and romance. Along with Rudyard Kipling, he influenced such contemporaries as Frank Norris, Jack London, John Reed, and Stephen Crane, while his legend was inherited by Vincent Sheean and Ernest Hemingway.

Davis's family background was hardly indicative of a future filled with travel in exotic lands, reports on warring nations, and wild adventures. From early childhood, his surroundings were literary. His father was editor of the *Philadelphia Public Ledger* and his mother was one of the prominent women novelists of her generation.

Davis's newspaper career began in 1886, when he was twenty-two. It was destined to make him the most widely known reporter of his generation. For a brief time, he was employed by the *Philadelphia Record* and then the *Press,* for which he reported the Johnstown flood disaster. His first foreign assignment was for the *Telegraph,* which sent him to England with the Philadelphia cricket team. Later he joined the staff of the *New York Sun,* his stories and special articles for that paper and *Scribner's Magazine* attracting wide attention. They also won for him attention from *Harper's Weekly,* where he became managing editor in 1890. He made a tour of the West fraternizing with Mexican murderers, Texas Rangers, old prospectors, and women who smoked and drank in public. Next he went on an extensive tour of the Mediterranean.

In the spring of 1896, the *New York Journal* sent Davis to Russia to cover the coronation of Czar Nicholas II, and to Cuba to report on the insurrection. He sent back some unusually dramatic stories, including several about the execution of Cuban revolutionaries.

The next war Davis covered was in the spring of 1897, when he was sent by the London *Times* to report on the battles between Greece and Turkey. He and a *Journal* correspondent were the only reporters present at one of the important engagements near the close of the war, the Turkish attack on Velestinos where the reporters narrowly escaped with their lives.

When the U.S. Navy landed in Cuba Davis decided to attach himself to the Rough Riders, an odd mixture of college athletes, cowboys, and New York society men, who had been recruited by Theodore Roosevelt and who were under his command as a lieutenant colonel. Even though they were not as well trained as regular army troops, Davis thought that he would see more action and excitement with the Rough Riders.

After marching all morning through the steaming Cuban jungle, a thundering fusillade came from a hillside just ahead and American soldiers began falling all around Davis. He helped to drag the injured to cover, and then grabbed a rifle from a fallen soldier and joined the attack on the snipers. Roosevelt shouted for a charge and the Rough Riders followed him up the hill. A few minutes later the Spaniards were in flight and the skirmish was over. Roosevelt thanked Davis personally for his help and offered him a commission in the Rough Riders, which he refused.

By 1900 Davis was ready for more military action and glory. He went to British South Africa to cover the Boer War, first with the British army and then with the Boer commandos, intrepid bush fighters and raiders. While with the Boer army, Davis visited a schoolhouse in Pretoria that had been converted into a prison camp for British Soldiers. Among the prisoners was a correspondent for the *London Morning Post,* young Winston Churchill.

In 1904 Davis went to Tokyo to cover the Russo-Japanese War, but permission by the Japanese to go to the front was so long delayed, he saw little of the fighting. Also somewhat tame from Davis's viewpoint was a trip to Mexico in 1914 to cover the outbreak there, although Davis was arrested by Mexican soldiers and came close to facing a firing squad before being released.

Then came the first World War. Davis went independently to Brussels, where he witnessed the German army marching through. Davis's dispatches on the highly efficient and ruthless German army on the march were smuggled to England and were hailed as one of the classics of war reporting.

At this time, everything written by war correspondents was severely censored by the Germans, British, and French. Davis did not live to know the full story of this war since he died at his home in Mt. Kisco, New York, in 1916, before the United States entered the conflict.

Davis was a prolific writer: he published eleven collections of short stories; *Soldiers of Fortune* (1897), a novel about an adventurous American engineer in South America; twenty-five plays, and seven nonfiction books based on his experiences.

In the opinion of a leading literary critic, Van Wyck Brooks, Davis's "writings were commonplace enough, efficient, surely, but undistinguished," as compared for instance with Stephen Crane's writings. Brooks agreed that Davis's Latin American stories had special color and feeling as he responded to "the land of guitars and gorgeous silent nights." As a correspondent, Davis was quick to see the picturesque and a genius in selecting features having news value. In all his journalistic work he tended to be sensational and dramatic.

FRANCIS WASHINGTON DAWSON
1840–1889

Francis Dawson was born in London and came to the United States in 1861 to enlist in the Confederate cause, first in the Navy and later in the Army. He fought in a dozen battles, was wounded three times, and suffered a term in prison.

Following the war, Dawson worked on the *Richmond Examiner* and later the *Richmond Dispatch.* In 1866 he was employed by the *Charleston Mercury.* The following year, Dawson and two partners purchased the

Charleston News. The *Charleston Courier* was acquired in 1873. The two papers were combined to form the *News and Courier,* with Dawson as editor.

BENJAMIN HENRY DAY
1810–1889

Benjamin Henry Day, born in Massachusetts, began his newspaper career in Springfield, his hometown. At age fourteen, he was apprenticed to Samuel Bowles of the *Springfield Republican,* and remained there for six years learning the printing trade. In 1830, Day moved on to New York to be a compositor for the *Evening Post,* the *Journal of Commerce,* and the *Commercial Advertiser.*

Until this time, several efforts to establish penny newspapers had failed. Day was convinced that such a paper could be made profitable. Accordingly, in September 1833 he founded the *New York Sun,* proving the feasibility of a popularly priced newspaper aimed at mass readership. The *Sun* was the first successful penny daily in New York. Within two months its circulation reached two thousand and four thousand within four months.

The *Sun's* popularity could be explained by Day's innovations. As Mott notes, "The fresh, even flippant, style of the *Sun's* news items, and its emphasis on local, human-interest, and often sensational events caught the town's fancy." The price, of course, was popular among readers of limited means. One of the features that won immediate popularity was its humorous treatment of police-court news. Copying methods used by the *London Morning Herald,* the *Sun* played up the tragicomic aspects of drunkenness, theft, assaults, and street walking observed in police courts.

Another device to increase circulation, original with the *Sun,* was to hire newsboys to hawk the paper on the streets. By 1836 the *Sun* claimed a circulation of thirty thousand, largest in the world at the time. Production of the paper was facilitated by using steam power to operate the printing press — its first trial in America.

After selling the *Sun* in 1838 for $40,000 (considerably below its true value), to his brother-in-law Moses Yale Beach, Day founded *Brother Jonathan,* a monthly magazine that reprinted English novels and later became the first American illustrated weekly, with Nathaniel P. Willis as an editor.

Day's son, Benjamin Day (1836–1916), a printer, invented the Ben Day process used in shading plates for printed color illustrations.

DOROTHY DAY
1897–1980

Dorothy Day, born in New York City, became a radical journalist and social activist. Her father was a sports journalist and editor. The family moved from New York to California and then to Chicago. From 1914 to 1916, Dorothy was a student at the University of Illinois, where she supplemented a scholarship by writing for a local newspaper. When her father became racing editor of the *Morning Telegraph,* the family moved to New York, where Day found a job as reporter and columnist with the socialist magazine *Call.* The following year she joined Max Eastman and others on the staff of the radical journal the *Masses,* which was suppressed after six months. Eastman began a new magazine, the *Liberator,* for which Day worked for a short time. She traveled in Europe for a year, then became a feature writer for the *New Orleans Item.*

After her conversion to the Catholic faith, Day began writing for the *Commonweal,* a weekly journal of opinion published by Catholic laymen. In 1933 she founded the *Catholic Worker,* concerned with race, labor, and other social problems. The paper was an immediate success, with circulation rising to one hundred thousand by 1934. In the beginning the *Catholic Worker* dealt mainly with current events, such as wage levels, strikes, evictions, and racial incidents. Soon it developed into the organ of an important social monument, advocating social change and a wide range of radical social activities. Day contributed regularly to the journal as a reporter and columnist. In addition, she wrote many articles for other magazines and a number of books.

FELIX GREGORY DE FONTAINE
1834–1896

Felix Gregory de Fontaine was born in Boston, the son of a French nobleman. His first journalistic assignment was in Washington, D.C., in 1859, to report on the notorious trial of a congressman for shooting a district attorney.

About 1860, de Fontaine founded in Columbia, South Carolina, the *Daily South Carolinian.* For reasons that are unclear, he became a violent partisan for all things Southern. In 1861, the *New York Herald* published his views on the antislavery agitation and the state of affairs in the South. The articles were completely Southern in viewpoint and opinions. Through his friendship with General Beauregard, de Fontaine was able to transmit to the *Herald* the first account to appear in the Northern press of the firing on Fort Sumter, the opening shots in the Civil War.

De Fontaine saw active service throughout the Civil War as a military correspondent covering most of the major campaigns for the *Herald, Charleston Courier,* and *Savannah Republican.* All his dispatches were written under the pseudonym "Personne," and were designed to praise the South and to downgrade the North. During General Sherman's march through the South as the war was ending, de Fontaine's press in Columbia was burned.

Soon after the war, de Fontaine moved to New York City to serve three years as editor of the *Telegram.* For the remainder of his active career he was the financial editor and later the dramatic and art critic of the *Herald.*

PAUL DEKRUIF
1890-1971

Paul DeKruif was born in Zeeland, Michigan, and became a bacteriologist who won fame as the author of such scientific works for laymen as *Microbe Hunters* (1926) and *Men Against Death* (1932). During World War I, DeKruif helped to develop a serum for gas gangrene. In 1925 he collaborated with Sinclair Lewis in providing the scientific background for *Arrowsmith.* After working for the Rockefeller Institute (1920–22), he became a full-time author.

JOSEPH DENNIE
1768-1812

Joseph Dennie, born in Boston, was called the "American Addison" by his contemporaries, because of his exceptional talents as an essayist. Like a number of journalists, he began practicing law and later changed his profession. Dennie started his newspaper career in 1792 by contributing short pieces to the *Morning Ray or Impartial Oracle,* in Windsor, Connecticut. Two years later, he joined another young lawyer, Royall Tyler, in writing satirical poetry and prose for the *Eagle: Or Dartmouth Centinel,* items widely reprinted. On a visit to Boston, arrangements were made for publication of a weekly newspaper, the *Tablet,* using the English *Spectator* and *Tatler* as models, and to carry Dennie's "Farrago" essays. The *Tablet* survived only thirteen weeks.

In 1795, Dennie moved to Walpole, New Hampshire, and began to contribute a series of essays entitled "Lay Preacher," to the *New Hampshire Journal; or the Farmer's Weekly Museum*. The popularity of these pieces established his literary reputation. In 1796, Dennie was appointed editor of the *Museum*. Recognition came in 1799, when the name of the paper was changed to the *Farmer's Museum, or Lay Preacher's Gazette.*

Dennie left Walpole in September 1799 to help edit John Fenno's *Gazette of the United States* in Philadelphia, and to serve as secretary to Timothy Pickering, secretary of state. After Pickering was dismissed by President Adams in 1800 and Fenno sold the *Gazette,* Dennie announced plans for "a new weekly paper." This turned out in 1801 to be the *Portfolio,* which became the most distinguished literary weekly of its time. The *Portfolio* published the works of the leading American essayists, storytellers, and poets, and reprinted the best-known English and French writers.

Dennie held extremist political views, reflected in his writings. He was fiercely antidemocratic, critical of the Declaration of Independence, and intensely disliked Thomas Jefferson.

JOHN DEVOY
1842–1928

John Devoy was born in Vill County Kildare, Ireland. After violent experiences as a Fenian leader with the Irish Republican Brotherhood, Devoy arrived in New York in 1871 and was received with honors by the Irish population there. He joined the staff of the *New York Herald,* first as a reporter, then as telegraph editor. He was later placed in charge of the foreign desk. After eight years, a disagreement with James Gordon Bennett caused his dismissal. Employment followed with the *Daily Telegraph* and *Morning Journal* of New York and the *Herald* and *Evening Post* of Chicago. In 1881 Devoy established a weekly newspaper, the *Irish Nation* in New York, to continue his agitation for Irish independence. The *Irish Nation* was forced to cease publication in 1885, but in 1903 Devoy founded the *Gaelic American* in New York and edited the paper until his death in 1928.

M. H. DEYOUNG, JR.
1849–1925

Michael Harry deYoung, Jr., was born in St. Louis but when he was still a child his family moved to San Francisco. He was in high school in 1865 when he and his nineteen-year-old brother Charles started the *San*

Francisco Chronicle. Over the next sixty years, until his death in 1925, deYoung built the *Chronicle* into one of California's major newspapers.

The *Chronicle,* produced by the two brothers in a job printing shop, began as a four-page tabloid called the *Dramatic Chronicle* and was intended as a program sheet for local theaters. It was distributed free.

The paper caught on quickly, and was soon circulating as many as two thousand copies, subsidized by theater owners. Two journalists living in San Francisco, Mark Twain and Bret Harte, were early contributors. Within two years, the *Chronicle* acquired its own equipment and its circulation increased to ten thousand. In September 1868 it became the *Daily Morning Chronicle.* Circulation was stimulated by crusades against various monopolies and sensational stories. Charles deYoung was killed in his office in 1880 in an election dispute. Thereafter, Michael deYoung took complete control of the paper.

Civic activities occupied much of deYoung's life in later years. He went to Paris in 1889 to represent the United States at the Paris Exposition, was a national commissioner to the World's Columbian Exposition in Chicago in 1893, and founded the Golden Gate Memorial Museum. DeYoung was among the last of the journalists who created and were always closely identified with their papers.

IRVING DILLIARD
1904-

Irving Dilliard was born in Collinsville, Illinois. For some forty years, he was associated with the *St. Louis Post-Dispatch.* He began as a correspondent in 1913 and progressed from there to editorial writer (1930–49, 1957–60). From 1949 to 1957, Dilliard edited the editorial page.

In addition to his newspaper career Dilliard was in demand as a lecturer at a number of colleges and universities in various parts of the country.

Dilliard was awarded a Bronze Star for his service in World War II and was cited by the British Empire and by France.

CHARLES PATTON DIMITRY
1837-1910

Charles Dimitry was born in Washington, D.C., and was a veteran of the Civil War on the Confederate side. At the conclusion of the war, he went to New York and held jobs at various times with the *World, Graphic,*

News, Star, and *Brooklyn Union.* Dimitry was a frequent contributor to a number of newspapers, including the *Alexandria Commercial Advertiser, New Orleans Bee,* and *Washington Daily Patriot.* His journalistic activities took him for short periods to Mobile, Richmond, and Baltimore. Late in his career he was on the editorial staff of the *New Orleans Picayune.* In addition, he wrote a series of articles on local history for various newspapers.

JACOB RICHARDS DODGE
1823-1902

Jacob Richards Dodge was born in New Boston, New Hampshire. He showed an early interest in journalism and was editor and publisher of the *Oasis* in Nashua, New Hampshire (1850-54), and of the *American Ruralist* in Springfield, Ohio (1857-61). Dodge's next move was to be Senate reporter for the *National Intelligencer* and the *National Republican* in Washington (1861-62).

When the U.S. Department of Agriculture was established in 1862, Dodge became its editor, responsible for editing the department's annual reports and the monthly reports of the Division of Statistics. In 1879, he was placed in charge of the agricultural statistics of the Tenth Census. Two years later the Department of Agriculture recalled him as its statistician.

SAMUEL ANDREW DONALDSON
1934-

In 1987, Sam Donaldson's fellow journalists voted him for the third consecutive time the best all-around television news correspondent in the nation's capital. This was ABC's aggressive and pugnacious reporter whom Jimmy Carter hoped would cause trouble for his successor, Ronald Reagan.

Before joining the White House press corps, Donaldson was a veteran journalist, with more than 30 years' experience in radio and television news. He was born March 11, 1934, and as a youth in his native Texas, had become fascinated with radio broadcasting. His first forays into that field were as a part-time disc jockey for a small station in El Paso, followed by a move to a larger local station to serve as news reader, occasional interviewer, and host of a one-hour program. After graduating from Texas Western College and completing a year of postgraduate study at UCLA, Donaldson went on active duty with the U.S. Army for a three-year tour (1956-59).

After his discharge from the Army, Donaldson found a job as a general announcer with a CBS affiliate in Houston. The next stop was New York City, where no opening could be had because of his lack of suitable experience. He was hired, however, by a CBS affiliate in Washington, WTOP-TV, as a temporary substitute. This position was soon changed to a permanent appointment.

As a general assignment reporter Donaldson covered a variety of stories for his stations. In time he was drawing such important assignments as the Cuban Missile Crisis, the civil rights movement, and Senator Barry Goldwater's 1964 presidential bid. A short time later, he left WTOP to join ABC News's Washington bureau. His expert reporting of the Democratic and Republican national conventions earned him a promotion to cover Capitol Hill. There was a three-month interlude while he served as a war correspondent in Vietnam. Another exciting story came out of the Senate Watergate hearings, where Donaldson acted as a member of the ABC news team.

From January 1977 to 1989 Donaldson was chief White House correspondent for ABC News. His irreverent, no-nonsense style is famous, a major irritant for some, approved by many. He anchors various ABC broadcasts and serves as a regular panelist the "This Week with David Brinkley," often anchoring in Brinkley's absence.

An autobiographical work, *Hold On, Mr. President* was published in 1987. It is an account of the leading events of some of the personalities he has met in a long and colorful career. Donaldson, with Diane Sawyer as co-anchor, began a different type of news program, "Prime Time Live," for ABC in 1989. During the two month Gulf War in 1991, he was the top reporter for ABC and was located in Riyadh, Saudi Arabia.

RHETA CHILDE DORR
1866–1948

Rheta Childe Dorr's entrance into journalistic activities did not start until after a somewhat stormy period during which she was trying to find a suitable outlet for her talents. She went to New York City in 1898, thirty-two years of age, determined to make a place for herself as a woman journalist. Three years later, she won a position on the women's page of the *New York Evening Post,* writing on women's club and charitable activities, fashions, and housekeeping. Her writing that attracted the most attention was a series of articles concerned with the condition of the working girls of New York's East Side.

Dorr left the *Evening Post* in 1906, convinced that a woman journalist had no future with the paper. The same year, she embarked on the first of nine trips to Europe. The *Post, Boston Transcript,* and *Harper's Weekly* had agreed to publish her account of the crowning of the king of Norway and of a trip to St. Petersburg, where she lived with revolutionary terrorists. Arriving home almost penniless, *Everybody's* magazine published a series of her articles entitled "The Woman's Invasion" about women in industry.

Dorr's next step was to join the staff of *Hampton's,* a reform magazine. In a series of articles for *Hampton's* she told of the women's club movement, the plight of the working girl, and the fight for women's suffrage. In 1916, she became the first editor of the *Suffragist,* the official organ of the Congressional Union for Woman Suffrage.

The coming of World War I changed the direction of Dorr's career. A second trip to Russia came in 1917, after which she denounced the Bolshevik Revolution. From 1917 to 1918 she returned to the *Evening Post* as a war correspondent. Her reports were syndicated in twenty or more newspapers.

A serious motorcycle accident in 1919 forced Dorr to withdraw as a journalist, from travel, and from practically all other activity except the authorship of several books.

FREDERICK DOUGLASS
1817–1895

Frederick Douglass, born at Tuckahoe, Maryland, was the son of an African American slave and a white man. He taught himself to read and write and escaped from slavery at age twenty-one, and spent the next fifty-seven years fighting the institution of slavery. At an antislavery convention in Nantucket in 1841, his brilliant speeches encouraged the Massachusetts Antislavery Society to appoint him as a lecturer in 1842. His eloquence as a speaker continued to be recognized and Douglass was invited to lecture to antislavery groups throughout the East for the next four years. His autobiography, published in 1845, *Narrative of the Life of Frederick Douglass, An American Slave,* became a best-seller.

To avoid being captured and returned to slavery, Douglass spent two years (1845–47) in England. During his absence, funds were raised to purchase his freedom. From 1847, after his return to the United States, until 1863, Douglass published his abolitionist newspaper, the *North Star,* in Rochester, New York. It was one of the most successful African American newspapers in the United States. Among his continued activities was leading a successful fight against segregated schools in Rochester, and he made his home a station on the underground railway to help runaway slaves reach freedom.

At the beginning of the War Between the States he helped to recruit African American boys and served as a consultant to President Abraham Lincoln. He used his lecture fees to aid fugitive slaves. He was active in many social reform movements including women's suffrage.

Douglass was a prolific writer and contributed not only to his own publications, but to the *Washington Evening Star, Journal of Social Science, North American Review, Harper's Weekly, Cosmopolitan, Our Day, Century Magazine, Woman's Journal, London Times,* and *Zion's Herald.*

From 1877–81 Douglass was U.S. Marshal for the District of Columbia, and was its recorder of deeds from 1881 to 1886.

Late in his career, Douglass served as American minister and consul general in Haiti (1887–91), and chargé d'affaires to Santo Domingo (1899–91). He remained in the limelight for nearly half a century until his death in 1895.

HUGH MALCOLM DOWNS
1922–

Hugh Downs was born in Akron, Ohio, and was a student at Wayne State University and Columbia. He began his journalistic career as a staff announcer on radio stations in Lima, Ohio, Detroit, and Chicago, from 1939 to 1954. Since 1954 he has been a freelance radio and television broadcaster. Downs is chairman of the U.S. Committee for UNICEF, and has had a long-time concern for refugee problems. He was coanchor with Barbara Walters on the popular television program, "20/20," aired by ABC.

THEODORE DREISER
1871–1945

Theodore Dreiser, born in Terre Haute, Indiana, was probably the greatest American writer of naturalistic fiction. He attended the University of Indiana for a short time in 1889–90. Although his first journalistic experiences were incidental for the next years, he did find a reporter's job with the *Chicago Globe,* when the Democratic national convention was meeting in that city. When the *Globe* had no permanent opening for him, Dreiser moved on to St. Louis to join the *Globe-Democrat.* Later he worked briefly for papers in Toledo and Pittsburgh. He began also to contribute to several magazines: *Munsey's, Ainslee's,* and *Cosmopolitan.* For a couple of years (1885–87), Dreiser edited *Every Month,* which printed miscellaneous material. He continued as a reporter until he became editor of a music magazine in New York City in 1895. He edited a magazine, *Smith's Magazine* in 1905 and the *Broadway Magazine* the following year.

After a period of depression over the lack of support for his first novel, *Sister Carrie* (1900), he became successful as an editor of Butterick's women's magazines, the most important one being *The Delineator.* He held this position until 1910.

In 1911, after the publication of *Jennie Gerhardt,* he devoted himself to writing novels, short stories, essays, plays, his autobiography, and later memoirs.

ELIZABETH DREW
1935–

Elizabeth Drew was born in Cincinnati, Ohio. She has been a writer for the *New Yorker* since 1973 and her "Letter from Washington," with her acute observations on the current political situation, appears regularly in that journal. She has also written for *Reporter, New Republic, Atlantic,* and *New York Times Magazine.* Early in her career she was an associate editor for the *Writer,* and then became senior editor with the *Congressional Quarterly.* Miss Drew served as Washington editor for *The Atlantic,* 1967–73.

Elizabeth Drew also won awards for her television broadcasts. Starting in 1971 she was host of "Thirty Minutes With," over WETA-TV in Washington. More than 150 PBS stations aired the program.

A daily record of the Watergate scandal, based on Elizabeth Drew's diary was published under the title of *Washington Journal: The Events of 1973–75.* It was followed up with *American Journal,* 1977, *Senator,* 1979, *Portrait of an Election,* 1981, *Politics and Money,* 1983, and *Campaign Money,* 1985.

ALLEN DRURY
1918–

Allen Drury was born in Houston, Texas. Before winning national repute as a leading American historian, Drury received the Delta Sigma Chi Editorial Award for 1941. He later reported national political developments for the *Washington Evening Star* and the *New York Times.* He won a Pulitzer Prize in 1960 for his novel about Washington politics, *Advise and Consent.* Other books on the same theme followed.

WILLIAM DUANE
1760-1835

William Duane was born near Lake Champlain, New York, and was taken by his mother to her native Ireland in 1774. He moved to India in 1787. Duane founded the *India World,* a liberal Calcutta journal, which brought him fame and fortune. It also brought him trouble. His criticism of the East India Company's practices and support of army officers' grievances led to Duane's arrest, deportation, and the confiscation of his property. Back in London, he served as parliamentary reporter for the *General Advertiser,* but was unable to obtain parliamentary approval for restoration of his property seized in India.

Unhappy with his situation in England, Duane went on to Philadelphia to join Benjamin Franklin Bache in editing the *Aurora.* When Bache died in 1798, Duane became editor and succeeded in making the *Aurora* both the most powerful organ of the Jeffersonians and Duane himself the most effective journalist of his time. Efforts by his enemies to silence him, including a murderous assault by armed men, failed.

The removal of the capital to Washington caused Duane's journal to lose influence, but he remained editor of the *Aurora* until 1822. It continued to be the leading national Republican paper throughout Jefferson's two terms.

In a letter to Duane, years after the violent controversies had died down, Jefferson wrote, "I have not forgotten the past, nor those who were fellow-laborers in the gloomy hours of federal ascendancy, when the spirit of republicanism was beaten down, its votaries arraigned as criminals, and such threats denounced as posterity will never believe."

Duane became adjutant general in the War of 1812. In the last years of his life, he traveled in South America and wrote extensively on military matters.

W. E. B. DU BOIS
1868-1963

In his *Negro Thought in America, 1880-1915,* August Meier concludes that of the great trio of Negro leaders, Frederick Douglass best expressed aspirations toward full citizenship and assimilation, Booker T. Washington interest in economic advancement, and W. E. B. Du Bois "most explicitly revealed the impact of oppression and of the American creed in creating ambivalent loyalties toward race and nation in the minds of American Negroes." Meier adds that of the three "Douglass was the orator, Du Bois the polished writer, and Washington the practical man of affairs."

A noted Negro poet and educator, James Weldon Johnson, expressed the view that W. E. B. Du Bois's *Souls of Black Folk* is "a work which, I think, has had a greater effect upon and within the Negro race in America than any other single book published in this country since *Uncle Tom's Cabin.*" The immense popularity of the book is demonstrated by the fact that since its publication in 1903, *Souls of Black Folk* has been issued in more than thirty English-language editions.

Du Bois was born in Great Barrington, Massachusetts, in 1868, the year that Ulysses S. Grant was elected president of the United States. The backgrounds of Booker T. Washington, born into slavery on a Virginia plantation, and the man destined to contest his leadership of the black race, W. E. B. Du Bois, could hardly have been more dissimilar. Du Bois conceived of himself as an aristocrat, and his personal history is atypical for an African American. In 1895 he became the first African American to receive a Ph.D. from Harvard University. He was a professor of economics and African American history at Atlanta University from 1896–1910, and head of its sociology department from 1932–44. Western Massachusetts had been a center of abolitionist sentiment. The twenty-five African American families in the valley from which Du Bois came, dated back to the War of 1812. As old residents, they mingled freely with farmers and townspeople, attended the same churches, went to town meetings, and otherwise participated fully in community affairs. On his mother's side, Du Bois was descended from Tom Burghardt, who was brought by Dutch slave traders to the Hudson Valley about 1740 and whose service in the Army during the Revolutionary War won freedom for himself and his family. On his father's side, Du Bois was a descendant of French Huguenots who migrated to America three centuries earlier.

As a journalist, Du Bois is best known as editor of a militant monthly periodical *The Crisis* (1910–34). The journal was an outgrowth of the National Association for the Advancement of Colored People started by Du Bois and a group of young African American intellectuals, an organization for which Du Bois became director for research. After World War II he was identified with the leftist peace movement. He was also editor of *The Encyclopedia of the Negro,* 1933–45. In 1960 Du Bois went to Ghana, and the next year he joined the Communist Party. His autobiography, *Dawn of Dusk,* was published in 1940.

For fifty years, Du Bois was a passionate fighter for full civil rights and equality of citizenship for the African American. By the time of his passing in 1963, his concept of the African American's proper status in America had gone far toward realization. His major writings are *The Philadelphia Negro: A Social Study,* 1899, and the *Black Reconstruction in America,* 1935.

MATTHEW DUNCAN
1785-1844

The first newspaper in Illinois, the *Illinois Herald,* was published by Matthew Duncan in 1814 at Kaskaskia. Duncan was a native of Virginia. He brought his press up from Kentucky. The paper was later moved to the new capital at Vandalia and in 1816 was renamed the *Western Intelligencer.* Like most pioneer papers, it had to depend on revenue from public printing.

JOHN DUNLAP
1747-1812

John Dunlap, a native-born Irishman, came to Philadelphia in 1757 as an apprentice to his uncle printer-bookseller, William Dunlap. Twelve years later, the uncle turned his printing house over to his nephew.

In 1771, John Dunlap began publishing a weekly, the *Pennsylvania Packet, or the General Advertiser.* The paper had serious financial problems, but survived by becoming loaded with advertisements. Competition was fierce during that period, for three other newspapers had recently started up in Philadelphia: Benjamin Towne's *Pennsylvania Evening Post,* James Humphrey, Jr.'s *Pennsylvania Ledger,* and the *Pennsylvania Mercury,* published by Enoch Story and Daniel Humphreys.

Through fortunate connections, Dunlap became official printer to the government in 1776. He was the first to print the Declaration of Independence. During the War of Independence and the British Army occupation of Philadelphia, Dunlap moved his printing plant temporarily to Lancaster in 1777. Within a few months, however, he found it safe to be back in Philadelphia.

Dunlap arranged for his associate, James Hayes, Jr., to ship printing materials to Virginia. Hayes began publishing the *Virginia Gazette, or the American Advertiser* in Richmond on December 22, 1781.

The *Packet* was published semiweekly in 1780 and triweekly in 1781.

A more revolutionary change occurred on September 21, 1784, when the *Packet* became a daily newspaper. Dunlap made journalistic history by being the first American to publish a successful daily newspaper, although an abortive attempt had been made in 1783 by Benjamin Towne's *Pennsylvania Evening Post.* The first printing of the new U.S. Constitution appeared in the *Packet* on September 19, 1787.

FINLEY PETER DUNNE
1867–1936

Finley Peter Dunne was the greatest American humorist of his time. His dialect essays for the *Chicago Evening Post* and the *Chicago Journal* featured the fictional Mr. Dooley, an opinionated Irish moralist, bartender, and crackerbarrel philosopher who commented on national and Chicago politics and on the Irish-American community. Writing for the *Chicago Tribune,* Dunne invented Martin P. Dooley, renowned as Mr. Dooley, whose wit, skepticism, and keen perceptions delighted a multitude of readers.

Dunne was born in Chicago, where he spent the first half of his life. The son of Irish immigrants, who were flooding into the United States by the thousands, Dunne was famous for his use of Irish-American dialect.

His newspaper apprenticeship was on three Chicago papers, as police and sports reporter and feature and editorial writer. He became city editor of the *Chicago Times* at age twenty-one. Later he was Sunday editor of the *Tribune,* editorial page editor of the *Evening Post,* and managing editor of the *Journal.* Using the Irish brogue as a vehicle for his ideas and observations, Dunne employed his humor and satire on such topics as Dooley's early life in Ireland, his career in Chicago as a barkeeper, and current affairs in general. He invented another character, Mr. Hennessy, to listen to his rambling comments.

In 1900 Dunne left Chicago and moved to New York. He became a regular contributor to *Collier's* magazine and for a short time edited the *New York Morning Telegraph,* a theatrical and sporting paper. In 1906 he joined Lincoln Steffens, Ida Tarbell, Ray Stannard Baker, and William Allen White as editors of the *American Magazine.* A series of articles was written in 1911 for *Metropolitan,* a moderate socialist magazine. Several collections of his essays were published in book form, the most popular of which was *Mr. Dooley in Peace and in War* (1898). A half-million dollar legacy from Payne Whitney in 1927 allowed Dunne to retire, ending his career as a journalist.

WALTER DURANTY
1884–1957

Walter Duranty was born in Liverpool, England, and graduated from Emmanuel College, Cambridge. For seven years he lived a Bohemian life in Paris and then was employed by the Paris bureau of the *New York Times*. At the outbreak of World War I he was attached to the French army and sent dispatches to the *Times*. Following the Versailles Peace Conference, Duranty reported on conditions in the Baltic states and Russia. He was unable to enter Russia, however, until 1922, when he was a member of Herbert Hoover's American Relief Association. The *Times* appointed him to be its Moscow correspondent. For the next nineteen years he wrote about every major event in the Soviet Union.

Among Duranty's top news stories from Russia were reports on two private interviews with Josef Stalin, the death of Lenin, the Soviet five-year plan, the Moscow purge trials, liquidation of the Kulaks, and famine in Eastern Europe. Duranty's opinion of communism was reflected in the statement "An ugly, harsh cruel creed this Stalinism." American diplomats and American reporters who came to Russia relied upon his advice.

Duranty's highly informed and detailed Russian dispatches helped to give the *Times* top rank for foreign coverage, but with the passage of time he became less effective and he left the *Times* in 1941. For a short time he reported for the North American Newspaper Alliance from Japan.

THEODORE DWIGHT
1764–1846

Theodore Dwight was born in Northampton, Massachusetts, a brother of Timothy Dwight, president of Yale and prominent clergyman. Dwight lived in New York City from 1817 to 1936, where he founded and edited the *New York Daily Advertiser*. He also wrote many articles and pamphlets for the Federalist party and served a term in the U.S. House of Representatives.

CHARLES GAMAGE EASTMAN
1816–1860

Charles Eastman was born in Fryeburg, Maine. While a student at the University of Vermont he wrote for the *Burlington Sentinel*. His first independent venture, the *Lamoille River Express* (1838), soon expired. In

1840 he started the *Spirit of the Age* at Woodstock (Vermont) to promote Jacksonian democracy. The paper sold out in 1845 and the following year Eastman became editor and part-owner of the Montpelier *Vermont Patriot,* a weekly that under his direction became the leading Democratic paper in the state. In 1851 he took over sole ownership of the *Patriot* and continued to edit it until his death in 1860.

Aside from his journalistic activities, Eastman achieved some reputation as a poet, served as a state senator and postmaster of Montpelier, and attended Democratic national conventions regularly.

MARY BAKER EDDY
1821–1910

The founder of the Christian Science movement, Mary Baker Eddy, was a controversial figure for a major portion of her nearly ninety years of life and remained so after her death. From infancy she was an odd child, given to "fits," temper tantrums, and hysteria. Because of delicate health, she remained out of school for long periods, and thus most of what she learned was absorbed from books at home. Her mind was filled with religion at an unusually early age, and she could hear voices calling her name. At the age of twenty-two, Eddy acquired the first of three husbands. None of the marriages was happy or successful, and her poor health continued. When her spells of depression were most profound, and morphine failed to relieve pain, the family called in a local mesmerist, "Boston John" Clark. Eddy, who was peculiarly suggestible, became fascinated with mesmerism — an omen of things to come — and developed a habit of falling into trances and began to receive messages from the dead.

Eddy was in her fiftieth year when the first draft was completed of the book that was to bring her fame and fortune. Three more years were spent in revisions before the volume appeared in print in 1875, a 456-page work. Quimby had called his method the "Science of Health"; Eddy entitled her book *Science and Health,* later adding a subtitle, *With Key to the Scriptures.* Two devoted students agreed to provide a subsidy of $1,500 demanded by the publisher.

The first edition of *Science and Health* consisted of one thousand copies, cheaply bound, crudely printed, and full of typographical errors. Today it is one of the rarest books in the world, for only a handful of copies survive; the remainder have been systematically destroyed.

One of Eddy's notable achievements was the founding in her eighty-seventh year of the *Christian Science Monitor,* which became a well-known international daily newspaper. She also established in 1883 a monthly magazine, the *Christian Science Journal.*

BENJAMIN EDES
1732–1803

Benjamin Edes, born in Charlestown, Massachusetts, was notably active and influential as a newspaper editor and political agitator during the Revolutionary period.

Edes, in partnership with John Gill, in 1755 founded the *Boston Gazette and Country Journal,* the third paper of that name in Boston. The *Gazette* became the organ of the Sons of Liberty opposing British acts considered oppressive by the colonists. It carried on a continuous battle against the Stamp Act, the Tea Tax, and the Boston Port Bill. Members of the Boston Tea Party assembled in Edes's home to don their Indian disguise. Edes published the *Gazette* with a skull and crossbones on the front page, in reaction to the Stamp Act.

British authorities responded to the criticisms. The arrest of Edes and Gill as instigators of sedition was proposed by the governor of the colony. During the siege of Boston, Edes secretly transferred his press to Watertown, a Boston suburb, and continued publication of the *Gazette.* The Boston Massacre in 1770 provided effective propaganda for the paper. A picture of four large coffins with the names of four men shot to death was printed.

Edes and Gill were the leading American printers in 1774 and 1775, especially of political pamphlets. The *Gazette's* circulation reached a record-breaking weekly total of two thousand. Governor Hutchinson commented, "The misfortune is that seven eights of the people read none but this infamous paper."

After this partnership with Gill was dissolved in 1775, Edes and his two sons continued the paper, but its influence waned because its patriotic mission was completed. Publication of the *Gazette* was discontinued on September 17, 1798, after a career of more than forty-three years.

GEORGE CARY EGGLESTON
1839–1911

George C. Eggleston was born in Vevay, Indiana. While still in his teens, he taught school, an experience that later inspired his classic work, *The Hoosier Schoolmaster.* He saw active service as a Confederate soldier during the Civil War. In 1870, he moved to New York and began a newspaper and editorial career that lasted for the next twenty years. His first job was as a reporter and later an editorial writer on the *Brooklyn Daily Union.* For a time, he was editor-in-chief of *Hearth and Home,* until the magazine was sold in 1874. While freelancing Eggleston wrote for the *Atlantic, Galaxy, Appleton's Journal,* and other periodicals.

In 1875 Eggleston became a member of the *New York Evening Post,* where William Cullen Bryant promoted him to the literary editorship. In the 1880s he was literary advisor to Harper & Brothers and literary editor (later editor-in-chief) of the *Commercial Advertiser.* Another change came in 1889. For eleven years Eggleston was on the editorial staff of Joseph Pulitzer's *New York World.*

WILLIAM ROBERT ESHELMAN
1921-

William Eshelman was born in Oklahoma City, Oklahoma, and holds degrees from the University of California at Los Angeles and Berkeley. After a business career (1941–48), he became a library assistant at Berkeley (1950–51), assistant periodicals librarian, Los Angeles State College (1951–52), serials librarian (1952–53), assistant librarian (1954–59), and librarian (1959–65). From 1965 to 1968 he served as librarian and professor of bibliography at Bucknell University. He was editor of the *Wilson Library Bulletin* (1968–78). He has served also as a consultant on library projects at Whittier College, the University of Nevada, and the University of West Florida, on accreditation teams for various colleges, and on numerous library association committees. He was president of the American Association of University Professors (1964–65), and editor of the *California Librarian* (1960–63). He was president of Scarecrow Press from 1979 to 1986. His specialities are planning academic library buildings, publishing for librarians, and academic library administration.

GEORGE HENRY EVANS
1805-1856

The *Journeyman Mechanics' Advocate,* published in Philadelphia for a short time in 1827, was the first labor paper, but the second, and most important, was the *Working Man's Advocate,* edited by George H. Evans, a famous leader in the early labor movement.

Evans was English-born and came to the United States in 1820. He was apprenticed to the printer of the *Ithaca Journal.* Evans had absorbed radical and free-thought ideas from reading Thomas Paine, Thomas Jefferson, and John Locke, and these were reflected in his writings and publications. Near the end of his apprenticeship, and having learned the printing trade, Evans joined another youth in 1824 in publishing a biweekly free-thought paper, *Museum and Independent Correction,* which continued until 1827. At that time, Evans went on to New York to aid in writing and printing the *Correspondent,* another free-thought periodical. Feeling the need for stronger support for labor, Evans brought out, on October 23, 1829, the first issue of the *Workingman's Advocate,* a four-page weekly. Later, Evans was one of the printers who produced the *New York Daily Sentinel,* the first daily devoted to the cause of labor. The *Sentinel* was taken over by Evans in 1832, but he discontinued it the following year because of "insufficient patronage."

Influenced by Benjamin Day's success in starting a penny paper, Evans decided in 1834 to publish his own "penny paper," the *Man,* which continued only until 1835. Later that year, he moved to Rahway, New Jersey, and published the *Advocate* there for several months.

Through the *Advocate,* a title later changed to *Young America,* Evans urged the formation of workingmen's political parties, fought such monopolies as the United States Bank, expounded his views as an atheist, and supported a number of humanitarian reforms. He is given chief credit for the passage of the Homestead Act, giving every man an inalienable grant of 160 acres—a plan advocated by Henry George a generation later. Evans's reforms helped to guide the labor movement for many years.

ROWLAND EVANS AND ROBERT NOVAK
1921–   1931–

Rowland Evans was born in White Marsh, Pennsylvania; Robert Novak does not reveal his origin in standard biographical sources. The two have been an inseparable team for a quarter of a century. Their twenty-fifth anniversary was celebrated in 1988.

The Evans–Novak column was born in 1963, after the *New York Herald Tribune* had gone on strike the previous year. The paper offered Evans a chance to write a column based on reporting to run six days a week. Evans felt the need for a partner and invited Novak, then with the *Wall Street Journal* to join him. Their column, starting in May 1963, appeared as a news story, not on the editorial pages.

Originally, the Evans–Novak column was considered leaning in a left-of-center position, but increasingly over the years it has moved right and is more generally viewed as conservative. How the team divides the labor of writing the column is a trade secret. It is generally believed, however, that Evans focuses major attention on foreign relations, while Novak's expertise is more in the area of economic and monetary policy and politics.

The exact number of newspapers that subscribe to the Evans–Novak column is uncertain. The authors themselves estimate that the total is between 110 and 150. The *Encyclopedia of American Journalism* notes that an Evans–Novak newsletter has about two thousand subscribers.

JOHN FENNO
1751–1798

Boston-born John Fenno, who failed in a business venture in Boston, took advantage of an opportunity when the federal government was operating in New York. He procured printing equipment and on April 11, 1789, launched the semiweekly *Gazette of the United States.* His only previous journalistic experience had been as an editorial assistant for Benjamin Russell, editor of the *Massachusetts Centinel.*

Fenno's *Gazette* was a kind of court paper, concerned mainly with government news. The paper was sponsored by U.S. Secretary of the Treasury Alexander Hamilton, who was also a frequent contributor. Other contributors included John Adams and Rufus King. The paper's first issue came out in time to announce preparations for George Washington's inauguration. Fenno was criticized from the first, as Mott states, by "his interest in ceremonies and titles, his sympathy with monarchism," and titles and toadying to the Federalist leaders. He was generally involved in acrimonious disputes with Republican journals, especially Philip Freneau's *National Gazette.* In Congress, Fenno was accused of inaccurate reporting.

When Congress moved to Philadelphia, Fenno did the same and from 1790 continued to publish the *Gazette* there. His financial situation was precarious, and publication was suspended for three months in 1793, partly for lack of funds and partly because of the yellow fever epidemic in Philadelphia. A loan from Hamilton enabled Fenno and the *Gazette* to survive. The paper became an evening daily in December 1793, with a slightly changed title: *Gazette of the United States and Evening Advertiser.*

Another disastrous yellow fever epidemic hit Philadelphia in 1798 and Fenno, who had refused to leave the city, was one of the victims. He died on September 14, 1798. His eldest son, John carried on the paper for two years, and it continued under various editors until 1818.

THOMAS GREEN FESSERDEN
1771-1837

Thomas Fesserden was born in Walpole, New Hampshire. While a student at Dartmouth, he contributed verse to the Dartmouth *Centinel* and the *Farmer's Weekly Museum* in Walpole. From 1806 to 1807, Fesserden edited the *Weekly Inspector,* a Federalist partisan magazine in New York. After retiring to Vermont, he edited the *Brattleboro Reporter* (1815-16), and the *Bellows Falls Advertiser* (1817-22). In 1822, Fesserden moved to Boston to establish the *New England Farmer,* which he edited until his death. At the same time, he managed three other periodicals devoted to agricultural matters.

Aside from his journalistic activities, Fesserden encouraged the introduction of silk culture in Massachusetts, patented inventions for heating devices, and served in the Massachusetts General Court as a Whig representative from Boston.

EUGENE FIELD
1850-1895

Eugene Field, known as the "poet of childhood" and "the first of the columnists," was born in St. Louis and grew up in Amherst, Massachusetts. While a student at the University of Missouri, he wrote humorous verse for the local newspaper, the beginning of his career in journalism.

Following a six-month tour of Europe, Field returned to St. Louis in 1873 to become a reporter on the *Evening Journal* from which he was later promoted to city editor. There were interim appointments as city editor of the *St. Joseph* (Missouri) *Gazette* (1875-76), editorial writer for the *St. Louis Times-Journal* (1876-80), managing editor, *Kansas City Times* (1880-81), managing editor, *Denver Tribune* (1881-83), and columnist, *Chicago Morning News* (1883-95).

Field's celebrated "Sharps and Flats" column was inaugurated in 1883 in the *Chicago Morning News.* Its combination of whimsical humor, satirical, farcical and pathetic stories, and verse became nationally famous. In the view of journalism historian, Frank Luther Mott, Field's work was "probably never excelled for its keen satire, its genuine wit, and the brightness of its literary torch." Field is particularly remembered for his poems of childhood. He was a prolific writer and his poems and other works were published in a twelve-volume edition in 1912. He was also an avid book collector, possessed a large library, and described his experiences as a collector in *Love Affairs of a Bibliomaniac* (1896), the final chapter of which was written the night before he died.

MARSHALL FIELD III
1893–1956

The Marshall Field family is best known as great American merchants and department store owners. During the 1930s, Marshall Field III developed an interest in political and social problems, supported the New Deal, and promoted U.S. intervention in World War II. In accord with these interests, he established a newspaper, the *Chicago Sun* (later the *Sun-Times*). Field also owned the New York daily newspaper *PM,* which accepted no advertising and ceased publication in 1948.

Marshall Field IV became president of Field Enterprises, publisher of the *Chicago Daily News,* and, after his father's death, the *Chicago Sun-Times.*

STEPHEN RYDER FISKE
1840–1916

Stephen Fiske was born in New Brunswick, New Jersey. He was a precocious youngster. Before age twelve he was being paid for his newspaper contributions. At fourteen he was editing a small paper. After leaving college he was employed by the *New York Herald* as editorial writer, special correspondent, and war correspondent during the Civil War. In 1862 and until 1866 he served as the *Herald's* drama critic.

In 1866, Fiske sailed for England on the *Henrietta* in the first Atlantic yacht race; was with Garibaldi in Rome during the revolution; and was active in the London theater world from 1873 until 1878.

Back in New York, Fiske founded the *New York Dramatic Mirror* in 1879 and during the last ten years of his life was associated with the *Spirit of the Times.* He was also a playwright of some distinction, writing a number of popular plays.

THOMAS FITZGERALD
1819–1891

Thomas Fitzgerald, New York-born, became interested in newspapers at an early age. As a teen-ager he went to work for the *Fredonian* of New

Brunswick, New Jersey, and then became a reporter with the *New York Commercial Advertiser.* At age twenty, Fitzgerald moved to Florida to accept an editorial job with the *Floridian,* in Tallahassee. Ever ambitious to own his own paper, in 1847 he and two associates founded a weekly *City Item* in Philadelphia, a paper that he continued until 1890. Fitzgerald eventually became the sole owner. The title was changed several times: to *Fitzgerald's City Item,* the *Evening City Item,* and the *Daily Item.* As a lively, crusading afternoon penny paper, it caught the public's fancy and attained the spectacular circulation of 182,000. The editor's interest in the theater, music, and fine arts insured full attention to those fields. Another interest, baseball, led the *Item* to be the first paper in Philadelphia to provide complete coverage of the sport. In 1890, Fitzgerald turned over operation of the newspaper to his three sons and retired.

DORIS FLEESON
1901–1970

Doris Fleeson was born in Sterling, Kansas. She was the first woman political columnist to be syndicated. Her first newspaper jobs were with the *Pittsburgh* (Kansas) *Star* and the society editor for the *Evanston* (Illinois) *News Index.* In 1926, she went on to Long Island, New York, to work for the *Great Neck News* and the following year she joined the *New York Daily News* staff, assigned to cover police courts and New York politics. Her political reporting began when she was sent to the Albany Bureau. In 1933 Fleeson moved to the Washington Bureau of the *News.* During the same year she helped to establish the American Newspaper Guild and served as a member of the guild's national executive committee. Franklin Roosevelt was the only president she deeply admired and she was the sole woman reporter permanently assigned to accompany Roosevelt on his campaign trips.

In 1943, Fleeson resigned from the *Daily News* and became a war correspondent for the *Woman's Home Companion.* In that capacity she covered battlefronts from Salerno to Omaha Beach.

When Fleeson came home after the war she began her outstanding career as a political columnist. The column was first carried in the *Washington Evening Star* and *Boston Globe,* but caught on quickly, and was distributed throughout the Bell Syndicate in 1945 and starting in 1954, by the United Features Syndicate, reaching about one hundred papers by the early 1960s.

Fleeson won many awards in recognition of her accomplishments as a professional journalist. The Johnson campaign of 1964 was the subject of her last column. She and her husband Dan Kimball, former secretary of the navy, died within a few hours of each other in 1970.

THOMAS FLEET
1685-1758

Thomas Fleet was born in Shropshire, England, and came to America to open a printing shop in Boston about 1712. He was the printer for the Massachusetts House of Representatives from 1729 to 1731. Thereafter, Fleet printed a news sheet, *Weekly Rehearsal* (1731–35). In 1735 he founded the *Boston Evening-Post,* which he published until his death in 1758.

Mott states that Fleet made the *Post* "the best and most popular paper in Boston, with carefully selected features and its news written with more wit and liveliness than most other colonial newspapers."

Fleet is credited with printing more than 350 other publications, among them numerous works by the Mathers.

CHARLES E. FLYNN
1912-

Charles Flynn was born in DuQuoin, Illinois, and holds degrees from the University of Illinois and the University of Missouri. He was a reporter and sports editor at the University of Missouri (1930–32). In the summer of 1933, he was a reporter for the *DuQuoin Evening Call.* From 1934 to 1937 he was managing editor of the *DuQuoin Daily News,* and special correspondent for the *St. Louis Globe-Democrat.*

From 1937 to 1944, Flynn was on the journalism faculty of the University of Illinois. During the period 1944–56, he was publicity director and supervisor of athletic publicity for the University of Illinois Athletic Association. In 1961 Flynn was named assistant to the president of the University of Illinois for institutional relations and development activities. From 1956, he had been director of public information.

In 1975 Flynn became editor-in-chief and general manager of the *Champaign-Urbana News Gazette,* a position from which he retired in 1984. He is the author of a syndicated newspaper column for chefs, "Mostly for Men."

PATRICK FORD
1835–1913

Patrick Ford was born in Galway, Ireland. As a child he was brought to America by friends who settled in Boston. While still a youngster, he worked in William Lloyd Garrison's newspaper office. His active career as a journalist began in 1855. In 1859–60 he was editor and publisher of the *Boston Sunday Times*. After the Civil War, Ford lived in Charleston, South Carolina, and edited the *Charleston Gazette*. He returned north to New York in 1870 to found a newspaper, the *Irish World*. The remainder of his career was devoted mainly to agitating the cause of Irish independence and to editing his paper. Gladstone once remarked, "But for the work the *Irish World* is doing and the money it is sending across the ocean, there would be no agitation in Ireland."

JOHN WIEN FORNEY
1817–1881

John Forney was born in Lancaster, Pennsylvania. At age seventeen he became an apprentice in the printing office of the *Lancaster Journal*. When he was twenty he took over the editorship and was part-owner of the *Lancaster Intelligencer,* a failing paper. Under Forney's direction, the paper became reasonably prosperous and united with the *Journal*. After campaigning for Buchanan, Forney sold the Lancaster paper to become editor and proprietor of the *Pennsylvanian* in Philadelphia. In 1852 he served as editorial writer for the *Washington Daily Union*. Forney was frustrated in his ambitions for political office and decided to return to Philadelphia to establish the *Press* in 1857. In 1861 he founded the *Sunday Morning Chronicle,* and the following year started a daily edition, the *Daily Morning Chronicle*. In 1878 Forney founded and edited, in Philadelphia, a weekly magazine called *Progress.*

Politically, Forney swung back and forth between the Democratic and Republican parties. The last ten years of his life were spent in journalism, travel, and lecturing.

T. THOMAS FORTUNE
1856–1928

One of the longest-lived and most important of newspapers founded by blacks in the United States was T. Thomas Fortune's *New York Age,* beginning in 1879. The original title was the *Globe,* changed to the *Freeman* in 1884, and the *Age* in 1887. Fortune, the editor until 1907, was a poet and essayist, born in Marianna, Florida, of slave parents. As a youth he learned printing, spending time in the shop of the *Jacksonville* (Florida) *Sentinel.* His printing apprenticeship continued with the *Jacksonville Daily Union,* where he became an expert typesetter. A move to Washington, D.C., followed. There he worked on a new black weekly, the *People's Advocate,* and met Frederick Douglass. After a short stay in Jacksonville as a printer on the *Daily Union,* Fortune took a job as a printer for the *Weekly Witness,* a religious newspaper in New York City.

Fortune's connection with the *Age* ceased in 1907. He then wrote for numerous black publications, some of them ephemeral, and returned to the *Age* from 1911 to 1914 as a salaried employee. From 1919 until his death in 1928 he wrote for the *Norfolk* (Virginia) *Journal and Guide,* and in 1923 he became editor of Marcus Garvey's *Negro World* in New York. He was always the black activist, unwilling to compromise with injustice and segregation, as was Booker T. Washington.

SAM WALTER FOSS
1858–1911

Sam Walter Foss was born in Candia, New Hampshire. As a student at Brown University, he contributed poems to the *Brunonian,* the college literary fortnightly, of which he became an editor. He and a friend, William E. Smythe, in 1883 bought the *Lynn* (Massachusetts) *Union,* changing its name to the *Saturday Union.* Humorous pieces written by Foss were picked up by *Puck, Judge,* the *Sun,* other New York publications, the *Christian Endeavor World* and *Youth's Companion.*

In 1887 Foss moved to Boston to become editor of the *Yankee Blade* and editorial writer for the *Boston Globe,* a joint appointment that he held for seven years. His last literary effort was writing the "Library Alcove" for the *Christian Science Monitor* (1909–11).

In 1898, Foss was appointed librarian of the Somerville (Massachusetts) Public Library and held that position during the rest of his life.

MAX FRANKEL
1930–

Max Frankel was born in Gera, Germany. The Frankel family was forced to leave Nazi Germany by way of the Soviet Union. The father was sent to Siberia by the Russians on suspicion of being a German spy. He was not reunited with his family until the end of World War II.

Mary Frankel and her son Max arrived in the United States in 1940, and Max became a naturalized citizen in 1948. He was editor-in-chief of the *Columbia Daily Spectator* and campus correspondent for the *New York Times* while a journalism student at Columbia University.

Frankel was hired as a full-time reporter for the *Times* in 1952. He served in the U.S. Army (1953–55), and then returned to the *Times* as a rewrite man and reporter. In 1956, Frankel was sent to Europe to cover the Hungarian and Polish rebellions. Following his return to the United States, he covered the United Nations and the Caribbean area, including Cuba. In 1961 he became diplomatic correspondent in the *Times's* Washington bureau. When invited by the *Herald-Tribune* Frankel was persuaded to stay with the *Times* by becoming chief correspondent. Another raise came in 1968 when he succeeded Tom Wicker as Washington bureau chief. In 1972, he accompanied President Nixon on his historic trip to China. One of the highlights among the news stories appearing in the *Times* under Frankel's direction was publication of the Pentagon papers, revealing the secret history of U.S. involvement in the Vietnam war.

Following a term as Sunday editor and editorial page editor of the *Times,* Frankel was named executive editor in 1986, succeeding Abe Rosenthal, who had held the position for seventeen years. The appointment met with full approval by the large *Times* staff.

BENJAMIN FRANKLIN
1706–1790

Benjamin Franklin is celebrated in American history as a printer, moralist, essayist, civic leader, scientist, inventor, statesman, diplomat, and philosopher. It has been noted that Franklin's name is the only one appearing on all four of the great documents connected with the founding of the United States: the Declaration of Independence, the Treaty of Alliance with France (bringing the French in on the American side in the Revolution), The Treaty of Paris that ended the war with England, and the Constitution. The present sketch will focus on one aspect of his varied career: printing and publishing.

At age twelve, Franklin was apprenticed to his older brother James in the printing business. James was a hard taskmaster. The brothers quarreled and Franklin ran away from home in 1723 to Philadelphia. He arrived penniless and unknown, but soon found employment with a printer named

Samuel Keimer. Philadelphia was to be Franklin's home for the rest of his life.

With the encouragement of Governor Sir William Keith, Franklin sailed for England in 1724, hoping to buy his own printing press. Lacking funds, which had been promised him by Keith, he went to work for Palmer's, a famous printing house, and later for Watt's Printing House. In 1726 he returned to Philadelphia, was again employed by Keimer, and two years later went into partnership in a printing business with Hugh Meredith. By 1730 Franklin was owner of the firm, including a newspaper, the *Pennsylvania Gazette.* The paper was his main source of livelihood for the next twenty years. Franklin's most successful printing venture was *Poor Richard's Almanack,* starting in 1734, which soon sold ten thousand copies annually. He also published numerous pamphlets on public issues, including a proposal for an academy that eventually became the University of Pennsylvania. He also founded a club, the Junto (later the American Philosophical Society), and the Library Company, a pioneer subscription library.

Franklin's first love was printing, and he always regarded himself first of all as a printer. He had established a press at Passy, and produced a number of imprints while living in France. Before he died, he directed that the following epitaph should be carved on his tombstone: "The body of Benjamin Franklin, Printer, (Like the Cover of an Old Book, its Contents Torn Out and Stript of Its Lettering and Gilding) Lies Here. Food for Worms, But the Work Shall Not be Lost. For It will (as he Believed) appear Once More In a New and More Elegant Edition Revised and Corrected By the Author."

JAMES FRANKLIN
1697–1735

James Franklin, another Bostonian like his younger brother Benjamin, was less distinguished than Benjamin, but he was noted for several achievements. His biographer Jeffrey A. Smith states that "James Franklin was American's first crusading editor and first major defender of press freedom."

Franklin learned the printing trade in England. He brought back with him a press, type, and other supplies. In 1719 he was employed by William Brooker to print the *Boston Gazette.* When the *Gazette* was sold and Franklin was not continued as printer, he started a rival paper of his own, the *New England Courant,* in 1721. Because of articles disrespectful of civil and ecclesiastical authorities, Franklin was sentenced to a month in jail.

During his absence the paper was carried on by Benjamin. Franklin was ordered to print nothing more without official approval. Unrepentant, he circumvented the order by contriving to publish the *Courant* under Benjamin's name.

Sometime in 1726, Franklin moved to the freer atmosphere of Rhode Island to establish the first press in that state, at Newport. In 1732 he started the *Rhode Island Gazette,* which was continued by his widow, daughters, and son after his death.

HAROLD FREDERIC
1856–1898

Harold Frederic was born in Utica, New York. At age fourteen he became an office boy on the *Utica Observer.* Later he joined the *Utica Morning Herald* as a proofreader. A term as proofreader on the *Observer* led to his promotion to reporter and editorial writer. In 1880, Frederic was elevated to managing editor of the *Observer.* About two years later, he accepted an offer to edit the *Albany Evening Journal.* That position was lost in 1884 when the *Journal* changed its political affiliation.

Frederic's important foreign career began in 1884 when he accepted a position as London correspondent for the *New York Times,* a post that he filled for the rest of his life. A major news story that broke just after his arrival abroad was a cholera epidemic in southern Europe, killing thousands. Displaying rare courage, Frederic plunged into the afflicted areas and sent back detailed stories — accounts that established his reputation as a correspondent. In 1891 he went to Russia to investigate the persecution of the Jews; his sweeping indictment of the Russian government closed the borders of that country to him forever after. Other notable dispatches led to Frederic becoming recognized as the leading foreign correspondent of his time.

In addition to his work as a journalist, Frederic was active as a novelist. During his ten years abroad, he composed ten volumes of fiction, works that caused him to be accepted in London literary circles.

DOUGLAS SOUTHALL FREEMAN
1886–1953

Douglas Freeman was born in Lynchburg, Virginia. After completing a doctoral degree at Johns Hopkins University in 1908, he turned to newspaper work. From 1915 to 1949, Freeman was editor of the *Richmond News-Leader* and was professor of journalism at Columbia University (1934–41).

After 1949, Freeman devoted himself primarily to writing historical biography. His life of Robert E. Lee won a Pulitzer Prize in 1934. Ambitious late works included *Lee's Lieutenants* (1942–44), and a seven-volume biography of George Washington (1948–54). Freeman showed a particular interest in and expert knowledge of military history.

LEGH RICHMOND FREEMAN
1843–1915

Legh Richmond Freeman, a native of Culpepper, Virginia, had a strange career in journalism. At the end of the Civil War, his regiment was in Kearney, Nebraska. Freeman acquired printing equipment though a novice as a printer, and established the *Kearney Herald* in 1865. Moving westward with his printing outfit, the next stop was to set up the *Ogden* (Utah) *Freeman,* which Freeman edited from 1875 to 1878, followed by the *Butte* (Montana) *Frontier Index* (1878–81); *Daily Inter-Mountains* and *Inter-Mountains Freeman,* renamed *Union-Freeman,* renamed *Butte City Union* (1881–84); and *Thompson Falls* (Montana) *Frontier Index* (1884). Freeman published newspapers under six different titles during his five years in Montana. Lee's *History of American Journalism* notes that the *Frontier Index* was published at all the temporary terminals of the Pacific railroad. Attracted by the Yakima Valley in Washington Territory, Freeman again picked up his printing equipment, moved to Yakima City, and began publication of the *Yakima Farmer,* renamed *Freeman's Farmer,* renamed *Washington Farmer,* published from 1884 to 1910. The *Washington Farmer* held by various owners over its span of twenty-six years was generally rated as a success among farmers and ranchers.

PHILIP FRENEAU
1752–1832

Philip Freneau, born in New York City and educated in the College of New Jersey (Princeton), one of the leading journalists of his day, was also celebrated as a poet, earning the title of "Poet of the Revolution."

Freneau was fascinated by the sea. In 1776–78 he spent two years in the Caribbean. In 1780 he was captured by the British, accused of being a privateer, and spent two years in prison. He spent the rest of the Revolutionary War period in Philadelphia, editing the *Freeman's Journal.* After peace came, Freneau went to sea as a captain of coastal vessels. For the next ten years much of his time was spent commanding a merchant ship, voyaging to the Canary Islands, and visiting various Caribbean ports.

During the war Freneau contributed to the short-lived *United States Magazine.* When Francis Bailey began a new paper, the *Freeman's Journal,* in Philadelphia, Freneau joined its staff as editor and contributor. He also began writing for the *Daily Advertiser* in New York City and accepted an editor's position with that paper in 1790. Freneau decided, however, that he would be happier editing his own paper. In October 1791, the first issues of the *National Gazette,* a semiweekly, appeared. The paper soon started to attack Hamilton and the Federalists. The question of monarchy was a hot issue and Freneau won George Washington's enmity by suggesting that he and some of his supporters, such as Hamilton, John Adams, and Fenno, were favorably inclined toward a monarchical form of government. Washington condemned him as "that rascal, Freneau," and urged Jefferson to fire him. Jefferson refused and in a famous letter to Washington stated: "No government ought to be without censors, and where the press is free none ever will."

Freneau edited the *Jersey Chronicle* in Monmouth County for a short time in 1795 and the *Time-Piece and Literary Companion* in 1797–98. His public career was over by 1800. During his editorship of the *National Gazette,* he produced the liveliest, most readable newspaper of his time.

FRED W. FRIENDLY

1915–

Fred Friendly was born in New York City. He adopted his mother's maiden name Friendly as his surname in preference to Wachenheimer, his father's surname.

Friendly began his long career as a radio-television announcer and newscaster with radio station WEAN in Providence, Rhode Island, in 1937, and remained in that position for four years. At the beginning of World War II, he enlisted in the U.S. Army and won medals for heroism in action.

In 1948, Friendly met and began an extended association with Edward R. Murrow. They collaborated in producing best-selling albums of the voices of notable personalities, entitled, "I Can Hear It Now." In 1951 the Murrow–Friendly team inaugurated a half-hour weekly news review on the CBS television network, "See It Now." The program had a seven-year run, dealt with many controversial subjects, and received numerous awards.

In 1964 Friendly was appointed president of CBS News, but he resigned two years later because of what he considered undue interference by upper-level CBS executives.

The day after resigning from CBS, Friendly accepted a position as advisor on communications to the Ford Foundation. Beginning in 1968 he served simultaneously as professor of journalism at Columbia University. In 1980 Friendly retired from his Ford Foundation position, although he continued as advisor and to work on seminars relating to the news media and public policy. The seminars brought together journalists and other representatives concerned with issues of social importance for dialogues discussing topics of mutual interest.

WILLIAM HENRY FRY
1815–1864

William Henry Fry was born in Philadelphia, son of the publisher of the *National Gazette*. He achieved some fame as a composer and music critic, but he never followed music as a profession. In 1829, he entered the field of journalism in his father's office and in 1844 he became editor of the *Philadelphia Public Ledger*.

From 1840 to 1852, Fry was in Europe as Paris and London correspondent of the *Public Ledger, New York Tribune,* and other newspapers. He returned to New York in 1852 as editorial writer and music editor of the *Tribune.* He continued to compose operas and concertos and is rated as the first successful American opera composer.

MARGARET FULLER
1810–1850

Margaret Fuller was born in Cambridgeport, Massachusetts. She was a friend of Ralph Waldo Emerson and through Emerson became involved in the Transcendental movement. From 1840 to 1842 she edited the transcendentalist periodical *Dial.* In 1844, Fuller joined the staff of Horace Greeley's *New York Tribune* as a book reviewer, and quickly established a reputation as one of the leading critics of her day.

In 1846, Margaret Fuller went to Europe as correspondent for the *Tribune.* While in Rome she met and married Giovanni Angelo, one of the revolutionists against the government of the Papal States. In 1850 she and her husband and son embarked for the United States. All three were drowned in a shipwreck off Fire Island, New York, on July 19, 1850.

EDWIN SAMUEL GAILLARD
1827–1885

Edwin Samuel Gaillard was born near Charleston, South Carolina, and studied medicine at the Medical College of South Carolina and in Europe. He served as a surgeon with the Confederate forces during the Civil War, losing his right arm in one of the battles. In 1865, Gaillard became a faculty member at the Medical College of Virginia at Richmond and there established the *Richmond Medical Journal.* Several years later he moved to Louisville, Kentucky, along with his publication, changing the title to the *Richmond and Louisville Medical Journal.* In 1874, Gaillard established the *American Medical Weekly,* continuing as its editor until 1883. After moving to New York City in 1879, he continued to publish the *American Medical Weekly* and added *Gaillard's Medical Journal.* Gaillard was a prolific writer and contributed numerous articles to his own and other medical papers.

THEODORE FREDERIC GAILLARDET
1808–1882

Theodore Gaillardet was born in France and came to New Orleans in 1837 with the intention of writing a book on the United States in the style established by de Tocqueville. The book was never written except in fragmentary fashion, but Gaillardet bought a nearly defunct French language paper *Courrier des États-Unis,* founded in New York in 1828. The new owner revived the paper and received a favorable response at once from French readers. Thus was created the oldest French newspaper in America, one that continued publication until 1937.

HUGH GAINE
1726–1807

When both the *Journal* and the *Evening Post* ceased publication, New York had only one newspaper, Parker's *Post-Boy* and *Evening Post.* A young Irishman, Hugh Gaine, recognized an opportunity and established the *New York Mercury* in 1768.

As a fourteen-year-old boy, Gaine had been apprenticed by his father to two Belfast printers, Samuel Wilson and James Magee. When the partners dissolved their partnership in 1744, young Gaine was free to sail for America. On his arrival in New York he was hired as a journeyman by James Parker for the next seven years, working on the publication of the *New York Evening Post.*

In the beginning, Gaine's *Mercury* (later renamed *Weekly Mercury*) was filled with news of fires, natural disasters, robberies, murders, and official proclamations. Then he branched out to carry essays on varied subjects. Many writings were political and Gaine was embroiled in political disputes most of his career. One of the controversies in which he was caught was between the Episcopalians and the Presbyterians over the control of King's College, later Columbia University.

Gaine's critics accused him of refusing to take firm stands on burning issues of the day. He took no position when the colonies were agitating for independence from Britain but when independence was declared he accepted it enthusiastically.

After New York had been abandoned by the Continental Army, two editions *(New York Gazette* and *Weekly Mercury)* were published for a short time, one in New York City favoring the Tory cause and the other in Newark, New Jersey, supporting the Whigs. The New York edition, however, was printed not by Gaine but by Ambrose Serle, a Royalist, using some of Gaine's equipment left in New York.

After the British evacuated New York, Gaine suspended publication of his newspaper on November 10, 1783. From that point he limited himself to printing and selling books. A variety of books were published by his firm, ranging from stories for children to political works. He also carried many imported books on his shelves.

According to Lee's *History,* Gaine was the first newspaper publisher to employ newsboys to deliver papers. This belief is based on an advertisement in the *Mercury* for September 14, 1761, offering employment to a "nice boy."

JOSEPH GALES
1786–1860

Joseph Gales was born in England and taken to America by his father in 1795. He attended the University of North Carolina and learned the printer's trade from his father, who also taught him shorthand.

In 1807 Gales went to Washington to report on congressional proceedings for S. Harrison Smith, editor of the triweekly *National Intelligencer.* From 1807 to 1820 he reported Senate proceedings. Gales took into partnership William W. Seaton, his brother-in-law. When the British captured the capitol in 1813, they destroyed Gales's library and equipment, but his building was spared.

Gales owned the *National Intelligencer* after 1810 and was responsible for most of the paper's editorials. He edited the *Annals of Congress,* covering the years 1798-1824, and the *Register of Debates in Congress* for 1825-37, important records of congressional debates.

GEORGE HORACE GALLUP
1901-

George Gallup, born in Jefferson, Iowa, turned his doctoral thesis at the University of Iowa into a career. His dissertation was entitled "A New Technique for Objective Methods for Measuring Reader Interest in Newspapers." From this study came the concept of polling public opinion. The Gallup methods were originally tested on newspapers in Des Moines, Cleveland, and St. Louis. For several years (1919-37) Gallup taught journalism at Drake, Northwestern, and Columbia. From 1932 to 1947 he directed research at Young and Rubicam Advertising Agency in New York, investigating the public's reaction to the firm's products.

In 1935 Gallup founded and became director of the American Institute of Public Opinion, organized to conduct public opinion polls. The institute has had uniform success in predicting the winners of presidential elections since 1936, except for 1948, when it predicted a landslide for Thomas E. Dewey.

Gallup also founded the Audience Research Institute in 1939, to measure the popularity of radio and television programs.

FRANK E. GANNETT
1876-1957

Frank Ernest Gannett was born in Bristol, New York. At nine years of age, he took a job delivering Rochester newspapers to subscribers in his hometown. Later he supplemented his income by selling newspapers. Before entering college, Gannett learned typing and shorthand, viewing them as assets for a future newspaperman. At Cornell University, he wrote for the college newspaper and became a paid correspondent for the *Ithaca Journal.* Throughout his time in college, Gannett wrote stories about Cornell for papers in Chicago, Boston, Philadelphia, and elsewhere.

In 1898 Gannett served as secretary of a commission appointed by

President McKinley to study the government of the Philippine Islands. On his return from Manila in 1900, Gannett was appointed city editor of the *Ithaca News,* a position in which he made the paper strong editorially and financially, earning him a promotion to managing editor and business manager.

Gannett worked briefly in New York as a subeditor for *Leslie's Weekly,* a pictorial magazine. He then took advantage of an opportunity in 1906 to buy a half-interest in the *Elmira* (New York) *Gazette.* This was the start of the growth of a newspaper empire. In 1907 Gannett and a young partner who owned the *Elmira Star* agreed to merge their papers, establishing the *Star-Gazette.* A competing paper, the *Elmira Herald,* was started. The rivalry lasted seven years, but eventually the *Herald* failed.

The next move to expand came in 1918 when two Rochester newspapers, the *Union and Advertiser* and the *Times* were bought and merged into the *Times-Union.* Gannett took over as business manager. In 1921, Utica was the next target; the *Democratic Observer* and the Republican *Herald-Dispatch* were bought and merged into the independent *Observer-Dispatch.* Gannett continued to increase his newspaper holdings. Between 1924 and 1929 he bought ten papers in New York cities and others in Plainfield, New Jersey, and Hartford, Connecticut. Between 1934 and 1937 Gannett added four more newspapers to his group. Altogether he built a network of twenty-one newspapers and seven radio and television stations.

Gannett was a staunch conservative, opposed to the New Deal and the Fair Deal; he favored states' rights, and was against dealings with the Soviet Union. He allowed his papers considerable leeway, however, in their political affiliations and policies.

WILLIAM LLOYD GARRISON
1805–1879

William Lloyd Garrison, born in Newburyport, Massachusetts, was given his first taste of journalism in 1818 at age thirteen, when he was apprenticed for seven years to the editor of the Newburyport *Herald.* In that office he developed into an expert compositor and when his apprenticeship was completed in 1826, Garrison became editor of the local *Free Press.* Two years later, when the *Free Press* failed, he joined Nathaniel H. White in Boston in editing the *National Philanthropist,* a temperance journal. While in Boston, Garrison met Benjamin Lundy, a Quaker, who converted him to the anti-slavery movement. Soon thereafter, Garrison went to Bennington, Vermont, to manage the *Journal of the Times,* an anti–Jackson organ.

Later in the same year, 1829, he was in Baltimore to join Lundy in editing the weekly *Genius of Universal Emancipation.*

Garrison's violent attacks on slavery led to his being sued for libel, and being imprisoned for seven weeks in a Baltimore jail. On January 1, 1831, Garrison established his famous periodical the *Liberator.* The paper was printed on a hand-press with borrowed type, a four-page folio scheduled to appear every Friday.

Garrison and his *Liberator* infuriated Southerners. The State of Georgia offered a reward of $5,000 for his arrest and conviction. On another occasion while giving an antislavery lecture in Boston, Garrison was attacked by a mob, dragged through the streets with a rope, and rescued with difficulty.

In 1833 Garrison presided over the meeting that organized the American Anti-Slavery Society and remained closely identified with the society as long as it existed. He is recognized, along with Wendell Phillips and John G. Whittier, as one of the great leaders in the war against slavery.

Garrison continued publication of the *Liberator* until the adoption of the Thirteenth Amendment ended slavery in 1865. The paper had been published continuously for thirty-five years. Thereafter Garrison devoted himself to other reform movements, notably women's suffrage, Prohibition, and advocating the rights of American Indians.

SYDNEY HOWARD GAY
1814–1888

Sydney Howard Gay was born in Hingham, Massachusetts. In Boston he joined the group of abolitionists led by Garrison and in 1843 went to New York to become editor of the *American Anti-Slavery Standard.* After fourteen years in that position, he joined the staff of the *New York Tribune* in 1857 and was appointed managing editor from 1862 to 1865, when ill health forced his retirement.

In 1867 Gay became managing editor of the *Chicago Tribune* and he remained in Chicago until the Great Fire of 1871. At that point, he returned to New York and from 1872 to 1874 was a member of the editorial staff of the *New York Evening Post* under William Cullen Bryant.

THEODOR SEUSS GEISEL
1904–

Theodor Geisel, who wrote under the pen name of "Dr. Seuss," was born in Springfield, Massachusetts, and became immensely popular as a writer of humorous verse for children. His own illustrations accompanied his delightful nonsense fantasies. Geisel also worked as a magazine illustrator and humorist. His *Cat in the Hat,* 1957, a book for young readers, is quite influential in encouraging them to learn to read. Perhaps his other best known work for children is *Horton Hears a Who!,* 1954, but the books most likely to become classics are *And to Think That I Saw It on Mulberry Street,* 1937, and *The Five Hundred Hats of Bartholomew Cubbins* (1938), a favorite with experienced storytellers.

HENRY GEORGE
1839–1897

Henry George's famous book, *Progress and Poverty,* was dedicated "to those who, seeing the vice and misery that spring from the unequal distribution of wealth and privilege, feel the possibility of a higher social state and would strive for its attainment." Here was the keynote of George's extraordinary career.

A native of Philadelphia, in his teens he went to sea. Soon after returning home, he settled on the Pacific Coast and there rotated among a variety of occupations: typesetter, tramp, peddler, printer, shop clerk, newspaper editor, weigher in a rice mill, ship steward, inspector of gas meters, gold-seeker, farm laborer. He married young, and family responsibilities together with the intermittent nature of his jobs caused him to lead a poverty-stricken existence, at times reducing him and his family to actual hunger. Thus George's knowledge of destitution and want was gained firsthand.

In his travels through Australia, India, England, Ireland, New York, San Francisco, and elsewhere, George was deeply disturbed by two paradoxical social phenomena: recurring depression and dire want in the midst of plenty. On one side, he observed a few people living in luxury, and, in contrast, the great masses barely subsisting. "This association of poverty with progress," he noted, "is the enigma of our times." On the West Coast he observed thousands of men mining, building railroads, and lumbering and the ownership of these natural and man-made resources eventually falling to a favored few. Those who held the land were rich, while those who worked it and made homes on it were poor.

Gradually, George became convinced that the concentration of land in the hands of the privileged rich was the bottom cause of depressions, the primary reason why poverty invariably accompanied a country's increasing wealth. Thus was born the theme of *Progress and Poverty.*

George began his book with a statement of the problem that long had "appalled and tormented" him: "where the conditions to which material progress everywhere tends are most fully realized—that is to say, where population is densest, wealth greatest, and the machinery of production and exchange most highly developed—we find the deepest poverty, the sharpest struggle for existence, and the most enforced idleness."

George's cure-all for this dilemma was to free the land, returning its ownership to the people as a whole. He argued that land is the physical foundation of the economic process and therefore its control is basic. To dominate land, he maintained, meant to dominate the entire economic structure. There was no more justification for private ownership and control of land than of air or sunshine. "The great cause of the inequality in the distribution of wealth is inequality in the ownership of land," George declared, for "the ownership of land is the great fundamental fact which ultimately determines the social, the political, and consequently the intellectual and moral conditions of a people."

George suggested that men should be allowed to use land in any amount they could reasonably manage, but never be permitted to hold it after their use of it had ceased. Rentals for use would be paid to the community for the expense of government. The anticipated yield would be fully adequate to make possible the abolition of all other forms of taxation—import duties, personal property taxes, inheritance taxes, and income taxes. Here would be the one and only tax—the Single Tax, a concept popularly associated with George's name. The fruits of the recommended reform were thus glowingly described by George:

> What I propose, therefore, is the simple yet sovereign remedy, which will raise wages, increase the earnings of capital, extirpate pauperism, abolish poverty, give remunerative employment to whoever wishes it, afford free scope to human powers, lessen crime, elevate morals, and taste, and intelligence, purify government and carry civilization to yet nobler heights is to appropriate rent by taxation.

George's experience as a journalist was limited. He worked as a typesetter in California for a brief time. Five years were spent as an editor for several newspapers, including the *San Francisco Chronicle.* In 1871 he and two partners started the *San Francisco Daily Evening Post,* but it was a financial failure and discontinued after four years.

The writing of *Progress and Poverty* was begun by George in 1877 during a serious national depression with widespread suffering and sporadic labor strikes. The manuscript was completed in eighteen months, but then had to be privately printed because no established publisher would accept it. A short while later D. Appleton agreed to take over publication. Through several favorable publicity breaks, the book quickly caught the public's fancy and it ultimately became one of the most widely distributed economic treatises of all time. How many copies have been sold in the intervening years is unknown. Estimates of worldwide circulation have varied from 2 to 5 million.

George's later years were spent in active promotion of his economic theories in England, Ireland, Australia, and the United States. He gained a tremendous following at home and abroad, and he narrowly missed election as mayor of New York City. George was largely responsible for the rise of socialism in England, a fact confirmed by George Bernard Shaw, who wrote that "five-sixths of those who were swept with me into the great socialist revival of 1882 had been converted by Henry George."

Borrowing a phrase from Theodore Roosevelt, Gerald W. Johnson in a recent series of biographic studies categorized Henry George as belonging to "the lunatic fringe." Despite this unflattering description, Johnson concluded that George was "in many respects remarkably right" and praised his reliance "on the eventual triumph of the good sense and innate decency of the masses of men." It is George's diagnosis of ills from which the modern economy suffers rather than his solution which remains of permanent interest and importance. His greatest accomplishment was to awaken in thinking people everywhere a hope for the abolition of poverty through public control of natural resources.

George returned to journalism in 1887 by beginning a weekly newspaper the *Standard*. It lasted until 1891.

GEORGIA ANNE GEYER
1935–

Georgia Anne Geyer was born in Chicago. She chose journalism as her profession early in life and graduated from Northwestern University's Medill School of Journalism. In her first overseas experience, she received a Fulbright Scholarship in history for a year's study at the University of Vienna. In 1958 she was a reporter on the *Southtown Economist* in Chicago, and then joined the staff of the *Chicago Daily News* as society desk reporter. While continuing to work for the *Daily News* she won a grant for six months in Latin America, starting in Peru and later including the Dominican Republic, Guatemala, Cuba, Chile, and Bolivia.

On the fiftieth anniversary of the Russian Revolution, the *Daily News* in 1967 sent Geyer to the Soviet Union, where she reported her observations on the country and its peoples. In 1969 she began her travels through the Middle East and was able to arrange interviews with leading personalities: Arafat, Quaddafi, Khomeini, Sadat, Peres, and others. In her opinion, the world leaders tend to be egomaniacs. Beginning in 1964 she spent nine months each year on foreign assignments to Latin America, the Soviet Union, the Middle East, the Far East, Vietnam, and Europe. In 1975 she became a columnist, based in Washington, for the Los Angeles Times Syndicate. In 1980 she moved again, to the Universal Press Syndicate and the *Washington Star.* Since then her columns on national and international affairs and various current issues have appeared three times a week in newspapers from coast to coast. One of her foreign excursions was in 1976 to Angola, where she was seized and imprisoned for a time by the Marxist government.

A knowledge of foreign languages has expedited Geyer's work abroad. She is proficient in German, Spanish, Portuguese, and Russian and has attempted to learn something about the language of each country she visits. She is a frequent guest on "Washington Week in Review."

FLOYD GIBBONS
1887–1939

Floyd Gibbons started in Washington, D.C. In Lucca, North Dakota, he was inspired to become a reporter by working for the editor of the local paper. While in Minneapolis in 1907 he was employed by the *Daily News* for a short time and then went on to be a police reporter for the *Milwaukee Free Press.* In 1910 Gibbons returned to Minneapolis to work for the *Tribune.* By 1912 he was ready to move on to Chicago, but the only job available was with the socialist paper *World.* A few months later he joined the *Tribune* as a reporter and began to demonstrate his unusual skill in gathering news.

In 1914 Gibbons began his colorful career as a roving correspondent. The *Tribune* sent him to report on Pancho Villa's raids along the Mexican border. He met and spent time with Villa and later accompanied the Pershing expedition. As a reward, the *Tribune* promoted him to its Washington bureau. Gibbons's next major assignment was as a war correspondent in Europe in 1917. The ship on which he was crossing, the *Laconia,* was sunk by a U-boat off the coast of Ireland and Gibbons wrote a dramatic account of the affair. While covering the Marine attack at Belleau Wood, he was badly wounded and lost his left eye. During his recovery he returned to the United States as a war lecturer.

Gibbons went back to Paris in 1919 to direct the *Tribune's* foreign news service for Europe, the Near East, and North Africa. In one news story he covered the Sinn Fein rebellion in Ireland. In 1920 he went to the front to report on the Polish-Russian war and the following year reported on the famine that was killing millions in Russia. At that time he gained an exclusive interview with Joseph Stalin.

Another spectacular Gibbons stunt, on assignment from the *Tribune,* was to lead a camel caravan across the Sahara Desert from Algeria to Timbuktu. After an around-the-world trip, Gibbons returned to Africa to report on the war against the Riff in Morocco. Back in Chicago, he made his first radio broadcast in 1925 over the *Tribune's* new station, WGN. During a roving assignment in Europe in 1926, he covered Marshall Pilsudski's coup d'état in Poland. Gibbons had a successful career as a radio commentator, but took time out to cover the Sino-Japanese War in 1931–32 for the International News Service. Reporting on events back on the home front continued until Gibbons died of a heart attack in 1939 as he was preparing to report on World War II.

JOHN GILL
1732–1785

John Gill was born in Charlestown, Massachusetts. Gill and Benjamin Edes were two young men who had set up a printing business in Boston and took over printing of the *Boston Gazette,* a weekly that had been established in 1719. The *Gazette* was the spokesman for radicals in the colony, and soon achieved a record-breaking circulation of two thousand. With such strong support, the *Gazette* became one of the most outspoken Patriot newspapers of the Revolution.

ELIZABETH MERIWETHER GILMER (DOROTHY DIX)
1861–1951

Elizabeth Meriwether Gilmer, better known as Dorothy Dix, was a precursor of Ann Landers and Dear Abby, pioneering the advice to the lovelorn column. She was born in Montgomery County, Tennessee, and had limited educational opportunities. Because of health problems, her father took her to Bay St. Louis near New Orleans. A next-door neighbor, Mrs. E. J. Nicholson, was the owner of the *New Orleans Picayune.* She encouraged Elizabeth to write and paid her for a short story. Elizabeth was given a minor job with the *Picayune* and started writing articles about domestic problems under the pseudonym "Dorothy Dix." Her columns and stories were noticed elsewhere and began to be reprinted in other papers.

An important break came in 1900 when Hearst's *New York Journal* asked permission to use some of her articles. The response from Hearst readers was so favorable that the *Journal* offered Dix a job. At first she declined but agreed to write a feature story about Carry Nation, the hatchet heroine. The next year, 1901, she joined Hearst's staff of writers and reporters. In that position she became a celebrated crime reporter, while continuing her five-times-weekly column. The *Journal* paid her an annual salary of $5,000, more than the salary of the governor of Louisiana. Later, as a syndicated writer, she earned more than $90,000 annually.

In addition to her newspaper pieces, Dix wrote regularly for Hearst's magazines, *Good Housekeeping* and *Cosmopolitan*. An immense correspondence was carried on with readers inspired by her column to write for advice.

At the end of 1917 Dix left the *Journal* and joined the nationwide Wheeler Newspaper Syndicate. She moved back to New Orleans, which remained her home for the rest of her life. The advice column was continued using the familiar question-and-answer format. After about 1910, she became an active suffragist. Time-out was taken for extended tours of Europe and the Orient.

In his *History of American Journalism,* James M. Lee quotes from a journalism lecture at New York University given by Dix: "Women spend the money of the world. Except for his vices and his outside clothes, the average man does not handle a penny of the money he earns. His wife spends it. She buys the groceries, the furniture, the piano, the jewelry — everything that is advertised in the newspapers. Therefore, surprising as it may seem to the uninitiated, it is the women readers and not the men who are considered first in the make-up of a paper."

MORRILL GODDARD
1865–1937

Morrill Goddard was born in Auburn, Maine. After graduating from Dartmouth in 1885 he went to New York, hoping to be hired by Joseph Pulitzer's *World*. Within a few weeks, several trial stories earned him a place on the staff. Placed in charge of the Sunday *World,* as city editor, Goddard hired artists and writers to expand the paper. One innovation was to use a new color press, bought to illustrate women's fashions, and to use for comics. Richard F. Outcault was hired to do the drawings, thus creating the first American newspaper color comic.

Goddard showed his imagination in other ways, such as originating the banner headline and using cutaway drawings to show interiors. These innovations caught the eye of William Randolph Hearst, who had just acquired the *Morning Journal*. Hearst hired away the entire *World* Sunday staff in order to persuade Goddard to shift his allegiance to the *Journal*. With the same sensational tactics that had proven so successful with the *World,* Goddard built up the Sunday *Journal's* circulation from less than 100,000 to 450,000 by 1896.

The *Journal* was renamed the *American* in 1901. The remainder of Goddard's life was occupied with the *American Magazine* (renamed *American Weekly* in 1916) issued as a supplement to the *Journal*. In 1911, Hearst decided to include the magazine with all of his Sunday newspapers. Eventually that resulted in a circulation of more than 5 million copies. The *Weekly* was reduced to tabloid size after 1937 and ceased publication in 1963, twelve years after Hearst's death. Mott's history called Goddard "the father of the American Sunday paper."

WILLIAM GODDARD
1740–1817

The Goddard family acted as a unit in printing and publishing. William Goddard's mother Sarah and his sister Mary Katherine were both expert printer-publishers and filled in for Goddard when he was otherwise engaged.

Goddard, at age fifteen, served as a printer's apprentice in the shop of James Parker, New Haven printer and publisher of the *Connecticut Gazette*. Parker also ran a printing shop in New York and published the *New York Weekly Post-Bay,* and Goddard was sent there to gain experience in printing almanacs and books. At the end of his period of apprenticeship, Goddard became a journeyman printer in New York for Samuel Farley, publisher of the *American Chronicle* newspaper. His next move was to Providence, Rhode Island, where in 1762, he established the state's third paper, the *Providence Gazette and Country Journal*. For financial reasons the paper suspended publication temporarily, and then resumed under the management of Sarah Goddard. In 1768, the *Providence Gazette* was taken over by John Carter, who had previously worked for Benjamin Franklin in Philadelphia.

The three Goddards proceeded to Philadelphia, where Goddard had begun the *Pennsylvania Chronicle and Universal Advertiser* in January 1767, as an organ of the Whig party. The *Chronicle* became one of the most successful colonial papers in terms of circulation, reaching a total of 2,500 by 1770. After several acrimonious disputes in Philadelphia, Goddard decided to move to Baltimore. There he established the *Maryland Journal and the Baltimore Advertiser* in 1773. Goddard engaged in and survived two major quarrels with the Whig Club, the local Patriot organization. The *Chronicle* continued under Mary Goddard's direction until 1774. At that time, Mary took over the *Maryland Journal* and made it one of the most influential voices of the American Revolution. She served as chief printer in Baltimore when the Continental Congress moved there and made a great coup in 1777 by printing the first official copy of the Declaration of Independence, with the names of the signers attached.

Goddard continued to publish the *Maryland Journal* until 1793, then sold out to his brother-in-law James Anzell and retired to Rhode Island.

LOUIS ANTOINE GODEY
1804-1878

Louis Godey was born in Philadelphia. In the 1820s he worked as a clerk and "scissors editor" of Charles Alexander's paper, the *Daily Chronicle.* In 1820 he and Alexander founded the *Lady's Book,* the first periodical for women in the United States. Alexander soon dropped out and Godey changed the title to *Godey's Lady's Book.* The magazine was largely devoted to women's interests, manners, morals, and fashions. Its most distinctive feature was its fashion plates, which for many years were hand-colored. These magazines have become collectors' items. They contain engravings of fashions of the times—great beruffled hoopskirts and Nankeen trousers with narrow waists. *Godey's* also contained stories and poems by such well-known American authors as Emerson, Longfellow, Poe, and Hawthorne. The circulation of the magazine reached 150,000 in the late 1850s.

From 1836 to 1877, Godey's coeditor was Sara Josepha Hale, author of "Mary Had a Little Lamb," a rhyme that first appeared in the *Juvenile Miscellany* in September 1830. Hale had been editor of the *Ladies' Magazine* in 1829. That was merged with *Godey's* in 1837. *Godey's Lady's Book* continued publication until 1898.

EDWIN LAWRENCE GODKIN
1831-1902

Edwin Lawrence Godkin was born in Ireland. His first journalistic experience was to serve as special correspondent for the *London Daily News* in the Crimean War and editor on the *Belfast Northern Whig.* He came to

New York in 1856, continued as correspondent for the London paper, and wrote editorials for the *New York Times.*

Godkin was offered a partnership in the *New York Times* by Henry Raymond, but elected instead to establish a weekly, the *Nation,* a liberal journal that he edited until 1899. The *Nation* was soon recognized as the country's foremost review. In 1881, the *Nation* was sold to Henry Willard, owner of the *New York Evening Post,* and became the weekly edition of the *Post.* Godkin was named associate editor. From 1883 to 1899, Godkin served as editor-in-chief of the *Post.*

Godkin retired from his editorial duties in 1899 and died in England in 1902.

HARVEY L. GOODALL
1836–1900

Harvey L. Goodall was born in Lunenberg, Vermont. Early in his career he did newspaper work in Harrisburg, Lancaster, Philadelphia, and New York. After the Civil War, in which he served, he returned to journalism by publishing the *Cairo* (Illinois) *Times* until 1868. In 1869 Goodall moved to Chicago to establish the weekly *Sun,* along with a job printing office.

Goodall's most important contribution as a journalist was to publish a livestock market paper, the *Drover's Journal,* starting in 1873, the first paper ever published in its field. It soon won an important place for itself in the livestock industry. A daily edition was started in 1877, and a semiweekly edition was also published. Until the end of his life, Goodall continued to publish the Chicago editions of the *Drover's Journal* and the *Sun,* which had become a daily.

HENRY WOODFIN GRADY
1850–1889

Henry W. Grady had a short but brilliant career as a journalist. A native of Athens, Georgia, a graduate of the University of Georgia, and a law student at the University of Virginia, Grady soon turned toward journalism. After leaving Charlottesville he went to Rome, Georgia, to edit the *Courier.* A disagreement with his employer over exposing local political corruption led to his resignation. He then bought two other papers and combined them under the title, the *Daily Commercial.* After that paper failed financially, Grady and two associates went to Atlanta to found the *Atlanta Herald* — another financial failure. For a time he wrote for the *Constitution* and the *Atlanta Chronicle* and also was a special reporter for the *New York Herald* (1876–77).

Grady's future was determined in 1879 when Cyrus W. Field lent him $20,000 to buy a fourth interest in the *Atlanta Constitution*. He became the paper's managing editor and was responsible for much of its news and editorial content. The format was changed and the number of pages increased. Grady's editorials were liberal and forward-looking, advocating social, economic, and political reforms in the South.

During the 1880s, Grady continued his efforts to make the *Constitution* one of the nation's best newspapers. His ability as an organizer and an effective executive was an important asset in this undertaking.

In addition to being a great journalist, Grady was a famous orator. He made a number of celebrated speeches, one of the most publicized on "The New South" to the New England Club of New York in December 1886. The speech helped to eliminate the North–South animosities of the post–Civil War period, and established Grady nationally as a spokesman for the South. Grady died of pneumonia at age thirty-nine after a trip to Boston to speak on the race problem.

FRED PATTERSON GRAHAM
1931–

Fred Patterson Graham was born in Little Rock, Arkansas. He entered journalism as the Supreme Court correspondent for the *New York Times* and remained in that position until he joined CBS in 1972. His voice became familiar to the large audience he reached on the CBS News from Washington. He has received an Emmy and other awards for his television broadcasts. He is presently anchor and senior editor of station WKRN-TV in Nashville, Tennessee.

KATHARINE MEYER GRAHAM
1917–

Katharine Graham was born in New York City. During her college years at Vassar and the University of Chicago she worked briefly as a newspaper reporter. Her father Eugene Meyer acquired the *Washington Post* at auction in 1933. It passed to Katharine's husband in 1948, and she gained control of the paper after her husband Philip Graham's suicide in 1963. Previously she had been a reporter on the *San Francisco News,* a Scripps–Howard paper, assigned to cover the waterfront, and then was called back to Washington by her father to join the editorial staff of the *Post* and to work in the circulation and editorial departments of the Sunday edition.

Graham has been called one of the most powerful women in America because of her ownership of the *Washington Post* and *Newsweek.* As president of the Washington Post Company, she has directed the newspaper, magazine, and radio-television enterprises since 1963.

In 1954, the company acquired a competing morning paper, the *Washington Times-Herald,* from Robert R. McCormick. *Newsweek* was purchased in 1961. In cooperation with Otis Chandler of the *Los Angeles Times* an international news service was established to provide information on world news to over three hundred U.S. and foreign newspapers.

The *Washington Post* with Graham as publisher has become the capital's most influential paper and consequently one of the most powerful in the United States. In some ways, it is a competitor of the *New York Times,* but their situation and audience, in Graham's view, are different.

SHEILAH GRAHAM
1904–1989

Along with Hedda Hopper and Louella Parsons, Sheilah Graham was one of Hollywood's most feared and powerful gossip columnists. She was born in London and came to the United States in 1933. She was an intimate friend of F. Scott Fitzgerald. Her Hollywood writings, widely syndicated, continued until the early 1970s.

HARRY J. GRANT
1881–1963

Harry J. Grant was born in Chillicothe, Missouri, and was introduced to publishing as an advertising salesman for student publications. He also worked for N. W. Ayers, publisher of business directories. In 1913 he joined an advertising firm handling newspaper placement. In that position, he became acquainted with the *Milwaukee Journal,* of which he was made business manager in 1916. Three years later Grant became vice president and treasurer of the Journal Company and then one of the company's three directors and publishers.

Under Grant's direction, the *Journal* provided thorough local, national, and international coverage. Correspondents were maintained in New York and Washington. Comics, pictures, features, columns, and puzzles were added. The broadcasting field was entered with radio and television stations.

Grant gave up control of the *Journal's* regular operations in 1937, although he remained chairman of the board. During his tenure he had made the *Milwaukee Journal* one of the leading American twentieth-century newspapers.

CHARLES H. GRASTY
1863–1924

Charles Henry Grasty was born in Fincastle, Virginia. The family moved to Missouri when he was a small child. His journalistic career started with a summer reporting job on the *Mexico* (Missouri) *Intelligencer* in 1880. A job offer from William Rockhill Nelson to join the *Kansas City Star* was accepted in 1882. Within eighteen months Grasty had been promoted to managing editor. He remained with the *Star* until 1889, at which time he became general manager of the *Manufacturers' Record,* a weekly business journal in Baltimore. He was eager to return to daily journalism, however, and in 1891 he bought the *Baltimore Evening News.* The paper soon became actively involved in Maryland state politics. A crisis faced Grasty when the great Baltimore fire of 1904 destroyed a large part of the city, including the *News* plant. With equipment borrowed from the *Philadelphia Times,* the *News* lost little time getting back into circulation.

In 1908 Grasty sold the *News* to Frank Munsey and bought the *St. Paul* (Minnesota) *Pioneer Press.* Shortly, he sold that paper also and seizing an opportunity to return to Baltimore, raised funds for the purchase of the *Baltimore Sun.* Both morning and evening circulation were dominated by adding the *Baltimore World* in 1910. H. L. Mencken was the *Evening Sun's* associate editor for four years.

In 1914, Grasty resigned as director of the Sunpaper Corporation. When World War I began, he went to Europe as a war correspondent for the *Kansas City Star* and the Associated Press, of which he had been a director from 1900 to 1910. Later, Grasty was in Europe as a special editorial correspondent for the *New York Times.* Many of his dispatches were printed in the *Sun* and other newspapers. The rest of his life was spent in that job. He returned to the United States for only a few weeks each year.

JOHN TEMPLE GRAVES
1856–1925

John Temple Graves was born in South Carolina, the son of a Confederate Army general. About 1882 he went to Jacksonville, Florida, first as editor of the *Daily Florida Union* and later of the *Florida Herald*. He served for a year as editor of the *Atlanta Journal* (1887), and then transferred to Rome, Georgia, to edit the *Tribune of Rome*. Several years were taken out for political activity. Newspaper work was continued with editorship of the *Atlanta News* (1902-6), and the *Atlanta Georgian* (1907). From 1907 to 1915 Graves was editor of the *New York American*. Thereafter he wrote special articles for the Hearst papers and for short periods edited the *Palm Beach Post* and the *Hendersonville* (North Carolina) *Times*.

JOSEPH W. GRAY
1813–1862

Joseph Gray was born in Bridgeport, Vermont. He became associated with Cleveland, Ohio, as a public school teacher in 1836. He and his brother purchased the *Cleveland Advertiser,* a Democratic evening daily, and changed its name to the *Plain Dealer,* a journal that has continued to flourish to the present day. The paper recruited a distinguished staff, and Gray took full advantage of the latest technological changes, such as steam presses, railroads, and telegraph. He was also a pioneer in illustrated journalism, especially in the use of cartoons. The *Plain Dealer's* circulation grew to forty thousand by 1860.

Gray served as postmaster of Cleveland from 1857 to 1858, on appointment by President Pierce.

HORACE GREELEY
1811–1872

Horace Greeley, journalist, author, lecturer, and political leader, has been characterized as America's greatest editor, perhaps its greatest popular educator, and certainly one of its greatest moral leaders.

There was little auspicious about Greeley's start in life. He was a native of Amherst, New Hampshire, the son of a poor farmer and day laborer, and one of seven children. His limited education in New Hampshire,

Vermont, and Pennsylvania country schools ended at age fourteen, as his family moved from place to place.

Greeley's first glimpse of his future came with his apprenticeship to the editor of the *Northern Spectator* in East Poultney, Vermont. Subsequently, he found employment as a printer at Jamestown and Lodi, New York, and Erie, Pennsylvania. Too ambitious to remain in jobs with poor prospects, Greeley proceeded on to New York City in 1831. After several weeks of searching, he accepted work setting up a New Testament in minute type. Over the next several years, there was other employment as a printer.

Greeley was always more fascinated, however, with writing than with the printing trade. He began early to contribute short paragraphs to newspapers and journals. In 1834, in partnership with James Winchester, he founded a weekly literary and news magazine called the *New Yorker.* Most of the material included was derived from other sources, including foreign and domestic newspapers and selected stories, reviews, and music, but original contributions were also made by Greeley and his associates. The enterprise attracted many readers, although it was a financial failure. To supplement his income, Greeley wrote constantly for the *Daily Whig* and other newspapers, and edited a campaign weekly, the *Jeffersonian.*

Another publishing venture began in 1840 with establishment of the *Log Cabin,* which was continued after the election as a general political weekly. It later was merged with the *New Yorker* and finally with the *New York Tribune.*

Greeley's greatest achievement in the journalistic field was the founding in 1841 of a new daily newspaper, the *Tribune,* to compete with twelve other dailies in the city. It was a period of great political excitement, and the *Tribune* soon appealed to a nationwide audience, with circulation rising at one time to a quarter of a million. The paper set a new standard in American journalism, with sound taste, high moral principles, and intellectual appeal. The indefatigable Greeley wrote as many as three columns for each issue. From the beginning the *Tribune* was stamped with his individual views, often regarded by contemporaries as radical. He was an egalitarian, believing that all Americans should be free politically and economically. He supported the Utopian socialistic ideas of Charles Fourier, a high tariff to protect American industry and labor, better working conditions for wage earners, free land for homesteaders, international copyright, and independence for Ireland. He vigorously condemned slavery and its expansion to new territory, and the Mexican War. Moral causes included opposition to capital punishment, a strong belief in the sanctity of marriage and against easy divorce, and support for the temperance movement. Greeley opposed women's suffrage on the ground that the majority of women did not want it, but he aided practical efforts to broaden the sphere of women's employment.

A distinguished group was gathered to write for the *Tribune:* Margaret Fuller, Charles Dana, Carl Schurz, Arthur Brisbane, Henry James, Whitelaw Reid, and others. After the *Tribune* became successful, Greeley's income was high. Nevertheless, his personal finances were in constant trouble, due to gullibility, overgenerosity, and generally poor judgment. He bought undeveloped lands, took stock in mining companies, dessicated egg companies, patent looms, and photolithographic companies, and was a ready prey for all new inventions. In addition he gave away money promiscuously to both deserving and undeserving causes and individuals.

In politics, Greeley began as a Whig, but then became one of the founders of the Republican party. His active support for Abraham Lincoln's nomination and election to the presidency was a key factor in the 1860 election. At the same time, he upheld the right of a state to secede from the Union if a majority of the people desired it. He held, however, that Southerners as a whole did not choose secession, and he vigorously supported the Northern cause.

The Reconstruction era following the Civil War involved Greeley in several controversies. His support for general amnesty and voting privileges for defeated Southerners was an unpopular stand; he also advocated suffrage for the freed blacks, and he was bitterly criticized for signing Jefferson Davis's bail bond.

Greeley made several ill-advised attempts to gain public office. He opposed Grant's campaign for a second term, convinced that the Grant administration was demoralized, corrupt, averse to civil service reform, and too illiberal toward the South. As a result, Greeley became the new Liberal Republican party's candidate for president. It was a disastrous experience for him. He spoke and wrote tirelessly in an exceptionally bitter campaign. His foes attacked him for his high tariff views, and he was called a traitor, a fool, an ignoramus, and a crank. Cartoonists, such as Thomas Nast, caricatured and ridiculed him. The abusive criticisms, added to a highly organized Republican campaign, distrust by financial interest, and popular doubts of Greeley's judgment resulted in a smashing defeat for him in the 1872 election.

It was a tragic end to Greeley's often brilliant career. The exhausting campaign had wrecked his health. He suffered a mental breakdown, and his wife died after a long illness. Greeley died on November 29, a few weeks after the election.

More tributes were paid to him in death than in life. His funeral was attended by the president and vice president of the United States, the chief justice of the Supreme Court, and numerous other eminent public figures. Despite his foibles, he was generally held in high esteem as a leader of opinion and a faithful public servant. Greeley is perhaps best remembered today for his slogan, "Go West, Young Man, Go West," which caught the public fancy and was thereafter associated with his name.

BARTHOLOMEW GREEN
1666-1732

Bartholomew Green was introduced to printing through assisting his brother in managing Sewall's press in Boston in 1682. He took charge of the press after his brother's death in 1690. For nearly forty years he was New England's leading printer. Green printed the *Boston News-Letter* from its start in 1704 until 1723, except for the period from 1707 until 1711, when John Campbell was publisher. The *Boston News-Letter* was passed on to his son-in-law John Draper when Green died in 1732.

DUFF GREEN
1791-1875

Duff Green, born in Kentucky, saw service in the War of 1812 under General William H. Harrison. His journalistic career, which lasted nearly fifty years, began in 1823, when he purchased the *St. Louis Enquirer,* previously owned by Thomas Hart Benton, one of Missouri's first U.S. senators. Green announced his support for Jackson in the 1824 presidential election.

The *Enquirer* was sold in 1825. Green moved to Washington, and bought the *United States Telegraph.* One of the paper's prime targets was John Quincy Adams, who was denounced on various economic and political issues. After Jackson was elected, Green became a member of his "kitchen cabinet," Jackson's inner circle of advisors and confidants. Green was rewarded with patronage contracts for government printing, earning $50,000 a year. His inflammatory editorials involved Green in several duels, on one occasion causing him severe injuries.

In 1830, Green broke with Jackson, supporting Vice President Calhoun. The Jackson administration retaliated by replacing the *Telegraph* with Francis P. Blair's *Globe* as the party organ and taking away Green's government printing patronage. Green gave up editorship of the *Telegraph* in 1836, although he remained as publisher until the paper ceased publication the following year. For a short time he founded and published the *Washington Reformer,* a state-rights journal, and started the *Pilot* in Baltimore in 1840 to support Harrison. After a mission to England and

France, Green established in 1844 the *Republic,* a radical free-trade, civil-service, and postal-reform journal. In 1857, Green undertook another publishing venture, the short-lived *American Statesman* in Washington.

THOMAS GREENLEAF
1755–1798

Thomas Greenleaf was born in Abington, Massachusetts. In 1773 his father established a printery in Boston and placed him in charge. Greenleaf had been taught the printing art in Isaiah Thomas's Boston shop. One of the Greenleaf printing house publications was the *Royal American Magazine, or Universal Repository of Instruction and Amusement,* which Greenleaf himself had begun. The title was later changed to *New York Journal and Weekly Register,* and issued daily starting in 1787, with another title change *(New York Journal and Daily Patriotic Register).*

On May 11, 1795, Greenleaf established the *Argus & Greenleaf's New Daily Advertiser,* which continued until 1800, two years after Greenleaf's death. The *New York Journal* was sold to David Dennison.

GILBERT HOVEY GROSVENOR
1875–1966

Gilbert Grosvenor was born in Constantinople (now Istanbul) Turkey, the son of an American professor. Alexander Graham Bell, president of the National Geographic Society from 1898 to 1903, appointed Grosvenor editor of the *National Geographic Magazine* in 1900, a position that he held for more than fifty years and used to create popular interest in geography and exploration. Under his direction as president the membership of the National Geographic Society grew from less than one thousand to over two million. Grosvenor married Bell's daughter in 1900.

During Grosvenor's administration the society sent out numerous expeditions to the North and South poles, into the stratosphere, to the ocean depths, and sponsored and financed many other investigations. Grosvenor was a leader in the conservation of natural resources and protection of wildlife.

Grosvenor retired as president of the National Geographic Society in 1954 and then became chairman of its board of directors.

WILLIAM MASON GROSVENOR
1835-1900

William Grosvenor was born in Ashfield, Massachusetts. He was a student at Yale for three years and a veteran of the Civil War. From 1859 to 1861 he was editor of the *New Haven Palladium*. He returned to New Haven for two years to edit the *Journal-Courier* (1864-66).

In 1866, Grosvenor became editor of the *St. Louis Democrat,* a position that he held almost continuously until 1875. While in St. Louis he was actively involved in local, state, and national politics. From 1875 to 1880 Grosvenor was economic editor of the *New York Tribune* and wrote editorials on national and international affairs. He edited *Dun's Review* from 1893 until his death.

BENJAMIN F. GUE
1828-1904

Benjamin Gue began his journalistic career in 1864 as editor and publisher of the *Fort Dodge* (Iowa) *Republican,* which he renamed the *Iowa North-West,* dedicated to Republicanism, temperance, and women's suffrage. In 1871, Gue took over editorial control of the *Iowa Homestead* in Des Moines, and a few months later became chief editor of the *Daily State Journal.* The latter part of Gue's life was devoted to the writing of history and biography, including a four-volume history of Iowa.

CURTIS GUILD
1827-1911

Curtis Guild was born in Boston. At age twenty he joined the staff of the *Boston Journal* and then transferred in 1849 to the *Boston Traveller.* In 1857 he arranged a merger of four Boston newspapers into the *Boston Morning Traveller* and *Evening Traveller,* with Samuel Bowles as editor-in-chief. The venture failed, leaving Guild heavily in debt, but he came back as manager and editor of the *Commercial Bulletin.* The new paper added such features as stock and market reports and general banking news and was an immediate success. Its influence established Guild's reputation as a financial authority. Later, he was the author of several books based on his European travels, first published as letters in the *Bulletin.*

JOHN GUNTHER
1901–1970

John Gunther was born in Chicago and began his writing career while a student at the University of Chicago, serving as literary editor of the student paper and contributing book reviews to a number of newspapers. After a trip to Europe in a cattleboat in 1922, he was employed for the next two years as a local reporter by the *Chicago Daily News*. Following a second trip to Europe he again became an employee of the *Daily News* and was given European assignments for the next twelve years, taking him to almost every nation on the Continent and to the Near East. From 1926 to 1929, he was stationed at various times in Paris, Moscow, Berlin, Rome, Scandinavia, Spain, Switzerland, and the Near East.

In 1930 Gunther became Central European and Balkan correspondent and chief of the *Chicago Daily News* Vienna bureau, a position in which he remained until 1935, when he was named chief correspondent in London. During those years he interviewed nearly every prominent government figure in Europe and was present at the notable events preceding World War II. His newspaper and magazine articles were widely read.

Gunther is best known for a series of informal histories, based on his observations and experiences abroad. His *Inside Europe* (1936) was followed by *Inside Asia* (1939), *Inside Latin America* (1941), *Inside U.S.A.* (1947), *Inside Africa* (1955), *Inside Russia Today* (1958), *Inside Europe Today* (1961), and *Inside South America* (1967). A memorial to his son, *Death Be Not Proud* (1948) was widely read and praised.

In 1937 and 1938 Gunther traveled throughout Asia, spent 1940 and 1941 in Latin American countries, covered the outbreak of the Second World War from London, represented the American press during the 1943 invasion of Sicily, revisited Central and Eastern Europe in 1948, traveled in Asia in 1950, and made his fourth visit to the Soviet Union in 1956—all of which provided a wealth of detail for his works of historical journalism.

SARAH JOSEPHA BUELL HALE
1788–1879

Sarah Hale was born in Newport, New Hampshire. She was always a champion of women's rights and for improved educational opportunities for women. To advance her ideas, she founded the *American Ladies' Magazine* and a children's periodical, the *Juvenile Miscellany*. Louis Antoine Godey, founder of *Godey's Lady's Book,* was impressed by Hale's editorial ability and offered to purchase the *American Ladies' Magazine,* an offer that she accepted. The first issue of *Godey's* under her editorship appeared in January 1837. Hale continued to promote the feminist views expressed in the *Ladies' Magazine,* but carefully avoided extreme or controversial topics, in accord with Godey's fixed policy. A critic, Elizabeth Oakes Smith, characterized Hale's career as "a tribute to the respectabilities, decorums and moralities of life, devoid of its enthusiasms." Nevertheless, she remained dedicated to advancing the interests of her sex, and the circulation of *Godey's Lady's Book* grew from 10,000 in 1837 to 150,000 in 1860.

Hale continued her editorship of *Godey's* until 1877, retiring at age eighty-nine. The magazine discontinued publication in 1898.

ABRAHAM HALL
1826–1898

Abraham Hall was born in Albany, New York. For a short time, he was a newspaper reporter in New Orleans. After a legal career, he was city editor of the *New York World* and then was abroad for five years as London representative of the *New York Herald,* under James Gordon Bennett. From 1890 to 1891, Hall held a similar position with the *New York Morning Journal.*

DAVID HALL
1714–1772

When Benjamin Franklin retired from printing the *Pennsylvania Gazette,* his successor was David Hall, whom Franklin had brought from London. In 1766, Hall became owner of the *Gazette.* Thereafter the paper was published by Hall and his sons and grandsons, with various partners, until it ceased publication in 1815. Hall was a native of Edinburgh, Scotland.

CHARLES GRAHAM HALPINE
1829–1868

Charles Halpine, born in Ireland, was the son of an Irish journalist. He emigrated to America in 1851, where his first job was writing advertisements and serving as secretary for P. T. Barnum. In 1852 he became coeditor of the *Carpet-Bag,* a humorous weekly. Several months later he went to New York for a job as French translator for the *New York Herald.* Halpine was successively correspondent for the *New York Times* in Nicaragua, Washington correspondent, and then associate editor of the *Times.*

He saw active service in the Civil War on the staff of General David Hunter. After his return from the army, Halpine assumed the editorship of the *Citizen,* an organ of the Citizens Association, aimed at the reform of municipal corruption.

MURAT HALSTEAD
1829–1908

Murat Halstead was born in Ross Township, Ohio, and began his journalistic career on the staff of the *Cincinnati Commercial* in 1853. He bought a part-interest in the paper, gradually took over its editorship, and in 1865 held the controlling ownership. As a newsman, he reported on the 1860 conventions, witnessed the hanging of John Brown at Harper's Ferry, and represented his paper at the front during the Civil War.

In the early 1880s the *Cincinnati Commercial* was merged with the *Cincinnati Daily Gazette,* with Halstead as editor-in-chief. The paper met strong competition from the new *Cincinnati Enquirer* and Halstead disposed of the *Commercial Gazette.* Halstead became editor of the *Brooklyn Standard-Union* in 1890, and contributed signed articles to newspapers and magazines. He was a war correspondent from the United States during the Franco-Prussian War (1870–71). Mott called the *Commercial Gazette* under Halstead's editorship "one of the greatest papers west of the Alleghenies."

ALEXANDER HAMILTON
1755?–1804

Alexander Hamilton was born on a Caribbean Island. At age seventeen he was sent to New Jersey to attend a grammar school and a year later he entered King's College (now Columbia University).

Hamilton was one of the most brilliant Americans of the eighteenth century. He was in the forefront of those who shaped the government of the United States during the Revolution and the postwar period. As a member of George Washington's cabinet, he served as the first secretary of the treasury and set the monetary policies for the new nation. It was his responsibility to establish credit for the federal government, representing the eleven united states that had recently emerged from a long war. The policies Hamilton implemented did as much to establish the form of the U.S. government as those of any other man.

Hamilton demonstrated his political philosophy by publishing numerous papers. Many of his concepts of government were published in the *Federalist* in 1788. In the same year, he led the struggle for ratification of the Constitution.

While still in college Hamilton made anonymous contributions to the *New York Journal.* His literary reputation was increased by his "Federalist" papers in the *Independent Journal.* Hamilton was the chief sponsor of John Fenno's *Gazette of the United States* and he was closely associated with Noah Webster's *American Minerva.* Another journalistic interest was the *Evening Post,* for which Hamilton was virtually the editorial director for several years.

Hamilton met his death in 1804 in a duel with Aaron Burr.

CHARLES HAMMOND
1779–1840

Charles Hammond was born near Baltimore and showed an early aptitude for writing. The first years of his career were in the legal profession. From 1813 through 1817 he published the *Ohio Federalist* while a member of the Ohio House of Representatives. In 1822 he moved to Cincinnati and became an editorial writer for the *Cincinnati Gazette.* From 1825 until his death he served as editor of the *Gazette.* For a time during the 1828 campaign, Hammond edited a monthly called *Truth's Advocate,* supporting Henry Clay. In his heyday, Hammond was recognized as one of the strongest Whig writers in the country.

FLETCHER HARPER
1806–1877

Fletcher Harper was born in Newtown, New York. His brother James originated *Harper's New Monthly Magazine* in 1850, but turned over the management to Fletcher. Harper also managed *Harper's Weekly,* established in 1857, and *Harper's Bazaar* (1867). Through the *Weekly,* he exerted a strong political influence and came to know the leading American and European literary figures.

BENJAMIN HARRIS
1673–1716

Benjamin Harris's claim to journalistic fame is based on the fact that he published the first American newspaper, *Publick Occurrences, Both Foreign and Domestick,* although it lasted for only one issue.

Before coming to America (ca. 1686), Harris had twice been in trouble with British authorities in London for violating the printing and bookselling laws. His newspaper appears to have been the offender. When his shop was raided again in 1686 and Harris was about to be arrested, he went to the American colonies.

In Boston, Harris set up his printing shop and published a couple of almanacs in 1687. One was printed in red, the first colonial publication to use color. His most successful venture in book publishing was the *New England Primer* (1687–90). On September 25, 1690, the single issue of *Publick Occurrences* was published. The paper was a small one, four pages, two columns to the page, and was to have been published monthly. As its publication had not been authorized, the governor and council ordered the suppression of the pamphlet, ordered all copies destroyed, and resolved that nothing further could be printed without a license. The only extant copy of *Publick Occurrences* is in the London Public Record Office.

Even though *Publick Occurrences* was suppressed, Harris won some favors from the colonial government. He was given an order for official printing in 1692. During 1692 and 1693 he was the official printer for Massachusetts, operating under a commission granted to him by the governor. Meantime, he was becoming homesick for London. About 1695, Harris returned to England, where he became the publisher of the *London Post* and supplemented his income by dealing in patent medicines.

JOEL CHANDLER HARRIS
1848–1908

Joel Chandler Harris, celebrated today as a great folklorist for his Uncle Remus and other plantation tales, was first of all a journalist. His birthplace was Eatonton, Georgia, and he never left his native state for any appreciable length of time.

Harris's journalistic apprenticeship began at age fourteen. He read in a weekly newspaper, the *Countryman,* a help-wanted notice for a boy to learn the printing business. In 1882 Harris became an apprentice printer, a "printer's devil" on the *Countryman* and occasionally inserted items of his own into the paper's columns. The *Countryman* discontinued publication in 1866. Harris's next position was a typesetter on the daily *Macon Telegraph.* During his five or six months with the *Telegraph,* he also reviewed books and magazines. One title that he found attractive was the *Crescent Monthly,* published in New Orleans by William Evelyn. For about a year Harris was Evelyn's private secretary, and then returned to Georgia. During the next three years Harris was on the staff of the *Monroe Advertiser,* a weekly, for which he set type, and ran off the pages on a hand-press. He also composed humorous paragraphs about Georgia life and characters.

In 1870 Harris was offered a position as associate editor of the *Savannah Morning News* at a phenomenal salary of $40 a week. For the *News,* Harris wrote a daily column first called "State Affairs" and later changed to "Affairs of Georgia," filled with humorous comments on personalities and current affairs. His six years with the *Morning News* established Harris as Georgia's leading humorist.

In 1876 Harris became associate editor of the *Atlanta Constitution.* He was destined to remain in Atlanta for the rest of his life. A series entitled "Roundabout in Georgia" was begun, including sketches in black dialect. The character of Uncle Remus appeared early and over the years Harris contributed many Uncle Remus stories to the *Constitution.* The tales were immediately popular and collections began to appear in book form. During the 1890s Harris had color sketches and stories published in newspapers and magazines outside the South, making him one of the best-known regional writers. In 1899, he began to contribute stories based on Civil War events to the *Saturday Evening Post.*

Harris resigned from the *Constitution* in 1900, in order to devote full time to his literary career. His last publishing venture, ill-advised, was to serve as editor of *Uncle Remus' Magazine,* a monthly first printed in 1907 and in 1908 merged with the *Home Magazine.* The journal was not a success and was soon discontinued.

GEORGE BRINTON MCCLELLAN HARVEY
1864–1928

George Harvey was a New Englander, born in Peacham, Vermont. His journalistic career began with the *St. Johnsbury Index* in 1879. From 1882 to 1886 he reported for the *Springfield Republican, Chicago News,* and *New York World.* He edited the New Jersey edition of the *World* for a time and in 1891 Joseph Pulitzer chose him to be managing editor of the New York edition.

In 1899 Harvey bought the *North American Review* and became its editor. His success in that venture persuaded Harper & Brothers to make him president of that company. In 1901 he became editor of both the *North American Review* and *Harper's Weekly*. His political involvement with Woodrow Wilson started when Harvey, through the *Weekly,* campaigned for Wilson for president. There was a break between the two men several years later, and Harvey became an outspoken critic of Wilson and the Democratic party.

Harvey was appointed ambassador to Great Britain by President Harding, but resigned in 1923 to become editor of the *Washington Post* (1924-25). He sold the *North American Review* in 1926.

PAUL HARVEY
1918-

Paul Harvey was born in Tulsa, Oklahoma. His career began in the 1940s with radio broadcasts over stations in Tulsa, Oklahoma; Salina, Kansas; St. Louis, Missouri; and Michigan, Indiana. Starting in 1944, Harvey became an analyst and commentator with the ABC network and a syndicated columnist with the Los Angeles Times Syndicate. By 1970, his morning broadcasts were rated first in the nation, his newspaper columns appeared widely in smaller newspapers, and he had a devoted following outside the large cities.

Harvey has been classified as a conservative, identified with the political right wing. He was a close friend of both Senator Joseph McCarthy and J. Edgar Hoover. He has won a number of awards from organizations connected with conservative causes.

JOHN ROSE GREENE HASSARD
1836-1888

John Hassard, born in New York City, gained some early experience as a journalist as a reporter for the *New York Tribune*. In 1865 he became editor of the newly established *Catholic World*. After a few months, Charles A. Dana persuaded him to accept the editorship of the *Chicago Republican*. When that paper failed, Hassard returned to the *New York Tribune* and was identified with the *Tribune* for the rest of his life. He was temporarily managing editor, but he was best known for his essays and music criticism. In his later years Hassard traveled widely to the Mediterranean, the Bahamas, France, and in the United States, sending back letters for publication in the *Tribune*.

FRANK HATTON
1846–1894

Frank Hatton was born in Cambridge, Ohio, the son of a frontier newspaperman who owned and edited the *Cadiz* (Ohio) *Republican*. Hatton began working in his father's printing office at age eleven and had a variety of experiences, ranging from printer's devil to local editor. During the Civil War he served as a drummer boy. In 1866 the Hatton family moved to Mount Pleasant, Iowa, where the father bought the *Journal* and published it with the assistance of his son until his death in 1869. Hatton and his brother then operated the plant for five years.

In 1874 Hatton acquired the *Burlington* (Iowa) *Daily Hawk's-Eye* and moved to Burlington. As a reward for his political support, he was appointed assistant postmaster-general by President Arthur and three years later became postmaster general.

While still holding national office, Hatton wrote extensively for the *National Republican* of Washington. He moved to Chicago in 1885, helped to reorganize the *Mail,* and served as its editor until 1888. In 1888, he joined Robert Porter in founding the *New York Press*. In 1889, in cooperation with former Congressman Beriah Wilkiers, he purchased the *Washington Post*. Despite his affiliation with the Republican party, the *Post* was edited as an independent paper.

WILLIAM RANDOLPH HEARST
1863–1951

William Randolph Hearst was born in San Francisco on April 29, 1863. His father, George Hearst, was a mining engineer, prospector, and eventually senator for California who owned such fabulous mineral properties as the Phir Mine in Nevada and Homestake Mine in South Dakota. The boy was tutored by his mother, then taken by her when he was only ten on a tour of Europe, where he began to form his compelling interest in antiques and art. Young Hearst was sent to St. Paul's preparatory school in New Hampshire but left without graduating. He was admitted to Harvard in 1882 and remained long enough to extricate the *Lampoon* from financial difficulties and to study the methods and problems of the press.

He was finally expelled for involvement in college pranks. After serving a brief apprenticeship on Joseph Pulitzer's *New York World,* he persuaded his father to give him the *San Francisco Examiner,* which the elder Hearst had bought in 1880. The first issue under the new editor appeared on March 4, 1887. From the beginning of his newspaper career, Hearst invested in superior equipment and employed a competent staff whom he paid well. He was not afraid to support the underdog, although sometimes his crusades were erratic and he was known as a liberal for much of his life. In San Francisco he attacked the Southern Pacific Railroad, publishing the excoriating articles of Ambrose Bierce for this purpose, and he often espoused the side of labor.

After George Hearst died in 1891, his wife, as sole heiress, sold the family interest in the Anaconda Copper Mining Company for $7.5 million, which she gave to her son. Hearst then bought the *New York Morning Journal* in 1895 and shortly thereafter began the *Evening Journal* in open rivalry with Pulitzer's *World.* He also employed S. S. Carvalho as business manager and Arthur Brisbane as editor. Brisbane was long associated with the Hearst enterprises and became known to millions of readers for his sententious columns. The troubles in Cuba soon attracted Hearst's attention, and he supported the insurrection in the island against Spanish hegemony. When the battleship *Maine* was blown up in Havana harbor, Hearst attributed the deed to Spain and urged an American declaration of war. After combat did occur, he sent the artist Frederic Remington to Cuba as a correspondent for the *Journal.* Hearst's journalistic treatment of the conflict was sensational and not always accurate. But the two New York papers sold 1.25 million copies daily.

About this time, Hearst began to expand his publishing empire. In 1900 he acquired the *Chicago American.* Later he purchased newspapers in Atlanta, Boston, and Los Angeles. He also became the owner of such magazines as *Cosmopolitan, Good Housekeeping,* and *Harper's Bazaar,* the last a women's magazine which Hearst converted in 1913 to a more modern and sophisticated periodical. His *American Weekly* syndicated supplement provided features and photographs to a variety of newspapers.

Hearst also manifested political ambitions, most of which were frustrated. He was elected twice to the House of Representatives from New York State (1903-7), and indicated his availability then as a candidate for the presidency. But he ran twice unsuccessfully for mayor of New York City in 1905 and 1909, and interspersed these campaigns with an equally futile quest for the governorship of the state. Hearst was not conspicuous as a legislator, but did favor public ownership of utilities, control of trusts, and popular election of U.S. senators. He was originally a supporter of Franklin D. Roosevelt, but eventually objected to the New Deal policies on taxes and labor and became stridently conservative.

Hearst married Millicent Wilson, formerly a Broadway dancer, on April 28, 1903; they had five sons. But in 1917 Hearst met Marion Davies, once a showgirl in the Ziegfeld Follies, and began a relationship that endured until his death. By this time he had begun to invest in film companies, and he saw to it that his papers gave Miss Davies suitable treatment. His wife refused him a divorce, however. His growing affluence stimulated him to construct an edifice worthy of his prominence, and in 1919 he began the building of a castle at San Simeon on his 375-square-mile California ranch. This was to be not only a Hearst showplace but a museum for his growing collection to art. Since his death, incidentally, it has become a mecca for tourists and is now by bequest part of the California park system. Other Hearst properties included at one time the Cerra de Pasco Copper Company of Peru and a castle in Wales. About 1935, however, Hearst's wealth began to show signs of shrinkage, probably due to the Great Depression. At any rate, an administrator was selected to consolidate the Hearst holdings, and some of the mines and publishing properties were sold. Even so, at Hearst's death on August 14, 1951, his estate was valued at almost $60 million and was divided among his five sons, his wife, and various philanthropies (Miss Davies had already received some Hearst stock).

Hearst was a flamboyant character not always treated with proper respect. Orson Welles used him as a prototype in his motion picture *Citizen Kane,* presenting him as a stark example of the crude, greedy, and culpable robber baron. Yet there is no question that Hearst was a competent newspaperman, conscious of constructive changes taking place in journalism, willing to exploit them, paying well for dedicated service, not averse to catering to the masses, responsive to flashy headlines and lurid stories. One of his biographers, James Boylan, has summarized his career astutely but somewhat ambiguously: "American journalism and politics are richer in legend and poorer in practice for Hearst's existence."

GABRIEL HEATTER
1890–1972

Gabriel Heatter was born in New York City and was a reporter by age thirteen for Manhattan's lower East Side while still in school. Two years later he was covering Brooklyn and serving as messenger for Hearst's *New York American.* He worked on the *Brooklyn Times,* reporting crime stories, before going to Hearst's *New York Journal* to report on the New York slums. From the *Journal,* Heatter went to the *New York Herald,* working as a political correspondent in Albany.

Shortly after World War I Heatter was sent abroad as the Paris representative of the Foreign Language Publisher's Association to report on conditions abroad. In 1932, he wrote a series of articles for the *Nation,* debating socialism with Norman Thomas. That brought an invitation to appear on radio as a news broadcaster. For years thereafter he was one of the nation's leading broadcasters, speaking over the principal radio and television channels.

BEN HECHT
1894-1964

Ben Hecht, born in New York City, spent his early years in Chicago, where he was a reporter for the *Chicago Journal* (1910-14). From 1914 to 1923, he worked on the *Chicago Daily News.* His news stories often dealt with the city's seamier side, such as police courts, jails, barrooms, and brothels. During his fifteen years as a newspaperman in Chicago he witnessed seventeen hangings. At the end of World War I, Hecht was sent to Germany and Russia (1918-20) as a foreign correspondent for the *Daily News* syndicate of seventy American newspapers.

Hecht took part in the Chicago Literary Renaissance along with Edgar Lee Masters, Sherwood Anderson, Carl Sandburg, and Harriet Monroe. He and Maxwell Bodenheim founded the short-lived *Chicago Literary Times* in 1923 (it ceased publication in 1924).

Hecht had his most lasting success as a dramatist, with two plays written in collaboration with Charles McArthur: the *Front Page* (1928), re-creating his newspaper days, and *Twentieth Century* (1932). The success of the first of these fast-paced, wise-cracking stage plays was duplicated in numerous screen plays. Hecht also wrote novels and numerous short stories and essays.

During the period preceding the formation of the State of Israel and in reaction to the Nazi Holocaust, Hecht became an active propagandist for the Zionist cause. British film exhibitors boycotted his films for five years because of his outspoken support of Jewish resistance movements in Palestine.

KARL PETER HEINZEN
1809-1880

Karl Peter Heinzen was filled with radical ideas. In 1848 he came to New York to establish a German language paper, and then returned to

Europe to take part in the 1848 Paris revolution. He came back to the United States in 1850 and founded in succession four newspapers, all full of radical articles and in German. All failed.

Looking for a new cause, Heinzen seized on the antislavery issue and moved to Louisville, Kentucky, to found the *Herald des Westens.* His establishment was burned. With the help of friends, a new paper, the *Pioneer,* was founded in 1854 and moved from Cincinnati to New York to Boston. To save expenses, Heinzen's wife served as typesetter and business manager. The *Pioneer* continued publication until the end of 1879, a year before Heinzen's death.

JOHN HERSEY
1914–

John Hersey was born in Tientsin, China, and was only ten years of age when he came to America. From 1942 to 1946 he was a war and foreign correspondent for *Time, Life* and the *New Yorker.* In 1937 Hersey joined *Time* as a staff writer, remaining there until 1944 when he became *Life's* senior editor. He won the Pulitzer Prize in 1945, and has been the recipient of other prestigious awards.

Perhaps Hersey's most famous work is *Hiroshima,* which filled an entire issue of the *New Yorker,* and soon appeared in book form. He is the author of a number of other books dealing with world affairs.

For five years (1975–80), Hersey was president of the Authors League of America and from 1981 to 1984 was chancellor of the American Academy and Institute of Arts and Letters.

SEYMOUR HERSH
1937–

Seymour Hersh, born in Chicago, is a foremost exponent of the latest newspaper trend, investigative journalism. His articles on the My Lai massacre, CIA domestic spying, Henry Kissinger's wiretaps on National Security Council aides, probes into chemical and biological warfare, and other exposés have won a Pulitzer Prize and other awards.

Hersh began his journalistic career in 1959 as a copy boy and later as a police reporter for the Chicago City News Bureau. Short periods were spent as a public information officer at Fort Riley, Kansas; trying to establish a suburban newspaper in Chicago; and as a reporter for United

Press International in Pierce, South Dakota. A longer connection was made with the Associated Press in Chicago starting in 1963. Hersh joined its Washington Press Corps in 1965 and was promoted to Pentagon correspondent in 1966. He quit AP in 1967 to become a freelance investigative reporter.

In 1972, to "accomplish more and reach more people" than he could as an independent reporter, Hersh joined the staff of the *New York Times*. He spent the next seven years working for the *Times* and turning up more top-level news scoops. In 1979 Hersh left the *New York Times* to allow more time for book writing and extensive research, although he continued to contribute articles to the *Times* from time to time. He is widely admired by his colleagues for his persistence in tracking down stories.

MARGUERITE HIGGINS
1920–1966

Marguerite Higgins was born in Hong Kong, China, and was educated in California, where her family settled after their return to the United States in 1923. She graduated with a degree in journalism from Columbia University.

Higgins's reporting experience was gained in California with the *Tahoe Tattler, Daily Californian,* and the *Vallejo Times-Herald.* She was Columbia's campus correspondent and later hired as a reporter for the *New York Herald Tribune.* She received her first foreign assignment in 1944, at age twenty-four, first in the London bureau and next in Paris. As bureau chief in Berlin in 1945, Higgins produced a number of headline stories.

In 1950 Higgins was sent to Tokyo as chief of the *Herald Tribune's* Far East bureau and immediately after went to Korea to cover the war there. She returned to the United States late in 1950, recognized as the best-known woman correspondent reporting on the Korean War, and received numerous honors. Higgins was the first woman to win a Pulitzer Prize for foreign correspondence for her coverage of the Korean War.

In 1955 Higgins settled in Washington, where she covered the State Department and wrote a weekly column. She continued to travel abroad, however, and in the 1950s and 1960s, covered international meetings and presidential trips.

Higgins left the *Herald Tribune* in 1963 to join the *Long Island Newsday,* where she wrote a triweekly column syndicated to ninety-two newspapers.

After a long tour in Vietnam, India, and Pakistan in 1965, Higgins died at age forty-five of a tropical infection picked up during the journey.

RICHARD HILDRETH
1807–1865

Richard Hildreth, historian and journalist, was born in Deerfield, Massachusetts. He was a founder (1832) and editorial writer (1832–38) for the *Boston Atlas.* From 1855 to 1861 he contributed to the *New York Tribune.* Hildreth's most important work is his six-volume *History of the United States* (1849–52).

JOHN HOLT
1721–1784

John Holt was a Virginian who had failed in business and turned later to journalism. In 1755, James Parker began printing the *Connecticut Gazette,* the first newspaper in that colony. The imprint listed Holt as resident partner and editor. It is probable that Holt learned the printing trade from his brother-in-law William Hunter.

In 1760, Parker called Holt to manage his printing business in New York, which included the *New York Gazette and Weekly Post-Bay.* Holt was again listed as junior partner. In 1762, Holt became sole publisher, leasing the plant and equipment from Parker. In addition to the newspaper, Holt published books, pamphlets, handbills, broadsides, and other materials. Most of the publications were political in nature, reflecting the struggle going on between the colonies and England. Holt also printed items dealing with such subjects as religion, Free Masonry, economics, history, biography, archeology, and poetry. His income was supplemented by selling books, ink, stationery, paper, and other supplies.

Holt was forced to leave his equipment behind him in New York in 1766 during the British invasion. He set up a new printing office in Kingston, New York, and began publishing the *New York Journal.* The new paper lasted fifteen weeks until the British army captured and burned Kingston. Part of the printing materials was destroyed. Holt's next move was to Poughkeepsie, where his paper was published, with occasional interruptions, until 1783. In 1766, a new title was adopted: the *New York Journal, or General Advertiser,* but Holt always considered the *Journal* a continuation of the *Gazette.*

Holt died in 1784, shortly after returning to New York. His family maintained the printing tradition. His widow published the paper until 1800, when it was sold. His son, John Hunter Holt, was publisher of the *Virginia Gazette, or the Norfolk Intelligencer* and his daughter Elizabeth married Eleazer Oswald, editor of the *Philadelphia Independent Gazetteer.*

JOHNSTON JONES HOOPER
1815-1862

Johnston Jones Hooper was born in Wilmington, North Carolina. The record shows that his father was a journalist. Hooper was working on a newspaper in Charleston, South Carolina, at age fifteen. For a time he edited the *Dadeville Banner* and for six months in 1846 he edited the *Wetumpha Whig*. He helped to establish the *Montgomery Journal*. A backwoods sharper, Simon Suggs, invented by Hooper, became widely popular and Hooper's writings about him were reprinted in the *New York Spirit of The Times* and in book form. About 1853 Hooper established a newspaper, the *Mail,* in Montgomery and he edited the paper until 1861.

LUCY HAMILTON HOOPER
1835-1893

Lucy Hooper was born in Philadelphia. Her first journalistic experience was on the editorial staff of *Lippincott's Magazine.* When her husband was appointed consul general, she and her family moved to Paris, France. Her connection with *Lippincott's* continued. She wrote articles on French theaters, art exhibitions, concerts, and fashions. In addition, Hooper contributed weekly letters to *Appleton's Journal* dealing with Parisian social and literary life, and for twenty years wrote for the *Philadelphia Evening Telegraph.* She died in Paris.

HEDDA HOPPER
1885-1966

Hedda Hopper, who became famous as a Hollywood gossip columnist, was born in Hollidaysburg, Pennsylvania. After a theater career, she became the fifth of DeWolf Hopper's six wives. In 1918 she adopted the name "Hedda Hopper," on advice of a numerologist.

In 1937, Hopper began to establish herself as a personality with a gossip radio program. The following year the Hopper column began appearing in the *Los Angeles Times* and a dozen other newspapers distributed by the Esquire Syndicate. In 1940 she switched to the Register-Tribune Syndicate and in 1942 to the Chicago Tribune-New York Daily News combine, with an enormous circulation of eighty-five metropolitan and three thousand small-town dailies and two thousand weeklies.

Hopper was always conservative, and her writing showed her political bias to such an extent that some publishers refused to run her column. Nevertheless, she was undisputed queen of Hollywood gossips after 1964, especially following Louella Parson's retirement.

ROY W. HOWARD
1883–1964

Roy W. Howard was born in Gano, Ohio. He helped supplement his family's income by delivering the *Indianapolis Star* in the morning and the *Indianapolis News* in the afternoon. He was also school correspondent for the *News*. After graduation from high school, the *Sun* hired him as a full-time reporter, but he moved to the *Star* as a sportswriter for a higher salary. His next job, in 1905, was assistant telegraph editor of the *St. Louis Post-Dispatch*. Failing to win a hoped-for promotion, Howard left St. Louis to be news editor of the *Cincinnati Post,* owned by E. W. Scripps. He was transferred to New York as a special correspondent for the Scripps–McRae League of newspapers. In 1906, when Scripps bought the Publishers Press Association, Howard was named general manager. In 1907, Scripps combined his several news-gathering organizations into the United Press Association, with Howard as New York manager.

Howard continued his climb by being made president and general manager of United Press in 1912. In 1921, he became business director and board chairman of the Scripps–McRae (later Scripps–Howard) newspapers and Newspaper Enterprise Association. In 1925 he became coeditor.

In later stages of his career, Howard was editor of the *New York World-Telegram* (1931–61), chairman of the executive committee of the Scripps–Howard newspapers, and a director of United Press International. Under his direction, Scripps–Howard came to own twenty-five daily papers in twenty-four cities. The *World-Telegram* was acquired in 1927, the *New York World* in 1931, and the *New York Sun* in 1950. The *New York World Telegram and Sun* ceased publication in 1967, three years after Howard's death.

Howard achieved fame as the "man who ended World War I four days early," when as a foreign correspondent he cabled an unconfirmed report of a false armistice on November 7, 1918.

E. W. HOWE
1853–1937

Edgar Wilson Howe was born in Indiana. Most of his career was spent in Atchison, Kansas, where he became known as the "Sage of Potato Hill."

Howe worked as an apprentice printer in Missouri, Iowa, Nebraska, and Utah before he founded the *Atchinson Daily Globe* (1877). He remained owner and editor of the *Globe* until 1911. From 1911 to 1933, Howe published the *E. W. Howe Monthly,* made up almost entirely of his homespun "commonsense" philosophizing.

Howe thought of himself as a country journalist. In some respects he resembled another Kansas editor, his friend William Allen White. Howe gained a national reputation for his quotable "paragraphs" and especially for his novel, *The Story of a Country Town.* The book was widely praised by critics as a grim, realistic portrait of the narrowness and dullness of life in Midwestern America. According to one biographer, William I. McReynolds, "Howe had an amazing repertory of prejudices, and he was famous for his blunt exposition of them, often expressed with laconic humor."

CLARK HOWELL
1863–1936

Clark Howell was born in South Carolina. His reputation as a journalist centers on one newspaper, the *Atlanta Constitution,* for which he was managing editor, editor, and publisher for forty-seven years (1889–1936). He succeeded a famous journalist, Henry W. Grady, and was followed by another, Ralph McGill.

Howell entered the newspaper world immediately after graduating from the University of Georgia in 1883. His apprenticeship was served with the *New York Times* and the *Philadelphia Press.* Returning to Atlanta, he became night city editor under Grady. By 1889, Howell had become assistant managing editor of the *Constitution.* When Evan Howell, his father, retired, Clark Howell was made editor-in-chief.

Howell was active in Georgia politics but failed to achieve his ambition to be governor of the state. He did win other distinctions, such as being a member of the official delegation to the Philippines in 1935, when Manuel Quezon was made president, being made a chevalier of the French Legion of Honor in 1936, serving as a member of the Democratic National committee for twenty-six years, and being a director of the Associated Press from its founding in 1900 until his death. From 1889 to 1937, the *Constitution's* daily circulation grew from 11,000 to 84,500, testimony to Howell's journalistic skill and leadership.

EVAN P. HOWELL
1839–1905

Evan P. Howell, a native of Warsaw, Georgia, became a journalist more or less by chance by acquiring a half-interest in the *Atlanta Constitution* in 1876. Howell was retained as the *Constitution's* attorney and when Edward Y. Clarke retired as editor his share of the newspaper was sold to Howell. At that time, Howell became editor-in-chief. He was fortunate, however, that the *Constitution* ranked high in general esteem and was growing steadily in circulation. Furthermore, Howell was not a novice. He had a brief apprenticeship as reporter and editor on the *Intelligencer* and as the *Constitution's* counsel. Another asset was a talented and dedicated staff, including Henry Woodfin Grady and Joel Chandler Harris.

Howell had high standards and the *Constitution* prospered under his direction. A eulogy by Joel Chandler Harris summed up his career as follows: "He made the *Constitution* the mouthpiece for or against every public measure that was proposed. His success was little short of marvelous, for he was not a professional journalist nor a trained writer in the technical sense." Clark Howell succeeded his father as editor of the *Constitution* in 1889.

WILLIAM DEAN HOWELLS
1837–1920

William Dean Howells, long regarded as the dean of American letters, was born in Marten's Ferry, Ohio. At the age of nine he began to learn the printer's trade, setting type in his father's printing shop. In 1840 the family moved to Hamilton, where the father, a printer, bought a weekly newspaper, the *Intelligencer,* which he edited for the next nine years. Another move was made in 1849 to Dayton, Ohio, where the father bought the *Transcript,* changing it from a semiweekly to a daily. Howells helped in the printing office, often worked at night, and rose early in the morning to deliver the paper. Howells was on the editorial staffs of several Ohio newspapers. In 1851 he went to Columbus, Ohio, the state capital, and worked as a compositor on the *State Journal*. The father bought the *Sentinel* in Ashtabula. In 1856, young Howells returned to Columbus and became a correspondent for the *Cincinnati Gazette*. Three years later he was made news editor of the *State Journal*. A campaign biography of Abraham Lincoln that he wrote was rewarded with an appointment as U.S. consul in Venice, where he served until 1865. When Howells returned to the

United States in 1865, he was appointed to the staff of the *Nation* under E. L. Godkin. A few months later, the subeditorship of the *Atlantic Monthly,* under James T. Fields, came open and Howells moved to Boston. Howells's connection with the *Atlantic* lasted fifteen years (1866–81). In 1871 he became editor-in-chief. He formed a lifelong friendship with Mark Twain and came to know Lowell, Emerson, Holmes, and Hawthorne. In his influential post with the *Atlantic* he promoted the careers of Stephen Crane, Frank Norris, Hamlin Garland, and other promising young authors.

Between 1880 and 1890, Howells left the *Atlantic Monthly* and wrote several novels for the younger and more popular *Century Magazine.* His most famous work during this period was *The Rise of Silas Lapham* (1885). Altogether he published about one hundred books, divided equally among fiction and literary criticism, travel, and biography.

Howells's later life was uneventful. For six months (1891–92) he edited the *Cosmopolitan Magazine.* A more permanent connection was a monthly department, "Editor's Study," in *Harper's* (1886–92), renamed "Easy Chair" (1900–20).

ALBERT R. HUNT
1942–

Albert Hunt was born in Charlottesville, Virginia, and graduated from Wake Forest University. He was a reporter for the *Wall Street Journal* in New York City (1965–67), for the *Journal* in Boston (1967–69), and for the *Journal* in Washington (1968–83). Since 1983 Hunt has been Washington bureau chief for the *Journal.* He received the Raymond Clapper Award in 1976. Hunt is married to another leading journalist, Judy Woodruff.

WILLIAM GIBBES HUNT
1791–1833

William G. Hunt was born in Boston. In 1815 he emigrated to Lexington, Kentucky, and became editor of the *Western Monitor,* a title changed later to *Western Monitor, Western Review and Miscellaneous Magazine,* which became the literary voice for the region. After the *Review* ceased publication, still another venture in 1821–23 was the *Masonic Miscellany and Ladies Literary Magazine.*

Hunt moved later to Nashville, Tennessee, to publish the *Nashville Banner,* merged in 1826 with the *Nashville Whig* to form the *Nashville*

Banner and Nashville Advertiser. Hunt remained in charge of the *Banner* until 1833.

CHARLAYNE HUNTER-GAULT
1942–

Charlayne Hunter-Gault was born in Due West, South Carolina. She was the first black woman admitted to the University of Georgia. Earlier she edited the student newspaper, the *Green Light,* at Spelman College in Atlanta. The University of Georgia had the only school of journalism in the state, and in 1959 she applied for admission. It was not until 1961 that the legal barriers were removed. Hunter-Gault received her journalism degree from Georgia in 1963. She had worked on weekends for the *Atlanta Enquirer.* The *New Yorker* employed her as a secretary for a year and then promoted her to staff writer. Other steps in her career included editing articles for *Trans-Action* magazine, and serving on the staff of WRC-TV, an NBC affiliate in Washington, as an investigative reporter and anchorwoman of the local evening newscast.

In 1968, Hunter-Gault joined the Metropolitan staff of the *New York Times,* specializing in covering the urban black community. She remained with the *Times* nine years.

Since 1978, Hunter-Gault has become widely known for her role in the "MacNeil/Lehrer News Hour," PBS's weeknight newscast. She became the program's national correspondent.

CHESTER ROBERT HUNTLEY
1911–1974

The Huntley-Brinkley NBC news reports ranked first in television ratings until Huntley retired in 1970. Huntley broadcasted from New York and David Brinkley from Washington. They always signed off with "Good night, David," "Good night, Chet." Huntley brought a considerable background of experience to the Huntley-Brinkley program.

He was born in Cardwell, Montana, and came from the famous Adams family on his father's side. His mother's side of the family brought him colorful coverage from his grandfather, W. R. Fatham, who crossed the plains in a covered wagon and was still active into his nineties. Huntley was interested in sports, oratory and debating. He attended Montana State College, studied pre-medical courses, and later attended the University of Washington at Seattle. He received the B.A. degree in 1934.

Huntley had performed on a Seattle radio station while still a student at the University of Washington and later on stations in Spokane, Portland, and Los Angeles. In 1939 he began a twelve-year connection with CBS in Los Angeles. For a special series on Mexican-Americans he won the George Foster Peabody Award in 1942, and later, other awards, including a medal in 1945 from the U.S. Treasury Department for his work in the bond campaigns during World War II. He moved to ABC in 1951, becoming, according to *Newsweek* (April 19, 1954), "one of broadcasting's best reputed interpreters of world and local scenes...."

In June, 1955, after some unpleasantries on the West Coast due to the "Communist scare," he was signed by NBC and went to New York. Huntley moved from radio to television, and raised the standards of broadcast journalism with keen analyses of controversial issues. His being paired with David Brinkley from 1956 to 1970 resulted in NBC's award winning nightly broadcast. After his retirement in 1970, Chet Huntley helped with various community projects and the development of the Big Sky Montana Recreational Complex.

WILLIAM HENRY HURLBERT
1827–1895

William H. Hurlbert was born in Charleston, South Carolina. In 1855 he was a writer on the staff of *Putnam's Magazine* and dramatic critic for the *Albion*. In 1857 he joined the *New York Times,* but in 1862 transferred to the *New York World.* As the *World's* representative in 1867, he attended the Paris Exposition and the Festival of St. Peter in Rome. Another *World* assignment, in 1871 was to serve as special correspondent accompanying the commission sent by President Grant to Santo Domingo. From 1876 to 1883, Hurlbert was editor-in-chief of the *World.* Thereafter, he spent most of his time in Europe, contributing many articles to American and British magazines.

RALPH M. INGERSOLL
1900–1985

Ralph M. Ingersoll was born in New Haven. He began as a reporter for the *New Yorker* in 1925 and for five years was its managing editor. In 1930 he became associate editor and later managing editor of *Fortune.* As a member of the staff of Time, Inc., he became vice president and general manager of *Time, Life, Fortune,* and *Architectural Forum,* and of the radio and cinema productions of "The March of Time." Ingersoll was also publisher of *Time.* He was the spirit behind *PM,* the daily that refused advertising to assure editorial purity.

RALPH INGERSOLL II
1946–

Ralph Ingersoll II was born in New York City. He began as a reporter on the family-owned newspaper in Pawtucket, Rhode Island. In 1982 he forced the resignation of his father in a power struggle. In 1986 he bought the *New Haven Journal-Courier and Register,* a morning-evening combination, and subsequently acquired other dailies on the outskirts of New York City, bringing his holdings of daily newspapers to forty. In 1987, Ingersoll bought an 80 percent share in the Chantry Communications on Long Island, holding sixty-seven papers.

Ingersoll emphasizes profitability above all else in newspaper publishing, it is charged by his critics, although he insists that good fiscal management is compatible with journalistic quality. He heads the fifteenth largest media conglomerate in the United States.

JOHN INMAN
1805–1850

John Inman, born in Utica, New York, began his career in journalism by serving on the editorial staff of the *New York Mirror,* a literary magazine (1828-31, 1835-36). For a short time in 1828 he had editorial charge of the *New York Standard.* A more important position came his way in 1837 as assistant editor of the *Commercial Advertiser.* He succeeded William L. Stone as editor-in-chief of the *Advertiser* in 1844. When the *Columbian Lady's and Gentleman's Magazine* was established in 1844, Inman was appointed its editor, a connection that continued until 1848. In addition to his other activities, Inman was a contributor to *Spirit of the Times* and *New York Review.*

WILL IRWIN
1873–1948

Will Irwin, who has been called one of the great reporters of the twentieth century, demonstrated amazing versatility, not only as a newspaperman but as a magazine writer and editor, novelist, playwright, and poet. He was born in Oneida, New York. In the 1880s the Irwin family moved to Denver, Colorado, and in 1894, Irwin went to Palo Alto, California, to attend Stanford University. There he formed a lifelong friendship with Herbert Hoover.

The month after graduating from college in 1899, Irwin began his newspaper career on the *San Francisco Wave,* with a variety of assignments. When the *Wave* was sold in 1900, Irwin went to work for the *San Francisco Chronicle.* Shortly, he was given the title of development editor and in 1902 he was named Sunday editor.

Irwin's next job was on the other side of the country, working for the *New York Sun,* in 1904. Despite its considerable variety, however, Irwin found the post frustrating, and he resigned to accept an appointment as writing editor of *McClure's Magazine.* He was unable to get along with Samuel McClure and therefore turned to freelancing, mainly for *Collier's.* After World War I began, Irwin made arrangements to cover the war for *Collier's* and the *American Magazine.* In an interim period he did publicity work for the Commission for Relief in Belgium. In 1915 he resumed his war correspondence for the *New York Tribune.* Censors barred him from battlefronts for a time, but David Lloyd George had his name removed from the blacklist. Irwin returned to France in 1916 as a correspondent for the *Saturday Evening Post.*

Irwin joined George Creel's Committee on Public Information in 1918. Through the Depression years and World War II he wrote for the North American Newspaper Alliance and other syndicates and for *Liberty* and other magazines, and published a number of books.

HENRY JAMES
1843-1916

Henry James, brother of the famous psychologist William James, was born in New York City. He is more celebrated as a novelist and critic than as a journalist, but his career had some journalistic aspects. While a student at Harvard in 1865, he began to contribute sketches to periodicals and over the next ten years a number of his short stories were published in the *Atlantic Monthly.* William Dean Howells encouraged him to write short stories. Some were published in magazines and later gathered together in *A Passionate Pilgrim and Other Tales,* 1871. Some of his short stories were considered masterpieces, and the best known was "The Turn of the Screw" published in 1898. In 1875, while completing a novel in New York City, he tried to write literary journalism for the *Nation*. Earlier, his book notices had appeared in the *North American Review*.

James never married but he enjoyed many friendships with women, some of them writers. Although he did not know her well, George Eliot's fiction provoked strong feelings, and, according to the writer, Millicent Bell, it was about her that in 1866 he wrote his first signed critical article. A life-long attachment filled with respect, pleasant experiences, and a deep, satisfying friendship was with Edith Wharton, who, while not so great a writer as Eliot, was definitely the most gifted and productive of female writers among his close friends.

MARQUIS JAMES
1891–1955

Marquis James was born in Springfield, Missouri. His career as a reporter began with working on several Midwestern newspapers before moving to New York City, where he joined the staff of the *Tribune*. He became national director of publicity for the American Legion and from 1923 to 1932 was editor of the *American Legion Monthly*. He also served on the staff of the *New Yorker* magazine.

James received Pulitzer Prizes for his biographies of Sam Houston and Andrew Jackson.

PETER JENNINGS
1938–

Peter Charles Jennings was born in Toronto, Canada. His father, Charles Jennings, was a distinguished broadcast journalist for the Canadian Broadcasting Corporation. Peter's first exposure to journalism was as a CBS broadcaster over various stations in Canada.

Jennings moved to New York City in 1964 to join the staff of ABC News. Though only twenty-six years of age, ABC executives decided to make him anchorman of the network's nightly fifteen-minute national newscast. Jennings anchored the ABC nightly newscast for three years and then returned to reportorial duties in 1968. The next ten years were mainly spent abroad where Jennings became known as a leading foreign correspondent, particularly expert on Middle Eastern affairs.

Jennings returned to the United States in 1974 to serve as ABC's correspondent and news reader for the early morning newscasts. In addition to major news stories on the domestic front, he has covered such international events as Sadat's assassination, the Falkland Islands War, the Israeli invasion of Lebanon, the civil war in Bangladesh, the Ayatollah Khomeini's overthrow of the Shah of Iran, and Pope John Paul II's visit to Poland in 1983. Since 1983 he has been anchorman and senior editor for ABC News.

GERALD WHITE JOHNSON
1890–1980

Gerald W. Johnson, born in Riverton, North Carolina, was described by H. L. Mencken as "the best editorial writer in the South, a very excellent critic, and a highly civilized man." He was involved with journalism from an early age. His father had edited a Baptist Church publication and Gerald established his own newspaper, the *Thomasville Davidsonian,* while a student at Wake Forest University. After college he was a reporter on the *Lexington* (North Carolina) *Dispatch* and music critic on the *Greensboro* (North Carolina) *News.* Johnson was in military service during World War I and following his return became a professor of journalism at the University of North Carolina.

From 1926 to 1943, Johnson wrote editorials, first for the *Baltimore Evening Sun* and then for the *Baltimore Sun.* During that period he was a prolific author, producing fourteen published books. In 1943 he left newspaper work to freelance. Subsequently, he was a news commentator on a Baltimore station (1952–54), and contributing editor to the *New Republic* starting in 1954.

Gerald Johnson spent more than six decades as a writer, ending up before his death at the age of ninety with more than forty volumes and innumerable articles. His published works were predominantly concerned with American history and politics.

JOHN HAROLD JOHNSON
1918–

John Harold Johnston was born in Arkansas City, Arkansas, and is a leading American publisher of books and magazines aimed at the black reader. His magazines included *Ebony,* a monthly picture and news journal; *Jet,* a weekly news magazine; *Tan,* a monthly women's magazine; and *Black World* (formerly *Negro Digest*), a monthly literary magazine.

Johnson began his publishing career in 1942 when he founded the Johnson Publishing Company in Chicago. He represented the United States on missions to Africa, Poland, and Russia.

WILLIAM ANDREW JOHNSTON
1871–1929

William Andrew Johnston was born in Pittsburgh, Pennsylvania. He spent two years reporting on local papers and then tried his own hand at publishing, with the *Williamsburg* (Pennsylvania) *Independent,* an unsuccessful venture. Next, from 1894 to 1897 he was in New York serving as a reporter on the *Morning Journal* and the *New York Press.* Johnston next spent three years on the editorial staff of the *New York Herald.* From 1900 until near the end of his life, he was associated with the *New York World.* Johnston also wrote many magazine articles and books, including a number of mystery and detective novels.

MARVIN KALB
1930–

Marvin Kalb was born in New York City. His parents had emigrated to the United States from the Ukraine and Poland to escape anti–Semitism. He was the first director of the Kennedy School of Government's Center for the Press, Politics and Public Policy at Harvard University. After receiving an M.A. degree in Chinese and Russian history from Harvard in 1953, Kalb served for two years in the U.S. Army. In 1955 he accepted an appointment as a translator in the Anglo-American Joint Press Reading Service in the American Embassy in Moscow. He took advantage of the opportunity to travel around the Soviet Union.

When Kalb returned to the United States in 1957, he joined the staff of CBS News in New York. In 1960, the network's officials decided to reopen the CBS news bureau in Moscow. Kalb's background made him the choice for the post and he returned to Moscow in the spring of 1960. For three years he contributed articles to the *New York Times* and other journals on a variety of topics relating to the Soviet Union.

In 1963 Kalb came back to the United States as chief diplomatic correspondent in CBS's Washington bureau. A return trip was made to Russia in 1965 to direct a film crew, which, with permission of the Soviet Foreign Ministry, visited cities and towns along the Volga River. After the United

States became involved in Vietnam, Kalb brought his brand of probing analytical journalism to an exhaustive investigation of the situation.

Kalb accompanied Henry Kissinger on his overseas travels to the Soviet Union, China, and the Middle East.

In 1980, after twenty-three years with CBS news, Kalb resigned to become chief diplomatic correspondent for NBC News. Part of the new assignment was to serve as moderator of "Meet the Press," a long-running weekly public affairs program. Kalb left NBC in 1987 to accept the previously mentioned Harvard position. He is also Edward R. Murrow Professor at Harvard.

Kalb won several Overseas Press Club awards for his radio and television analysis.

HANS VON KALTENBORN
1878–1965

H. V. Kaltenborn was born in Milwaukee, Wisconsin. He served in the Spanish-American War and began his newspaper career as city editor of the *Merrill* (Wisconsin) *Advocate* in 1899. In 1902–5 and 1910–30, he was a reporter and editor for the *Brooklyn Eagle*. He graduated from Harvard in 1909.

Kaltenborn became a radio news analyst in 1922 and after 1924 he was the first regularly scheduled radio commentator. From 1929 to 1940, he was with the Columbia Broadcasting System and after 1940 with the National Broadcasting Company. During his career he covered political conventions, international crises, World War II overseas, and the civil war in Spain. He contributed to many magazines and was author of a number of books based on his observations and experiences.

JOHN MCLEOD KEATING
1830–1906

John McLeod Keating was born in Ireland and learned the printing trade as an apprentice in a print shop. At age eighteen he became foreman of the printing office of the *Dublin World*. He emigrated to America in 1848, settled in New York, and again became foreman in a newspaper plant. In 1854 Keating moved to New Orleans and later to Nashville, Tennessee, to be foreman of the composing room of what became the Methodist Publishing House. Still restless, he went on to Baton Rouge to serve as superintendent of state printing. Later he returned to Nashville as managing editor of the *Daily News.* In 1859 he settled in Memphis, where he was employed as commercial and city editor of the *Daily Morning Bulletin.*

At the end of the Civil War, Keating served as city editor of the *Memphis Daily Argus,* then the city's only Democratic newspaper. In 1865, he established the *Memphis Daily Commercial,* combining it with the *Argus* the following year to create the *Commercial and Argus.* In 1868 he bought a half-interest in the *Memphis Appeal,* which he edited for twenty-one years.

Keating was a political liberal. He attacked carpetbaggers, and advocated enfranchisement of former Confederate soldiers, the education of emancipated slaves, and the political equality of women.

Among Keating's memorable news stories are his accounts of the yellow fever epidemic that struck Memphis in 1878. His vivid daily stories have been compared to Daniel Defoe's *Journal of the Plague Year* in its graphic detail.

In 1889 Keating became editor of the *Commercial* until 1891 when he left Memphis for Washington, D.C. He died in Gloucester, Massachusetts.

JAMES KEELEY
1867–1934

James Keeley was born in London and emigrated to America in 1883. Before leaving England he had worked for his uncle who operated a book and stationery store. His job was to fold and deliver newspapers in the mornings and evenings. While living in Wyandotte, Kansas, Keeley began supplying news items to the *Kansas City Journal* and soon became a regular reporter. Between 1887 and 1889, he also worked for the *Memphis Commercial* and the *Louisville Commercial.* In 1889 he went to Chicago, and was employed by the *Tribune.* He remained with that paper for the next twenty-five years, until 1914. Keeley began with the *Tribune* reporting on the night police beat. After two years he was promoted to general assignment reporter.

Keeley made the front page of the *Tribune* in 1892 reporting on a "rustler's war" in Wyoming; again in 1896 covering a tornado that struck St. Louis; and in 1898 with a news scoop on Admiral Dewey's battle with the Spanish fleet in Manila Bay. He demonstrated himself to be a great reporter, and in 1898 was promoted to be the *Tribune's* managing editor. Previously he had served as assistant city editor and city editor.

Keeley's marriage in 1895 was to a journalist, Gertrude Small, who had been a reporter on the *Boston Post* and had worked on the *Tribune* for two years.

Along with William Randolph Hearst, Keeley "departmentalized" the *Tribune,* introducing separate divisions relating to health, advice to the lovelorn, sports, dietetics, travel, and cooking.

In 1910 Keeley became general manager of the *Tribune* with complete authority over all of its operations. A royal battle erupted when the paper set out to expose political corruption and bribing of leading politicians, but Keeley survived libel suits and came out with increased standing.

In 1914, Keeley's long tenure with the *Tribune* ended. Joseph Medill Patterson and Robert R. McCormick were ready to take control. With support from wealthy bankers, Keeley bought the *Chicago Record-Herald* in 1914. Four years later, he sold the *Herald* to Hearst, who combined it with his paper to become the *Herald and Examiner.* Keeley never held another newspaper position.

SAMUEL KEIMER
1688–1739

When Ben Franklin, runaway apprentice, went to Philadelphia he planned to start a newspaper. Another Philadelphia printer, Samuel Keimer, got the jump on him by establishing a paper in 1728 with the strange title of *The Universal Instructor in All Arts and Sciences: and Pennsylvania Gazette,* a major portion of which was filled with material reprinted from *Chamber's Cyclopaedia.* Extracts were printed, too, of *Defoe's Religious Courtship,* the first serial story in an American newspaper. In 1729, Franklin bought the paper and changed the title to *Pennsylvania Gazette.* Keimer was an eccentric and religious enthusiast.

ANSEL NASH KELLOGG
1832–1886

Ansel Nash Kellogg was born in Reading, Pennsylvania, but grew up in New York. He went to Portage, Wisconsin, in 1854 to work for the *Northern Republic.* The following year he moved to Baraboo (Wisconsin), where he edited and published the *Baraboo Republic* until 1862.

The numerous local newspapers in the Midwest, such as the *Republic,* were mainly four-page weeklies with small circulations. Ordinarily, there would be a page of local news, some political comments, and the remaining space would be filled with fiction, poetry, and entertainment features clipped from other newspapers and magazines. In 1861 Kellogg made arrangements with the *Wisconson State Journal* in Madison to supply him with supplements reporting war news. The supplements were folded into the *Republic.* The idea spread quickly and other papers began to adopt this economical device. A competing syndicate was set up by the *Evening Wisconsin* in Milwaukee. By 1880 more than three thousand weeklies were being supplied with readyprints by twenty-one companies.

Kellogg decided that it was a strategic time to establish a syndicated service independent of any newspaper connection. He sold the *Republic* and moved to Chicago, where he bought the *Chicago Western Railroad Gazette,* and began a new venture, readyprint "insides." Orders for the service began to come in and by August 1865 Kellogg's organization became the first continuous independent syndicate to print from typeset exclusively for weekly papers. The sheets were filled with features and entertainment items, to which were later added news and advertisements. In 1865, Kellogg began publishing the *Publishers' Auxiliary* containing trade news of interest to publishers. By the end of the year Kellogg was supplying his sheets to fifty-three papers in four states. In 1972 he bought a St. Louis syndicate that was supplying 116 papers.

At the time of Kellogg's death in 1886, the Kellogg corporation was providing about 1,400 papers with readyprints and thousands more with stereotyped plates, a technological device improved by Kellogg and his associates in the 1870s. The service was viewed with contempt by "all home print" papers, but as Mott notes, the material "was sometimes of excellent quality to the small country publisher with slender resources."

MURRAY KEMPTON
1918–

Murray Kempton was born in Baltimore. After graduating from Johns Hopkins University he became an organizer for the International Ladies Garment Workers Union in Peekskill, New York. In 1941, he worked as publicity director for the American Labor party. The following year he joined the staff of the *New York Post* as a labor reporter. Almost at once, however, Kempton entered the U.S. Army and saw two years of combat service in the Pacific.

After his discharge from military service, Kempton was a reporter for the Wilmington (North Carolina) *Star* (1946–47). He returned to the *Post* from 1947 to 1949 as assistant labor editor and columnist. Topics of main concern for him were the McCarthy era, the black struggle for civil rights in the South, the activities of right-wing extremists, and other liberal causes.

In 1963, Kempton left the *Post* to accept a job with the *New Republic* as an editor and columnist-at-large, but the following year he signed on as a columnist with the *New York World-Telegram.* When the *World-Telegram* ceased publication in 1966, Kempton returned to the *New York Post* as a columnist. In 1967 he again resigned from the *Post.*

In addition to his regular columns, Kempton has contributed numerous articles to various magazines. He has also appeared as a CBS radio news commentator.

FRANK R. KENT
1877–1958

Frank R. Kent was born in Baltimore. His grandfather owned the *Baltimore Republican.* Kent began his newspaper career as a sportswriter for the *Columbus Enquirer Sun* in Columbus, Georgia. He came back to Baltimore as a reporter for the *American.* In 1900 he joined the *Baltimore Sun,* covering the police beat. When he won promotion to city hall, Kent soon became recognized as a top political reporter. He was sent to Washington in 1910 as the *Sun's* correspondent, but later in the year was brought back to Baltimore to be managing editor of the *Sun.* In 1911, Kent was given added duties as managing editor of the *Evening Sun,* a new paper.

Near the end of World War I, Kent went abroad to cover the closing days of the war and the Paris Peace Conference. His controversial reports stirred up considerable furor in the United States. In 1921 he became the *Sun's* first London correspondent. At the same time he was elected vice president of the company that published the *Sunpaper,* a position he held until age seventy.

Kent's political commentary began in 1922 on the front page of the *Sun.* The column was syndicated to 140 newspapers across the country, starting in 1934. The daily columns were discontinued in 1947, but Kent continued to write a weekly column until his death in 1958.

JAMES J. KILPATRICK
1920–

James J. Kilpatrick was born in Oklahoma City, Oklahoma. He is one of the principal advocates of conservative thought in the nation. According to a recent report, his column, "A Conservative View," is syndicated to four hundred newspapers. His views are being further spread as a contributing editor of the *National Review* and as a television news commentator.

In 1949, Kilpatrick became chief editorial writer of the *Richmond News Leader* and two years later editor-in-chief. As a spokesman for the "Old South," he was a staunch defender of white supremacy and opposed to racial integration in the schools.

Kilpatrick's column, "A Conservative View," began appearing in the *Washington Star* in 1965. The following year he left the *News Leader* and moved to Washington to devote full time to writing. In addition to his thrice-weekly columns and serving as contributing editor of the ultraconservative *National Review,* Kilpatrick wrote regularly for *Human Events, Saturday Review of Literature,* and other periodicals, and a monthly column for *Nation's Business.*

Despite his conservative opinions, Kilpatrick believes in civil rights. In the early 1950s, for example, he campaigned successfully to win a pardon for a black man wrongly sentenced to life imprisonment for a murder he did not commit. When Harper Lee's novel *To Kill a Mockingbird* was banned by a school board, Kilpatrick distributed free copies of the book to children of the school district.

HENRY KING
1842–1915

Henry King was born in Salem, Ohio. He learned the printer's trade after his parents moved to Illinois. For a time he edited and published a weekly newspaper in his hometown of Laharpe. After the Civil War began, he served four years in the Union Army. Soon thereafter he moved to Quincy, Illinois, to serve as editor of a newspaper. In 1869 King went on to Topeka, Kansas, where he edited in succession the *Kansas State Record,* the *Weekly Commonwealth,* and the *Topeka Daily Capital.* He was also at one time editor of the *Kansas Magazine,* a periodical concerned with the literature of the West.

In 1883 King joined the staff of the *St. Louis Globe-Democrat* as editorial writer. He became editor after 1897, making it a conservative force in American journalism. He remained editor of the *Globe-Democrat* until three weeks before his death.

King was keenly interested in education for journalism and wrote and lectured on the subject, promoting the idea of a school of journalism at the University of Missouri.

WILLIAM BURNET KINNEY
1799–1880

William Kinney was born in Speedwell, New Jersey. In the beginning he considered careers in the military and law, but his interest was in the direction of literature. In 1820 he became editor of the *New Jersey Eagle,* a weekly in Newark, New Jersey. He moved to New York in 1825 to serve as literary advisor to Harper & Brothers. One of his interests in New York was to aid in the organization of the Mercantile Library, of which he was librarian for a time. About ten years later he returned to Newark as editor of the *Newark Daily Advertiser,* the only daily paper in the state. Kinney became the largest stockholder and merged the paper with the *Sentinel of Freedom.*

As a reward for his newspaper's strong support of the Whig party, President Tyler appointed Kinney as the U.S. representative to the court of Sardinia at Turin in 1850. He returned to Newark in 1865, but did not again engage in journalism.

GEORGE KNAPP
1814–1883

George Knapp was born in Montgomery, New York. At the age of twelve he became an apprentice in the business office of the *Missouri Republican,* the oldest newspaper in English west of the Mississippi River. Knapp later was proprietor of the book and job printing department and in 1837 succeeded to part-ownership of the paper. He was publisher of the *Republican* until his death, making it the most influential paper in the Midwest and a leader in the nation. At the time of his death in 1883, he was the oldest newspaperman in St. Louis, and for years afterward his family continued to direct the policies of the *Republican.*

Knapp was a public-spirited citizen. He was mainly responsible for the building of the Eads bridge, the first Mississippi bridge at St. Louis.

SAMUEL KNEELAND
1697–1769

What Mott calls "the true successor" of the *Boston Courant* was Samuel Kneeland's *New-England Weekly Journal of Boston,* started in 1727. After a few months, Kneeland turned the printing over to a partner and devoted himself to editing. The *Journal* attracted contributions from leading New England literary figures and ran human interest stories, rather than dealing with politics. It also printed a good deal of news from abroad and from the other colonies. In 1741, the *Journal* bought the old *Gazette* and merged it with the *Journal,* the first American newspaper consolidation. Kneeland was a native of Boston.

JOHN S. KNIGHT
1894-1981

John S. Knight was born in Akron, Ohio. One of his claims to fame was to assemble the largest newspaper chain in the United States. His father was a prominent Akron editor, controlling the *Beacon-Journal.* Knight saw military service in World War I. After some delay he went to work for his father's paper in 1920 and in 1925 he was named managing editor of the *Beacon-Journal.* Stiff competition had to be faced at once from a Scripps–Howard newspaper, the evening *Times-Press.* Other problems resulted from the death of Knight's father in 1933, but Knight kept his paper operating amid the severe economic depression that struck Akron.

The Knight newspaper chain began in 1937, when Knight bought a Florida paper, the *Miami Herald.* The next year, the rival paper, the *Times-Press* was added. The next step was the *Detroit Free Press,* secured in 1940. In 1944, after Frank Knox's death, the *Chicago Daily News* was offered for sale and joined the Knight empire. In 1959, the *Chicago Daily News* was sold to Marshall Field IV, but two Philadelphia papers, the *Inquirer* and the *Daily News,* were bought in 1970. Further, in 1974 the Knight papers acquired the Ridder group of nineteen newspapers, mainly in Western states. By the late 1970s the Knight–Ridder chain held thirty-five dailies in seventeen states, with a total circulation of 25 million and annual revenues of more than a billion dollars. A number of rival papers in Chicago, Detroit, Philadelphia, and Miami had been forced to suspend publication in the face of this strong competition.

FRANK KNOX
1874-1944

William Franklin Knox (later shortened to Frank Knox) was born in Boston. He had three periods of military service, first in the Spanish-American War as one of Theodore Roosevelt's Rough Riders; second, during World War I as a major in the 78th Division; and finally as secretary of the navy in World War II.

Knox's first newspaper experience was as a reporter for the *Grand Rapids Herald*. This job gave him basic training as a reporter, city editor, and circulation manager. In 1902 he and a partner purchased the *Evening Journal* in Sault Ste. Marie, Michigan, changing the title later to the *Evening News*. About 1912, Knox moved east and founded a new progressive paper, the *Manchester* (New Hampshire) *Leader*. A competing paper, the *Manchester Union,* was taken over. The *Union* covered state news while the *Leader* concentrated on local news.

In 1927 Knox accepted an offer to become publisher of the Hearst newspapers in Boston, the *Boston American, Sunday American,* and *Advertiser*. Knox resigned this position in 1930 when he disagreed with Hearst's business methods. The step by which Knox made his most permanent impact on American journalism was taken in 1931 when he bought a controlling interest in the *Chicago Daily News*. He revitalized that major newspaper during the Depression years.

In 1940 Knox was appointed secretary of the navy by President Franklin Roosevelt. He was directed to create a two-ocean navy and his administration was successful in making the U.S. fleet the most powerful in history. Knox died in office in 1944. The *Chicago Daily News* was sold first to John S. Knight and then to Marshall Field IV, in 1959. It ceased publication in 1978.

JOHN ARMOY KNOX
1850–1906

John Armoy Knox, born in Armoy, Ireland, belonged to a breed of American humorists popular in the nineteenth century, such as Bill Nye, Opie Read, Robert J. Burdette, and Eugene Field. With a partner, Alexander Edwin Sweet, Knox began a weekly paper, *Texas Siftings,* in Austin in 1881. The paper printed some local news, but it was mainly filled with humorous anecdotes and proverbs. The *Siftings* soon attracted a national audience; popular pieces from the paper were often reprinted. The partners moved to New York in 1885; Knox joined the Sunday *World* and Sweet the Sunday *Herald*.

Knox contributed weekly letters to papers in Boston, New York, San Francisco, Chicago, Toronto, Milwaukee, Philadelphia, and elsewhere. In 1888, the letters were collected and published in London under the title of *Texas Siftings Afloat,* a great literary success. In the same year, Knox scored a hit with a lecture on humor in Steinway Hall, New York.

Knox and Sweet sold *Texas Siftings* in 1895. Knox moved to Atlanta to become editor-manager of the *Herald,* but after two years returned to his home in New York. He spent his last years writing articles for newspapers and magazines.

MOSES KOENIGSBERG
1879–1945

Moses Koenigsberg had a remarkable journalistic career, editing, owning, or reporting for twenty newspapers, and established the first modern newspaper features and comics syndicates, reaching a circulation of 16 million readers on weekdays and 25 million on Sundays. He became a reporter for the *San Antonio Times* in 1891, after adventures in Mexico. He lost his job after he exposed crooked prosecuting attorneys. For a short time Koenigsberg worked for the *Houston Age.* He was then editor of the *Texas World.* He moved east and became a reporter for the *New Orleans Item,* followed by a project with three partners to launch a newspaper, the *Evening Star,* in San Antonio. The *Star* was a financial failure and Koenigsberg jumped from one newspaper to another in Kansas City, St. Louis, Chicago, Pittsburgh, and New York City.

In 1903 Koenigsberg became city editor of Hearst's *Chicago American,* specializing in sensational stories. Later he was sent on by Hearst to work on the *New York Journal* and then to Boston to manage the *Boston American.* The Boston paper was a financial disaster and Hearst sent Koenigsberg on a tour of the nation's larger cities to appraise newspapers that could be bought. Hearst's ambition was to own a paper in every major urban center.

At age thirty-five, Koenigsburg decided to establish his own feature syndicate. Still allied with Hearst, the Newspaper Feature Service began in 1913 and in 1915 another Hearst service, King Features Syndicate was established. Koenigsberg was given another assignment in 1919, when Hearst placed him in charge of the International News Service. Soon he was managing eight different Hearst services.

Disagreements with Hearst led to Koenigsberg's resignation from the organization in 1928. His final undertakings were trying to build a newspaper chain with the backing of a wealthy department store owner, serving as executive director of the Song Writers' Protective Association, and helping to produce a Sunday magazine for the *Philadelphia Inquirer.*

SHEPARD KOLLOCK
1750–1839

Shepard Kollock was born in Lewes, Delaware. He learned the printing business in the office of the *Pennsylvania Chronicle* under his uncle
William Goddard. In 1779, Kollock began publication of a newspaper, the
New Jersey Journal, at Chatham, New Jersey, to support the Revolutionary cause. He also published the *United States Almanac* from 1779 to
1783.

After the evacuation of New York, Kollock moved there and for three
years published the *New York Gazetteer,* starting in December 1783. In
partnership with his brother-in-law, Shelly Arnett, he also began the *Intelligencer* in New Brunswick, New Jersey. The paper was moved to
Elizabethtown, New Jersey, in 1785, and renamed the *New Jersey Journal.*
Kollock continued to publish the *Journal* until 1818. During a period from
1789 to 1791, he also issued the *Christian's, Scholar's, and Farmer's
Magazine,* mainly consisting of serials.

Kollock was active as a book publisher, especially of religious books.

EDWARD JAMES KOPPEL
1940–

Ted Koppel was born in Lancashire, England, the son of Jewish
parents who had fled Nazi Germany in 1938. When Koppel was thirteen the
family emigrated to New York City. At Syracuse University he had his first
broadcasting experience on the campus radio station. He obtained his
Master's degree in journalism in 1962 at Stanford University. The following
year he joined the staff of WABC radio in New York. Soon he was assigned
to do general news summaries.

In 1964 Koppel covered his first presidential nominating conventions
and the same year he reported on the civil rights movement in Selma,
Alabama. In 1967 ABC News transferred him to Vietnam and he changed
from radio to television broadcasting over the network's Saigon bureau.
Coming back to the United States, Koppel was promoted to Miami bureau
chief, where he reported on political developments in Latin America. He
was sent back to the Far East as Hong Kong bureau chief in 1969. For a
year and a half, he traveled throughout the Pacific region, from Vietnam
to Australia.

In 1971, Koppel was promoted by ABC News to be chief diplomatic
correspondent, with Washington as his home base. Global travels thereafter included accompanying President Nixon to China in 1972, return to

China with President Ford in 1975, and accompanying Secretary of State Henry Kissinger in his shuttle diplomacy missions around the world. In addition to his other assignments, Koppel accepted the post of anchorman for the evening program, "ABC Saturday Night News."

In 1980 ABC producers transferred Koppel's program to the ABC News "Nightline," focusing on late-breaking stories, with some emphasis on foreign policy matters. He accompanied President Reagan on his trip to China in 1984.

JOSEPH KRAFT
1924-1986

Joseph Kraft was born in South Orange, New Jersey. He had an early start in journalism serving as an editorial writer for the *Washington Post* (1951–52), and then as a staff writer for the *New York Times* for four years. Kraft returned to Washington in 1962 as the Washington correspondent for *Harper's*. The following year his column began to be syndicated. Beginning in 1984 he started to work for the *Los Angeles Times,* while continuing to write from Washington. He was a speech writer for John F. Kennedy.

ARTHUR KROCK
1886-1974

Arthur Krock was born in Glasgow, Kentucky. His first newspaper job was as police reporter for the *Louisville Herald*. The following year he became an assistant to the Kentucky correspondent of the *Cincinnati Enquirer*. Krock left the *Herald* in 1908 and joined the Associated Press in Louisville as night editor, and from there proceeded to be Washington correspondent for the *Louisville Courier-Journal* and the *Louisville Times*. Krock returned to Louisville in 1915 as editorial manager of both papers. The 1918–19 peace conference took him to Paris, from where he contributed syndicated articles to various newspapers.

In 1919 Krock became editor-in-chief of the *Louisville Times,* a position that he held until 1923, when he became assistant to Ralph Pulitzer, president of the *New York World*. He remained with the *World* until 1927, when he joined the editorial staff of the *New York Times,* a change that shaped the remainder of his career. Krock was Washington correspondent for the *Times* from 1931 until 1966. In addition to supervising the twenty or more reporters in the Washington office, Krock wrote a column of analytical and interpretive comment, "In the Nation," three times a week for the *Times*'s editorial page. The column became a widely read and influential newspaper feature. During the course of his career Krock won four Pulitzer Prizes for his reporting.

CHARLES KURALT
1934–

Charles Kuralt was born in Wilmington, North Carolina. After high school he entered the University of North Carolina where he edited the campus newspaper, the *Daily Tarheel.* He became a reporter on the *Charlotte* (North Carolina) *News* in 1955. Two years later he was recruited by CBS to handle general assignments. His report on Cuba impressed the network's top management, leading them to choose him as head of the newly established Latin American bureau, a post that he held until 1963. The next step was appointment as chief West Coast correspondent.

In the mid–1960s, Kuralt spent much time abroad, in the Middle East, and served four tours of duty in Vietnam.

Kuralt became famous for his "On the Road" stories (dealing with human-interest matters) that turned up during his extensive tours around the country. In 1980, he became anchorman for CBS's "Sunday Morning" news program.

WILLIAM MACKAY LAFFAN
1848–1909

William Laffan was born in Dublin, Ireland. At age twenty he went to San Francisco and became city editor of the *San Francisco Chronicle* immediately after it was established in 1868. Later he was managing editor of the *San Francisco Bulletin.*

Laffan moved to Baltimore in 1870, first as a reporter and then editor of the *Baltimore Daily Bulletin.* This newspaper, later entitled the *Evening Bulletin,* was mainly concerned with art, literature, and science and was subsequently acquired by Laffan.

In 1877 Laffan went on to New York to serve as drama critic on the *New York Sun,* under Charles A. Dana. Thereafter, except for two years as art editor and general representative of Harper Brothers in London, his career was with the *Sun.* With the aid of J. Pierpont Morgan, he bought control of the *Sun,* supervised every department, and wrote occasional editorials.

GEORGE THOMAS LANIGAN
1845–1886

George Lanigan was a native of St. Charles in Canada. As a boy, he had learned telegraphy and had sent special correspondence to the *New York Herald*. Later he moved to Chicago and became a writer for the *Chicago Times*. About 1870 he was employed in St. Louis by the *St. Louis Daily Globe* and then returned to Chicago, where he wrote for the *Chicago Tribune* and was appointed Western correspondent for the *New York World*. In 1874 Lanigan joined the *World's* editorial staff, where he remained for the next eight years. His fluency in French led him to specialize on foreign news, but he also wrote editorials, political and literary articles, and humorous verse.

In 1883 Lanigan became editor of the *Rochester Post-Express*, although he resigned the next year in a political dispute and joined the staff as editor of the *Philadelphia Record* shortly before his death.

RING LARDNER
1885–1933

Ringgold Wilmer Lardner, popularly known as Ring Lardner, was born in Niles, Michigan. His start in journalism came with the *South Bend* (Indiana) *Times,* supposedly as a sports editor, but his actual duties were broader: drama critic, courthouse and police station activities, and anything else related to news. More specialized was Lardner's next job, the sports desk of the *Chicago Inter-Ocean*. At the end of the 1908 season, he transferred to the *Tribune* and in 1910 to *Sporting News* in St. Louis, where he remained only two months before becoming a baseball writer for the *Boston American*. His stay in Boston was also brief and Lardner returned to Chicago, first as a copyreader for the *Chicago American* and then as a sports reporter on the *Examiner*. In 1913 he was approached by the *Tribune* to write a popular column "In the Wake of the News." Lardner accepted and his inimitable style attracted many readers. From then on he produced both his daily column and short stories. When Lardner's contract with the *Tribune* expired in 1919, he did not renew it. Instead, he signed with the Bell Syndicate to write a weekly column. During the next eight years, he traveled widely over the country covering major sporting events. He also tried his hand at writing plays. His *June Moon,* in which he teamed with George S. Kaufman, was a Broadway success. In 1932 Lardner wrote a series of autobiographical articles for the *Saturday Evening Post* and the following year a series of columns on radio for the *New Yorker*.

Lardner was widely admired for his use of American vernacular slang, such as in his book *You Know Me, Al,* letters from an ignorant and arrogant baseball player. In such writings he displayed his familiarity with colorful American character types and his mastery of the American vernacular speech.

DAVID LAWRENCE
1888–1973

David Lawrence was born in Philadelphia. For three years he earned money for his college education by working as a reporter for the *Buffalo Express*. While a student at Princeton, he wrote about sports and college activities for several newspapers, and following graduation was employed by the Associated Press on its Washington staff. For two years he covered White House affairs, and was sent to Mexico (1911–12), to report on the Madero and Orozco revolutions. Later assignments were Woodrow Wilson's presidential campaign and the White House during the Wilson administration. After the start of World War I the Associated Press placed Lawrence in charge of all war news emanating from Washington.

Lawrence resigned from the Associated Press in 1915 to become Washington correspondent for the *New York Evening Post,* a position that he held for four years. After the 1918 armistice, he covered the peace negotiations in Paris and accompanied Wilson on his trips to Italy and England. The *Evening Post* connection ceased in 1919 and Lawrence organized the Consolidated Press Association to furnish a feature and financial news service for large dailies. Another enterprise by Lawrence, in 1926, was the *United States Daily,* limited to news of government and texts of official actions. In 1929 the paper added news of state governments.

Lawrence's several organizations were changed in 1933. The Associated Press and the North American Newspaper Alliance took over the Consolidated Press and the daily newspaper became the weekly *United States News.* In 1946, the *World Report* was launched and in 1948 the Lawrence publications were merged to create *U.S. News & World Report.*

Lawrence was highly criticial of the New Deal and liberal government policies. His views dominated his columns, magazine articles, and five books that he published.

VICTOR F. LAWSON
1850–1925

Victor Lawson, son of Norwegian parents, was born in Chicago and spent his entire life in that city. When his father died in 1874 his estate included a partnership in the *Skandinaven,* a Norwegian-language daily. Lawson took over the business management. His interest in newspaper work began as a youth when he was employed in the circulation department of the *Chicago Evening Journal.*

By coincidence, the *Chicago Daily News* occupied the same building as the *Skandinaven* and was facing serious financial problems. Within six months Lawson bought the struggling paper, retaining Melville E. Stone, one of the founders as editor. Under Lawson's efficient management the *News* made rapid progress. In 1878 the *Evening Post and Mail* was taken over with its Associated Press franchise. A morning edition, the *Chicago Record,* was brought out in 1881. By 1885 the *Daily News* had reached a regular circulation of one hundred thousand, exceeded only by the *New York World.* From the beginning the *News* included popular fiction, household tips, consumer advice, and other information designed to appeal to a majority of readers. By 1894 the *Daily News* reached a circulation of two hundred thousand and dominated the afternoon field.

Lawson was a strong supporter of the Associated Press, of which he was president from 1894 to 1900 and director for the remainder of his life. In 1898 he turned his attention to the development of a foreign news service — a gap that he recognized at the time of the Spanish-American War.

The independent policy of the *Daily News* in politics and civil reform, under Lawson's direction, made the paper a powerful influence in Chicago.

ESTHER PAULINE LEDERER
1918–

Esther Pauline Lederer, who writes under the name of "Ann Landers," was born in Sioux City, Iowa. She is the author of one of the most widely read advice columns, appearing in over nine hundred newspapers across the country. Ann Landers receives about a thousand letters daily and dispenses advice on a vast variety of marital and other personal problems.

One of Ann Landers's chief rivals in the advice business is Abigail Van Buren, "Dear Abby," who is her identical twin sister, Pauline Esther Friedman Phillips. The two sisters began their columns in the mid-1950s.

JAMES LEHRER
1934–

Jim Lehrer was born in Wichita, Kansas. While in high school in Beaumont, Texas, he covered sports for the school newspaper. Later, in San Antonio, he edited Jefferson High School's student newspaper. Lehrer graduated in 1956 from the University of Missouri with a degree in journalism. A tour of duty in the Marine Corps, mainly spent on Okinawa, followed.

After his discharge, Lehrer was hired as a political reporter for the *Dallas Morning News.* Angered by the paper's refusal to publish certain controversial articles, he resigned and was immediately employed by a rival paper, the *Dallas Times Herald.* In 1968 he was named city editor of the *Times Herald,* but remained only a year, expecting to support himself by writing fiction. He entered the field of broadcast journalism in 1970 as consultant for a public television station in Dallas. In 1972 he moved to Washington, D.C., for a position with the Public Broadcasting Service, but resigned within a year due to lack of funding for his program.

A turning point for Lehrer came in 1973 when he met Robert MacNeil, who had been a reporter for NBC-TV and the BBC. MacNeil and Lehrer coanchored the PBS telecasts of the Senate Watergate hearings. In 1975 WNET, the public television affiliate for New York, offered MacNeil the opportunity to produce a nightly news program. MacNeil chose Lehrer as his coanchorman. The plan was to focus on a major news story each night and to interview a limited number of guests. When the program was inaugurated in 1975, it was entitled "The MacNeil/Lehrer Report," and later "The MacNeil/Lehrer News Hour." It was regarded as an alternative to network news. The success of the program was demonstrated by the fact that it was reaching a viewing audience of 12 million a week within a few years. Judy Woodruff and Charlayne Hunter-Gault were added to the team. The program has received numerous awards for broadcasting excellence.

In the first of the 1988 debates between presidential candidates George Bush and Michael Dukakis, Jim Lehrer acted as moderator.

MAX LERNER
1902–

Max Lerner has successfully combined journalism and teaching during his long career. He was born in Minsk, Russia, and brought to the United States at age five. Representing the "Left Wing of American democracy," Lerner is recognized as an outstanding political commentator. He holds degrees from Yale, Washington University in St. Louis, and Brookings. At age twenty-five he joined the editorial staff of the *Encyclopedia of the Social Sciences,* first as assistant editor and then as managing editor. For two years, starting in 1936, Lerner was editor of the *Nation,* the country's oldest liberal journal. Teaching appointments at Sarah Lawrence College, Wellesley, Harvard, Williams College, and Brandeis University filled some of the years from 1932 to 1943.

Lerner's journalistic activities continued. He was a contributor to the *New Republic, Yale Law Journal,* and *Harvard Law Review,* and author of several books expounding his economic and political views. In 1943 Lerner became editorial director for the New York newspaper *PM,* an idealist journal that only lasted eight years.

FRANK LESLIE
1821–1880

Frank Leslie, born in Ipswich, England, showed his genius as a wood engraver by age thirteen. "Frank Leslie" was a pseudonym; his real name was Henry Carter. His engravings caught the attention of the *Illustrated London News* and at age twenty-one he became superintendent of that journal's engraving department.

Persuaded that there was wider scope for his talents in the United States, Leslie emigrated to New York in 1848. Many of his full-page engravings appeared in 1852 in *Gleason's Pictorial,* published in Boston. By 1853 he was back in New York to become superintendent of a new publication, the *Illustrated News.* Shortly, the *Illustrated News* merged with *Gleason's Pictorial* and a new publication was born: *Leslie's Ladies' Gazette of Fashion and Fancy Needlework of Paris, London and New York,* first issued in January 1854. The next venture, destined to insure Leslie's enduring fame, *Leslie's Illustrated Newspaper,* was launched on December 15, 1855. The emphasis, for the first time, was on current news events, presented in both pictures and text.

The Civil War brought Leslie his greatest opportunity. A corps of correspondents and artists was employed and scattered all over the country to illustrate battles, sieges, marches, and other war incidents. Leslie's paper became phenomenally popular, making the owner wealthy.

A new method was introduced in Leslie's engraving department, making it possible to reproduce scenes and occurrences in the shortest possible time.

Leslie's establishment grew. At one time he was publishing eleven different magazines and newspapers, employing several hundred persons:

the *Ladies Journal,* the *Boys and Girls Weekly, Chimney Corner, Boys of America, Pleasant Hours,* the *Budget of Fun,* the *Jolly Joke, Chatterbox, Illustrated Almanac,* the *Sunday Magazine,* and the *Popular Monthly.* A German-language magazine, *Illustriek Zeitung,* was begun in 1857.

After the Civil War, Leslie's magazine campaigned against social ills but also became a scandal sheet. The *New York Times* described it as "a most wicked and disgusting sheet." Leslie retorted that he was indebted to the *Times* for the news items on which his pictures were based.

Following Leslie's death in 1880, his publishing empire was taken over by his second wife, Miriam Folline Leslie. She reduced the number of periodicals to six. In 1889 she sold the *Illustrated Newspaper.* Altogether, as one critic noted, "she was a better editor, marketer, and business manager" than her husband (who had ended up in bankruptcy) had been.

FRANCIS ELLINGTON LEUPP
1849–1918

Francis Leupp was born in New York City. After graduating from Williams College and the Columbia Law School, he served under William Cullen Bryant, as assistant editor of the *New York Evening Post.* In 1878 he bought an interest in the *Syracuse Herald* and became its editor. In 1889 Leupp was placed in charge of the *Evening Post's* Washington bureau. At the same time he represented the *Nation.* He held this position until 1904. From 1892 to 1895 Leupp also edited *Good Government,* the official organ of the National Civil Service Reform League, and wrote for the *Outlook.*

Throughout his career Leupp took a keen interest in the American Indian. As Indian commissioner (1903–9), he worked for justice and betterment of the Indian population.

Leupp's reputation is based chiefly on his articles for the *Evening Post* and the *Nation,* giving him a high rating among Washington correspondents.

ALFRED H. LEWIS
1857–1914

Alfred Henry Lewis, born in Cleveland, Ohio, began his career in law, serving as Cleveland's prosecuting attorney in 1880. Later he roamed the Southwest gathering the stories and experiences that he eventually wove into his popular newspaper fiction, the "Old Cattleman" stories.

In New Mexico, Lewis had his first experience with newspapers when he became editor and staff of the *Mora County Pioneer.* While the regular editor was ill, he also took charge of the *Las Vegas* (New Mexico) *Optic.* In 1885, Lewis went on to Kansas City and at the urging of his brother, city editor of the *Kansas City Times,* he began to write his "Old Cattleman" stories. William Rockhill Nelson offered him a reporting job on the *Kansas City Star* in 1890.

After a year on the *Star,* Lewis went to Washington, D.C., as correspondent for the *Chicago Times.* When the *Times* was sold to the *Chicago Herald* he became chief of the Washington bureau of Hearst's *New York Journal.* In 1898 Lewis moved to New York, planning to devote his time to freelance political, crime, and fictional writing. For about two years, he edited the *Verdict,* a weekly Democratic paper. Lewis was a vitriolic and sensational writer whose style was in tune with the tastes of middle-class readers of his time.

ANTHONY LEWIS
1927–

Anthony Lewis was born in New York City. From 1952 to 1955 he was a reporter for the *Washington Daily News.* He then joined the *New York Times* Washington bureau, where he remained until 1964. An overseas assignment followed, as chief of the *Times's* London bureau (1965–72). Lewis began writing his column in 1969 and has continued it.

Lewis won Pulitzer Prizes for national reporting in 1955 and 1963. He is also the winner of the Lovejoy Award and the Heywood Broun Award.

ABBOTT JOSEPH LIEBLING
1904–1963

A. J. Liebling was once described as "the *New Yorker's* press critic, gourmand, boxing writer, war correspondent, labor reporter, medievalist, Francophile, Chronicler of Broadway, and resident epicure." He was a person of amazing versatility.

Previous to signing on with the *New Yorker,* Liebling had been on the staff of the *New York World Telegram* under Roy Edward. Earlier he had worked for the *Providence Evening Bulletin and Journal.* At one time he worked for Hearst — apparently a disillusioning experience.

After joining the *New Yorker,* Liebling was sent abroad during World

War II as a correspondent in France, England, and North Africa. After 1945 and until his death he wrote a series of columns for the *New Yorker* entitled "The Wayward Press." The columns, highly critical of the American Press, were widely read and provoked much comment, pro and con.

SARA JANE CLARKE LIPPINCOTT
1823–1904

Sara Jane Lippincott, born in Pompey, New York, wrote under the pen name of "Grace Greenwood." Her first published poems appeared in Nathaniel P. Willis's magazine, the *New Mirror*. Willis also published in his *Home Journal* a series of "Letters" by Grace Greenwood—not aware that they were by the same person. Her name became familiar to readers of *Graham's Magazine, Union Magazine,* and other periodicals. In 1849 Grace Greenwood became an editorial assistant for *Godey's Lady's Book,* but she lost the job by offending Southern readers with her antislavery writings. For the next two years she lived in Washington, contributing to the *National Era* and *Saturday Evening Post,* the latter carrying her "Washington Letters," a series that was to continue for the next half-century.

In 1952–53, Grace Greenwood toured Europe, sending back to the *National Era* and *Saturday Evening Post* a series of travel reports, impressions, and interviews with celebrities, later published in book form. Her interest in juvenile literature inspired her in 1853 to establish in Philadelphia the *Little Pilgrim,* one of the first American magazines for children. It continued until 1875.

In the early 1870s, Grace Greenwood settled again in Washington as a correspondent for the *New York Times* and newspapers in Philadelphia, Chicago, and elsewhere. She also contributed stories and essays to *Hearth and Home,* the *Christian Union, Ladies' Home Journal,* and other popular magazines of the postwar period. In 1875 she made a second trip to Europe and contributed a series of letters to the *Independent* on current political and literary affairs.

WALTER LIPPMANN
1889–1974

Walter Lippmann is widely regarded as one of the most influential journalists of the twentieth century. His syndicated column, "Today and Tomorrow," dealing with foreign affairs, politics, and economics, had millions of faithful readers. He was twice awarded a Pulitzer Prize for his reporting on international matters.

Lippmann was a native of New York City, the only son of a wealthy Jewish manufacturer, and a graduate of Harvard University. His exceptional ability was demonstrated early. He was, for example, one of the founders of the *New Republic*, a journal of liberal opinion, in 1914. At the outbreak of World War I, he was appointed assistant to the secretary of war, aided President Wilson in drafting his Fourteen Points, and in July 1918 went to France as a captain of the U.S. Army Intelligence.

From the beginning, Lippmann wielded a facile pen. At age twenty-four he wrote and published *A Preface to Politics*, the first of his many books on politics, morals, economics, personalities, and social life. Theodore Roosevelt was an enthusiastic admirer of the work, and a warm friendship developed between him and Lippmann.

Lippmann's newspaper career began in 1921, when he joined the *New York World*—the last three years as editor. During this period, he wrote brilliant editorials on the Harding scandals, the Scopes evolution trial, the Dawes Plan for German war reparations, and the defects of the Hoover administration. As a result the *World's* editorial page was described as "the brightest lighthouse in United States journalism."

When the Great Depression forced the *World* out of business, Lippmann became a columnist of the *New York Herald-Tribune* "to provide in its ample pages a little corner of mild left-wing philosophy to offset its own conservative columns." He agreed to write four columns weekly on whatever appealed to him in the news of the day. The Lippmann column was syndicated to a large number of newspapers.

Lippmann's most widely read and probably most influential book was *The Good Society*, published only two years prior to the outbreak of World War II. Lippmann's thesis was that America had to make a choice between communism and fascism on the one hand, or unplanned democracy on the other.

Other books by Lippmann included *Public Opinion* (1922), *A Preface to Morals* (1929), *The Cold War* (1947), *The Public Philosophy* (1955), *The Communist World and Ours* (1959), *The Coming Tests with Russia* (1961), and *Western Unity and the Common Market* (1962).

Another famous journalist, James Reston, wrote, "No doubt Walter Lippmann would prefer to be judged by his books on political philosophy, but while philosophy may be his love, journalism has been his mistress, and the amazing thing is that he has managed to be so faithful to both. I know that he has given my generation of newspapermen a wide vision of our duty. He has shown us how to put the event for the day in its proper relationship to the history of yesterday and the dream of tomorrow."

During a career that spanned six decades, Lippmann wrote more than four thousand columns.

DAVID ROSS LOCKE
1833-1888

David Ross Locke, noted American humorist and political satirist, became known under his pen name of "Petroleum Vesuvius Nasby." He was born in Vestal, New York. He began newspaper work at the precocious age of twelve. For five years he was apprenticed with the *Cortland Democrat.* After that he became an itinerant printer and drifted among a number of cities, North and South, including Cleveland and Pittsburgh.

In 1852, with a partner, Locke founded a newspaper at Plymouth, Ohio, the *Plymouth Advertiser.* Later he was publisher of the *Bucyrus* (Ohio) *Journal* and editor of the *Jeffersonian* in Findlay, Ohio. It was there that he first signed a letter, a bitter attack against slavery, with the name Petroleum Vesuvius Nasby. Nasby was an illiterate, hypocritical, cowardly, loafing, lying, dissolute, country preacher, a Copperhead designed to ridicule Copperheads and Democrats. Locke also supported such reform movements as women's rights and Prohibition.

The Nasby letters were immensely popular, making Locke rich and famous. He became principal owner of the *Toledo* (Ohio) *Blade* and managing editor of the *New York Evening Mail.* Offers of political office from Lincoln and Grant were refused. The Nasby letters continued to appear until two months before Locke's death and collections of them in book form were best-sellers.

RICHARD ADAMS LOCKE
1800-1871

Richard Adams Locke was born in Somersetshire, England, and was a graduate of Cambridge University. Two journalistic ventures, the London *Republican,* a prodemocratic journal, and the *Cornucopia* were failures. In 1832, Locke brought himself and his family to New York, where he became a reporter for the *Courier and Enquirer.* There he covered a variety of stories, including the sensational murder trial of Matthias the Prophet in White Plains, New York. Benjamin Day, editor of the *New*

York Sun, was impressed with Locke's talents as a reporter and offered him a job as editorial writer for the *Sun,* an offer he accepted.

In August 1835, Locke wrote for the *Sun* the famous "Moon Hoax" story. The wild tale told of the discovery by Sir John Herschel, with his new telescope at the Cape of Good Hope, of winged men and animals on the moon. The account was sprinkled with astronomical terms and was so well written that it deceived readers. The articles were widely reprinted and the *Sun's* circulation shot up.

Locke resigned from the *Sun* in 1836 and started a penny daily, the *New Era.* When that paper failed to win acceptance, Locke became an editorial writer for the *Brooklyn Daily Eagle* in 1841. He wrote extensively for other papers before dropping out of journalism entirely.

WILLIAM LOEB
1905–1985

William Loeb was born in Washington, D.C., the son of Theodore Roosevelt's private secretary. He described himself as a "nineteenth-century liberal" and a "Teddy Roosevelt conservative." To the world at large, he was viewed as a rock-ribbed right winger.

Loeb began his journalistic career while at Williams College, editing the campus newspaper and working part-time for Springfield (Massachusetts) papers and the *New York World.* Later he was a reporter for the Hearst National News Service. In 1941, he bought the *St. Albans* (Vermont) *Daily Messenger* and the next year the *Burlington* (Massachusetts) *Daily News.* The paper that was to establish his reputation, the *Manchester Union Leader,* was added in 1946. Another acquisition, in 1948, was what became the Sunday edition of the *Union Leader,* the *New Hampshire Sunday news.* Years later in 1957, Loeb founded the *Haverhill* (Massachusetts) *Journal.*

Under Loeb's editorship the *Union Leader* consistently supported conservative causes, defending what Loeb viewed as the traditional American way of life. For similar reasons, he backed conservative candidates for political office, such as Robert Taft, Barry Goldwater, and Senator Joseph McCarthy. Loeb is credited with destroying the presidential candidacy of Senator Edmund Muskie in 1972 by publishing fabricated charges against him and his wife. Loeb made the *Union Leader* the dominant newspaper in New Hampshire and a national force despite the fact that his candidates generally lost.

ROBERTUS DONNELL LOVE
1867-1930

Robertus Donnell Love was born in Irondale, Tennessee. After his family moved to Louisiana, Missouri, Love, at age nineteen, became local editor of the *Louisiana Press,* with wages of five dollars a week. About ten months later he was appointed city editor of the *Wichita* (Kansas) *Daily Journal.*

Love had a forty-three-year career of itinerant journalism, taking him to a variety of cities coast to coast. He was editor of the *Asbury Park* (New Jersey) *Press* (1892–95); Coast correspondent of the *New York Sun* (1895); founder of the *Asbury Park Daily Star* (1896); established *Seashore Life* at Asbury Park; managing editor of the *New London* (Connecticut) *Day* (1896–99); and reporter for the *St. Louis Post-Dispatch* (1900–1903).

Love was in charge of press bureaus at the Louisiana Purchase, Lewis and Clark, and Jamestown expositions in 1905. In 1905 he was an editorial writer for the *Portland Oregonian* and columnist for the *Los Angeles Times.* He returned to the *Post-Dispatch* as feature writer (1911–13). From 1913 to 1918, Love was in Oklahoma as Sunday editor of the *Tulsa Democrat* (1917–18), and editor of the *Ardmore Admoreite* (1918–20). For a short period in 1921 he was on the editorial staff of the *Kansas City Post,* and then returned to St. Louis, where he was Sunday magazine writer (1922–25) and literary editor (1925–26) of the *Post-Dispatch.* Love's final position was with the *St. Louis Globe-Democrat* first as Sunday magazine writer (1926–28) and then literary editor until his death in 1930.

ELIJAH PARISH LOVEJOY
1802-1837

Elijah Lovejoy was born in Albion, Maine, and graduated from Colby College in 1826. He then moved to St. Louis to begin newspaper work. In 1829 he became editor of a political paper supporting Henry Clay for president. Thereafter he turned to the ministry, studied at Princeton Theological Seminary, and was licensed as a Presbyterian minister. He returned to St. Louis in 1833 to edit a Presbyterian weekly, the *St. Louis Observer.* The paper carried on a campaign against slavery, intemperance, and "popery." The idea of gradual emancipation of slaves, advocated by Lovejoy, was wholly unacceptable to Missouri slaveowners.

Threatened by mob violence, Lovejoy removed his paper to Alton, Illinois, across the river from St. Louis, where his press was destroyed three times in one year. A fourth press was received on November 6, 1837, but the following night a mob attacked the building. Attempts were made by Lovejoy and his friends to resist the attack. He was shot five times and expired immediately.

The news of Lovejoy's death made a tremendous stir in the North and greatly strengthened abolitionist sentiment. Some historians are inclined to believe that Lovejoy's death was the beginning of the Civil War. President John Quincy Adams called Lovejoy America's first martyr to press freedom. Lovejoy's brother, Owen, was elected to Congress in 1856 and became one of the most ardent abolitionists.

The sesquicentennial of Lovejoy's martyrdom was marked by a special convocation at Colby College, his alma mater. Since 1952, Colby has awarded the Elijah Parish Lovejoy award to a newspaper reporter, editor, or publisher who continues the Lovejoy tradition. Former award winners include some of the nation's most distinguished journalists.

CLARE BOOTHE LUCE
1903-1987

Clare Boothe Luce, who achieved fame as a playwright, journalist, and political figure, was born in New York City. She entered the field of magazine publishing in 1928 and became associate editor of *Vogue* in 1930. She was managing editor of *Vanity Fair* (1933-34). A turning point in her life was her marriage to Henry R. Luce in 1935.

As a war correspondent during World War II, Luce traveled in Europe as a journalist under contract to *Life*. She toured China with her husband in 1941 to report on war conditions there. In February 1942, she visited Africa, India, and Burma, where she interviewed leading personalities and visited front lines wherever possible.

In 1940 Luce became an active Republican and in 1943-47 served as a congresswoman from Connecticut. President Eisenhower appointed her ambassador to Italy (1953-56), but she resigned the post in 1956 because of ill health. She was confirmed as ambassador to Brazil in 1959, but resigned the appointment because of a political controversy.

Luce was a successful Broadway playwright; she was author of *The Women* (1936) and other popular plays.

HENRY ROBINSON LUCE
1898-1967

Henry Luce was born in Tengchow, China, the son of a Presbyterian missionary. He spent his early years there. He attended Yale and Oxford and spent a short time as a reporter for the *Chicago Daily News* and the *Baltimore News.* In cooperation with Briton Hadden, in 1923, he founded the weekly news magazine *Time.* After Hadden's death, *Fortune* was established in 1930, *Life* in 1936, and *Sports Illustrated* in 1954. *Architectural Forum, House and Garden,* and Time-Life Books were added, to make Luce head of one of the world's largest publishing empires.

Luce's strong conservative convictions were reflected in his publications. He was a staunch Republican, a defender of big business, a foe of big labor, a strong supporter of Nationalist China, and an aggressive opponent of Soviet Russia and Communist China in the Cold War.

Luce's varied enterprises — which included his magazines, eight radio and television stations, paper companies, and real estate investments — made him enormously wealthy. At the time of his death in 1967, his publishing empire was estimated to have a market value of $690 million. The combined circulation of his four leading magazines exceeded 14 million copies.

JAY ANTHONY LUKAS
1933-

J. Anthony Lukas was born in New York City. While at Harvard he was assistant managing editor of the *Harvard Crimson,* the campus daily newspaper. After a two-year tour of military service in Tokyo, he joined the staff of the *Baltimore Sun,* covering stories of local interest over a four-year period. In 1962 he was hired by the *New York Times* and sent to Zaire to report on the emerging nation of West Africa. Next, Lukas was transferred to the *Times* India bureau, where he watched developments in India, Pakistan, and Sri Lanka, with occasional side trips to Australia, Japan, and Korea, from 1965 to 1967.

After five years overseas, Lukas returned to the United States, to be assigned to the *Times's* metropolitan bureau. He took a year off (1968–69) for study on a Nieman Fellowship at Harvard. When he returned to the *Times* he was appointed a roving national correspondent, based in Chicago. Lukas left daily reporting in 1970 to become staff writer for the *New York Times Magazine.* He resigned from that position in 1971 and was associated with two short-lived journals: *More,* a monthly magazine designed to take a critical view of the news media, and *New Times,* an "alternative" news magazine.

Over the next several years, Lukas devoted many hours to interviews and to writing a kind of social history, entitled *Common Ground: A Turbulent Decade in the Lives of Three American Families* (1985).

MATTHEW LYON
1749-1822

Matthew Lyon was born in Dublin, Ireland. At an early age he was apprenticed to a printer and bookbinder in Dublin. In 1749 he emigrated to America. His extraordinary career thereafter marked him as an inventor, soldier, politician, publisher, founder of the town of Fair Haven, Vermont, player of a key role in creating the state of Vermont, two terms as a U.S. congressman, and casting the decisive vote that made Thomas Jefferson U.S. president. He was a member of the Green Mountain Boys, a revolutionary troop who defeated the British in several important engagements. When war was declared, Lyon was commissioned a second lieutenant under General Horatio Gates.

In 1793, Lyon started a weekly newspaper in Rutland, Vermont, the *Farmers' Library,* which was sold the following year and the title changed to *Rutland Herald: A Register of the Times.* The *Fair Haven Gazette,* was established by Lyon in 1795. He was adamantly opposed to the Sedition Act, and used the *Vermont Journal* for his political criticism. Lyon also began publishing a magazine as a vehicle for his news, the *Scourge of Aristocracy and Repository of Important Political Truths.*

Two days after the first issue of the *Scourge* appeared, Lyon was sued for libel, arrested, found guilty and sentenced to four months in prison and fined $1,000. Still in jail, he was elected to Congress, campaigning while serving time. A momentous act as a congressman was a vote for Thomas Jefferson to break the tie in the House between Jefferson and Aaron Burr.

Disenchanted with the political situation in Vermont, Lyon moved in 1801 to Eddyville, Kentucky, where he established a papermill, a book business, and the first printing office in Kentucky, hauling the type by horseback over the Allegheny Mountains. In 1803, he was elected to Congress from his Kentucky district, and served until 1811. The final phase of Lyon's career, by appointment of President James Monroe, was to serve, in 1820, as federal agent to the Cherokee Indians in the Arkansas Territory.

CHARLES McARTHUR
1895-1956

Charles McArthur was born in Scranton, Pennsylvania. His mother was one of seventeen children and his father was a hell-and-brimstone evangelist. McArthur became a model for the tough, wise-cracking reporter.

In 1915 McArthur went to Chicago looking for a newspaper job. He was hired by a small publication called *Oak Leaves* in suburban Oak Park and he worked briefly on the *City Press.* In a military interlude he went to Mexico with the Illinois militia and during World War I served in France with the Rainbow Division.

As a reporter McArthur worked with the *Chicago Herald and Examiner* and then switched over to the *Chicago Tribune.* Two stints in New York City were with Hearst's *New York American* and as a special writer for *International Magazine.* In 1928 McArthur married the actress Helen Hayes.

McArthur achieved his greatest fame as a playwright during a twenty-year collaboration with Ben Hecht. Best known is the Pulitzer Prize-winning play *Front Page,* based on the authors' adventures as Chicago newspapermen. The pair collaborated also on a number of screenplays, including *The Scoundrel,* which won an award from the Academy of Motion Picture Arts and Sciences for the best original story of the year.

McArthur's last venture in journalism was as editor of *Theatre Arts,* a magazine of the stage and a financial loser, from which he resigned in 1950.

C. K. McCLATCHY
1858–1936

Charles Kenny McClatchy, born in Sacramento, entered journalism by way of his father, who owned the *Sacramento Bee.* He became a cub reporter on the *Bee* in 1875, rose to be full partner on his twenty-first birthday in 1879, and took the editorship after his father's death in 1883. His brother Valentine acted as publisher until 1923, when his interest was sold to McClatchy.

The *Bee* extended its coverage in 1904 by establishing a Northern California section with 125 special correspondents. The *Fresno Bee* began in 1922; the *Sacramento Star* was bought in 1925 and merged with the *Bee;* and the *Modesto News-Herald* was purchased in 1927 and renamed the *Modesto Bee.* In 1922 McClatchy began to establish a chain of radio stations in Sacramento, Stockton, Modesto, Fresno, Bakersfield, and Reno, Nevada.

McClatchy's strong convictions were reflected in personal columns and editorial policies. They included crusades against powerful railroad interests, for progressive Era legislation (which he saw as an alternative to socialism), opposition to radical labor leaders; he was against the League of Nations and Prohibition, and supported the 1924 Exclusion Act barring Asians from California on economic grounds. He blamed Herbert Hoover for the Depression that struck in the 1930s and endorsed the New Deal programs to stimulate the economy and help the unemployed.

At the time of McClatchy's death in 1936, the *Bee's* circulation was fifty thousand compared to ten thousand for its rival, the *Union.*

SARAH MCCLENDON
1910–

Sarah McClendon, was born in Tyler, Texas, the last of nine children. She attended the University of Missouri School of Journalism. Afterward she worked for a Beaumont newspaper, where she covered the Women's Army Corps. Enlisting in the WAC, she became a public relation's officer at Fort Oglethorpe, Georgia, and then was sent to the Pentagon in Washington. The White House became part of her regular beat and she covered presidential press conferences from Franklin Roosevelt to Ronald Reagan. She became celebrated for asking embarrassing questions about causes with which she was deeply concerned. Eventually she acquired the reputation of being one of Washington's most enduring nonconformists, with a career spanning four decades and the terms of nine chief executives in the White House.

SAMUEL SIDNEY MCCLURE
1857–1949

Samuel McClure was born in Ireland. His family emigrated to America when he was a child, and settled in Illinois. McClure graduated from Knox College and then went on to New York City. After two years in minor editorial positions, he founded the McClure Syndicate, the first newspaper syndicate in the United States.

McClure achieved his greatest fame as founder (1893) and editor (1893–1949) of *McClure's Magazine,* one of the first muckraking periodicals. In a campaign for social reforms, the magazine published Ida M. Tarbell's, *History of the Standard Oil Company,* Lincoln Steffens's *Shame of the Cities,* and Ray Stannard Baker's *Right to Work.*

The writers for *McClure's* included the leading authors and journalists of its time: Rudyard Kipling, Sir Conan Doyle, Robert Louis Stevenson, William Dean Howells, Mark Twain, O. Henry, Finley Peter Dunne, Jack London, and William Allen White. With such an array of authors and appealing subject matter, *McClure's* became a leader among low-priced news and literary periodicals. It ceased publication in 1929.

ANNE MCCORMICK
1889–1954

Anne O'Hare McCormick was born in Wakefield, England, of American parents, and brought to the United States as an infant. She began her career in journalism as an associate editor of the national Catholic weekly, the *Catholic Universe Bulletin*. As a freelance writer she also began contributing articles to the *New York Times Magazine, Atlantic Monthly,* and other publications.

About 1920 McCormick wrote to the managing editor of the *New York Times* expressing her desire to send some dispatches from abroad. The response was favorable and articles by her began appearing in the *Times*. The first stories were concerned with the rise of fascism in Italy and Mussolini's accession to power. After 1922, McCormick became a regular correspondent and from 1925 on she wrote exclusively for the *Times,* except for a series in the *Ladies' Home Journal* (1933–34).

In 1939, McCormick studied conditions in thirteen countries during a five-month period. Eventually, the *Times* scheduled her for a three-times-a-week column, entitled, "In Europe," and later "Abroad."

In June 1936, McCormick became the first woman member of the *Times's* editorial board, a seat that she occupied for the rest of her life. In 1937, she won a Pulitzer Prize for European correspondence, the first woman to be awarded a major Pulitzer Prize in journalism.

JOSEPH MEDILL MCCORMICK
1877–1925

Joseph Medill McCormick was born in Chicago. He was the grandson of Joseph Medill, editor of the *Chicago Daily Tribune*. After graduating from Yale in 1900 he returned to Chicago to begin his career as newspaper editor and publisher. He began as police reporter for the *Tribune,* but by 1908 he had taken over management of the paper. Foreign travel took him to the Philippines and elsewhere in the Far East. During that period, McCormick also became associated with Charles A. Otis in the ownership of two Cleveland papers, the *Leader* and the *News*.

McCormick was active in politics, starting in 1908, elected a member of the Illinois State Legislature, U.S. congressman (1916–19), and U.S. senator (1919–25). While in the Senate, he introduced the bill creating the Bureau of the Budget, supported the proposed "Great Lakes to Gulf Waterway," and favored the child-labor amendment. He was an ardent Republican but generally avoided extreme positions.

ROBERT R. MCCORMICK
1880–1955

Robert R. McCormick, born in Chicago, one of the giants of American journalism, represented the body and soul of the *Chicago Tribune* for forty-five years. He came from a distinguished family. His father and two brothers were wealthy from manufacturing the McCormick reaper, invented by his uncle, Cyrus Hill McCormick, and his father had served as ambassador to Austria-Hungary, Russia, and France. His mother was the daughter of Joseph Medill, editor and publisher of the *Chicago Tribune* for forty-four years.

McCormick was versatile, famous not only as a journalist, but also known as a lawyer, public official, historian, soldier, radio performer, amateur polo player, and world traveler. In 1910 he and his cousin, Joseph Patterson, became coeditors of the *Chicago Tribune*. McCormick served in France during World War I and was promoted to colonel in the 61st Field Artillery. Starting in 1918, McCormick became editor and publisher of the *Tribune*. At the start, the *Tribune* ranked third among Chicago papers in circulation, but by the time of McCormick's death it ranked first among Midwest papers with a daily sale of more than a million and a Sunday circulation of a million and a half copies. The two cousins adopted the slogan "The World's Greatest Newspaper." McCormick called the city and five surrounding states "Chicagoland."

An innovation, introduced by McCormick was to invest in Canadian forests, build paper mills in Quebec and Ontario, and buy a fleet of lake ships to transport the paper to Chicago. The Tribune Company was thereby able to produce newspapers from the log to newsprint. Improvements in color presses were also made by the *Tribune*.

McCormick and Patterson undertook other journalistic ventures. They established the *New York Daily News,* a tabloid, which came to have the largest circulation of any newspaper in the United States. From 1948 to 1954, McCormick was publisher of the *Washington Times-Herald.*

McCormick was an adamant Republican and a relentless foe of Franklin Roosevelt, the New Deal, Harry Truman, the Fair Deal, the Tennessee Valley Authority, and everything that they stood for. The Colonel's prejudices and preferences were strong and were reflected daily in the *Tribune's* editorials and news columns. A biographer, Julian S. Rammelkamp, called McCormick "perhaps the last of the great personal editors in the tradition of Pulitzer, Hearst and Scripps."

JOSEPH B. MCCULLAGH
1842-1896

Joseph B. McCullagh, born in Dublin, Ireland, came to the United States as a cabin boy on a ship to New York in 1853. His first job in America was as an apprentice printer on a Catholic weekly, the *Freeman's Journal.* At age sixteen he went on to St. Louis to be a compositor for the *Christian Advocate,* a Methodist weekly. A year later, he was hired by the *St. Louis Democrat* as a proofreader. When tried as a reporter, he was so proficient that he was appointed to the *Democrat* staff as a permanent reporter.

In 1860, McCullagh accepted an offer from the *Cincinnati Gazette,* but returned to St. Louis for a year, and then became war correspondent for the *Gazette.* In the course of the Civil War, he gained the reputation of being one of the war's best reporters. He resigned from the *Gazette* when it refused to publish an article critical of the conduct of certain Northern officers. His next assignment was capital correspondent for the *Commercial* in Washington, D.C. A knowledge of shorthand landed him the additional job of Senate reporter to the New York Associated Press. He became acquainted with members of Congress and interviewed President Andrew Johnson on several occasions.

After Washington, McCullagh became managing editor of the *Daily Republican* in Chicago in 1869, but that post was terminated by the disastrous fire of 1871. McCullagh returned to St. Louis as managing editor and part-owner of the *St. Louis Democrat.* A competing paper, the *St. Louis Globe,* started in 1872; McCullagh was fired by the *Democrat* over a staff dispute and immediately was appointed managing editor of the *Globe.* The *Democrat* was failing, was bought and merged with the *Globe,* and on May 20, 1975, the first issue of the *St. Louis Globe-Democrat* was published. Under McCullagh's direction, the *Globe-Democrat* became the leading paper in St. Louis, with the largest circulation of any paper in St. Louis until the end of the century. National recognition for the paper was assured by McCullagh hiring and training hundreds of correspondents across the country to supply news from major regions, Ohio to the Rockies and south to Louisiana and Texas. McCullagh controlled the *Globe-Democrat* completely and reporters were expected to carry out his instructions without question.

A biography by Ellen M. Mrja concluded that McCullagh "was one of the truly great newspaper editors to dominate the Midwest during the last decades of the 1800s."

DWIGHT MACDONALD
1906–1982

Dwight Macdonald was born in New York City. For four years (1920–24), he was a student in the Phillips Exeter Academy in New Hampshire, and then entered Yale. At Yale, he was editor of the *Yale Record,* columnist of the *Yale News,* and managing editor of the *Yale Literary Magazine.* In 1929 he obtained a job as associate editor of *Fortune* magazine, about to be launched by Henry Luce. The journalistic apprenticeship with *Fortune* continued for seven years.

In the mid–1930s, Macdonald became associated with liberal and radical movements. In cooperation with several associates, he revived the *Partisan Review,* which was made a politically independent journal but favored revolutionary socialism. Macdonald resigned from the *Partisan Review* in 1943. Meanwhile, in 1938, he had begun contributing to the *New International,* organ of the Trotskyist party. He also wrote for the *New Yorker,* the *Nation, Harper's,* and other periodicals.

In 1944 Macdonald started a "little" magazine, *Politics,* of which he was editor, owner, publisher, and chief contributor. The circulation of *Politics* grew to five thousand by 1945, but publication was stopped in 1949, because Macdonald wanted more time for his own writing.

Macdonald began spending more time writing articles for the *New Yorker,* and in 1951 he became a staff writer for that magazine. While continuing with the *New Yorker* (1960–66), Macdonald held the post of movie critic for *Esquire.* After 1966, his articles for *Esquire* changed from moving pictures to exploring the political scene.

CHARLES RICE MCDOWELL, JR.
1926–

Charles McDowell was born June 24, 1926, in Danville, Kentucky. He graduated from Washington & Lee University with a B.A. degree in 1948; with an M.S. from Columbia University in 1949. He served in the U.S. Navy from 1944–45. He is a member of Phi Beta Kappa.

McDowell was a reporter for the *Richmond Times-Dispatch* in 1949–57; columnist in 1957 and has been a Washington correspondent since 1965. He has written several books and is one of the honored panelists on *Washington Week in Review* aired by Public Broadcasting System.

BERNARR MACFADDEN
1868–1955

Bernarr Macfadden, famous or infamous, according to different critics, as a physical culturist, was born near Mill Spring, Missouri. A puny youth, he developed his physique with dumbbells, long walks, and periodic fasting, key ingredients of his later career.

In 1899 Macfadden founded *Physical Culture,* a magazine that stressed exercise, fresh air, rest, cleanliness, an almost meatless diet, and opposed alcohol, tobacco, coffee, and overeating. He also produced a five-volume encyclopedia and more than a hundred books. The most successful of his magazines was *True Story,* started in 1919, melodramatic confessions "written from life by ordinary people." In less than a decade, sales exceeded 2 million copies and the magazine was earning over $2 million a day.

At various times during his career, Macfadden added other magazines: *True Romances, True Experiences, True Detective Mysteries, Dream World, The Dance, Fiction Lovers, Modern Marriage, Muscle Builder, Love and Romance, Master Detective, Own Your Own Home, Ghost Stories, Photoplay,* and *Liberty.* Between 1924 and 1932 Macfadden also published a daily tabloid newspaper, the *New York Evening Graphic* (called by critics the "Pornographic") featuring sex and violence. He also owned newspapers in several other cities. His publications reached an annual circulation of 35 to 40 million.

Macfadden had frequent clashes with censors, especially Anthony Comstock and John S. Sumner of the New York Society for the Suppression of Vice. Doctors were opposed by Macfadden on the ground that only natural methods cured and physicians' drugs poisoned patients. This brought him into conflict with the medical profession. To demonstrate his virility, in his eighties he flew his own plane, played tennis, and celebrated his birthdays with parachute jumps. He died at age eighty-eight, however, of jaundice, convinced that he could beat the ailment with a regimen of fasting.

W. O. McGEEHAN
1879–1933

William O'Connell McGeehan, born in San Francisco, was called by Paul Gallico "the greatest sports writer that ever lived." Virtually McGeehan's whole career was spent reporting baseball, boxing, and other sporting events. His first job, following military service in the Spanish-

American War of 1898 and the Philippine Insurrection of 1899, was with the *San Francisco Call,* to cover prizefights throughout the region. Later, McGeehan moved from the *Call* to the *Chronicle,* then to Hearst's *Examiner,* and finally to the *Evening Post,* first as city editor and later managing editor.

In 1914, McGeehan went on to New York to be sportswriter for Hearst's *Evening Journal,* writing mainly about boxing. The next year he joined the *New York Tribune.* After a military tour of duty in 1917, he was promoted to be the *Tribune's* managing editor, and subsequently transferred to the *Herald* when the *Tribune* and *Herald* merged two years later. McGeehan remained as sports editor. His writing was not limited, however, to sports. Often he commented on the day's news and public affairs. His column was one of the most popular features of the newspaper. He also wrote numerous articles and short stories for some of the leading magazines of his time.

RALPH MCGILL
1898–1969

Ralph McGill was born in an eastern Tennessee farming community. He served in the Marine Corps during World War I, but the war ended before he was sent to France. At Vanderbilt University, he wrote for the school newspaper, founded the campus humor magazine, and worked part-time for the *Nashville Banner* as a copyboy and occasional sportswriter.

In 1922 McGill became a full-time reporter for the *Banner,* a job he held until 1928. His next move was to Atlanta to become assistant to the sports editor of the *Atlanta Constitution.* For years the names of Ralph McGill and the *Atlanta Constitution* were inseparable, as he progressed from sports editor to later editor and publisher. The *Constitution's* owner-publisher assigned McGill to political reporting, to make better use of his talents. After traveling around the state with economists and agricultural experts, McGill did a series of articles on Southern farm problems. His knowledge of the subject was increased by travels in Great Britain and Europe, especially Scandinavia. Back in the United States, McGill was promoted to executive editor of the *Constitution* and wrote a daily column on a variety of subjects.

In 1942, McGill was named editor-in-chief of the *Constitution,* giving him full control of the paper's editorial policies. He traveled widely, including a world tour visiting twenty-two countries. Among the highlights were the new Jewish State in Palestine, the Nuremberg trial of war criminals, and a trip to Russia with Vice President Nixon in 1959. McGill was a leading social critic, taking stands on controversial issues that inspired much hate mail. The Ku Klux Klan named him "Southern enemy number one" for his stand on civil rights and segregation, but he was honored with a Pulitzer Prize, the Presidential Medal of Freedom, and university honorary degrees.

O. O. MCINTYRE
1884-1938

Oscar Odd McIntyre was born in Plattsburg, Missouri. He entered newspaper work at age eighteen as a reporter for the *Gallipolis* (Ohio) *News*. Several other jobs followed in succession: city editor of the *Gallipolis Journal,* feature writer for the *East Liverpool* (Ohio) *Morning Tribune,* and political writer and managing editor of the *Dayton* (Ohio) *Herald*. In 1906, McIntyre was appointed telegraph editor and later city editor and assistant managing editor of the *Cincinnati Post*. His next move was to New York in 1911 to be associate editor of *Hampton's Magazine*. When that job terminated, McIntyre joined the *New York Evening Mail* as drama editor.

A radical turn in McIntyre's career occurred when he inaugurated independently a newspaper column entitled "New York Day by Day," dealing with life in the metropolis. He wrote on such topics as Bowery lodging houses and drifters, speakeasies, fake jewelry auction sales, chop houses, and antique shops, all designed to bring the sights and sounds of New York to readers around the country. By 1918 there were fifty-seven subscribers to the series. By the time of McIntyre's death in 1938, his column was syndicated in 375 dailies and 129 Sunday papers, bringing him an annual income of $200,000. After 1922, the column was distributed by the McNaught Syndicate. McIntyre was also a contributor to *Cosmopolitan, American Magazine,* and *Life*. Some of his favorite columns were collected and printed in book form.

WILLIAM V. MCKEAN
1820-1903

William Vincent McKean was a native Philadelphian. His first contact with printing was at age sixteen, when he was apprenticed to a firm of type-founders; there his work began with hand-mold casting. Later he began writing articles for the *Pennsylvanian* and in 1850 joined that journal as associate editor. After several years as clerk of the U.S. House of Representatives, McKean returned to Philadelphia, where he joined the *Philadelphia Inquirer* as an editorial writer. At the same time, he did some editorial work for publisher George W. Childs. When Childs bought the *Public Ledger* in 1864, McKean was appointed general manager and editor-in-chief. He remained with the *Public Ledger* for nearly thirty years, until his retirement in 1891. During that time, McKean was actively involved in many civic activities and in various philosophical and literary societies in Philadelphia.

JOHN R. MCLEAN
1849–1916

John R. McLean was more or less born into the newspaper world. He learned journalism by working for the *Cincinnati Enquirer* (his father was part-owner). The McLeans built up a large printing business, but the newspaper was not successful, failing to achieve a circulation commensurate with the size of the city. After a year at Harvard and foreign travel, young McLean went to work at the *Enquirer* as an office boy. Later, he became an excellent police reporter.

In 1881 McLean acquired full ownership of the *Enquirer,* but in 1886 he decided to establish his home in Washington. From that time until his death, he supervised the *Enquirer* from Washington, while keeping his legal and political base in Cincinnati.

In 1895 McLean purchased the *New York Morning Journal.* The paper was a financial failure. In 1895 he sold it to William Randolph Hearst, who was just beginning to enter the New York newspaper field. McLean had long been interested in the *Washington Post* and in 1905 he bought a half-interest in the paper. He considered himself editor-in-chief of both the *Enquirer* and the *Post.*

Because of McLean's manifold interests in business and politics, the affairs of the *Post* failed to receive proper attention and its circulation declined. Even more disastrous was the management by Ned McLean, who succeeded his father as owner of the *Post.* The son drove the paper into bankruptcy and it was sold at auction in 1933 to Eugene Meyer, who transformed it into one of the nation's great newspapers.

WILLIAM L. MCLEAN
1852–1931

William Lippard McLean was born in Mount Pleasant, Pennsylvania, and his career was spent entirely in that state. At age twenty, he was employed by the *Pittsburgh Leader's* circulation department and gained wide experience.

A major opportunity came for McLean when in 1878, at age twenty-six, he became secretary and treasurer of the *Philadelphia Press,* a paper founded in 1847, which had a circulation of about 6,000 at the time, lowest of Philadelphia's thirteen newspapers. McLean introduced advice columns on etiquette and other subjects. During his first year, the *Press's* circulation jumped to 33,615. In 1895, McLean purchased the *Evening Bulletin,* the oldest afternoon daily in Pennsylvania. Speed of delivery was emphasized and the paper announced that the entire city would be "covered by *Bulletin* wagons drawn by fast horses, by messengers on foot and in trolley cars, and by sturdy-legged young men" to deliver the news quickly. In 1899 two Daimler electric wagons were imported from France, making the *Press* the first American publisher to distribute papers by automobile. The *Bulletin* was delivered to outer reaches of the city within thirty minutes after it came off the press. By 1904 the *Bulletin* had the largest circulation of any Philadelphia paper, over 200,000 daily. By the time of McLean's death in 1931 circulation had increased to 560,000, due to policies adopted by McLean: thorough coverage of local news, but never neglecting national and international news, excellent editorial material, and attractive features.

McLean died in 1931. After various changes in management and drops in circulation, the *Bulletin* ceased publication in January 1982.

ROBERT MACNEIL
1931–

Robert MacNeil was born in Montreal, Canada. He tried various occupations before coming to journalism: the Navy, acting, and playwrighting. In 1955 he joined the London bureau of Reuters News Service as a rewrite man. NBC-TV in 1960 recruited him as a London-based roving foreign correspondent. In that capacity, he covered the major international news events of the 1960s, including a visit to Cuba, where he was imprisoned for a short time for entering the country without special accreditation.

In 1965, MacNeil was transferred to New York to anchor a sixty-minute nightly newscast for WNBC-TV, to complement the "Huntley–Brinkley Report." He left that job in 1966 to become a reporter for Panorama, BBC's documentary series, where he spent the next four year dealing with leading American and foreign news stories. MacNeil resigned from the BBC in 1971 and returned to the United States to become senior correspondent for the Public Broadcasting Service. For a brief period he served as moderator for "Washington Week in Review," PBS's weekly discussion of national news.

The highly popular "McNeil/Lehrer News Hour" was launched in 1975, with McNeil, Jim Lehrer, and Charlayne Hunter-Gault constituting its regular staff. Later, Judy Woodruff joined the team. The program was designed to supplement the commercial networks' nightly news broadcasts. By the end of its fourth season the "McNeil–Lehrer Report" was being watched by an average of 4 million people on more than 230 PBS stations.

JOHN MCPHEE
1931–

John McPhee was born in Princeton, New Jersey, and graduated from Princeton University in 1953. As a student he wrote articles for the *Nassau Literary Magazine,* the *Princeton Tiger,* and the *Princeton Alumni Weekly.* After a year in England reading literature at Cambridge University, McPhee moved to New York and joined *Time* as a contributing editor. For five years he wrote the magazine's "Show Business" column and wrote biographical sketches of theater personalities. He contributed freelance articles to various publications.

In 1965, the *New Yorker* hired McPhee as a staff writer. The choice of subjects was left open to him and over the years he has covered many fields. His articles are based on extensive reading, careful research, and interviews. His contributions include many pieces for the *New Yorker's* "Talk of the Town" section and articles on subjects as diverse as ecology, basketball, Alaska, geological history, and aeronautical engineering.

MARIE MANNING
1873–1945

Marie Manning was the daughter of English immigrants, and was born in Washington, D.C. It appears that Manning was employed by the London bureau of the *New York Herald* in 1897 and the following year joined the *New York World.* Her first news scoop was an interview with President Grover Cleveland. In 1898 Manning moved to Hearst's *Evening Journal.* One of her first assignments was to answer letters asking for advice on personal problems. Thus began the column by "Beatrice Fairfax," the pen name adopted by Manning, beginning on July 20, 1894. Her love forum is the oldest surviving uninterrupted advice column in any American newspaper, preceding Dorothy Dix's by nineteen years, and continuing under various authors to date.

The "Beatrice Fairfax" column was an immediate success, attracting at one time 1,400 letters daily. Manning was dissociated from the column (1905–29), but returned to it in 1930. When she resumed her connection the column was being distributed to 200 newspapers throughout the country. "Beatrice Fairfax" continued writing until her death in 1945. During her later years she was also a columnist for International News Service, serving as a reporter covering Washington.

DON MARQUIS
1878–1937

Don Marquis, who is ranked by most critics as an important American humor columnist, was born in Walnut, Illinois. His newspaper experience began with two unnamed Illinois weeklies, for which he performed practically every duty associated with production. While working for the Census Bureau in Washington, Marquis became a reporter for the *Washington Times.* His next move was to Atlanta in 1902, as associate editor of the *Atlanta News,* under John Temple Graves. Two years later he transferred to the *Atlanta Journal,* mainly as an editorial writer, but occasionally acting as a reporter or theater critic. From 1907 to 1909 he was coeditor with Joel Chandler Harris of *Uncle Remus' Magazine.* When that enterprise failed, Marquis went on to New York.

As a member of the staff of the *New York Sun* (1912–22), Marquis became known for his humorous column, "The Sun Dial" and after he joined the *New York Tribune* (1922–25), "The Lantern." In his columns, Marquis introduced the characters of Hermione and her "little Group of Serious Thinkers," Clem Hawley, a philosophical drunkard, "The Old Soak," Mehitabel the Cat, and Archy the Cockroach. Marquis is best remembered for these satirical newspaper pieces.

E. B. White summarized Marquis's many talents as a "parodist, historian, poet, clown, fable writer, satirist, reporter, and teller of tales."

JUDITH MARTIN
1938–

Judith Martin was born in Washington, D.C., graduated from Wellesley College in 1959, and was given her first journalistic job as a copygirl at the *Washington Post.* In 1960 she became a reporter and feature writer for the *Post*. At first she was society columnist, covering such events as White House dinners and Embassy Row cocktail parties. Later she wrote reviews of books, plays, and movies. She was banned from the Nixon White House for her behavior and writing about the Nixon family.

A new avenue for Martin's talents was opened in 1978, when she was authorized to write a column on etiquette for the *Post*. Using the nom de plume of "Miss Manners," the column was distributed by United Features Syndicate, and began to appear internationally in over 250 newspapers. Her writing for the press and in several books draws on her Washington experience and social observation. The column answers questions on a wide range of subjects.

In 1984 Martin resigned her position as a reporter for the *Post* to devote full time to her "Miss Manners" column and other writing, including serving as critic-at-large for *Vanity Fair*. She has also presented television shows since 1985 in more than one hundred U.S. and Canadian cities.

FRANKLIN MATTHEWS
1858-1917

Franklin Matthews was born in St. Joseph, Michigan, and graduated from Cornell University. In 1886 he was employed as a reporter by the *Philadelphia Press* and four years later he became editor of the *Press*. A short service with the *New York World* was followed by twenty-two years with the *New York Sun,* where his duties ranged from reporter to copy reader, telegraphic editor, city editor, and special correspondent.

Matthews's foreign experience began when he was sent to Cuba by *Harper's Weekly* to report on conditions after the Spanish-American War; to the Orient to report on the Russo-Japanese War; and in 1907 to accompany the Atlantic fleet on its cruise around the world as special correspondent for the *Sun.*

In 1912, Matthews joined the staff of the *New York Times,* first as Sunday editor and then night city editor. His last years were spent as a member of the faculty of Columbia University's school of journalism.

HERBERT L. MATTHEWS
1900-1977

Herbert Matthews was born in New York City. He joined the *New York Times* in 1922 and remained with that paper for forty-five years. A good portion of his time was spent in foreign service and as a war correspondent. He was in Peking in 1929, and traveled with the Italian army in Addis Ababa in 1936. During the late 1930s, Matthews reported on the Spanish civil war. He then covered World War II.

Following postwar service in London, Matthews returned to New York and worked on the *Times* editorial staff from 1949 to 1967. His interviews with Fidel Castro in Cuba were widely publicized. He received a number of citations for his reporting, and was the author of books on current politics and world affairs.

ROBERT C. MAYNARD
1937–

Robert Maynard was born in Brooklyn, New York, and grew up in the mostly black Bedford-Stuyvesant section. While in high school, Maynard frequented the offices of the black weekly paper, the *New York Age*. At sixteen he was working as a reporter for the *Age*. Later, while living in Greenwich Village, he met prominent black writers who encouraged his literary efforts. For a time Maynard was a reporter for the *Baltimore Afro-American*.

In 1961 Maynard was hired as a reporter by the *York* (Pennsylvania) *Gazette and Daily*. He took a year out as a Nieman Fellow at Harvard, and then returned to the *Gazette* as night news editor. In 1967 he was offered a position with the *Washington Post,* to become its first black national correspondent and was given free rein in reporting metropolitan and national news.

While continuing to write for the *Post* Maynard began in 1972 to serve part-time as a senior editor for a new black monthly, *Encore,* the aim of which was to report world news from a black perspective. In the same year, Maynard was appointed associate editor and ombudsman of the *Post*.

In 1977 Maynard left the *Post* to found the Institute for Journalism Education at the University of California, Berkeley. In that position, he was hired as an affirmative action consultant by the far-flung Gannett newspaper chain. In 1979 he was the first black in the United States to edit a major daily newspaper when the Gannett company appointed Maynard editor of the *Oakland Tribune*. During his first three years as editor, he increased staff, news space, and local coverage. A morning edition was successful, but later was united with the regular daily edition. In 1983, Maynard bought the *Oakland Tribune* from Gannett.

JOSEPH MEDILL
1823-1899

Canadian-born Joseph Medill moved with his parents to Ohio in his childhood. He first tried the legal profession, but soon changed to journalism. About 1849 he joined with three brothers in purchasing an Ohio Village weekly, the *Coshocton Republican.* In 1851, he founded the *Daily Forest City* in Cleveland, renaming it the *Cleveland Leader.* His most decisive move was made in 1855 when he and four partners purchased the *Chicago Tribune,* founded in 1847.

Medill was long a key political figure. He was elected mayor of Chicago after the disastrous 1871 fire and directed the rebuilding of the city. As one element of the reorganization, plans were made to establish the Chicago Public Library. Nationally, Medill originated the name "Republican" for the new party to replace the moribund Whigs. He strongly supported Abraham Lincoln for president, and was a relentless opponent of slavery. The *Tribune* circulation rose during its full reporting of the Lincoln–Douglas debates.

In 1874, after resigning as mayor of Chicago and touring Europe, Medill acquired a controlling interest in the *Tribune,* and became its editor, a position that he held for the rest of his life. The paper's editorial policies were increasingly conservative. Medill championed a free hand for business and fought liberal reformers and labor unions. Under his leadership, the *Tribune* became one of the most powerful papers in the nation.

The Medill family continued to be prominent in the history of journalism. Joseph's grandson, Robert R. McCormick, won control of the *Tribune* after 1914. Another grandson, Joseph M. Patterson, founded the *New York Daily News,* and his granddaughter, Eleanor M. Patterson, was publisher of the *Washington Times-Herald.* A great-granddaughter, Alicia Patterson Guggenheim, founded Long Island's daily *Newsday.* The Medill School of Journalism at Northwestern University was endowed by the family.

HENRY LOUIS MENCKEN
1880-1956

Since the end of World War I, a strong breeze of iconoclasm has blown through American literature. Biographers have stripped the national heroes of all legend and romantic glamor. Historians have been chiefly preoccupied with debunking America's past. No less irreverent in tearing down accepted dogma, destroying sacred cows, and wrecking popular images have been the novelists, poets, playwrights, and essayists.

Setting the tone for the new breed of social critics, and by far the most influential of the lot was H. L. Mencken, the "Sage of Baltimore." Among his prolific writings, the six-volume *Prejudices* (1919–27) is representative of Mencken's extremely catholic interests and of subjects on which he held vehement views, pro and con. A satirist, humorist, devastating critic, and word juggler supreme, Mencken attracted readers by the thousands as he damned ignorance and dishonesty in American politics, hypocrisy in the church, sham in the educational system, puritanism in every form, provincialism, artsy art, do-goodism among social reformers, racial discrimination, and superpatriotism, while defending with equal vigor the right of the individual to live life without interference from bureaucrats, prohibitionists, censors, bluenoses, and the like. Through his editorship of the *American Mercury, Prejudices,* and other writings, Mencken became a rallying point for the literature of protest in the United States; at one time he was described by the *New York Times* as "the most powerful private citizen" in the country.

For Mencken, a native of Baltimore, journalism was always his first love. At nineteen he was on the staff of the *Baltimore Morning Herald,* began writing a weekly column the following year, and within a short time was successively city editor and managing editor. After the *Herald* suspended publication in 1906, Mencken went over to the *Sun* papers of Baltimore and remained there intermittently and in various capacities for the next thirty-five years.

Mencken's greatest impact on the literary scene of his time was as a book reviewer and commentator on authors—in essence, creating literary trends and reputations. He championed Dreiser, Cabell, and Hergesheimer, contributed to Sinclair Lewis's early success by his enthusiasm for *Main Street* and *Babbitt,* and praised Sherwood Anderson and F. Scott Fitzgerald. His verdicts were by no means infallible, however, as, for example, in his rating of George Ade ahead of Ring Lardner as a humorist, and his characterization of Robert Frost as "a Whittier without the whiskers," while extolling minor poets John McClure and Lizette Woodworth Reese.

In long-range significance, present-day critics are agreed that Mencken's vitalizing effect on the American language as writer and lexicographer is preeminent. The first edition of his monumental *The American Language* appeared in 1919 and grew steadily in size. The fourth edition (1936) filled 798 pages, and was followed by two sizable supplementary volumes (1945–48). As Noah Webster had done a century earlier, Mencken argued that the American language was separate and different from the English, and he assembled a wealth of material and information to support his case.

Mencken has been compared, in each instance with considerable justification, with Juvenal, Dryden, Swift, Voltaire, Ambrose Bierce, and Philip Wylie. Most aptly, however, the current tendency is to liken him to Dr. Samuel Johnson, who played a similar role in eighteenth-century English literary circles. Edmund Wilson summed up the case with his comment, "It is astonishing that one independent critic, writing mainly in newspapers and magazines, should have fought so many successful fights and grown to be so powerful a figure," frequently in the face of powerful opposition. Mencken loved a good fight. His magazine, the *American Mercury,* was famous for debunking hallowed icons of American culture. When he published the memoirs of a prostitute, nicknamed "Hatrack," in the April 1926 issue of the *Mercury* and was later arrested and tried for peddling such "pornography" in Boston, he relished the chance to take on the "wowsers" (Puritans) and the "smellers" (post office censors) of New England.

Mencken later wrote his own memoirs of the "Hatrack" case — one of the landmark censorship cases of the twentieth century. Oddly, his account sat unpublished for more than fifty years, on a shelf with some scrapbooks of newspaper clippings about the case. In the spring of 1988, Carl Bode, Mencken's biographer, edited the manuscript and it was published as *The Editor, the Bluenose, and the Prostitute.*

EDWIN THOMAS MEREDITH
1876–1928

Edwin Meredith was born on a farm near Avoca, Iowa. His grandfather owned a weekly county farm paper, the *Farmer's Tribune,* with which his grandson assisted. In 1896, his grandfather gave him the paper as a wedding present. Meredith transformed the *Tribune* into a nonpartisan farm paper with a statewide circulation. A more ambitious venture was the founding in 1902 of *Successful Farming.* In 1922 he purchased the *Dairy Farmer* and also founded *Fruit, Garden and Home,* which in 1924 became *Better Homes and Gardens.*

Meredith set high ethical standards for his journals, refusing tobacco, liquor, and patent medicine advertisements, the backbone of advertising income for most magazines and newspapers of the period.

Meredith was appointed U.S. secretary of agriculture by President Wilson in 1920 and served with distinction until the end of the Wilson administration.

AGNES ELIZABETH ERNST MEYER
1887–1970

Agnes Meyer was born in New York City. After graduating from Barnard College, she became one of the first women reporters on the *New York Sun*. A year later, she left the *Sun* for study at the Sorbonne in Paris. Returning to New York in 1910, she married Eugene Meyer, international financier and multimillionaire.

In 1933, Eugene Meyer bought the *Washington Post*. Agnes was part-owner, but was given no role in the paper's management. The Meyers's son-in-law, Philip L. Graham, became publisher in 1946 and was succeeded by his wife, Katharine Meyer Graham, in 1963.

Meyer promoted the establishment of the Department of Health, Education, and Welfare. She was actively concerned with such social issues as health, education, and the status of women.

EUGENE MEYER
1875–1959

Eugene Meyer came to journalism late in his career, after distinguishing himself as creator of the Reconstruction Finance Corporation, serving as governor of the Federal Reserve Board, and being active in high finance. Meyer was born in Los Angeles, the son of a Jewish merchant who had emigrated from Alsace-Lorraine, France.

In June 1933 Meyer bought the *Washington Post,* one of five Washington dailies. The *Post* had been losing a million dollars a year. By enlivening the editorial page and adding special columns, Meyer reversed the trend. Circulation and advertising increased substantially. Meyer set out to establish a vigorous, independent newspaper with a national reputation. Well-known columnists included Walter Lippmann, Sumner Welles, and Marquis Childs. George Gallup's public opinion polls were featured. By 1938, circulation had gone from fifty thousand to one hundred thousand, and by 1943 the paper showed a small profit. In 1954 circulation grew to two hundred thousand. Meyer purchased the *Times-Herald* from Robert R. McCormick and combined it with the *Post* to create a morning newspaper monopoly.

Meyer retired as publisher of the *Post* in 1946, turning the job over to his son-in-law, Philip Graham, but he remained as board chairman.

DREW MIDDLETON
1913–

Drew Middleton was born in New York City. He began his long career in reporting when he was sports editor on the *Poughkeepsie* (New York) *Eagle News*. Shortly he moved to the *Evening Star* in the same city, and in 1939 joined the Associated Press in New York, writing about sports.

Middleton covered World War II for the Associated Press, starting with the British forces in 1939. He transferred to the *New York Times* London staff in 1942. In addition to his continued war coverage, he reported on the Nuremberg trials after the war. Before returning to the United States in 1965, he worked for the *Times* in Russia, Germany, London, and Paris. From 1970 until 1984, he remained a military correspondent. In 1984 he became a columnist attached to the *New York Times* syndicate.

WEBB MILLER
1892–1940

Webb Miller was born in Pokagon, Michigan. He had an early ambition to become a newspaper reporter. He was hired as a cub reporter by the *Chicago American* in 1912 and was especially successful in covering the proceedings of criminal courts. For a time he did freelance reporting, following the Pancho Villa raids in 1916 along the Mexican-American border. His longtime association with the United Press began when the head of the UP staff along the border offered him a regular job. During the next thirty years Miller traveled in more than thirty countries on news assignments and reported on practically every war and international controversy.

Miller covered World War I before and after U.S. involvement. Following the war he became a foreign correspondent. From 1925 to 1935 he was assistant manager of United Press's European division. During that period he traveled around the world, visiting sixteen European countries, South America, Africa, and Asia. He interviewed Hitler and Mussolini, and reported on Mahatma Gandhi's rebellion in India, the Italian invasion of Ethiopia, the Spanish civil war, the Nazi takeover of Czechoslovakia, and the Russo-Finnish War.

More peaceful stories included the abdication of Edward VIII, the coronation of George VI, and the wedding of the Duke of Windsor to Wally Simpson, a divorced American women. In 1938, Miller was appointed general European manager of the United Press, a position that he held until his death.

From his years of reporting, Miller became thoroughly disillusioned about war—its futility, horror, and obscenity. In a cry of despair he exclaimed, "poor human race."

HARRIET MONROE
1860-1936

Harriet Monroe was born in Chicago. She wrote several volumes of poetry, but her most notable achievement was founder and editor (1912-30) of *Poetry: A Magazine of Verse,* which published the early works of many American and English poets such as Carl Sandburg, Rupert Brooke, Robert Frost, Ezra Pound, T. S. Eliot, Wallace Stevens, Vachel Lindsay, W. B. Yeats, James Joyce, William Carlos Williams, Edgar Lee Masters, Marianne Moore, and Edwin Arlington Robinson, in most cases before they became famous. Monroe became a key figure in the development of modern verse, although her own poetry was not distinguished.

Monroe was chosen to write and to recite the *Columbian Ode* at the opening of the World's Columbian Exposition in Chicago in 1893. She was active for more than twenty years as a correspondent and reviewer of art, drama, and other subjects for various Chicago and New York papers. She was also widely traveled, including a world tour in 1910; England, France, and Spain in 1923; Mexico in 1929; and Asia in 1934. In 1936 she was an American delegate to the Congress of the International Literary, PEN, in Buenos Aires, Argentina.

ERIC MOON
1923-

Eric Moon is a native of Yeovil, England. He attended the Loughborough College of Further Education School of Librarianship in England (1947-49). Before coming to the United States, he was an assistant in the Southampton Public Library (1939-48), area librarian with the Hertfordshire County Library (1949-51), district librarian, Finckley Public Library (1951-54), deputy borough librarian and curator, Brentford and Chizwick Public Library (1954-56), head of technical processes, Kensington Public Library (1956-58), and director of public library service and secretary of the public library board at St. Johns Newfoundland, Canada (1958-59). From 1959 to 1968 he was editor of the *Library Journal.* He has had an active role in library associations in the United States, England, and Canada, and served as president of the American Library Association (1977–78). He was winner of the Joseph W. Lippincott Award in 1981. Earlier he was president of Scarecrow Press from 1969 to 1978. Moon has been a prolific writer on censorship and collection development.

EDGAR ANSEL MOWRER
1892–1977

Edgar Ansel Mowrer was born in Bloomington, Illinois. He was a brother of Paul Scott Mowrer, the first Pulitzer Prize winner for foreign correspondence. Mowrer, too, became a prize-winning foreign correspondent. When World War I began he took charge of the *Chicago Daily News* bureau in Paris, acting for his brother who had gone to the war front to cover the action. After Paul's return, Mowrer went to the war front himself. Later he went to Rome as chief correspondent for the *Daily News.*

Italy entered World War I on the Allied side shortly after Mowrer's arrival, and he witnessed the Caporetto battle. In 1915 he interviewed Benito Mussolini, and watched the Italian fascists take over the country.

In 1934, Mowrer replaced his brother in Paris. From there he covered the Spanish civil war. His Pulitzer Prize-winning book, *Germany Puts the Clock Back* (1932) was prophetic in its warning of the threat of Nazism. On his return to the United States, Mowrer was deputy director of the Office of Facts and Figures and Office of War Information until 1943. He made trips to Moscow and China, and reported the war first-hand in Europe. Mowrer resigned his government posts in 1943 and became a commentator on world affairs for the *New York Post.* He also wrote a syndicated newspaper column and was a consultant to Radio Free Europe. Altogether Mowrer worked as a journalist for fifty-five years, and, as he said, "occupied a ringside seat at most of the major scenes of history."

PAUL SCOTT MOWRER
1887–1971

Paul Scott Mowrer was born in Bloomington, Illinois, as was his brother Edgar. The two brothers spent much of their journalistic careers with the *Chicago Daily News.* Mowrer joined the newspaper as a reporter in 1905, was Paris correspondent (1907–10); war correspondent assigned to French General Headquarters (1914–18); diplomatic correspondent, political analyst, and head of European Service (1919–33); associate editor

(1934–35); and editor-in-chief (1935–44). He also had a term (1945–49) as European editor for the *New York Post.*

From Paris, Mowrer covered World War I with a network of *Daily News* correspondents that he organized, and at considerable personal risk entered Brussels, then occupied by German troops, and made repeated forays to the French front. When the United States entered the war in 1917, Mowrer was officially accredited to the French armies as correspondent until the end of the war. His detailed accounts of battles were celebrated.

Following the war, Mowrer reported on the peace negotiations, traveled through Eastern Europe, plagued by revolution and starvation, and the Riff-Spanish War in North Africa. After his return from Morocco, Mowrer observed the impact of Russian communism on neighboring countries, the ominous growth of fascism in Europe, and the danger of war posed by Germany, Italy, and Japan.

BILLY DON MOYERS
1934–

Bill Moyers was born in Hugo, a small town in the southeastern corner of Oklahoma. As a student he reported school news for the *Marshall* (Texas) *News Messenger,* and by fifteen he became a general assignments reporter, covering everything from school board meetings to courtroom trials. As a college student, Moyers wrote editorials for the campus newspaper and spent his summer vacations as a reporter for the *News Messenger.*

In 1961, Moyers became associate director for public affairs of the Peace Corps and two years later he was nominated to be deputy director of the Peace Corps. Instead, he was appointed special assistant to president Lyndon Johnson. In 1964 Moyers became White House chief of staff. In addition to his regular duties in that office, he coordinated the president's television advertising campaign for the 1964 national election. In 1965 he was named Johnson's press secretary.

In 1966 Moyers returned to journalism as publisher of *Newsday,* the largest circulation suburban daily newspaper in the United States. Within three years, *Newsday* had won a number of important journalism awards, including two Pulitzer Prizes. Moyers left *Newsday* in 1975.

After 1970 Moyers turned his attention mainly to television, starting with a weekly public affairs program on New York's WNET-TV. In 1975 he presented twenty one-hour programs on international affairs for the Public Broadcasting Service, a series entitled *Bill Moyers' Journal, International Report.* During America's Bicentennial year of 1976, Moyers covered a variety of contemporary domestic problems, and for the past few years has done special programs for the Public Broadcasting System.

ROGER MUDD
1928-

Roger Mudd was born in Washington, D.C., and has always remained close to his birthplace. To learn more about the newspaper business, he joined the staff of the *Richmond* (Virginia) *News Leader* in 1952 as a reporter and has been a journalist ever since. After leaving the *News Leader,* Mudd became news director of radio station WRNL in Richmond for three years, then moved to Washington, D.C., as a reporter for WTOP, a CBS-affiliated radio and television station. There he was assigned in 1961 to cover Congress—an ideal post for his talents as a reporter.

Mudd was narrator for the documentary series "CBS Reports" in the early 1970s. The most controversial program of the hard-hitting series was entitled "The Selling of the Pentagon," a muckraking attack on the Pentagon's extravagant and wasteful public relations program. Other leading stories included the Watergate scandal, President Nixon's resignation, and an interview with Edward Kennedy on his campaign for president.

Mudd had hoped to succeed Walter Cronkite on "CBS Evening News" in 1980, but was disappointed when Dan Rather was chosen by the network. Mudd received offers from ABC and NBC. He finally signed with the latter because NBC would allow him to continue working in his native Washington, D.C. He continues to produce feature programs for PBS.

FRANK A. MUNSEY
1854-1925

Frank Andrew Munsey was the most spectacular, free-wheeling newspaper and magazine executive of his time. A native of Mercer, Maine, he went to New York in 1882 to start a juvenile weekly, the *Golden Argosy.* Much of the writing for the magazine came from British children's magazines, or Munsey himself. Six years later the title was changed to *Argosy Magazine,* and it became a monthly for adults. In 1889 another magazine was founded, *Munsey's Weekly,* which later was changed to a monthly. In 1891, Munsey bought his first newspaper, the *New York Star,* renaming it the *Daily Continental* (later the *Morning Advertiser*). It was New York's first tabloid newspaper. When the paper began losing money after only four months, Munsey sold it.

To attract more customers for his magazines, Munsey started cutting prices. *Munsey's Magazine* was offered at ten cents a copy. Circulation jumped to five hundred thousand, and advertising revenue experienced a tremendous increase. Every issue was profusely illustrated and contained popular fiction. By 1905, Munsey's publications were earning over a million dollars a year.

In 1901 Munsey became a newspaper publisher again, buying the *New York Daily News* and *Washington Times.* During the next twenty-five years, he was busily engaged in buying and selling newspapers. In 1902, he purchased the *Boston Journal* with its morning, evening, and Sunday editions. Among newspapers he bought, merged, or discontinued were the *New York Morning Sun,* the *New York Press,* the *Herald* (sold to the *Tribune*), the *Daily Continent,* the *Globe,* the *Baltimore Star,* and the *Philadelphia Times.* Later he sold the *Boston Morning Journal, Washington Times, Baltimore American,* and *Baltimore News.*

Other magazines were launched by Munsey: *Scrap Book, Quaker, Railroad Man's Magazine,* and *All-Story Magazine.* He destroyed, merged, or renamed a number of magazines: *Scrap Book, Quaker, Puritan, Godey's Magazine, Peterson's Magazine, Live Wire, Junior Munsey Woman, Cavalier, Railroad Man's Magazine,* and the *All-Story Magazine* – several of his own creation. Munsey's fixed policy was to kill or merge financially unsound or competitive publications.

At Munsey's death he owned the *New York Sun* and *Evening Telegram* among the newspapers, and three magazines. He left an estate estimated at $20 million, which he willed to the Metropolitan Museum of Art.

EDWARD ROSCOE MURROW
1908–1965

Ed Murrow was born near Greensboro, North Carolina. He joined CBS in 1935 and was assigned to Europe, where he served as the network's one-man news staff. He won fame during World War II for his radio broadcasts describing German bombing attacks on London. He accompanied twenty-five bombing missions over Germany and was aboard a mine-sweeper on sea duty. After eleven years as an outstanding war correspondent, Murrow returned to the United States to become vice president of CBS news operations.

Murrow narrated the television program "See It Now," from 1951 to 1958, dealing with many important issues. Two of the most famous and controversial were his attack on Senator Joseph McCarthy and his investigations of communism, and "Harvest of Shame" on the plight of migratory workers. He was in Korea in 1950 to cover the conflict there and reported on the Berlin air lift. Other programs assayed American problems, policies, and personalities. Some "See It Now" subjects were concerned with the progress of decolonization in Africa, the Suez war, the Budapest uprising, presidential politics, nuclear testing, and school desegregation. From 1953 to 1959 Murrow conducted a different kind of television program, "Person to Person," which made weekly "visits" to the homes of celebrities. From 1958 to 1960 he also produced a program entitled "Small World."

Murrow became the most honored man in American broadcasting. He retired from the field in 1960, apparently disillusioned with its current state. He joined the Kennedy administration in January 1961 as director of the U.S. Information Agency, and served for three years until ill health forced his retirement in 1964, a victim of lung cancer, perhaps a consequence of excessive smoking.

THOMAS NAST
1840-1902

Thomas Nast, the son of a musician in a Bavarian military band, was brought to the United States at the age of six by his parents. Nast developed an early passion for drawing, after receiving a gift of crayons from a neighbor. There followed a period of art study with private teachers and at the National Academy of Design in New York. At age fifteen, some of his sketches were shown to Frank Leslie, who promptly employed him as a draftsman for *Leslie's Illustrated Newspaper,* at four dollars a week. Working with other artists on the Leslie staff gave young Nast invaluable technical training and experience.

The establishment of *Harper's Weekly* in 1857 opened a new outlet for Nast. His first important drawings, a savage satire on a police scandal in New York, appeared in 1859. Later in the same year, the *New York Illustrated News* started publication. It gave Nast a number of assignments, including John Brown's funeral, and then a foreign tour to cover the Heenan–Sayers prizefight in England and Garibaldi's revolt in Italy.

The outbreak of the Civil War, shortly after Nast's return to the United States, provided him with a chance to establish a permanent niche in history as a political cartoonist. His first drawings relating to the war appeared in the *New York Illustrated News,* briefly in *Leslie's,* and finally in *Harper's Weekly.* Fletcher Harper, the magazine's manager, recognized Nast's talents and employed him in 1862 as a staff artist. The Nast cartoons quickly became a favorite feature with *Harper's* readers. Nast's Civil War drawings were credited with helping to stimulate patriotism in the North. One of the first to receive wide attention was entitled "Peace," aimed at Northerners who opposed prosecution of the war. The impact of this and other Nast drawings led President Lincoln to describe Nast as "our best recruiting sergeant."

Among notable Nast works of the Civil War era were cartoons condemning guerrilla warfare in the border states; the "Emancipation" drawing of January 24, 1863, depicting black life of the past and the future; a dramatic sketch "On to Richmond"; and a sardonic drawing "Compromise with the South," showing a triumphant Southerner clasping hands with a crippled Northern soldier over the grave of Union heroes. All made a powerful impression on Northern sentiment.

After the war, Nast devoted himself to political cartoons. His drawings for the Reconstruction period were badly slanted, portraying President Andrew Johnson, for example, as a bully and dictator, and Southerners as mistreating defenseless blacks. Starting in 1866, Nast adopted an effective device of using Shakespearean situations for satirical purposes.

The most telling of Nast's cartoons, from 1869 to 1872, were aimed at destroying "Boss" William Tweed's corrupt political rule in New York City. At this time he created the elephant and the donkey as symbols of the Republican and Democratic parties, respectively, and also popularized the tiger as the emblem of Tammany Hall, the regular Democratic party organization in New York. Famous were his "The Tammany Tiger Let Loose," "Who Stole the People's Money?" and "A Group of Vultures Waiting for the Storm to Pass Over," all in 1871. The final triumph for Nast was a cartoon of Tweed so realistic that he was easily recognized and arrested in Spain, where he had fled as a fugitive from justice.

Nast was a staunch Republican most of his career, supporting Lincoln and Grant, ridiculing Horace Greeley's presidential ambitions, and defending Hayes against Tilden. In 1884 and 1888, however, he backed Grover Cleveland for president, after which he returned to the Republican fold.

By the mid-1880s, the vogue for Nast's work had passed. He continued for a short time to draw for other journals and to illustrate a few books, but his great days were over. In 1902, President Theodore Roosevelt appointed Nast as consul at Guayaquil, Ecuador, where he succumbed to yellow fever and the rigors of the climate.

VICTOR NAVATSKY

1932–

Victor Navatsky was born in New York City. An early evidence of his interest in writing was his editorship of the *Swarthmore Phoenix,* while a college student. Later as a student at Yale, he and two associates started a political satire magazine, *Monocle,* as a hobby. The magazine was moved to New York in 1961, and published intermittently as a commercial venture. Also published was a radical political weekly, *Outsiders' Newsletter.*

From 1970 to 1972, Navatsky was manuscript editor of the *New York Times Magazine* and for four years he wrote a monthly column on publishing "In Cold Print" for the *New York Times Book Review.*

A group of investors headed by Hamilton Fish III bought the *Nation* in 1977 and recruited Navatsky as editor. Though it had been and remained a money losing proposition, the *Nation* under Navatsky's management tripled its circulation.

MILO GABRIEL NELSON
1938–

Milo Nelson was editor of the *Wilson Library Bulletin,* 1978–88. He graduated from Drake University and holds an M.S. degree from the University of Wisconsin Library School. From 1970 to 1978, he was Humanities Librarian of the University of Idaho. He saw military service in the United States Army, 1962–63. He was author of *Idaho Local History* (1976), and coeditor of the *Bookmark,* 1970–78.

WILLIAM ROCKHILL NELSON
1841–1915

William Rockhill Nelson was born in Fort Wayne, Indiana. Initially, he had managed the family farm, practiced law, raised cotton on a large plantation near Savannah, and had been a building contractor in Indiana. All these ventures were losers.

In 1878, Nelson acquired part ownership of the *Fort Wayne Sentinel,* the local Democratic organ. The following year, he and a partner, Samuel E. Morss, became full owners. Ambitious for larger fields to conquer, the two sold the *Sentinel* in 1880 and moved to Kansas City, Missouri. Together they founded the *Kansas City Star.* Nelson remained as editor and publisher until his death in 1915. In 1880, Kansas City was a sprawling meat-packing town, a railroad point for western immigration, with mud streets, wooden sidewalks, and mule-drawn streetcars. It had two morning and two evening papers in English and two German papers. The *Star* began as a four-page paper selling for two cents or ten cents a week, compared to six cents each for its competitors. The *Star* flourished and by the end of its third year was printing ten thousand copies. A weekly edition circulated widely through the Southwest at twenty-five cents a year.

The *Star* led a crusade for municipal reform in Kansas City, campaigning for a modern street railway system, against corruption in municipal affairs and fraud in elections, for a system of city parks and boulevards, and for improving the residential sections of the city. The *Star* carried on public-service activities in many other areas, all designed to upgrade Kansas City.

Nelson acquired his afternoon rival, the *Evening Mail,* in 1882, bringing with it a much-needed Associated Press franchise, and in 1901, he bought the *Kansas City Times,* which became the morning edition of the *Star.* By 1915, the *Star's* circulation reached two hundred thousand — larger than the population of Kansas City.

ALLEN H. NEUHARTH
1924–

Allen Neuharth was born in Eureka, South Dakota. He began working at age eleven as a newsboy delivering the *Minneapolis Tribune.* At thirteen he had a part-time job in the composing room of the weekly *Alpena Journal.* During his junior year in high school he was editor of the school newspaper. After military service in the South Pacific and Europe during World War II, Neuharth entered the University of South Dakota to study journalism. There, too, he edited the campus newspaper, and in addition held summer jobs as a reporter for two South Dakota papers, the *Rapid City Journal* and the *Mitchell Daily Republican.*

Neuharth moved to Florida in 1954 to join the reporting staff of the *Miami Herald.* He demonstrated exceptional ability as an investigative reporter and in 1960 was promoted to be assistant executive editor of the Knight newspaper chain's *Detroit Free Press.* Another step up occurred in 1963 when the Gannett Company persuaded Neuharth to move to Rochester, New York, to become general manager of its two papers, the *Times-Union* and the *Democrat and Chronicle.* Three years later Neuharth was named executive vice president of the Gannett chain and president of Gannett Florida. In 1978 he assumed the additional title of chairman of Gannett, but in 1984 gave up the title. He remained chief executive officer of Gannett, the largest and most profitable newspaper chain in the United States, holding and operating ninety-three daily newspapers, thirty-eight other newspapers, eight television and sixteen radio stations. It is now a media conglomerate estimated in value at $2.5 billion.

One of Neuharth's recent ventures is the publication of *USA Today,* a daily, nationally distributed newspaper, which quickly became the nation's third-highest circulation paper.

ROBERT PEEBLES NEVIN
1820–1908

Robert Nevin was born in Shippensburg, Pennsylvania. At an early age he began writing poems and sketches for newspapers and magazines and became a correspondent for the *Washington Reporter* during the 1844 presidential campaign. Later he contributed to the *Atlantic, Lippincott's,* and other magazines.

In 1870 Nevin purchased an interest in the *Weekly Leader,* a Sunday paper, and changed it to a daily. Ten years later, he founded the *Pittsburgh Times,* but sold it four years later. His primary interest was in petroleum and oil refining, a field in which he was a leader.

LUCIUS W. NIEMAN
1857–1935

Lucius W. Nieman, born in Bear Creek, Wisconsin, is popularly known by journalists for two distinctions: as founder and editor of a major American newspaper, the *Milwaukee Journal,* and for the Nieman fellowships at Harvard University for working newspapermen.

Nieman was given a start in the newspaper business, at age twelve, with a job as a printer's devil at a weekly paper, the *Waukesha Freeman.* There he learned to set type and to carry on the variety of duties assigned to a printer's devil. At age fifteen Nieman proceeded to Milwaukee for a job in the *Milwaukee Sentinel's* composing room. While a student at Carroll College, he was the *Sentinel's* Waukesha correspondent and then became a full time reporter for the paper. After reporting on the 1875 state legislative session in Madison, Nieman was promoted to be city editor and a year later managing editor of the *Sentinel,* a job he held until 1880.

Nieman left the *Sentinel* briefly to take charge of a failing paper, the *St. Paul Dispatch* in Minnesota, where his genius as a newspaperman was shown. He was so successful that he was offered a one-third interest in the paper, but declined to return to the *Sentinel.* In 1882 Nieman went to the rescue of another newspaper in trouble, the *Milwaukee Daily Journal,* in which he bought a half-interest and became coowner, editor, reporter, and even occasionally typesetter.

The *Journal* under Nieman's direction adopted a policy of reporting all the news, whether favorable or unfavorable, to the political party that it supported; issued a sports summary as a feature section printed on green paper; hired women reporters to cover news of interest to women; and with the aid of a translator provided thorough coverage of German propaganda aimed at influencing American opinion.

When Nieman died in 1935, he left an estate valued at $10 million. His wife survived him by only four months. Her will left the bulk of her estate to Harvard University to "promote and elevate the standards of journalism." About twelve Nieman fellowships have been awarded to working journalists annually since 1938.

HEZEKIAH NILES
1777–1839

Hezekiah Niles, one of the important figures in early American journalism, was born in Pennsylvania, but grew up in Wilmington, Delaware. When he was seventeen, Niles was apprenticed to Benjamin Johnson, a Philadelphia printer, bookseller, and bookbinder. While still in his teens, he began contributing articles to the *Aurora* and other Philadelphia newspapers. Back in Wilmington, in partnership with Vincent Bonsal, a number of job printing orders were filled and the *Delaware Gazette* was printed.

In 1805, Niles founded his own magazine, the *Apollo,* the Delaware weekly magazine that published articles, poems, newsletters, and humorous essays written by Niles himself. The *Apollo* lasted for less than a year, after which Niles moved to Baltimore to become editor of the *Evening Post.*

Of historical importance was Niles's decision to publish speeches, letters, official documents, and similar material in a weekly news magazine, entitled variously *Weekly Register, Niles' Weekly Register,* or *Niles' National Register.* The paper was devoted primarily to politics, leaving no doubt about the editor's antislavery views and belief in a protective tariff, but scrupulously fair in presenting all sides of issues and avoiding endorsing candidates for office. The *Register* was indexed and is regarded by scholars as an invaluable source for the study of American history, especially contemporary events.

The *Register* exercised great influence in its day, was widely read, and by the end of its first year had more than 3,300 paying subscribers. After the death of the founder in 1839, the *Register* was continued for a time by his son William Ogden Niles, but ceased publication in 1849.

WILLIAM PENN NIXON
1833–1912

William Penn Nixon was born in Fountain City, Indiana. He began in the legal profession, but later switched to journalism. In 1868 he joined his brother in establishing the *Cincinnati Daily Chronicle,* an evening newspaper that was merged with the *Cincinnati Times* in 1872. Nixon became business manager of the *Chicago Inter-Ocean* in 1872, gained a controlling interest, and in 1875, took over as general manager and editor.

MORDECAI MANUEL NOAH
1785–1851

Mordecai Noah was born in Philadelphia. He entered the field of journalism in New York City in 1817 by becoming editor of the *National Advocate,* a daily paper founded by the Democratic party's Tammany faction. In 1826 Noah left the *Advocate* and established the *New York Enquirer,* merged in 1829 with the *Morning Courier* to form the *Morning Courier* and *New York Enquirer.*

After serving as a surveyor of the Port of New York (1829–33), Noah resigned to found the *Evening Star,* to support the new Whig party. Another political appointment followed. Then Noah became editor, first, of the *Union* and next *Noah's Times and Weekly Messenger.* He remained as editor of the latter until the end of his life.

LYN NOFZIGER
1924–

Lyn Nofziger was born in Bakersfield, California. After three years in the U.S. Army, he enrolled in the University of California at Los Angeles and graduated from San Jose State College, where he edited the school's paper. After several short stays in other jobs, he became Washington correspondent for Copley's chain of California newspapers. In 1966, Nofziger became Ronald Reagan's press secretary. He left the Reagan team two years later and established himself as an independent political consultant in Sacramento. He continued to advise Reagan on a part-time basis and served as an aide to President Nixon and the Republican National Committee. Nofziger has been described as a tough-minded, pragmatic, and aggressive Republican activist.

CHARLES NORDHOFF
1830–1901

Charles Nordhoff was born in Germany and brought to America at the age of five by his parents. At age thirteen he was apprenticed to a printer. In 1857, he was hired by Harper & Brothers as an editor and four years later he became managing editor of the *New York Evening Post*. Nordhoff retired from the *Post* in 1871 and spent two years visiting California and Hawaii. In 1874 the *New York Herald* appointed him its Washington correspondent, a position that he filled with distinction until his retirement in 1890.

CROSBY S. NOYES
1825–1908

Crosby S. Noyes was born in the obscure Maine village of Minot. At age fifteen he produced a small handwritten paper of four pages, the *Minot Notion,* which soon suspended publication. He also wrote items for various New England publications. In 1847 he decided to move to Washington, D.C., described at the time as a "struggling country village, with zig-zag grades, no sewerage, no water supply except from pumps and springs, unimproved reservations, second-rate dwellings and streets of mud and mire." For a livelihood, Noyes worked in a bookshop, ushered in a theater, and was route agent for the *Baltimore Sun*. By 1848, however, he began reporting for a weekly paper, the *Washington News,* over the next six years covering Congress, other branches of government, and local news.

During a year off in Europe, in 1855, Noyes sent back articles to the *Portland* (Maine) *Transcript*. Back in Washington he worked for the *Evening Star,* a small four-page paper started in 1852. His reporting duties for the *Star* were comprehensive. In 1867 Noyes and several partners bought the *Star* and he became editor-in-chief—a title that he retained until his death forty-one years later.

As editor and publisher, Noyes promoted numerous causes to improve Washington, notably, prevention of the use of parklands as sites for federal buildings, reclamation of Potomac River flats, clean streets, stopping the dumping of garbage in the Potomac River, construction of more bridges and public playgrounds, and removal of railroads from city streets. Most of the reforms were eventually achieved.

By the time of Noyes's death in 1908, the *Star* was a dominant force in Washington journalism and its editor was recognized, in Theodore Roosevelt's words, as "one of the two or three leading citizens and most distinguished men of Washington."

Noyes's sons, Frank and Theodore, also became journalists. Frank was later president of the Associated Press and Theodore was editor of the *Star* after his father's death.

THEODORE W. NOYES
1858–1946

Theodore Williams Noyes was born in Washington, D.C., and inherited his interest in journalism from his father, Crosby Noyes, long-time editor of the *Washington Evening Star*. His younger brother, Frank Brett Noyes, was the first president of the modern Associated Press in 1900.

At age nineteen, Noyes became a reporter on the *Star*. Later he lived in the Dakota Territory and wrote a weekly column for the *Sioux Falls Press*. He returned to Washington in 1886 to become associate editor of the *Star*. In that position, he crusaded for various civic reforms and fairer treatment by the federal government of District of Columbia citizens.

Noyes traveled extensively, to Europe, the Arctic, the Orient, the Philippines, and Australia, and sent reports back for publication in the *Star*. He was a leader in the 1898 campaign to gain the Hawaiian Islands for the United States.

Noyes served as editor-in-chief of the *Washington Evening Star* from 1908 to 1946, only two years less than his father.

EDGAR (BILL) WILSON NYE
1850–1896

Edgar Wilson Nye, popularly known as Bill Nye, was born in Shirley, Maine, and grew up in Wisconsin. In 1876 he moved to Wyoming territory. In Laramie City he became a reporter for the *Daily Sentinel*. Five years later he founded and edited the *Laramie Boomerang,* named after Nye's pet mule. His broadly humorous stories of frontier life first appeared in that publication. The tales were widely reprinted and made the author internationally famous. Occasional contributions were also made to other Western papers, such as the *Cheyenne Daily Sun* and the *Denver Tribune*.

Nye rivaled Mark Twain, Finley Peter Dunne, Artemus Ward, Josh

Billings, Petroleum V. Nasby, and Ambrose Bierce as a popular humorist in his days. Unlike some of his contemporaries, he avoided the dialect form, which was once considered amusing.

In 1886 Nye moved East and accepted a position on the staff of the *New York World,* where his writings gained national circulation. He also became a highly popular lecturer, teamed up with James Whitcomb Riley. His stories were republished in a number of volumes from 1881 to 1896.

ADOLPH SIMON OCHS
1858–1935

Adolph Ochs's parents were German Jewish refugees, who had settled in Knoxville, Tennessee. Their son's journalistic career began at age eleven as an office boy on the *Knoxville Chronicle.* As printer's devil on the *Chronicle* he learned the newspaper business from the ground up. Two years later he became a practical printer on the *Louisville Courier-Journal.* At age nineteen he moved to Chattanooga to take a job on a new paper, which soon failed. With $250 of borrowed money, Ochs bought a controlling interest in the *Chattanooga Times,* assumed its debts, and in 1878 began his career as a newspaper publisher—before he was old enough to vote.

The *Chattanooga Times* under Ochs's guidance set a pattern later applied to the *New York Times*—in his words, "clean, dignified, and trustworthy." Gradually, as Chattanooga grew, Ochs succeeded in raising his paper to a position of prosperity and prestige. His reputation was further enhanced by chairmanship (1891–94) of the Southern Associated Press and later affiliation with the old (Western) Associated Press, from which developed the nationwide organization of that name.

Early in 1896 came Ochs's opportunity to achieve fame and fortune on a much larger scale. He was informed that the *New York Times* was for sale. The *Times,* established in 1851, once prosperous and powerful, had been running down for years. Its circulation had dropped to nine thousand, it was losing a thousand dollars a day, and it was facing bankruptcy. After a thorough investigation, Ochs concluded that the paper could be saved. Using $75,000, which he mostly borrowed, a reorganization was arranged whereby Ochs would become publisher of the *Times,* with full control, and a majority stockholder, if he could make the paper pay for three consecutive years.

The competition Ochs faced in New York was rich and powerful. *Pulitzer's World* and *Hearst's Journal* (later the *New York American*) had built up enormous circulation by setting a sales price of one cent, while the *Times* and other papers were selling for three cents. Ochs refused to indulge in the typographical pyrotechnics, comic strips, and emphasis on crime and sex featured by Pulitzer and Hearst. The war with Spain almost finished the *Times,* for it could not afford to employ the special correspondents needed to report the news.

At this stage, as the *Times* was almost ready to go on the rocks, some of its executives proposed to reach a "quality public" by raising the price to five cents. Ochs was convinced, however, that many people bought the *World* and the *Journal* because they were cheap and would buy the *Times* instead if they could get it at the same price. It was a stroke of genius. Within a year the *Times's* circulation had trebled and the paper was making money. From there on, the record of Ochs's career is one of steadily increasing influence and prosperity.

Most basic to the *Times's* reputation and future greatness were the policies firmly established by Ochs. He believed that a large segment of the reading public is composed of intelligent, thoughtful people. His main object, therefore, was to give all the news, especially "all the news that is fit to print," and to reject coarse, vulgar, and inane features, muckraking, and any kind of crusade. As Benjamin Stolberg, writing on the history of the American press, stated, "The *Times* has no leg shows, side shows, or circuses. It employs no middle-aged, rundown newspaper men to grind out advice to the lovelorn. It peddles no funny sheets, Krazy Kats, Nize Babies, or humor by Andy Gump, Mutt and Jeff, and FPA." As Ochs himself expressed it, *"The Times* is the sort of newspaper which no one needs to be ashamed to be seen reading."

An important policy set by Ochs was to exclude advertising considered fraudulent or improper, and to refuse to let powerful and wealthy advertisers influence the *Times's* editorial and news policies, regardless of the loss of revenue. These high standards eventually raised the standards of both news and advertising in the news world as a whole.

To its usual news columns the *Times,* under Ochs's direction, added three innovations: a book review supplement, treating newly published books as news; a Sunday magazine section, devoted mainly to news of an informative nature; and a weekly financial review, presenting a detailed survey of worldwide economic, financial, and commercial trends. Also innovative were the ways in which the *Times* extended the scope of the news, as the paper set out to print happenings in every area of possible interest to its readers. There was emphasis on pure and applied science. Beginning with World War I, the *Times* began publishing in full the speeches of the leaders of all European governments, the "white papers" of the British and German governments, and other diplomatic records. In that way, the *Times* became over the years an invaluable source of original documentary records pertaining to current history.

Editorials in the *Times* have the reputation of being innocuous and somewhat colorless, carefully avoiding firm stands. Ochs may have planned it that way, because of his respect for things as they were; he was temperamentally convinced that there was merit on most sides of most questions and taking a firm editorial position was often unwise. One commentator, Silas Bent, in his book *Strange Bedfellows,* suggested that Ochs's early experience in a small town where his readers were also his friends had taught him to get out "a paper that hurt nobody's feelings." Ochs himself never wrote editorials, although he presided over the daily editorial council and directed general editorial policy. His editorial writers often disagreed with him and he gave them considerable freedom in stating their views in the paper. His editors-in-chief Charles R. Miller and Rollo Ogden were usually in harmony with him. In any case, Ochs always felt that editorial opinion should be kept subordinate to the news. The Ochs concept of news was greatly strengthened after 1904 by C. V. Van Anda, a genius as a managing editor, who was interested in everything and made a major contribution to the paper's success.

There has been no lack of critics of Ochs and the *Times,* ranging from the moderate differences expressed by Silas Bent, Benjamin Stolberg, and Elmer Davis to the extreme views of Upton Sinclair in *The Brass Check* and *Crimes of the Times.* The liberal opinions are well summarized by Oswald Garrison Villard in a chapter of *The Disappearing Daily.* After praising the dispatches of Walter Duranty from Russia, Herbert L. Matthews from Ethiopia, Italy, Spain, and India, Anne O'Hare McCormick for her distinguished foreign correspondence, Hanson W. Baldwin's military and naval commentaries, Arthur Krock's Washington reporting, and others, Villard maintains that the *Times* was biased and unfair in its reporting on the Soviet Union, the Spanish revolution, and in its handling of matters relating to the Jews. "Standing up for the privileged was part of Ochs's philosophy," according to Villard, "a great secret of his business success— that and his unending devotion to the god of things as they are."

Nevertheless, Villard concedes, "Ochs was a remarkable newspaper manager, the most successful in the whole history of American journalism. As such he created our foremost daily, which will never lose its commanding position if its directors but realize their responsibilities and their duties to this country and all of its people, and rise to them." Unquestionably the political and economic opinions of the *Times* have remained conservative, as they were under Ochs. But the *Times's* concept of news has deeply impressed the newspaper world, providing the American people with the most comprehensive information in their history. It raised the standards of American journalism and broadened the outlook of the American people. Thus, whatever his weaknesses, the *Times* remains a monument to Adolph Ochs's memory.

Some of his coreligionists never forgave him his opposition to Zionism;

he believed Judaism was a religion, not a separatist racial culture. Yet Judaism was no perfunctory faith expressed merely in benefactions; it colored his whole life. In later years he was happiest at his summer home on Lake George, surrounded by his family and a circle of old friends. He died, as perhaps he would have wished, on a visit to Chattanooga.

FREMONT OLDER
1856-1935

Fremont Older, born in Freedom Township, Wisconsin, was described by one biographer, Billy E. Deal, as "a muckracker, a crusader, a cigar-chewing bombastic, ferocious teacher who had a reverential respect for truth and decency." He was named for the explorer Fremont, the Path-finder.

At age thirteen, Older dropped out of school and took a job as a printer's devil at the *Courant* in Berlin, Wisconsin. He had a restless disposition and moved around Wisconsin, Illinois, and Minnesota, employed as a printer's devil on several newspapers. He even ran the *Oconto* (Wisconsin) *Free Press,* while the editor was serving a jail term for libel. Finally, Older went on to California, arriving in San Francisco in 1873. For a short time he worked for the *Territorial Enterprise* in Virginia City, Nevada, and then returned to San Francisco. He was with the short-lived *Daily Mail* and afterward was a reporter for the *Weekly Journal* in Redwood City, followed by a job as editor and business manager of the *Times-Gazette.*

In 1884 Older was offered and accepted a job with the *Alta California* in San Francisco. Next he moved on to the *Morning Call,* a paper on which he had worked as a printer when he arrived in San Francisco. Fremont became the *Call's* city editor. The *Call* was sold. Older then was appointed managing editor of the *Bulletin,* a failing paper. Fremont's stories of San Francisco police, mobs, political bosses, and political graft were soon reflected in increased circulation for the *Bulletin.* A year after Older took over the *Bulletin,* it was filled with highly readable names, articles, poetry, editorials, and fiction. It added a separate page and a women's section, and gave full attention to art and drama. Six-inch type and sensational headlines caught the reader's eye.

Older became actively involved in politics, trying first to rid San Francisco of graft and corruption, fighting the Southern Pacific Railroad, a dominant force in California, and campaigning for prison reform and abolition of capital punishment. The *Bulletin's* circulation rose to more than one hundred thousand.

Disagreements with the *Bulletin's* owner caused Older to accept an offer from Hearst to transfer to the *Call* as editor. In 1929 the *Call* and the *Bulletin* merged and Older became editor-in-chief. For several years he was also fiction editor of the Hearst chain.

BRADLEY SILLICK OSBON
1827–1912

B. S. Osbon, born in Westchester County, New York, was the most famous naval correspondent of the Civil War. Something of a juvenile delinquent, he ran away from home at age eleven to work on Hudson River Canal boats. Two years later he joined the crew of a ship for a trip between New York and Liverpool. Many Irish immigrant passengers died of typhoid on the return trip to New York. Osbon never seemed happy far away from the sea. He enrolled in a private school in Brooklyn to study navigation. For a time he enlisted in the U.S. Navy but found the routine too tame. Looking for more excitement, Osbon in 1847 sailed from New Bedford, Massachusetts, aboard a whaler bound for the Arctic Ocean and Antarctica. He was gone for more than five years. In 1853 he became captain of a schooner in the Argentine navy. He spent time in the merchant marine (1857–58) as quartermaster on a steamboat.

Osbon's fame as a journalist came with the Civil War. He wrote an eyewitness account of the siege and surrender of Fort Sumter at Charleston, South Carolina, for the *New York World*. Osbon was a signal officer aboard the U.S. carrier *Harriet Lane*. The Fort Sumter story made a journalistic hero out of Osbon and he was offered the position of naval editor of the *New York Herald* by James Gordon Bennett. The *Herald* gave its new reporter a roving commission to accompany naval expeditions to the South. In that capacity, Osbon covered the battle of Port Royal from the U.S. transport ship *Matanzas*. A full report was sent to the *Herald* and an illustration of the battle scene went to *Harper's Weekly* for the November 30, 1861 issue. In 1862, Osbon covered Admiral David Farragut's naval expedition against New Orleans. The expedition came under heavy fire from Confederate forts south of New Orleans. The last of his Civil War naval battles was covered by Osbon in 1863 when he witnessed the ironclad *Monitor's* unsuccessful assault on Fort McAllister in Georgia. Osbon was wounded in the battle. Altogether, he had many hair-breadth escapes.

After the war's end, in 1871, Osbon established what he described as a bureau of naval intelligence. He also founded an eight-page weekly, the *Nautical Gazette,* the first maritime journal in America. By 1873 the *Gazette* had seven thousand subscribers and its size was increased to sixteen pages. The paper was published by Osbon for thirteen years and then sold in 1884.

ELEAZER OSWALD
1755-1795

In a fairly short lifespan of forty years, Eleazer Oswald managed to achieve notoriety in a number of ways. His biographer, Dwight L. Tepler, Jr., lists the following occupations Oswald pursued: printer, soldier, publisher, duelist, coffee shop proprietor, free press theorist, fighter in the French Revolution, and unsuccessful revolutionist in Ireland.

Oswald was born in Falmouth, England, the son of a sea captain. At age fifteen he emigrated to New York City, where he was apprenticed to John Holt, owner of the *New-York Journal, or General Advertiser*. During the Revolution, Oswald volunteered and served with distinction in several engagements, including the battle of Monmouth. After leaving military service, he became a partner of William Goddard in Baltimore in a paper-making and printing business (1779). The firm's *Maryland Journal* was attacked by a mob for publishing an article critical of George Washington.

Oswald moved on to Philadelphia and in 1782 began publishing the *Independent Gazetteer*. More trouble resulted from attacks on Pennsylvania's Chief Justice Thomas McKean. Oswald was arrested and tried for seditious libel. He was released after putting up a surety bond, but was soon back in custody for publishing an account of his experience. He was bailed out of jail by his friends. McKean brought charges against Oswald on two other occasions, but a grand jury refused to indict. The *Independent Gazetteer* was one of the few newspapers of the time that opposed adoption of a new federal constitution.

Oswald became publisher of newspapers in America's two largest cities by buying the weekly *New York Journal* in 1786. The following year, however, he sold the *New York Journal* to an associate, Thomas Greenleaf. In a complicated case, again brought before McKean, in 1788, Oswald was charged with contempt of court, fined ten pounds, and sentenced to a month in jail. Oswald brought an impeachment suit against McKean in the General Assembly, a move defeated by conservatives.

Oswald went to England in 1792 and the next year volunteered for military service in the French Revolution. In 1793 he went to Ireland to try to stir up a revolt against the British. Soon after returning to New York, he died of yellow fever. This was the end of what McKean described as a "seditious turbulent man," one of the earliest fighters for freedom of the press in America.

OSWALD OTTENDORFER
1826–1900

Oswald Ottendorfer was a refugee, born in Morenia, who had been involved in revolutionary uprisings in Austria and Germany in 1848. After several narrow escapes, he left for New York, without friends and knowing no English. He was given a subordinate job with the German-language paper, the *Staats-Zeitung*, which had grown from a triweekly to a daily, with a circulation of 15,300. There was a great wave of German immigration into the United States in the 1870s and 1880s. In 1880 the *Staats-Zeitung* claimed that its circulation of 50,000 was larger than that of any other German-language daily in the world.

Ottendorfer was made editor of the *Staats-Zeitung* in 1858. The following year he married Anna Uhl, widow of the founder. Under their joint management the paper became an influential, widely read metropolitan organ, circulation increased, and the latest mechanical improvements were installed. The front page was usually filled with telegraphic news and reports from European correspondents. Other features were articles written by Ottendorfer, serial novels, and local news. The staff included many immigrants who, like Ottendorfer, were fugitives from Europe. After Ottendorfer retired in the late 1880s, he spent most of the remainder of his life in Europe.

RICHARD FELTON OUTCAULT
1863–1928

R. F. Outcault was born in Lancaster, Ohio, and studied art in Cincinnati and Paris. Some of his early cartoons appeared in *Truth, Life,* and *Judge.* Outcault pioneered the newspaper colored comic supplement and the cartoon strip. His "Origin of a New Species," featuring an anaconda and a yellow dog in the *New York World* in 1894, was the beginning of the "funny paper." It was followed by "Hogan's Alley," which led to the "The Yellow Kid," believed to be the first comic strip.

Outcault left the *World* to join the *New York Journal,* leading to a dispute that became known as "yellow journalism." One of his series, "Buster Brown," began in the *New York Tribune* in 1902 and was long popular. It reputedly inflicted Buster Brown suits, collars, and haircuts on small boys.

THOMAS PAINE
1737–1809

Few figures in American history are as controversial as Thomas Paine and few made contributions as notable as his toward the beginning of the United States as a nation. To dismiss Paine, as did Theodore Roosevelt, as "a filthy little atheist" (he was none of the three) is totally unfair to a man who played a major role in inspiring the American Revolution, who had a direct hand in drafting the Declaration of Independence, and who was instrumental in maintaining the morale of George Washington's troops at their lowest ebb.

The first thirty-seven years of Paine's career were marked by a series of failures, giving virtually no evidence of future greatness. He came into the world in 1737 in the village of Thetford, England, the son of Quaker parents. At the age of thirteen, he left the local grammar school to serve an apprenticeship in his father's trade of corset making. Soon tiring of the dullness and drudgery of the work, Paine staged his first rebellion, running away to join the crew of a privateer. His father overtook him on board and brought him back to stay making. Again the boy ran away and this time saw enough service at sea to cure any romantic illusion. In the years that followed, matters went from bad to worse: two unfortunate marriages, one ending in his wife's early death and the other in separation; two periods of employment in the excise service, the last leading to discharge for serving as a spokesman for the grossly underpaid customs officers; earning a pittance as schoolmaster; operating an unsuccessful tobacco shop; and ending up in London in hiding to avoid imprisonment for debt.

While in London, Paine had the good fortune to meet Benjamin Franklin, stationed there as political agent for the American colonies. Franklin was attracted by Paine's character and abilities and urged him to migrate to America and make a new start. Paine's interest in science, electrical experiments, and practical inventions had drawn the two men together. Paine accepted Franklin's advice and arrived in Philadelphia in late 1774, armed with a letter of introduction to Franklin's son-in-law, Richard Bache.

The New World produced a transformation in Paine. Prior to coming to America, he had written only one piece of propaganda, *The Case of the Officers of Excise,* in which he had argued for better pay for the excisemen. His varied experience in England, as shopworker, sailor, tradesman, revenue officer, and teacher, however, had fitted him well for the part of master propagandist, which he would play in the future. He had witnessed first-hand the misery, poverty, and insecurity of the lower classes in England, in contrast to the conspicuous wealth of the royalty and nobility.

During his term of government duty, Paine had also become acquainted with widespread public corruption. He sailed for America disillusioned with the European scene, but filled with dreams of liberty, ready to fight for democratic principles.

Within a short time after Paine's arrival in Philadelphia, a printer and bookseller named Robert Aitken began publication of the *Pennsylvania Magazine.* Paine wrote extensively for the first issue of the new periodical, following which he was appointed its editor. During the ensuing eighteen months, he wrote on a variety of radical causes denouncing slavery, the custom of dueling, cruelty to animals, and hereditary titles, and advocating women's rights, old-age pensions, rational divorce laws, national and international copyright, international federation, and republican equality. One of Paine's first articles condemned slavery as a monstrous evil.

On January 10, 1776, Paine published an anonymous pamphlet of forty-seven pages, priced at two shillings, and entitled *Common Sense.* In three months, 120,000 copies had been bought. Estimates of total sales have ranged up to half a million, equivalent in terms of population to a sale of 30 million copies in the United States today. Virtually every literate person in the thirteen colonies is believed to have read the fiery pamphlet.

Probably nothing comparable to *Common Sense* in its immediate impact is to be found in the history of literature. It was a clarion call to the American colonists to fight for their independence — without compromise or vacillation. Revolution was the only solution of the conflict with Great Britain and George III. *Common Sense* ran the gamut from down-to-earth realistic, practical arguments to emotion-charged, violently partisan, and biased appeals of the born agitator. Less than six months after Paine's famous pamphlet came off the press, the Continental Congress, meeting in Philadelphia, proclaimed the independence of "The United States of America," a phrase first used by Paine.

Soon after the Declaration of Independence, Paine composed a series of papers, entitled *The American Crisis,* designed to inspire the colonial forces. After the war, Paine went to Europe, became an enthusiastic supporter of the French Revolution, and wrote another landmark book, *The Rights of Man.* He was also author of *The Age of Reason,* a controversial work attacking Christianity. It stirred up anger among conservatives.

JAMES PARKER

1714–1770

Frank Luther Mott, historian of journalism, called James Parker "one of the most enterprising of colonial printers." A financial partnership with

Benjamin Franklin enabled Parker to establish the first newspapers in Connecticut and New Jersey, to publish a magazine, and to serve as public printer in New York and New Jersey.

Parker was born in Woodridge, New Jersey, and was William Bradford's apprentice for a time in publishing the *New York Gazette.* In 1742, Parker and Franklin became partners in carrying on a printing business in New Jersey. Franklin supplied the press, type, and other equipment. In 1743 Parker founded a new paper, the third in New York, the *New-York Weekly Post-Boy.* The title was changed later to *New York Gazette,* revived as the *Weekly Post-Boy,* and changed again in 1753 to *New York Gazette; or The Weekly Post-Boy.*

Another area was entered by Parker in 1746, when he became librarian of the corporation of the City of New York. He set up a system of circulation and fines and printed a catalog of the library's collection.

A printing office was established by Parker in 1751, the first printing plant in New Jersey. He also became engaged in magazine publishing, printing four periodicals in New York: the *Independent Reflector, Occasional Reverberator, Instructor,* and *John Englishman.* The Parker printing empire was extended to Connecticut, where he became printer to Yale College and in 1755 founded the *Connecticut Gazette,* New Haven's first newspaper.

Another Parker venture in periodical publishing was the *New American Magazine,* a successor to Andrew Bradford's *American Magazine.* It lasted only twenty-seven numbers and was a financial failure. The Woodbridge press also published New Jersey's first newspaper, the *Constitutional Courant,* in 1765.

Book publishing was another Parker interest. He printed works of poetry, fiction, science, history, religion, husbandry, and almanacs.

Some of Parker's apprentices and journeymen became prominent in printing and publishing, notably William Goddard and Hugh Gaine.

WILLIAM PARKS
CA. 1698–1750

William Parks was a native of Ludlow, Shropshire, England. From the point of view of American journalism history, he holds two signal distinctions: he printed the first newspapers in both Maryland and Virginia. Before coming to America, he began his printing business in England, becoming the first printer in three English towns and publishing the first newspapers in Ludlow and Reading, England.

In 1726, Parks was invited to be the public printer for Maryland. In

1727 he started the *Maryland Gazette,* the first newspaper published south of Philadelphia and the seventh in the American colonies. In addition, Parks encouraged literary efforts by publishing essays, poems, and other writings in the *Gazette,* many coming from faculty and students of William and Mary College. His press produced books and poetry, almanacs, and works on politics, economics, and religion.

After 1730 Parks made Williamsburg, Virginia, his home. The *Maryland Gazette* suspended publication for a short time and then resumed in 1732 under a slightly revised title, *Maryland Gazette Reviv'd,* before going out of business in 1734. In 1736 Parks founded the *Virginia Gazette,* the first newspaper in that colony. Like its predecessor, Parks made the *Virginia Gazette* an important medium for disseminating news, ideas, and literature.

Shortage of paper was a chronic problem for early printers. In 1744 a paper maker, John Conrad Sheets, helped Parks set up the first paper mill south of Pennsylvania, in Williamsburg. Apparently the mill supplied paper to other colonial printing presses as well. Parks was a skilled bookbinder. The *Virginia Gazette* under that name was discontinued in 1750, a few months after Parks's death, although after changes of editors and brief suspensions, it continued until near the end of the century.

LOUELLA PARSONS
1881–1972

Louella Parsons was born in Freeport, Illinois. While still in high school she began newspaper work as drama editor and assistant to the city editor of the *Dixon* (Illinois) *Morning Star.* She went on to Chicago and landed a job as reporter on the *Tribune.* In 1914, she started a movie column in the *Chicago Record-Herald.* A move was next made to New York, where Parsons became movie critic on the *Morning Telegraph* and then for the *New York American.* Hearst signed her to a three-year contract and made her movie editor for Universal News Service.

While in California recovering from a serious illness, Parsons moved to Hollywood in 1926. Her columns, thereafter, were filled with details about the lives and careers of actors and actresses. While writing a daily column, she contributed to movie magazines and hosted a number of successful radio programs, especially "Hollywood Hotel" from 1934 to 1938. A network of informers kept her supplied with material for her column about marriages and divorces and all varieties of gossip. Three secretaries were employed to receive telephone messages. Her column appeared in over four hundred newspapers, both U.S. and foreign.

SARA PAYSON WILLIS PARTON
1811-1872

Sara Parton, who wrote under the pen name of "Fanny Fern," was born in Portland, Maine, and came from a family with a long tradition of journalistic activity. Her grandfather, Nathaniel Willis, edited a Whig journal in Boston during the Revolution and her father published an anti-Federalist organ, the *Eastern Argus,* in Portland. Parton's father moved to Boston soon after her birth, set up a printing business, and established the *Boston Recorder,* one of America's first religious newspapers. More memorably, her father was the founder in 1827 of the *Youth's Companion.* An older brother, Nathaniel Parker, edited the *New York Mirror,* and a younger brother, Richard Storrs, edited the *Musical World and Times.*

Personal tragedies forced Parton to depend upon her own resources. She contributed pieces in 1831 to small Boston magazines: the *Mother's Assistant,* the *True Flag,* and the *Olive Branch,* none of which paid well. Many newspapers reprinted these amusing paragraphs, and they were collected in *Fern Leaves from Fanny's Port-Folio,* a book that became an instant best-seller. Two other popular series followed. Impressed by "Fanny's" success, Robert Bonner, owner of the *New York Ledger,* contracted with her in 1855 to write a regular weekly column, at $100 a column. Thus she became one of America's first women columnists. Parton remained with the *Ledger* for the rest of her life, reaching an estimated half a million readers. Her chatty pieces dealt with domestic problems, supported equality of the sexes, opposed excessive housework and large families. They have other aspects of interest for social history, such as her belief in women's suffrage, and criticism of conventional religion. Otherwise, Parton's writings are not rated by literary critics as having great merit.

ALICIA PATTERSON
1906-1963

Alicia Patterson was born in Chicago, a member of a dynasty of newspaper editors and publishers. Her father, Joseph Medill Patterson, was an editor of the *Chicago Tribune* and later founder of the *New York Daily News;* her grandfather, Robert W. Patterson, was an editor of the *Tribune* under Joseph Medill; and she was a great-granddaughter of Joseph Medill, who directed the *Tribune* from 1855 to 1899.

After varied educational experiences in Germany, Switzerland, Rome, and Virginia, Patterson's father gave her a low-level job on the *New York*

Daily News, but she was a failure as a reporter and was sent back to Chicago.

Later, Patterson and her third husband, Harry F. Guggenheim, purchased the plant of a defunct paper, the *Nassau Daily Journal,* in Hempstead, Long Island, and started *Newsday* in 1940. Under Patterson's aggressive and able management, the paper was a success. It expanded to a larger plant in Garden City, New York, in 1949. As a measure of its success, *Newsday* became the largest suburban newspaper in the country and the twelfth largest evening newspaper in the United States. It won a Pulitzer prize for public service in 1954.

In her will, Patterson established the Alicia Patterson Fund, a large endowment to provide many young journalists with a year of travel and study.

ELEANOR MEDILL PATTERSON
1881–1948

Eleanor Medill Patterson was born in Chicago, the granddaughter of Joseph Medill, owner of the *Chicago Tribune,* and the daughter of Robert Wilson Patterson, the *Tribune's* managing editor. Her brother, Joseph Medill Patterson, was later founder of the *New York Daily News.* Joseph nicknamed his sister "Cissy."

Patterson made a disastrous marriage to a Polish count, Joseph Gizycki, a fortune hunter twice her age. The couple separated in 1907, but a custody battle over their daughter was not settled until President Taft intervened. A second marriage, in 1925, to a New York attorney, ended in 1929, when her husband suffered a fatal heart attack.

Patterson did not become active in journalism until she was forty-six. In 1930 her friend Arthur Brisbane persuaded William Randolph Hearst to give her a trial as editor-publisher of the failing *Washington Herald.* Patterson threw herself into the challenge with tremendous energy and enthusiasm. She hired or fired seven editors in ten years, campaigned for popular local causes, interviewed Al Capone, and filled the paper with gossip. By 1936 circulation had doubled. In 1939 she bought the *Herald* and evening *Times* from Hearst, and combined them into a single all-day paper with six editions, the *Washington Times-Herald.* By 1945 the paper was clearing a million dollars a year. Patterson supported Franklin Roosevelt for a third term in 1940. Then, perhaps influenced by Robert R. McCormick and his *Chicago Tribune,* she became a relentless critic of the Roosevelt administration.

Patterson's will, when she died in 1948, dispersed an estate valued at

$16 million. In 1949 the *Times-Herald* was sold to the *Chicago Tribune,* and in 1954 it was sold again to Eugene Meyer, who merged it with the *Washington Post.*

EUGENE CORBETT PATTERSON
1923–

Eugene Patterson was born in Valdosta, Georgia. He is unrelated to the Chicago Pattersons. He graduated from the University of Georgia with a degree in journalism in 1943, but joined the U.S. Army and saw active service in World War II. After resigning his commission in 1947, he entered newspaper work as a reporter for the *Temple* (Texas) *Daily Telegram,* then with the *Macon* (Georgia) *Telegraph* in 1948. He then became South Carolina manager for the United Press. Patterson was transferred to New York City in 1949 as night bureau manager of UP and in 1953 went to England as UP's London bureau manager and chief correspondent for the United Kingdom.

After returning to the United States, Patterson became vice president and executive editor of the *Atlanta Constitution* and the *Atlanta Journal.* In 1960 he was made editor of the *Constitution,* a position that he held until 1968, when he moved to Washington to be managing editor at the *Washington Post.* In 1971–72 he was on the Duke University faculty. He returned to newspaper work as president of the Times Publishing Company in St. Petersburg, Florida, and editor of its newspaper, the *Times.* Beginning in 1972, Patterson also served as president and editor of the *Congressional Quarterly.* He has been an active member of the American Society of Newspaper Editors.

GROVE HIRAM PATTERSON
1881–1956

Grove Patterson was born in Rochester, Minnesota, and graduated from Oberlin College. His journalistic career began as associate editor at the *Lorain* (Ohio) *Times-Herald* (1905–8), followed by copyreader and night city editor of the *Cleveland Plain Dealer* (1908–9); managing editor of the *Toledo Times* (1909–10); news editor of the *Toledo Blade* (1910–17), managing editor (1917–19), executive editor (1920–26), editor (1926–46), editor-in-chief (1946–56); editorial manager of *Newark* (New Jersey) *Star Eagle* (1916–24), and *Detroit* (Michigan) *Journal* (1919–22). He was president of the American Society of Newspaper Editors, honored by Spain's order of Isabella (1934) and Poland's Gold Cross of Merit (1938), and earned a number of honorary degrees from colleges and universities.

JOSEPH MEDILL PATTERSON
1879–1946

Joseph Medill Patterson was a native of Chicago and a Yale graduate. During his junior year at Yale he spent a summer in China running dispatches for an American correspondent covering the Boxer Rebellion. There was a long journalistic tradition in his family. His father, Robert Wilson Patterson, was editor and publisher of the *Chicago Tribune,* succeeding another famous newspaperman, Joseph Medill, and his mother was Joseph Medill's daughter.

In 1901, Patterson went to work for the *Chicago Tribune,* progressing from reporter to editorial writer, assistant Sunday editor, and assistant editor. He devoted several years to political activities and the writing of books and plays. Coming back to the *Tribune,* he was copublisher and coeditor with Robert R. McCormick, his cousin (1914–25). During World War I, Patterson was a war correspondent for the *Tribune* in Germany and Belgium (1914), and in France (1915). He served on the Mexican border in 1916, and after the United States entered the war he was sent overseas with the Rainbow Division in 1917. His unit was engaged in military action in five major engagements and he was discharged with the rank of captain.

While overseas, Patterson had interviewed Lord Northcliffe, a London newspaper publisher, and was inspired to establish a tabloid newspaper similar to Northcliffe's *London Daily Mirror.* As a result, he began publication in June 1919 of the *New York Illustrated News,* a title changed later to the *New York Daily News,* a tabloid that made extensive use of photography and sensationalized sex and crime. By 1925, the *News* passed a million circulation, making it the country's largest paper and the first successful American tabloid.

In 1925, Patterson turned over full control of the *Chicago Tribune* to Robert R. McCormick. Like his sister, Eleanor Medill Patterson, he had begun as a supporter of Franklin Roosevelt. Later he became an isolationist and a bitter critic of the Roosevelt administration.

In 1924, Patterson, in association with Robert R. McCormick, founded a weekly five-cent magazine in New York entitled *Liberty.* It was sold to Bernarr Macfadden in 1931 and was liquidated in 1932.

JANE PAULEY

1950–

Jane Pauley was born in Indianapolis, and graduated from Indiana University. In the course of five years she went from being a cub reporter on WISH-TV in Indianapolis to becoming a regular cast member of the popular morning program "Today." In 1980 she married the Doonesbury cartoonist Garry Trudeau. Pauley currently hosts her own show, "Real Life with Jane Pauley."

DREW PEARSON

1897–1969

Drew Pearson was born in Evanston, Illinois. He became famous as cowriter, along with Robert S. Allen, of the widely read and syndicated "The Washington Merry-Go-Round" in the early 1930s.

Before he became a newspaperman, Pearson served as director of the American Friends Service Committee in Serbia, Montenegro, and Albania after World War I. He traveled in Australia, New Zealand, Japan, China, and Siberia. Following that experience, Pearson began reporting for a newspaper syndicate on such events as the Washington Arms Conference and the Geneva Naval Conference. From 1926 to 1933, he worked on the *United States Daily* owned by David Lawrence. During some of those years Pearson reported for the *Baltimore Sun* (1929–32).

GEORGE WILBUR PECK

1840–1916

George W. Peck was a newspaper humorist who achieved success both as a writer and as a politician. He was born in Henderson, New York, but grew up in Whitewater, Wisconsin. Peck's first exposure to journalism was as a printer's devil for the *Whitewater Register*. After military service in the Civil War, he established a weekly newspaper, the *Representative,* in Ripon, Wisconsin. His first humorous stories, Irish dialogue skits satirizing political events, appeared in that paper.

In 1874 Peck founded a weekly paper, the *Sun,* and in 1878 moved it to Milwaukee. The first of the "Peck's Bad Boy" sketches appeared in the *Sun* and won a national audience for the paper and its publisher.

Probably because of his popularity as a writer, Peck was elected mayor

of Milwaukee in 1890 and served two terms as governor of Wisconsin, starting in 1891. His humorous pieces were published in a series of books.

WESTBROOK PEGLER
1894–1969

Westbrook Pegler was born in Minneapolis, the son of a star reporter
in Minneapolis, Chicago, and New York. After graduation from high
school, Westbrook was employed as a reporter for the United Press in Des
Moines, St. Louis, and Texas. In 1916 he was sent to London as a foreign
correspondent. In 1925 he was hired by the *Chicago Tribune* to write a daily
sports story. While abroad, he wrote scathing stories about Hitler and
Mussolini, before his point of view became common. Attacks on prominent personalities on the home front were equally ferocious. He has been
described as rich in salty abuse, and strongly convinced that in every controversy both sides are wrong. At the height of his popularity it was
reported that he was being read by over six million people in 114 newspapers
throughout the United States.

ARTHUR PLOTNIK
1937–

Arthur Plotnik was born in White Plains, New York, and earned
degrees from the State University of New York, Iowa State University, and
Columbia University. In 1962–63 he was a reporter for the *Albany Times-
Union,* spent several years as a freelance journalist, served as assistant
editor of the *Library of Congress Information Bulletin* (1967–69), and in
1969 became associate editor of the *Wilson Library Bulletin.* In November
1974 Plotnik became editor of *American Libraries,* the official organ of the
American Library Association. He is the author of *Library Life—American Style* (1975) and *The Great American Library Success Story* (1976). He
left his position as editor of *American Libraries* in 1989 to become associate
publisher, new products, for the American Library Association.

BENJAMIN PERLEY POORE
1820–1887

Benjamin Poore was born on a farm northeast of Boston. Rebelling
against his father's desire for him to have a military career, young Poore

ran away from home for two years to learn the printer's trade in a Worcester shop. His first job as a journalist, at age eighteen, was to serve as editor of the *Southern Whig* in Athens, Georgia. The atmosphere was uncomfortable, however, for a Yankee from Massachusetts and in 1841 he gave up control of the paper. Several years of travel in the Middle East followed, during which Poore sent back letters for publication in the *Boston Atlas* and *Hartford Courant.* When he returned to the United States in 1847, he became Washington correspondent for the *Atlas*—a short-time appointment, for in 1848 he went back to Boston to take over editorial management of the *Boston Daily Bee.* After another brief stint as correspondent for the *Atlas* in Washington, he founded the *Sunday Sentinel* in Boston. Poore sold the *Sentinel* in 1851, at which time it was merged with the *Yankee Nation.*

In 1854, Poore returned to Washington, this time as correspondent for the *Boston Journal,* a leading Republican newspaper. It was a long-lasting relationship, during which Poore became nationally known. His articles on military, political, and social affairs were published in newspapers and magazines throughout the United States.

Because of illness and a dispute over salary, Poore resigned from the *Journal* in 1883. His career continued with writing for the *Boston Commonwealth,* the *Chicago Tribune,* the *New Orleans Daily Times,* and other newspapers and several magazines. He also edited the *Congressional Record* and other government publications. During the last four years of his life, Poore represented the *Boston Budget, Albany Evening Journal,* and the *Omaha Republican,* supplying them with weekly letters reporting on congressional activities. Poore's prolific pen produced biographies of Zachary Taylor, Andrew Johnson, Ulysses S. Grant, and other famous men of his time. He also compiled *A Descriptive Catalogue of Government Publications of the United States* (1885).

Sylvia Porter

1913–1991

Sylvia Porter was born in Patchogue, Long Island, New York, the daughter of Russian-Jewish immigrants. An estimated 40 million readers followed her nationally syndicated newspaper column, entitled simply "Sylvia Porter." In 1934 she conducted a weekly column in the *American Banner,* on U.S. government bonds. The *New York Post* ran her occasional column on financial news and in 1938 appointed her its financial editor. About 1942, the *Post* decided that her feminine gender was an asset and changed the byline from "S. F. Porter Says" to "Sylvia F. Porters Says."

A broader market for her articles was thereby opened up in mass circulation magazines, such as *American* and *Woman's Home Companion.* Her articles were increasingly concerned with changing fiscal conditions.

After more than thirty years with the *New York Post,* Porter switched to the *New York Daily News* in 1978, and her five-times-a-week column was syndicated by the Field Newspaper Syndicate. She was a contributing editor of the *Ladies' Home Journal* from 1965 until her death. Also, she occasionally made guest appearances on television. The enemy always, in her mind, is economic ignorance.

WILLIAM TROTTER PORTER
1809–1858

William Trotter Porter inherited his devotion to horses and horse racing from his grandfather and father, both of whom had a passion for horses and land in New Hampshire. Porter popularized the American sporting magazine, at first concentrating on providing full news coverage of horse racing and later expanding to cover field and river sports.

Porter's first taste of journalism was as an apprentice to printers in Andover, Massachusetts, about 1823. His second job was with the *Farmer's Herald* at St. Johnsbury, Vermont, and from there to Norwich as editor of the *Enquirer.* A short stay as foreman for the John T. West printing office in New York preceded Porter's launching his own magazine. In December 1831 the first issue of the weekly sporting paper, the *Spirit of the Times and Life in New York,* appeared. Horace Greeley was on the staff for several months. The contents of the magazine was varied at first; it did not catch on with readers and was sold by Porter. In 1835, however, he repurchased the paper and changed the title to the *New York Spirit of the Times.*

Porter immediately began exploiting the growing popularity of horse racing and recruited a number of well-known writers as contributors. Included were horse racing names of all kinds, advertisements for horse medicines and items likely to interest sportsmen, and tips on trout fishing. In 1839 Porter purchased the *American Turf Register;* the *Spirit of the Times* increased in size, added color prints of famous race horses, and began to publish local color sketches such as the "Big Bear" series.

Due to financial problems, Porter sold the *Spirit of the Times* and *American Turf Register* in 1842, but continued as editor-in-chief, a position he held until 1856. Porter's *Spirit of the Times* survived until 1858. A rival publication, *Wilkes' Spirit of the Times,* continued until 1902.

EMILY POST
1873–1960

Emily Post, who became the American dictator of correct behavior, was born in Baltimore to wealth and social position.

Post's *Etiquette: In Society, in Business, in Politics, and at Home,* issued in 1922, in a modest printing of five thousand copies, immediately caught the public fancy, and in successive versions the work attained a position of commanding authority in its field. By 1970, twelve editions and ninety-nine printings had been published, and more than a million copies had been sold. Generations of brides have arranged their wedding plans according to Post's rules, thousands of teenage swains have followed her advice about corsages, and countless American matrons have placed the fish forks where Post said they belonged.

Post's venture into the etiquette field came about by chance. Not without considerable persuasion, Richard Duffy, a Funk and Wagnalls editor, convinced her that existing books on etiquette were of miserable quality and that she should undertake to write a better one. The rest is history. Within a year, Post's *Etiquette* was at the top of the nonfiction, best-seller list. "No social climber should be without one," suggested one critic.

Since she was writing about the kind of society she had known so intimately, Post inevitably filled the first edition with advice concerning the right livery for footmen, the order of procedure at formal dinners, the duties of a kitchenmaid, and other problems of the fashionable life.

Not until after publication of *Etiquette* did Post discover the true nature of her mass audience, when letters began pouring in from all over the country. Responsive to lacks in her book, Post endeavored to clarify such matters in later editions. From the first to the twelfth edition, a series of revisions have kept *Etiquette* in tune with changing social mores.

In 1932, Post began a syndicated column that eventually appeared in about two hundred newspapers.

GEORGE D. PRENTICE
1802–1870

James M. Lee, in his *History of American Journalism,* rated George Denison Prentice as "not only the foremost journalist of Kentucky and the entire south, but also one of the greatest editors of the middle nineteenth century."

A native of Connecticut, Prentice began his career in 1828 on the *New*

England Review as an associate of John Greenleaf Whittier, a Quaker fighter against black slavery. Prentice edited the *Review* from 1828 to 1830. In 1830 he was sent to Kentucky to start a paper attacking Jacksonian democracy. The first issue of the *Louisville Journal,* with Prentice as editor, appeared on November 30, 1830. The editor was aggressive, always ready to fight with sword or pen. He was almost killed when fired upon by George J. Trotter, editor of the *Kentucky Gazette.* The *Journal* gained a national reputation with its witty editorial columns and was much quoted by other papers, especially the Whig press.

With the coming of the Civil War, Prentice was strongly pro–Union and anti–Confederacy. His influence was exerted to keep Kentucky from seceding. In 1868 his *Journal* stock was sold. Shortly thereafter the title was changed to the *Courier-Journal* and Henry Watterson assumed the editorship. Prentice died two years later.

Joseph Pulitzer

1847–1911

Joseph Pulitzer was one of a small number of nineteenth-century newspaper editors and owners (Horace Greeley and William Randolph Hearst are others) whose impacts on American journalism have been long-range. A major newspaper, the *St. Louis Post-Dispatch,* founded by Pulitzer more than a century ago, is still a flourishing institution, and his name is regularly recalled by the Pulitzer prizes awarded in journalistic fields, literature, history, drama, and music.

Pulitzer was of Jewish-German parentage, born in Hungary and educated in Budapest. He emigrated to the United States at age seventeen and promptly enlisted, in 1864, in the New York Cavalry. A few minor skirmishes were the extent of his participation in the Civil War.

Unable to find employment in New York after his discharge from military service, young Pulitzer went on to St. Louis, where he eventually joined the staff, as a reporter, of a German-language daily newspaper, the *Westlicher Post.* After three years, in 1871, he became part-owner of the paper. From the beginning, Pulitzer showed a genius for journalism, with his unbounded energy, resourcefulness, keen nose for news, and personal fearlessness. Opposition to and exposure of political corruption in St. Louis and Missouri brought him into local prominence, leading to his election to the state legislature in 1869. Previously, he had studied for and been admitted to the bar. His principal achievement as a legislator was to lead a movement to reform the corrupt county government of St. Louis. When the revolt against Grant as president led to the organization of the Liberal

Republicans in 1871–72, Pulitzer helped to organize the party in Missouri and was a delegate to the Cincinnati convention that nominated Horace Greeley. Disillusioned by Greeley's defeat, he joined the Democratic party.

The next step in Pulitzer's journalistic career came after he sold his share in the *Westliche Post* and made an extended tour of Europe. When he returned, he bought a moribund German newspaper, the *St. Louis Staats-Zeitung* and sold its Associated Press franchise to the *Globe*. The proceeds were used to purchase at auction the *St. Louis Dispatch,* which soon merged with the *Post* to form the *Post-Dispatch*. The new paper immediately became a financial success and soon dominated the St. Louis evening field. Politically, the *Post-Dispatch* under Pulitzer was independent, noted for its strong advocacy of "hard money" and tariff reform.

A sensational duel in which the *Post-Dispatch's* chief editor shot and killed a local lawyer brought unfavorable publicity to the paper, as a result of which Pulitzer left St. Louis and in 1882 moved to New York. There he took over the ownership of the *New York World*. Under his management the *World* became a highly profitable enterprise, with annual earnings of $500,000. These financial resources enabled Pulitzer to establish another paper, the *Evening World,* which also became a popular success.

A powerful competitor entered the New York newspaper field in 1882, when William Randolph Hearst purchased the *Journal*. Nevertheless, the *World* maintained a large circulation, aided by aggressive editorial independence and active support for the labor movement. Another factor in building circulation was a resort to "yellow journalism," a term reportedly derived from the "Yellow Kid," a comic strip character in the *World*. Pulitzer and Hearst tried to outdo each other in advocating war with Spain, motivated in Pulitzer's case by a genuine sympathy with the Cuban struggle for liberty.

Ill health and failing eyesight forced Pulitzer to give up most of his editorial duties after 1887, although he maintained general control of his newspapers until a few months before his death in 1911. In its later years, under his guidance, the *World* abandoned sensationalism and yellow journalism and built a solid reputation for an international point of view, sound information, support for free speech and personal liberty, and democratic principles in general.

In his will, Pulitzer left $2.5 million for the establishment of a school of journalism at Columbia University and for annual awards for "prizes or scholarships in the encouragement of public service, public morals, American literature, and the advancement of education." Prizes in journalism, fiction, drama, poetry, history, biography, and music have been presented regularly since 1917. The cash awards are small, but are high in prestige value.

Pulitzer's son, Ralph, was president of the company that published the

World and *Evening World,* purchased by the Scripps–Howard organization in 1931. The *Evening World* was merged with the *New York Telegram* as the *New York World-Telegram.*

Another son, Joseph Pulitzer, Jr. (1885–1955), was editor and publisher of the *St. Louis Post-Dispatch* from 1912 until his death, and his son, Joseph Pulitzer III became editor and publisher of the *Post-Dispatch* in 1955.

JOSEPH PULITZER, JR.
1885–1955

Joseph Pulitzer, Jr., was born into the newspaper business. He was the son of one of the most famous figures in journalistic history, but found that no handicap as he went on to achieve national distinction himself as editor and publisher of the *St. Louis Post-Dispatch* for forty-three years.

Pulitzer was born in New York City, where his father had made the *New York World* the most powerful and richest newspaper in the country. Young Pulitzer was sent to St. Louis in 1906 to learn the newspaper business from the editor-in-chief of the *Post-Dispatch.* The older Pulitzer had little confidence in his son's ability and left him only one-tenth of the family trust. Nevertheless, in 1912, the family named Joseph, Jr., editor and publisher of the *Post-Dispatch.* Among innovations, the paper pioneered the development of rotogravure photography sections, maintained strict standards for advertising, established the first commercial radio stations in Missouri, and later operated a television station. Particular attention was paid to the *Post-Dispatch's* news and editorial departments.

In 1951, Pulitzer bought the *St. Louis Sun-Times,* a long-time rival to give the *Post-Dispatch* a monopoly in the afternoon field. Pulitzer's older son, Joseph Pulitzer III, succeeded him as editor and publisher of the *Post-Dispatch.*

ERNIE PYLE
1900–1945

Ernest Taylor Pyle, known universally as "Ernie," was born near Dana, Indiana. He served a short time in the U.S. Navy during World War I and then entered Indiana University. From there on, his chief interest was journalism. He was a staff reporter, city editor, news editor, and later editor-in-chief of the university paper the *Student.* He also became editor of the *Smokeup,* a monthly humor magazine.

Pyle began his journalistic career as a reporter for the *LaPorte* (Indiana) *Herald*. After three months he found a better job as a reporter for the *Washington* (D.C.) *Daily News*. In 1926, Pyle resigned and he and his wife went on a ten-week car tour of the United States. Following their return, Ernie was employed on the copydesk of the *New York Evening World* and later on the copydesk of the *New York Evening Post*. In 1927, he returned to the *Washington Daily News* as telegraph editor. Two years later the paper made him full-time aviation editor for the Scripps–Howard chain, a field that had long fascinated him.

Pyle became famous as a world traveler and his newspaper accounts of his trips were widely read. While still in college, he visited Manila and Hong Kong. As a roving reporter for the Scripps–Howard papers, he roamed over the United States, Canada, Mexico, Alaska, Hawaiian Islands, and Central and South America.

When World War II began Pyle went to England and reported the British war experience, especially the German bombing of London. In 1942, he spent several months with the American troops training in England and Ireland and joined the American-British expedition in North Africa. More than any other American war correspondent, Pyle became a sympathetic spokesman for the common soldiers, living with them and bringing to the American people an understanding of the hardships of men in the armed forces. He remained with the American Army until the end of the war.

In 1945, Pyle set out on his last journey, to cover the Pacific campaign with the U.S. Navy and Marine corps. He went ashore at Ryukyus, near Okinawa, in a Jeep and was killed when a Japanese sniper opened fire with a machine gun. During his notable career he had won a Pulitzer Prize and many other awards and honors.

LEMUEL ELY QUIGG
1863–1919

Lemuel Quigg was born near Chestertown, Maryland. He had a brief newspaper apprenticeship in Montana Territory. At age seventeen he went on to New York and was employed as a reporter on the *New York Times*. Before age twenty-one, he was editor of the *Flushing* (Long Island) *Times* (1883–84), and in 1884 transferred to the *New York Tribune* to write special articles. He remained on the *Tribune* staff for ten years.

Quigg was elected to Congress in 1894 and served in the House until 1899. No longer connected with the *Tribune,* he spent a year as editor and publisher of the *New York Press,* an organization Republican newspaper. His time thereafter was devoted to his legal practice.

JULIAN RALPH
1853–1903

Julian Ralph was called, by a fellow reporter on the *New York Sun,* "the greatest newspaper reporter who ever lived." Certainly he was present or covered most of the major news stories of his time. Ralph was born in New York City and left school at an early age to become an apprentice in the office of the *Red Bank* (New Jersey) *Standard,* where he learned the printing and newspaper business. Still under twenty, Ralph founded a competing paper, the *Leader.* When that failed, he became local editor of a weekly, *Tom's River* (New Jersey) *Courier,* and an editor of the *Webster* (Massachusetts) *Times.* In 1873, he returned to New York to serve as a reporter for the *New York Daily Graphic.*

In 1875 Ralph attracted the attention of Charles A. Dana and began a connection with the *New York Sun* that lasted twenty years. Feature stories by him covered an amazing variety of subjects: conflicts in the Pennsylvania coalfields, presidential inaugurations, theater safety in New York City, political corruption, the funeral of Ulysses S. Grant, the 1888 blizzard, the trial of Lizzie Borden, and the Sino-Japanese War.

Ralph's association with the *Sun* ended in 1895 when William Randolph Hearst enticed him away to work for the *New York Journal.* For three years he was the *Journal's* European correspondent, reporting on the coronation of Czar Nicholas in St. Petersburg, the Greco-Turkish War, and Queen Victoria's Diamond Jubilee.

Ralph left the *Journal* in 1899, but continued as correspondent in London for the *New York Herald* and *Brooklyn Eagle,* and wrote regularly for *Harper's.* An extensive trip to Japan and China was undertaken for *Harper's.* Late in 1899, Ralph went to South Africa to cover the Boer War for the *London Daily Mail* and *Collier's* magazine. While with the British army in South Africa, Ralph and other correspondents published a daily newspaper, the *Friend,* to entertain and inform the troops. This was Ralph's last important foreign assignment. He died in 1903 from a variety of ailments, perhaps incurred during his African trip.

JAMES RYDEN RANDALL
1839–1908

James Randall was born in Baltimore. After the Civil War he became associate editor of the *Constitutionalist* in Augusta, Georgia. Later, he acted as Washington correspondent for the *Augusta Chronicle.* He also wrote for the *Catholic Mirror* in Baltimore and the *New Orleans Morning Star.*

Randall was author of a well-known state song, "Maryland, My Maryland," and received a number of honors for its composition.

DAN RATHER
1931–

Dan Rather was born in Wharton, Texas, and graduated from Sam Houston State College with a degree in journalism. While in college, he held a part-time job as a writer and sportscaster for the local radio station. Later he worked for United Press International and for the *Houston Chronicle*. For four years, in the mid-1950s, he was on the staff of KTRH, a CBS affiliate in Houston, as news writer, reporter, and subsequently news director, and then served as director of news and public affairs for KHOU-TV. In 1961, Rather was named chief of CBS's southwestern bureau in Dallas. Top news stories covered by him during that period were the civil rights movement and the assassination of President Kennedy.

In 1964, Rather was appointed CBS News White House correspondent. Ten months later he was sent abroad as chief of the London bureau. After a year he was moved again to report on the Vietnam War. Back in Washington, Rather found it difficult to cover the Nixon administration because of the president's hostility to the press. As part of his White House assignment, he accompanied the president on his travels to the Mideast, the Soviet Union, and China. Rather also chronicled the political developments leading up to the Watergate affair.

In 1974, Rather was named anchorman-correspondent for "CBS Reports." In 1981, he was selected to replace Walter Cronkite on the "CBS Evening News." He has received wide recognition for his outstanding reporting, including five Emmy awards.

HENRY RAYMOND
1820–1869

Henry Jarvis Raymond was born in Lima, New York, and showed early signs of being a child prodigy. While a student at the University of Vermont, he began contributing verse, book reviews, and news items to the *New Yorker*, edited by Horace Greeley. After receiving his degree, Raymond became Greeley's assistant in editing the *New Yorker*. When Greeley launched a one-penny Whig paper, the *Tribune*, in 1841, Raymond was appointed chief assistant editor at a salary of eight dollars a week.

For more than two years Raymond gained experience as a reporter and editor. Then the *Courier and Enquirer* offered him an editorship at five dollars a week more than his *Tribune* salary. Raymond accepted.

Raymond always had a passionate interest in politics. In 1849 he was elected to the New York State Assembly and the Whigs selected him to be assembly speaker. Raymond was elected lieutenant governor of New York in 1854, helped to organize the Republican party in 1856, wrote the party's statement of principles, and served in Congress (1865-67). While keeping up his *Courier* duties, he was named the first managing editor of the new *Harper's* magazine, a position he held for six years.

Raymond's greatest achievement from the point of view of the history of journalism was the founding of the *New York Times,* the first issue of which appeared on September 18, 1851, with Raymond as editor and George Jones as business manager. It was a large sheet (four pages, six columns wide) and sold for one cent a copy. In a preliminary prospectus, Raymond outlined the *Times* editorial policies: print local news, cover European affairs, report congressional and legislative proceedings, review books, devote space to music, drama, and art, and avoid sensationalism. The paper's circulation grew rapidly, although there were financial problems. In 1852 the size of the *Times* was doubled to eight pages and the price increased to two cents.

Because of his interest in thorough coverage of foreign news, Raymond went to Italy to cover the War of 1859, in which the French and Italians were trying to drive the Austrians out of the Piedmont area of Italy. Raymond distinguished himself as an excellent war correspondent. Civil War news was likewise fully reported.

In the years that followed Raymond's death in 1869, the *Times* went through a series of ups and downs until 1896, when it was bought by Adolph Ochs.

OPIE READ
1852-1939

Opie Read, born in Nashville, Tennessee, was celebrated for his use of local color in newspaper writing and numerous books, and as a popular lecturer.

Read's first experience in journalism came at age nineteen when the editor of the *Franklin Patriot,* Andrew Kelley, taught him the printer's trade and how to set type. Shortly thereafter he was hired as a typesetter for the *Pen,* a local college magazine. A stint back with the *Patriot* followed after which Read bought a half-interest in the *Statesville* (Kentucky) *Argus.*

That venture proved a fiasco, leaving Read looking for another job. For a time he worked for the Methodist Book Concern in Nashville, set type for a book in Carlisle, and then teamed with a partner to publish the *Prairie Farmer*. That paper, too, was doomed to failure. Proceeding first to Little Rock, Read later took the editorship of the *Bowling Green* (Kentucky) *Pantograph*. There was part-time work with Henry Watterson's *Courier-Journal*. Back in Little Rock, Read became city editor of the *Evening Democrat,* a job that came to a quick end. Immediately after, the *New York Herald* hired him to report on the yellow fever epidemic in Memphis. Back in Little Rock, Read was appointed an editor for the *Gazette*. Still restless, in 1881, he accepted an offer to work for the *Cleveland Leader*.

Read discovered his true forte, when his brother-in-law, P. D. Bentham, proposed that they start a weekly, the *Arkansas Traveler*. Publication began in 1882 and the paper was an immediate success. By the end of the third year circulation rose to 85,000. The paper's sketches of back-country scenes and characters made a great hit with readers throughout the country. In 1887, the *Arkansas Traveler* moved to Chicago. There was some resentment against the paper in Arkansas, where it was accused of making fun of the natives.

About 1891, Read lost interest in contributing to the paper that he and Bentham had founded. The *Arkansas Traveler* was taken over by the Review Printing Company.

Commenting on Opie Read's career, the *New York Times* noted that "Opie Read made country humor into a national institution."

HARRY REASONER
1923–1991

Harry Reasoner was born in San Marcos, Texas. His name became familiar to millions of television viewers as a member of the CBS "60 Minutes" show.

Reasoner began his career on the *Minneapolis Times*. He returned to Minneapolis after World War II military service to join WCCO, a CBS radio affiliate. Three years were taken out to work for the U.S. Information Agency in Manila. Another stint in Minneapolis, this time with KEYD-TV, preceded Reasoner going on to join CBS-TV in New York, where he quickly won a reputation for being an outstanding newscaster and commentator. He died shortly after retirement, in 1991.

JOHN REED
1887–1920

John Reed was born in Portland, Oregon. While a student at Harvard, he served on the editorial boards of the *Lampoon* and the *Harvard Monthly*. After graduation he joined the staff of the *American Magazine* in 1911.

Reed's serious interest in social problems appears to have been aroused by becoming acquainted with Lincoln Steffens and Ida Tarbell, but his beliefs were much more radical than theirs. In 1913, he joined the staff of the *Masses,* edited by Max Eastman. The *Metropolitan Magazine* sent Reed to Mexico for four months to follow Pancho Villa's army. After World War I began, he was successively with the armies of Germany, Serbia, Bulgaria, Romania, and Russia.

In 1917, Reed and his wife went to Russia to observe the October Revolution in Petrograd. He became a close friend of Lenin and wrote much of the Bolshevist propaganda dropped over the German lines.

After the Socialist party divided into two hostile factions in 1919, Reed headed the Communist Labor party and edited its papers, the *Voice of Labor.* To escape arrest for sedition in the United States, Reed escaped to Finland and then went to Russia. He died of typhus in 1920, and was buried in the Kremlin.

WILLIAM CHARLES REICH
1864–1924

William Reich was born in Philadelphia. Just out of high school, he joined the staff of the *Philadelphia North American* and spent five years as a reporter and correspondent. On a trip to Paris, he met James Gordon Bennett, who was so impressed with Reich that he put him in charge of the *Herald's* London and Paris offices and a year later sent him to New York as the Herald's city editor. Reich remained city editor of the *Herald* for fourteen years. The Spanish-American War was covered by a fleet of dispatch boats and a correspondent was on Admiral Dewey's flagship at the battle of Manila Bay.

In 1903, Bennett made Reich president of the New York Herald Company, publisher of the *Herald* and *Evening Telegram*. Reich preferred editorial work, however, and resigned in 1907 to join Adolph Ochs, publisher of the *New York Times* and *Philadelphia Public Ledger*. In 1911, Reich bought a controlling interest in the *New York Sun,* where he remained for ten years. In 1921, he became president of the company publishing the *New York Journal of Commerce* and the *Commercial Bulletin,* a position that he held until the year before his death.

HELEN ROGERS REID
1882–1970

Helen Rogers Reid was born in Appleton, Wisconsin. She was one of the first Midwest students to enroll in Barnard College, New York. In 1911, she married the son of Whitelaw Reid, owner of the *New York Tribune.*

In 1918, Reid became an advertising solicitor of the *Tribune,* which was experiencing financial problems. Her success substantially reduced the paper's deficit and she became director of the advertising department in 1922, a position that she held for the next twenty-nine years. In 1924, she promoted acquisition of the *New York Herald,* combining it with the *Tribune* into the *New York Herald Tribune,* one of the nation's major newspapers.

As vice president of the *Herald Tribune* from 1924 to 1947, Reid emphasized news of interest to suburban readers and features for women, such as gardening, an experimental test kitchen, and a food writer. Among women staff writers added were Irita Van Doren (book reviews) and Dorothy Thompson (foreign affairs). Reid became a power in the Republican party.

When her husband died in 1947, Reid succeeded him as president of the *Herald Tribune* corporation until 1953 and chairman of the board of directors (1953–55). Her son, Ogden Reid, became president, publisher, and editor in 1953. The paper failed to prosper under the new management, was sold in 1957 to John Hay Whitney, and finally expired in May 1967. The paper was merged, at that time, with Scripps–Howard's *World-Telegram and Sun* and Hearst's *Journal-American* to form the *World Journal Tribune.*

WHITELAW REID
1837–1912

Whitelaw Reid achieved his greatest fame for his eyewitness accounts of Civil War battles and as editor of the *New York Tribune* for more than thirty years. He was born in Xenia, Ohio. While still a student in Miami University, Ohio, he began contributing articles to three local papers: the

Xenia News, the *Oxford Citizen,* and the *Hamilton Intelligencer.* Shortly thereafter, Reid became editor of the *Xenia News,* but two years later the paper failed.

In 1860, Reid traveled several thousand miles through Minnesota and along the Mississippi River, sending back his observations and experiences to the *Cincinnati Gazette.* After his return, he reported on the Ohio Legislature for the *Cincinnati Times.* Reports were prepared also for the *Cleveland Herald* and the *Cincinnati Times.*

While in Columbus, Reid saw the outbreak of the Civil War. The *Gazette* had appointed him city editor and with the rank of captain he accompanied Union forces, seeing the opening battles and writing highly realistic stories of the death and destruction. His graphic accounts of the battles of Shiloh and Gettysburg are regarded as classics. His work as war correspondent closed with an article about Richmond immediately after its fall and a description of Lincoln's funeral.

In 1868, Reid joined the *New York Tribune* and the following year succeeded John Russell Young as managing editor. Under his direction, the paper's foreign news service was improved and the list of distinguished American contributors was enlarged. In 1872, upon the death of Horace Greeley, Reid became the principal proprietor and editor-in-chief of the *Tribune.*

Reid also had an outstanding career as a diplomat. He served as minister to France from 1889–92; special ambassador of the United States at Queen Victoria's jubilee in 1902, and the coronation of Edward VII in 1905; and U.S. ambassador to Great Britain (1905–12). President McKinley appointed him a member of the American Commission to negotiate peace with Spain in 1898. In 1892, Reid was the unsuccessful Republican candidate for vice president on the ticket with Benjamin Harrison.

JAMES RESTON
1909–

James Reston was born in Scotland and brought to the United States as a child in 1920. After graduating from the University of Illinois in 1932 in the journalism program, he began his newspaper career (1932–33) with the *Springfield* (Ohio) *Daily News,* and then became a reporter (1934–39) for the Associated Press.

A lifetime association for Reston began in 1939, when he joined the *New York Times* as its London correspondent. After 1941 he was stationed in the Washington bureau of the *Times.* He advanced from chief Washington correspondent (1953–64), to associate editor (1964–68), to executive editor (1968–69), to vice president (1969–74), of the New York Times Company. After 1974, Reston continued as a *Times* columnist and second consultant.

Reston won Pulitzer Prizes in 1945 and 1957 and three Overseas Press Club awards. His Washington column appears in more than three hundred newspapers.

His foreign experience was expanded in 1971 when Reston filed a series of articles and columns from the People's Republic of China, shortly before President Nixon's visit.

FRANK REYNOLDS
1923–1983

Frank Reynolds was born in East Chicago, Indiana, and attended Indiana University and Wabash College. He worked for WJOB, Hammond, Indiana (1947–50); and for WBBM-CBS, Chicago (1951–63), before joining ABC as Washington correspondent (1963–78). He held the position as chief anchorman of ABC's "World News Tonight" from 1978 until his death. Reynolds covered every national political convention and major campaign after 1965. He received the George Foster Peabody Award in 1969. His early death was sincerely mourned by his many friends, viewers, and colleagues.

ROBERT BARNWELL RHETT
1800–1876

Robert Barnwell Rhett, born in Beaufort, South Carolina, "the father of secession," a Southern firebrand, was a rabid advocate of states' rights, nullification, and secession. He was part-owner of the *Charleston Mercury* and his influence was exerted mainly through fiery editorials in that journal. He was also famous, as a member of Congress, for delivering sensational speeches filled with emotion.

Rhett was ambitious to become president of the Confederacy, and was incensed when passed over. The *Mercury* was the aggressive leader of the Southern states' rights press. Most of its editorials were written by Rhett. After the outbreak of the Civil War, the *Mercury* published editorials, poems, and news accounts to strengthen Southern morale. But Rhett was repudiated by voters in 1863 when he ran for election to the Confederate Congress. The *Mercury* was suspended in 1865, revived in 1866, and failed again in 1868.

GRANTLAND RICE
1880–1954

Grantland Rice was born in Murfreesboro, Tennessee. His widely syndicated column, "The Sportlight," started in 1930, made him America's favorite sportswriter. His love of athletics began early. At Vanderbilt University he played both football and baseball, spending three years as shortstop and his senior year as captain of the Vanderbilt baseball team. After graduation he was on the staff of the *Nashville News,* wrote for the *Forester Magazine,* spent three years (1902–4) with the *Atlanta Journal,* umpired and refereed games from 1907 to 1911, and was on the staff of the *Nashville Tennessean* from 1906 to 1910. After his Southern experience, Rice came North, where he worked on the *New York Mail* from 1911 to 1914, and then transferred to the *New York Herald* (1914–20), except for a period in France (1918–19) with the American Expeditionary Force.

Rice was a skilled athlete himself. He shot low scores in golf, hunted wild game, and caught salmon and trout in Canada. He saw thousands of sporting events and wrote about football, baseball, racing, golf, tennis, hunting, polo, rowing, track and field, and yachting. He knew the techniques and fine points of practically every American sport. He estimated at the end of his career that he had written 67 million words, 22,000 columns, 7,000 verses, and 1,000 magazine articles. He chose the All-American Football Team for *Collier's,* called Notre Dame's backfield the "Four Horsemen," and nicknamed Red Grange the "Galloping Ghost."

In 1930, Rice left the *Tribune* to join the Bell Syndicate and later the North American Newspaper Alliance. It has been noted that he knew more top sports figures than any other sportswriter in American history. Most of them attended a memorial service for him when he died in 1954.

WILLARD RICHARDSON
1802–1875

Willard Richardson was born in Massachusetts and moved to Texas in 1837. For a short period in 1842 he was acting editor of the *Houston Telegraph* and then became editor of the *Galveston News.* His chief aim as editor was to promote the annexation of Texas by the United States. Richardson acquired ownership of the *News* in 1845 and built up the paper to become the most widely circulated and influential newspaper in Texas. He was a pioneer in the South in the field of nonpolitical, independent journalism. Despite great difficulties, Richardson maintained continuous publication of the *News* during the Civil War. His printing plant was destroyed by fire after a forced move to Houston.

Another Richardson publication was the annual *Texas Almanac,* starting in 1857, one objective of which was to encourage immigration to Texas.

JACOB AUGUSTUS RIIS
1849-1914

Jacob Riis was a native of Denmark who came to America in 1870. His reputation was established by his campaign to clean up slum conditions in New York City. He worked at various trades until 1877, when he became a police reporter for the *New York Evening Sun* and the *New York Tribune* for more than twenty years. In that position he gained a thorough knowledge of the poverty and squalor of the city's slum areas. A new approach used by Riis was to document his stories by photographs of the crowded tenement districts. He also exposed graft, vice, and crime in the slum areas.

When Theodore Roosevelt became Police Commissioner of New York City he accompanied Riis on all-night tours of investigations. Partly as a result of Riis's campaigns, schools and playgrounds were established in slum sections, pollution of the water supply was stopped, and many tenement house abuses were corrected.

Riis was author of a number of books. *The Making of an American* is his autobiography. Another book, *How the Other Half Lives,* was an indictment of slum conditions and was highly influential in bringing about reform.

GEORGE RIPLEY
1802-1880

George Ripley was born in Greenfield, Massachusetts. He was a leader, with Ralph Waldo Emerson, Margaret Fuller, and others, in the Transcendentalist movement and helped to found the group's magazine, *Dial.* In addition, he edited a Fourierite magazine, the *Harbinger.* Ripley was also literary editor of the *New York Tribune* from 1849 to 1880, and editor of several reference works: *Specimens of Foreign Standard Literature, A Handbook of Literature on the Fine Arts,* and the *New American Cyclopedia.*

In his later years, Ripley was a journalist and publisher in New York City.

ROBERT LEROY RIPLEY
1893–1949

Robert Ripley was born in Santa Rosa, California. In 1918 he created the "Believe It or Not" cartoons, a series of unusual, little-known, sometimes questionable facts. The series was syndicated in newspapers around the world and continued by others after Ripley's death.

THOMAS RITCHIE
1778–1854

Thomas Ritchie was a native Virginian. He became a journalist more or less by chance when Thomas Jefferson and other leaders of the Republican party in 1804 persuaded him to take over the *Richmond Enquirer.* Ritchie continued the paper for forty-one years, writing ringing editorials, presenting the news in well-edited form, doing most of the reporting himself and making the *Enquirer* a powerful influence. The *Enquirer,* under Ritchie's editorship, was the most famous newspaper of the period — a national rather than a regional paper.

Ritchie was occupied with other publishing ventures. While still publishing the *Enquirer* during 1840, he edited a weekly paper, the *Crisis,* dealing with educational issues. In 1845, at the request of President Polk, Ritchie left his son, William, to edit the *Enquirer* and moved to Washington to become editor of the *Washington Union,* a national administration organ. The Washington interim was not a happy or successful time for Ritchie. Because of advancing age and financial problems, he was forced to sell the *Union* in 1851, and to retire.

JOHN COOK RIVES
1795–1864

John Cook Rives was born in Franklin County, Virginia. In 1832, he was employed by Francis Preston Blair of the Washington *Daily Globe* as a partner and financial manager. The editorial columns of the *Globe* were filled with his writings.

Rives's most important contribution was creating the *Congressional Globe,* to report congressional debates, from 1833 to 1864, and from then until 1873 his son continued this work, prior to the beginning of the *Congressional Record.*

JAMES RIVINGTON
CA. 1724–1802

James Rivington, born in London, was the best known and most influential Tory editor during the American Revolution. After squandering his fortune by gambling in England, he came to America to regain his wealth. He opened a bookstore in New York and subsequently a well equipped printing office was added.

In 1773, Rivington began publishing a newspaper entitled *Rivington's New-York Gazetteer; or the Connecticut, New-Jersey, Hudson's River, and Quebec Weekly Advertiser.* This unwieldy title was shortened in 1777 to *Rivington's New York Loyal Gazette,* renamed *Royal Gazette,* and finally, in 1782, *Rivington's New-York Gazette and Universal Advertiser.* According to Mott, "it was one of the best and most widely circulated papers published in the colonies," attractive in appearance, excellent foreign news coverage, and thorough local and colonial news reporting.

Rivington with his paper, however, quickly aroused resentment among the colonials by his support of the Royalists. He was hanged in effigy in New Brunswick. His office was twice mobbed, and his plant virtually destroyed by the Sons of Liberty from Connecticut. Rivington was arrested and forced to sign a statement of loyalty to the Continental Congress. He soon fled to England. After General Howe took control of New York, Rivington returned and resumed publishing the *Royal Gazette* until the end of the war. At that time, the newspaper ceased publication on December 31, 1783, though Rivington remained in New York to operate a bookstore until his death.

WILLIAM ERIGEN ROBINSON
1814–1892

William Robinson was born in Ireland and emigrated to the United States in 1836. While a student at Yale, he founded the *Yale Banner* and contributed to the *New Haven Daily Herald.* From 1844 to 1848 he contributed dispatches from Washington to the *New York Tribune,* and served for a brief period in 1846 as editor of the *Buffalo Daily Express.* From 1850 to 1853, Richardson was editor of the *Newark Daily Mercury.* Other journalistic connections were his membership on the editorial board of the *Irish World* in 1871, and publication the following year of the *Shamrock,* a Brooklyn weekly publication.

Robinson was active in politics, serving as a member of Congress, holding several offices by appointment, and agitating the cause of Irish independence.

WILL ROGERS
(WILLIAM PENN ADAIR ROGERS)
1879-1935

During the 1920s and until his death in a plane accident in 1935, with the aviator, Wiley Post, Will Rogers was widely known and admired as a homespun philosopher and political satirist. He was successful as a syndicated newspaper columnist and radio commentator. His humor dealt mainly with current political affairs.

He was born in Oklahoma: part Cherokee Indian and proud of his Indian blood. His formal education stopped at nineteen, when he traveled to Argentina, South Africa, and Australia. His stage career began in 1905 when he exhibited his skills learned as a cowboy. At one time he was a star with the Ziegfeld Follies. He also starred in several motion pictures including *A Connecticut Yankee, David Harum,* and *Steamboat 'Round the Bend.*

His son, Will Rogers, Jr., born in 1911 in New York City, was at one time publisher of the Beverly Hills, California, *Citizen.* He was also active as an entertainer performing in television.

Will Rogers's home is now a museum in the Will Rogers State Historic Park in Pacific Palisades Verdes, California. He wrote several books including his autobiography, . . . *Will Rogers,* composed of selections from his many famous impressions and sayings.

ELEANOR ROOSEVELT
1884-1962

Eleanor Roosevelt, wife of President Franklin D. Roosevelt, was the most politically active First Lady in the nation's history. For a period of thirty-four years, from the election of her husband as governor of New York in 1928 until her death in 1962, she was in the limelight, a dynamic and frequently controversial figure. Through her extensive travels at home and abroad and myriad activities, she became one of the best-known women in the world.

She was born in New York City, a daughter of Elliott Roosevelt, younger brother of President Theodore Roosevelt. Her education came largely from private tutors in the United States and Europe. Her marriage to Franklin Roosevelt, a distant cousin, occurred in 1905. They had six children.

Franklin Roosevelt appeared to have a mother fixation. His father died early. His mother, Sara, was a forceful, determined personality, and for years she dominated Franklin's life, even after his marriage to Eleanor, a match she had strongly opposed. Sara made all decisions about where they were to live, selected and paid for all furnishings, engaged servants, selected nursemaids for the Roosevelt children, and even arranged the family's vacation plans. The clash of wills went on for many years, with Eleanor usually submitting. It was not until Franklin reached high political office that Eleanor began to assert her independence.

In Franklin's early political career, Eleanor played a modest role, but following his near fatal attack of poliomyelitis in 1921, she became invaluable to him. Bound as he was to his wheelchair, she served as his eyes, ears, and legs, keeping him informed of popular hopes and fears and national reactions to his policies. During the dark days of the Great Depression and afterward, Eleanor found time also to champion the rights of minorities, to work for improved living conditions for the poor, to encourage youth disillusioned by the economic breakdown, and to fight for the rights of women. In the course of World War II, she visited a number of foreign countries to improve relations with allies and raise the morale of American servicemen.

Eleanor Roosevelt was generally considered homely in appearance, and throughout her youth she thought of herself as an "ugly duckling." This belief was the source of her feeling of shyness and insecurity. Under the guidance of Franklin's long-time associate, Louis Howe, her attitude gradually changed and she developed the drive and force that characterized her later career. Howe trained her in public speaking and taught her how to get rid of a high, nervous giggle. Useful experience came to her in addressing many groups, particularly of women, until she became one of the most articulate spokespersons for the Democratic party. The nation soon came to expect Eleanor to be constantly on the move; she seemed to be everywhere, watching, speaking, inspecting, writing, and reporting back to the president. She began a newspaper column, called "My Day," and prior to the coming of television, broadcast regularly on the radio. "My Day" was syndicated nationally to newspapers having a total circulation of 5 million.

In April 1945, Franklin Roosevelt died at Warm Springs, Georgia, of a massive cerebral hemorrhage, at the age of sixty-three. In the seventeen years that remained of her life, Eleanor was the most active First Lady on record. Rather than retiring, she continued her concern for youth and minorities, lectured, traveled widely, and wrote columns and books. President Truman appointed her, in 1946, as an American delegate to the United

Nations. By unanimous vote, she was selected as chairperson of the United Nations Commission on Human Rights. Under her guidance, the UN's covenant for human rights was developed. In 1961 she was appointed by President Kennedy as a delegate to the General Assembly of the United Nations.

Eleanor Roosevelt died in 1962, at age seventy-eight. She had often been a controversial figure during her long and active career and she had many critics, but these were far outnumbered by the millions around the world who admired her for her ceaseless dedication to human welfare.

ABRAHAM M. ROSENTHAL
1922–

Abraham Rosenthal was born in Sault Ste. Marie, Ontario, Canada. Later the family moved to New York City. At City College, Rosenthal was editor-in-chief of the *Campus,* the undergraduate newspaper, and college correspondent for the *New York Times.* After two years of local reporting for the *Times,* he was assigned to the United National Bureau of the *Times* in Lake Success, New York.

The first of Rosenthal's foreign assignments came after eight years of covering UN proceedings. In 1954, he was sent to New Delhi as the *Times's* correspondent in India and Pakistan. His four years of reporting in that position brought him a citation from the Overseas Press Club. In 1958, Rosenthal was transferred to Warsaw to cover Poland and other Eastern European countries. When he filed stories that could not be published by the heavily censored Polish press, he was expelled from the country in 1959. For his reporting from Poland he was awarded a Pulitzer Prize in 1960.

Rosenthal's next stop was in Geneva, where he reported on the negotiations between the United States and Soviet Russia, summit conferences, and other events occurring in Western Europe.

In 1983, Rosenthal became executive editor of the *New York Times,* an association that had begun in 1944.

HAROLD ROSS
1892–1951

Harold Ross was born in Aspen, Colorado, and from the first showed an affinity for journalism. In 1908 he visited California. Over a seven-year period he was employed by the *Marysville* (California) *Appeal* (1910); the

Sacramento Union (1911); the Republic of Panama *Star and Herald* (1912); and from 1915 to 1917 the *New Orleans Item,* the *Atlanta Journal,* and the *San Francisco Call.*

During World War I, Ross was in the Army and became editor of *Stars and Stripes* (1917–19). After the war he edited the *American Legion Weekly* (1919–23), and for a year (1924) was editor of *Judge.*

In 1925, Ross founded the *New Yorker* and continued as editor until his death in 1951. He created the "Profile," the "Talk of the Town," letters from abroad, and clever cartoons. Ross assembled a remarkable staff of editors and writers for the magazine, among them Wolcott Gibbs, James Thurber, E. B. White, and Emily Hahn. One critic commented, "Rarely has an editor had such a profound effect on American reportage and fiction."

GEORGE ROULSTONE
1767–1804

George Roulstone, the first printer in Tennessee, was born in Boston. His first venture, the *Salem Chronicle and Essex Advertiser,* was short-lived (March to August 1786). Three years later he was in Fayetteville, North Carolina, employed by the *Gazette,* later the *North Carolina Chronicle.* Roulstone then moved to Tennessee and on November 5, 1791, issued the first number of the *Knoxville Gazette,* a three-column, four-page sheet. The *Gazette* was published by Roulstone until his death in 1804. His wife was public printer for several years, and married William Moore, also a public printer, who continued the *Gazette.*

RICHARD H. ROVERE
1915–1979

Richard Rovere was born in Jersey City, New Jersey. While a student at Bard College, he edited the college newspaper, the *Bardian.* After graduating from college, Rovere became an associate editor of *New Masses* (1937–39); assistant editor of the *Nation* (1940–43); and an editor for *Common Sense* (1943–44). In 1944, he was offered and accepted a job at the *New Yorker.* His assignment was to write lengthy profiles of political and other prominent personalities. Over the years, Rovere contributed hundreds of biographical accounts to the *New Yorker.* In the course of his work, he interviewed numerous public figures. One of his most controversial pieces was about Senator Joseph McCarthy of Wisconsin.

In 1948, Rovere began writing his "Letter from Washington" column for the *New Yorker,* usually commenting on the contemporary political scene. His articles for the *New Yorker* and other periodicals have frequently been collected and published in book form.

CARL THOMAS ROWAN
1925–

Carl Rowan was born in Ravenscroft, Tennessee. He earned a Master's degree in journalism at the University of Minnesota while writing for two black weeklies, the *Minneapolis Spokesman* and the *St. Paul Recorder.* He did public opinion surveys for the *Baltimore Afro-American* in 1948 and in the same year joined the *Minneapolis Tribune* as a copyreader. A series of articles entitled "How Far from Slavery," based on Rowan's travels through the South, drew a large response from readers.

As evidence that racial prejudice and discrimination was not limited to the black race, Rowan wrote a series of fifteen articles for the *Tribune* on problems of the American Indian. These contributions, too, were highly praised for their assessment of the causes and effects of the Indians' dilemma.

Rowan was director of the U.S. Information Agency (1964–65), and he was the first black to serve on the National Security Council. He was also deputy assistant secretary of state for public affairs (1961–63), and ambassador to Finland (1963–64). He has been a syndicated columnist for the New American Syndicate (formerly Field Syndicate) since 1965.

HOBART ROWEN
1918–

Rowen was a reporter first with the New York *Journal of Commerce* in 1938, and was its Washington correspondent from 1941–42. He was with the War Production Board for several years before going to *Newsweek,* in 1944, where he remained its Washington correspondent for twenty-one years. During this time he was also editor of *Business Trends.* Hobart Rowen went with the *Washington Post* in 1966 as its financial editor. Since 1975 he has been a columnist and economic editor there.

He has won many honors, awards, and citations, among them the John Hancock Award. He has also served as president of the Society of American Business Writers. He is an author and appears as one of the most respected panelists of "Washington Week in Review" for PBS. He has been described as "...a seasoned business and economic writer and editor."

ANNE ROYALL
1769-1854

Anne Royall, on whose tombstone is inscribed "Pioneer Woman Publicist," was born near Baltimore. After her husband's death in 1812, she spent a number of years wandering about and writing down her observations of life and customs throughout the country. The end result was publication of a number of travel books. Her letters were published by several newspapers.

In 1820, Royall stopped her wanderings and settled down in Washington to start a newspaper, a weekly entitled *Paul Pry.* Her stated policy was "to expose all and every species of political evil and religious fraud without fear or affection." In following that policy, Royall has been described as the first of the muckrakers and her paper as the forerunner of the modern Washington gossip columns.

In 1836, Royall replaced *Paul Pry* with the *Huntress,* differing little from the earlier paper in content or purpose, but in which she proposed to introduce "amusing tales, dialogues, and essays upon general subjects." She was editor of the *Huntress* for the remaining fourteen years of her life.

The Royall papers supported the trade labor movement and states' rights, and exposed post office frauds and Indian land frauds. They were anti–Presbyterian and pro–Free Mason, praised worthy public servants, and called attention to political graft and corruption.

MIKE ROYKO
1932-

Mike Royko was born in Chicago. He has become celebrated as a chronicler of events in that city. Early in his career, Royko worked as a reporter on Chicago's North Side newspapers, with the City News Bureau, and on the *Chicago Daily News* (1959–78). In 1978, he became a columnist on the *Chicago Sun-Times.*

Royko won a Pulitzer Prize for commentary in 1972 and other awards for his journalistic achievements.

VERMONT CONNECTICUT ROYSTER
1914-

Vermont Royster was born in Raleigh, North Carolina, and graduated from the University of North Carolina at Chapel Hill, where his father was a member of the faculty. As a student, Royster edited the university newspaper. After graduation he went to New York city and began his career as a reporter for the New York City bureau. In 1936, he joined the staff of the *Wall Street Journal* as a correspondent in Washington, reporting on the White House, Congress, the Supreme Court, and the Treasury.

Royster enlisted in the Navy in 1941; he saw active service in the Pacific and was discharged in 1945 with the rank of lieutenant commander.

After returning to the *Wall Street Journal* following the war, Royster became chief correspondent in charge of the Washington bureau, was made associate editor in 1948, senior associate editor (1951–58), and editor (1958–71).

LOUIS RUKEYSER
1933-

Louis Rukeyser was born in New York City into a family of journalists. His father was former financial editor of the *New York Herald Tribune* and was the Hearst Newspapers' syndicated economic columnist for more than thirty years. One brother is executive vice president for public information at NBC; another is managing editor of *Fortune* magazine, and a third is public affairs director at American Brands Corporation.

Millions of listeners hear the popular "Wall Street Week" program, and its host's, Louis Rukeyser, analyses of the week's financial news. Before joining "Wall Street Week" for its first broadcast in 1970, Rukeyser worked for more than ten years as a reporter for the *Baltimore Sun* and served as an economic correspondent for ABC news. Rukeyser is also an award-winning columnist and recently launched *Louis Rukeyser's Business Journal.* His weekly column of economic commentary, begun in 1978, is syndicated to about two hundred newspapers by the McNaught Syndicate.

The format of "Wall Street Week" does not vary. It begins with a humorous monologue by Rukeyser, followed by a panel discussion of three financial experts, and concludes with a guest interview.

DAMON RUNYON
1884–1946

Damon Runyon was born in Manhattan, Kansas, the son of an itinerant printer and newspaper publisher, who operated newspapers in various Kansas towns.

When Runyon was fourteen, the Spanish-American War began. Despite his youth he enlisted in the Army and spent two years in the Philippines. Back home, he held a succession of jobs on small papers all over Kansas and also on the *Denver News, Post,* and *Republic.* After a short period of writing for the *San Francisco Post,* Runyon went on to New York to report sports for the *New York American.* Over the next twelve years, he traveled with the Giants and other New York baseball clubs.

In 1912, Runyon was sent to Mexico to cover the Madera revolution. He returned to Mexico in 1916 as an accredited correspondent to accompany the Pershing Expedition in pursuit of Pancho Villa. A year later, with the outbreak of World War I, Runyon went overseas, as a war correspondent with the First Army, and was present for some of the major operations. After the war he worked for the Hearst Syndicate, writing sports columns.

Runyon is remembered for his short stories about Broadway characters. His highly individual style used Broadway slang and metaphor. Beginning in 1933, Runyon worked as a screenwriter in Hollywood and a few years later became a writer-producer.

Aside from his short stories and movie scripts, Runyon thought of himself first of all as a newspaperman, called by Arthur Brisbane "the best reporter in the world." His sports column, "Both Barrels," was carried in the *American.* His general interest column, "As I See It," starting in 1937, was syndicated to sixteen Hearst papers and in the same year, "The Brighter Side" was syndicated by Hearst's King Features Syndicate to hundreds of newspapers all over the United States.

Runyon married a society reporter on a Denver paper, herself the daughter of a newspaperman.

BENJAMIN RUSSELL
1761–1845

Benjamin Russell has been compared to Benjamin Franklin, Isaiah Thomas, William Goddard, James Gordon Bennett, and Horace Greeley as one of the giants of eighteenth- to nineteenth-century journalism.

Russell was born in Boston and was given his first taste of journalism by frequenting Isaiah Thomas's printing office and learning to set type. Later he was taken to Worcester and apprenticed to Thomas. When Thomas was drafted for military service in 1780, he sent Russell as his substitute. As Russell reached age twenty, he became a full-fledged journeyman. Ambitious to set up a newspaper in Boston, the first number of his *Massachusetts Centinel and the Republican Journal* was issued on March 24, 1784. Russell continued as its editor until 1828, when he retired from journalism. The title of his paper was soon shortened to the *Massachusetts Centinel,* and in 1790 to *Colombian Centinel.*

The *Centinel* adopted a vigorous editorial policy, marked by strong support for adoption of the new Constitution, praise for George Washington, and, later, opposition to Thomas Jefferson. The paper became recognized as a leading Federalist champion. Along with political activity, the *Centinel* provided excellent news coverage, including summaries of foreign news, and was often copied by other newspapers. The appearance of the paper was made more attractive by the plentiful use of printers' devices, pictures, and mechanical arrangement of types. Russell printed the famous gerrymander cartoon, drawn by Gilbert Stuart, and perhaps coined the word "gerrymander."

The *Centinel* backed a variety of social reforms, such as temperance, education, and food preservation, and took stands on such issues as capital punishment, government secrecy, and profanity.

Twelve years after Russell's retirement, the *Centinel* became a part of the *Boston Daily Advertiser.*

CHARLES EDWARD RUSSELL
1860-1941

Charles Edward Russell was born in LeClaire, Iowa, and came naturally into journalism, since his father was a newspaper publisher. Russell rose early in the morning, aged twelve, to wrap papers in the mailing room of the *Davenport* (Iowa) *Gazette.* By age twenty he had become the paper's managing editor while his father wrote editorials. Time out was taken for education and then young Russell returned to Davenport in 1881 to manage the paper. From 1883 to 1886 he moved from one newspaper to another: writing editorials for the *St. Paul Pioneer Press,* reporter and night editor of the *Minneapolis Tribune,* and managing editor of the *Minneapolis Journal.* There was a brief stopover with the *Detroit Tribune* in 1886 before Russell moved on to New York.

Russell went to work as a reporter for the *New York World.* One of his first assignments was in Chicago to cover the Haymarket bombing and the hanging of strike leaders in 1887. He also reported the 1888 Republican nominating convention in Chicago. The following year he joined the *New York Herald,* then owned by James Gordon Bennett, Jr., reporting on the Johnstown flood and other sensational events. A promotion to assistant city editor came in 1872, but Russell returned to the *World* as city editor from 1894 to 1897. A star cast of editors and authors directed by Russell and Arthur Brisbane brought a large increase in the *World's* circulation, which exceeded six hundred thousand by 1897. An attractive offer from Hearst persuaded Russell to become managing editor of the *New York Journal* in 1897 and publisher of Hearst's *Chicago American* in 1900.

For several years, Russell contributed a series of muckraking articles to *Everybody's* magazine, *Hampton's,* and *Pearson's,* beginning in 1905. He became an active socialist and was nominated by the Socialist party for governor of New York, mayor of New York City, and U.S. Senator, none of which he won. In 1916, Russell went to Europe for the Newspaper Enterprise Association, aided George Creel with the wartime news bureau, and helped the Non-Partisan League to establish a newspaper, the *Non-Partisan Leader,* in Fargo, North Dakota. In 1918, he was a member of the Root Commission to Russia as a representative of U.S. socialists and American workers.

MORLEY SAFER
1931–

Morley Safer was born in Toronto, Canada. His initial experience as a journalist was in Canada and London. During the 1960s, he covered practically every major story in Europe, the Middle East, and Africa, and did two tours of Vietnam. After being appointed chief of the CBS London bureau in 1967, Safer reported on the Arab-Israeli War, the Soviet invasion of Czechoslovakia, religious strife in Northern Ireland, the Nigerian civil war, and the American withdrawal from Cambodia. He made a three-week tour of China during the Great Proletarian Cultural Revolution.

In 1970, Safer replaced Harry Reasoner as coeditor of "60 Minutes," CBS's news magazine, and began contributing his colorful essays on the many topics covered by the program. The top feature was Safer's interviews with prominent personalities. The "60 Minutes" show was popular from the beginning and was on a full fifty-two-week schedule. Some of Safer's "national disgrace stories" inspired government investigations.

WILLIAM SAFIRE
1929–

William Safire was born in New York City. His well-known conservative views induced the *New York Times* to hire him as a columnist in 1973 to counterbalance its more liberal reporters Tom Wicker, James Reston, and Anthony Lewis.

Before joining the *Times* staff, Safire had worked as a researcher and writer for the *New York Herald Tribune;* been a roving reporter for WNBC radio and WNBT-TV in Europe and the Middle East; was in Moscow at the American National Exhibition in 1959; was a speech writer for Richard Nixon during the 1968 presidential campaign; and moved into the White House as special assistant to the president in 1969.

The *New York Times* appointment met with some criticism from both liberals and conservatives. One commentator suggested that it was "a little like letting a hawk loose among the doves." One of Safire's immediate concerns was to defend Nixon's role in the Watergate crisis.

ADELA ROGERS ST. JOHNS
1894–1988

Adela Rogers was born in Los Angeles and throughout her journalistic career was associated with William Randolph Hearst's newspapers. She began as a cub reporter on the *Los Angeles Herald* and worked briefly on the *San Francisco Examiner.* Feature writing, "inside stories," and profiles for *Photoplay* magazine followed, and articles were contributed to a number of general interest magazines. Newspaper writing, however, was St. Johns's primary interest and during her years with Hearst, she was on the staffs of the *Chicago American, New York American,* and International News Service.

St. Johns called herself the first woman sportswriter. Her assignments from Hearst included the World Series, Kentucky Derby, Rose Bowl, Olympic Games, and the Forest Hills Tennis Tournament. Among the major stories covered by her was the 1935 trial of Bruno Richard Hauptmann for the kidnapping and murder of the Lindbergh baby. In the mid–1930s, she went to Washington to cover political stories, including a report on Huey Long's activities. Among later assignments were the abdication of Edward VIII, the Dempsey–Tunney prize fight, the assassination of Senator Huey Long, the 1940 Democratic national convention, and a series on Mahatma Gandhi shortly before his assassination.

Early in her career, St. Johns was called the veteran "sob sister" of

American journalism and she was also described as "mother confessor of Hollywood," for her stories about movie stars. In her more mature years she went far beyond that type of writing.

In 1976, at age eighty-two, St. Johns covered the bank robbery and conspiracy trial of William Randolph Hearst's granddaughter, Patty Hearst, for the *San Francisco Examiner.*

PIERRE SALINGER
1925–

Pierre Salinger was born in San Francisco, California, a piano prodigy as a child and the son of a musician. He entered San Francisco State College at age fifteen, edited the college newspaper, and worked nights as a copyboy with the *San Francisco Chronicle.*

Salinger enlisted in the U.S. Navy in 1942 and was sent to the Pacific on a submarine chaser. By age nineteen, he was made captain of the ship, with a crew of twenty-four.

After the war, Salinger continued in college and to work for the *Chronicle.* When he graduated in 1947, he became a full-time reporter and in 1950 was promoted to night city editor. He left the *Chronicle* in 1955 to become the West Coast editor of *Collier's* magazine. Salinger's articles on the Teamsters Union were used by Attorney General Robert Kennedy in an investigation of labor racketeering. In 1960, President-elect John F. Kennedy appointed Salinger as his press secretary. He represented the president on trips to France and Moscow. Soon after Kennedy's assassination, he left the White House.

In the intervening years, Salinger worked intermittently on several journalism stories. In 1979 he was made head of the ABC Paris news bureau. He was credited with some major international stories for ABC news and in 1983 was promoted to be ABC's chief foreign correspondent. In 1983 and 1984 he covered President Reagan's trips to Japan, England and France, and in 1985 to Europe. During 1986 he covered the Reagan–Gorbachev meeting in Geneva, the Gorbachev–Mitterrand meeting in Paris, and the Tokyo economic summit meeting. Salinger's permanent residence is in Paris and he has long been noted for his fluent French.

HARRISON E. SALISBURY
1908–

Harrison Salisbury was born in Minneapolis, Minnesota. He began his journalism career early by editing his high school's weekly newspaper and later at the University of Minnesota as editor of the campus daily. While still a student, he was employed (1928–29) as a cub reporter on the *Minneapolis Journal.* After his graduation in 1930, Salisbury joined United Press as a reporter and rewrite man. At various times, he worked in Chicago, Washington, and New York City before being sent to London in 1942. He was named manager of the London bureau in 1943 and foreign news editor (1944–48).

Salisbury was sent to the Soviet Union in 1944, expecting to remain for six weeks, but actually staying for eight months, reporting on conditions in Russia during the final days of World War II. It was here that he began to establish his reputation as the best-informed American reporter of his generation on the USSR. Salisbury spent the rest of his career with the United Press as its foreign news desk in New York City.

Salisbury transferred to the *New York Times* in 1949 for its Moscow bureau. In spite of strict censorship he sent back revealing reports on the Soviet Union during the Cold War Period. In 1954, tailed by security agents, he took a 12,000-mile tour through Siberia, the most extensive of any American up to that time. For that feat, Salisbury was awarded a Pulitzer Prize in 1955 for international reporting. In 1957, he surveyed conditions in Eastern Europe, visiting all of the Iron Curtain countries and Yugoslavia. A 1961 book by Salisbury, *The End of Stalin,* speculated that Stalin was murdered.

In 1966, Salisbury fulfilled a long ambition to visit China. A 30,000-mile tour was made through the People's Republic of China and North Vietnam.

After his return to the New York office, Salisbury covered such domestic stories as the problem of garbage disposal, Brooklyn street gangs, and the civil rights movement.

Since his retirement in 1973, Salisbury has contributed to the *New York Times Magazine* and book sections, and for four years edited the *Times's* Op. Ed page.

BENJAMIN FRANKLIN SANBORN
1831–1917

Benjamin F. Sanborn was born in Hampton Falls, New Hampshire, graduated from Harvard in 1855, and moved to Concord, Massachusetts. He became deeply involved in the abolition movement and had legal difficulties by supporting John Brown.

Sanborn was a correspondent of the *Springfield Republican* from 1856 until 1914. He succeeded Moncure Daniel Conway as editor of the *Boston*

Commonwealth (1863–67), and was a resident editor of the *Springfield Republican* (1868–72).

ROBERT CHARLES SANDS
1799–1832

Robert Charles Sands was born in New York City. In 1821, in association with several friends who called themselves the "Literary Confederacy," he published *St. Tammany's Magazine,* consisting largely of literary parody and burlesque. In 1824, Sands was, for a short time, editor of the *Atlantic Magazine,* and after its merger in 1825 with the *New York Review,* became William Cullen Bryant's assistant. The magazine was discontinued in 1826, and in 1827 Sands joined the editorial staff of the *New York Commercial Advertiser,* a position he held until his death. He had some reputation as a student of the Spanish language and as a minor poet.

EPES SARGENT
1813–1880

Epes Sargent was born in Gloucester, Massachusetts. He accompanied his father, a Gloucester shipmaster, on a voyage to Russia. In the early 1930s, he joined the editorial staff of the *Boston Daily Advertiser* and later was on the *Boston Daily Atlas* staff. He was Washington correspondent for the *Atlas,* giving him an opportunity to know prominent political figures, especially among the Whigs.

Sargent contributed to many periodicals during his active career and composed some verse. He assisted in the preparation of the Peter Parley books.

GEORGE HENRY SARGENT
1867–1931

George Henry Sargent was born on a farm near Warner, New Hampshire. He went West in 1887 and began his life work in journalism as a reporter on the *St. Paul Daily Pioneer Press.* He served as editor of the *Press* from 1890 to 1895. In 1895 he returned East to join the staff of the *Boston Evening Transcript.* He remained with that paper the rest of his life, as reporter, writer of special articles, and for twenty-seven years author of a department entitled "The Bibliographer," in every issue.

JESSICA SAVITCH
1947–1983

Jessica Savitch was born in Kennett Square, Pennsylvania. While in high school she was hired by a radio station in nearby Pleasantville as a disc jockey and news reader for its Saturday afternoon program. While in college she had a job as a weekend disc jockey at WBBF-AM in Rochester. In 1969, CBS hired her as an all-purpose assistant. Leaving New York, she was hired by KHOV-TV, a CBS affiliate in Houston, as a general assignment reporter. She became the first anchorwoman in the South. In 1977, NBC appointed Savitch to its Washington bureau, to cover the U.S. Senate. Later she was transferred from Capitol Hill for general assignments.

Savitch died in an automobile accident in rural Pennsylvania on October 23, 1983.

DIANE SAWYER
1945–

Diane Sawyer was born in Glasgow, Kentucky. In high school, she served as editor-in-chief of the campus newspaper. After college graduation, she went on to Louisville and held a job as a "weather girl" and part-time reporter for WLKY-TV, the local ABC affiliate. Another move was made in 1970 to Washington, where she found a job as assistant to Jerry Warren, White House deputy press secretary. Her assignment at first was to write press releases, but she went on to drafting some of President Nixon's public statements, to becoming administrative assistant to the White House press secretary, Ron Ziegler, and finally to staff assistant to the president. When Nixon resigned in 1974, Sawyer accompanied him in exile to San Clemente, California, as a research assistant.

After four years, Sawyer returned to Washington and joined the Washington bureau of CBS as a general assignment reporter. When CBS decided to expand its morning news show from sixty to ninety minutes, Sawyer was chosen to coanchor the program.

In 1984, CBS announced a major reorganization of the morning newscast, and the reassignment of Sawyer to the staff of "60 Minutes," where she joined Mike Wallace, Harry Reasoner, Morley Safer, and Ed Bradley, and continued to be a fixture on the program, until early in 1989, when she resigned to accept a position as coanchor with Sam Donaldson to create a new type of news program for ABC.

BOB SCHIEFFER
1937–

Bob Schieffer began as a reporter on the *Fort Worth* (Texas) *Star-Telegram* before turning to television at WBAP-TV in the Dallas-Fort Worth area. Since 1964, he has been with CBS News in various roles, such as Sunday evening anchorman. He has worked on many specials, including reporting on national political conventions.

For his superior ability as a reporter, Schieffer has won awards from Sigma Delta Chi, the Associated Broadcasters, and the Associated Press Managing Editors.

DANIEL LOUIS SCHORR
1916–

Daniel Schorr was born in New York City. From his days as a high school student, Schorr was engaged in journalistic activity. After college he joined the *New York Journal-American* and in 1941, the Netherlands News Agency. During World War II, he served in the Army. Edward Murrow was impressed by Schorr's ability and in 1953 hired him for CBS News. Schorr reopened the CBS Moscow Bureau in 1955, covered Europe until 1966, and for the next ten years served as chief of CBS's Washington bureau.

Schorr left CBS News in 1976 when he turned over to the *New York Village Voice* a copy of a suppressed report of the U.S. House Committee of Intelligence telling of illegal CIA and FBI operations. He was suspended by CBS and then resigned.

After leaving CBS, Schorr became a columnist for the Des Moines Register-Tribune Syndicate. From 1980 to 1985 he was senior Washington correspondent for the Cable News Network. Since 1985 he has been senior analyst for National Public Radio.

CHARLES M. SCHULZ
1922–

Charles Schulz was born in Minneapolis. In 1943, he was drafted into the U.S. Army. After the war ended he returned to St. Paul and obtained a job lettering the comic pages of a religious magazine published in St. Paul. He began to draw a weekly cartoon for a St. Paul newspaper and in 1948 sold his first cartoons to the *Saturday Evening Post.* The next step for Schulz was to sell his idea of a comic strip to United Feature Syndicate. It was then, in 1950, that "Peanuts" was born.

Featuring child characters who talk and think like adults, "Peanuts" soon became one of the most popular comic strips in the United States and in a number of foreign countries, syndicated to hundreds of newspapers.

CARL SCHURZ
1829–1906

Carl Schurz, a native of Germany, participated in the unsuccessful revolution of 1848, and was forced to flee to Switzerland to avoid arrest. He came to the United States in 1852 and settled in Philadelphia. Moving to Wisconsin in 1856, Schurz became a leading antislavery Republican and campaigned for Abraham Lincoln. During the Civil War he was commissioned a brigadier general, in command of a division. His troops saw action at Chancellorsville, Chattanooga, and Gettysburg.

After the war, Schurz began his journalistic career. He established the *Westlicher Post,* a German-language newspaper in St. Louis, Missouri, a journal that soon became a powerful influence in the West. President Hayes appointed Schurz secretary of the interior in 1877, a post that he held until 1881. Later, he became editor of the *New York Evening Post* (1881–82), and from 1892 to 1898, was chief editorial writer for *Harper's Weekly.*

As secretary of the interior, Schurz worked for a civil service merit system, supported fair treatment for the Indians, and encouraged the development of national parks.

GEORGE S. SCHUYLER
1895–1977

George S. Schuyler was born in Providence, Rhode Island. He had the distinction of becoming one of the first black journalists to gain national prominence and to have his writings appear in many newspapers and magazines and one of the first black reporters to serve as a foreign correspondent for a major newspaper.

As a youngster, Schuyler "carried" a newspaper route and sold newspapers to add to the family income. While in military service in Hawaii he made his first attempts to write for a newspaper with irregular pieces for the *Honolulu Commercial Advertiser* and the *Service* magazine. There followed some years of rather aimless drifting after discharge from the military, where Schuyler had attained the rank of first lieutenant. In 1923, he was offered and accepted the job of assistant manager on the *Messenger,* the official journal of the Friends of Negro Freedom. At the same time, Schuyler began freelancing. An important opportunity came in 1924 when he was asked to write a regular column for the *Pittsburgh Courier,* which had the second largest circulation of black weeklies. Schuyler was associated with the *Courier* for over forty years.

Schuyler remained with the *Messenger* until it ceased publication in 1928. He became friends with H. L. Mencken, who solicited contributions from him for the *American Mercury.* He also became the *Courier's* chief editorial writer for thirty-eight years. The *Courier* sent him on a tour of the Southern states to report on the condition of blacks in that region. A similar mission was a trip to Liberia, arranged by George Palmer Putnam, to write a book about the slave trade there. A series of articles on the Liberian situation were published by the *New York Evening Post,* the *Washington Post,* and the *Philadelphia Ledger.*

From 1937 to 1944, Schuyler was business manager of *Crisis,* the NAACP magazine. In 1943, he became associate editor of a monthly magazine, the *African.* For the *Courier,* he wrote about racial intolerance in America, the rise of communism, the civil rights situation, and living conditions in Harlem. In 1948 he was sent on a tour of a number of Latin American countries to investigate racial attitudes and discrimination. Another foreign mission took him to Berlin in 1950 as a U.S. delegate to the Congress of Cultural Freedom.

Schuyler's increasingly conservative views caused him to lose influence. His association with the *Courier* ended in 1966. At the height of his journalistic career his readers numbered hundreds of thousands. When he died in 1977, he had become an obscure figure in the newspaper world.

MONTGOMERY SCHUYLER
1843–1914

Montgomery Schuyler was born in Ithaca, New York. He went to New York City in 1865 and became a member of a brilliant group of young writers recruited by the editor of the *New York World*. Schuyler remained on the staff of the *World* until 1883, and then transferred to the *New York Times,* where he remained until his retirement from active journalism in 1907. Prior positions were managing editor of *Harper's Weekly* (1885–87), and reader for Harper & Brothers (1887–94). Schuyler contributed book reviews and articles on literary subjects to the *New York Sun* after 1912. He also wrote for magazines, mainly dealing with literature and architecture. He was recognized in his time as the leading critic and historian of American architecture.

HARVEY W. SCOTT
1838–1910

Harvey W. Scott was born in Illinois, but went West as a boy, graduating from Pacific University in Oregon. Originally he was headed for a legal career. Some pieces that he wrote for the *Portland Oregonian* were so well received, however, that he was appointed editor of the paper in 1865. Twelve years later he became owner of the *Oregonian* and continued to serve as editor until his death in 1910, forty-five years later.

In the seven states north of San Francisco and west of Minneapolis there were no large papers when Scott took over, and the *Oregonian* held a preeminent position in that extensive area. Scott's editorials were influential far beyond the thousands of *Oregonian* readers and became nationally recognized.

Editorially, Scott took strong stands on many issues. He was an ardent Republican and was credited with converting Oregon from a Democratic to a Republican state. He believed in the supremacy of the white race, opposed black suffrage and the enfranchisement of women, opposed the organization of labor and protective legislation for workers, fought for "sound money" (the gold standard), and was against prohibition.

Prior to the *Oregonian,* the *Oregon City Spectator* became the first U.S. newspapers west of the Rocky Mountains. Scott had no serious competition, however, until the establishment of the *Oregon Journal* in 1902. The *Journal* and the *Oregonian* were on opposite sides on most issues. The *Journal,* for example, was Democratic and battled for the enfranchisement of women.

Aside from his editorial influence, Scott achieved some reputation as a regional historian, especially of Oregon and the Northwest. He also regarded himself as a schoolmaster, contributing to the education of his readers by instructing them in morals, philosophy, theology, literature, and history. His lifetime habit of voracious reading provided endless material for these essays.

One honor that came to Scott late in life was to serve as director of the Associated Press from 1900 to 1910.

JAMES WILMOT SCOTT
1849–1895

James W. Scott was born in Walworth County, Wisconsin, the son and grandson of newspapermen. He learned the printer's trade in his father's office and he and his father founded the *Industrial Press* in Galena, Illinois. In Chicago, Scott bought an interest in the *National Hotel Reporter,* but he was ambitious to start a paper of his own. The Chicago Herald Company, in which Scott later gained a controlling interest, was organized in 1881 and began publishing the *Chicago Herald.* The paper became highly successful under Scott's management. Measurement of his standing in the journalism profession was his election as president of the American Newspaper Publishers' Association, president of the Chicago Press Club, and president of the United Press.

E. W. SCRIPPS
1854–1926

Edward Willis Scripps was born on a farm near Rushville, Illinois, the last of his father's thirteen children. At eighteen he began his newspaper work as an office boy on the *Detroit Tribune,* of which his half-brother James was manager. In 1873 he helped James start the *Detroit Evening News,* the first cheap evening paper in the United States. With financial support from James and half-brother, George, Scripps began, in 1878, the *Cleveland Penny Press.* Two years later he and his brothers bought the *Evening Chronicle* in St. Louis, a two-cent paper, and then the *Penny Post* of Cincinnati, with other papers in Ohio and Missouri, thus setting up the first chain of daily newspapers in the country. Subsequently, Scripps gave up control of the papers to his brothers, except for the *Cincinnati Post.*

Scripps founded the Scripps–McRae League of Newspapers in 1895, which in 1897 became the Scripps–McRae Press Association, merged in 1904 with International News Service, and in 1907 formed United Press International. Before Scripp's death, United Press was providing a daily service to nine hundred newspapers, U.S. and foreign. In 1920, the Science Service, to provide popular scientific news, was added.

Scripps moved to San Diego, California, in 1891, bought an interest in the *San Diego Sun,* the first of the Scripps Coast League of Newspapers, a chain of newspapers that included Seattle, Tacoma, Spokane, Portland, Denver, San Francisco, Los Angeles, Fresno, and Sacramento.

By the end of his career, Scripps's estate was valued at $50 million. His wealth enabled him to be philanthropic. The Scripps Institution of Oceanography, now part of the University of California, was endowed by him in 1903. He and his sister, Ellen, another journalist, founded Scripps College at Claremont, California. Another endowment provided for the Scripps Foundation for Population Research at Miami University, Oxford, Ohio.

Two of Scripps's sons, James and Robert, followed him in the profession of journalism, and his sister Ellen was associated with various journalistic enterprises over a long lifetime.

WILLIAM WINSTON SEATON
1785–1866

William Seaton, born in Virginia, reported debates in the U.S. Senate for fifty-two years, while his partner and brother-in-law, Joseph Gales, covered the House of Representatives. Seaton made an early start as a journalist at age eighteen by becoming editor of the *Virginia Patriot* in Richmond. In 1806, he moved to Raleigh to assist William Boylan on the *Minerva.* A year later, Seaton took over the editorship of the *North Carolina Journal,* a Republican newspaper in Halifax. Although apparently successful in that position, he returned to Raleigh in 1809 to assist Joseph Gales on the *Register.*

The Washington connection began in 1810, when Joseph Gales, Jr., became publisher of the *National Intelligencer.* In 1812, Seaton went to Washington as his partner. Under Gales and Seaton, the *Intelligencer* became the recognized government organ for the presidents until the inauguration of Andrew Jackson. Both Seaton and Gales were expert stenographers, masters of shorthand, recording the speeches of Daniel Webster, Henry Clay, John Calhoun, and other leading members of Congress. The *Register of Debates,* published from 1825 to 1837, included presidential messages and important executive documents.

Various difficulties hampered publication of the *Intelligencer.* It was suspended for a time during the War of 1812, when the British invaded Washington. The partners lost the Senate printing contract in 1827 and the House contract in 1829. Several major series, based on shorthand reports and other records, were published by Gales and Seaton: *Annals of Congress* (1789–1824, 42 vols.); *Register of Debates in Congress* (1824–37, 14 vols.); and *American State Papers* (1832–61, 38 vols.).

Gales died in 1860 and Seaton in 1866. The latter retired from editorial work in 1864. The *National Intelligencer* continued to be published in Washington until 1870, when it was moved to New York and soon suspended.

ARNOLD ERIC SEVAREID
1912–

Eric Sevareid was born in Velva, North Dakota. As a journalist for more than three decades he was a reporter, editor, war correspondent, radio newscaster, television commentator, and columnist.

Sevareid's interest in journalism began early. He was editor of his high school paper. After a canoe trip of 2,200 miles for which he and a friend were paid one hundred dollars by the *Minneapolis Star,* Sevareid found a job with the *Minnesota Journal* as a copyboy; six weeks later he was made a reporter. He lost his job with the *Journal* in 1937, went to Europe to study, and in 1938, was hired as a reporter for the Paris edition of the *New York Herald Tribune.* Sevareid also worked as night editor for the United Press.

In 1939, Sevareid joined Edward R. Murrow in London to broadcast radio news. Sevareid traveled with French armed forces in France, Belgium, Holland, and Luxembourg to broadcast war news back to the United States. He left Paris just before it was taken by the Germans, and then moved to London to join Murrow and report on the Battle of Britain.

Sevareid returned to the United States in 1940 and was assigned to the CBS bureau in Washington (1941–43).

In the summer of 1943, Sevareid set off for an assignment in China. The Army plane over the Himalayas from India to China had engine trouble and the twenty persons aboard, including Sevareid, had to bail out and make their way through the jungle to civilization a month later. After spending several months in the China-Burma-India area, Sevareid again returned to the United States.

In January 1944, Sevareid decided to return to Europe as a correspondent for CBS News. He took part in the Italian campaign, spent time with Marshall Tito's fighters in Yugoslavia, and accompanied American troops through France and into Germany.

After the war ended in Europe, Sevareid held a variety of CBS assignments: attended the organization of the United Nations in San Francisco; spent two years (1959–61), as roving European correspondent for CBS; national correspondent for CBS News in Washington; and moderator for CBS telecasts. His many achievements have won Sevareid numerous awards.

ROBERT SHAPLEN
1917–1988

Robert Shaplen worked as a writer and reporter for fifty years for the *New York Herald Tribune, Newsweek, Fortune,* and from 1950 until his death for the *New Yorker.* Most of his career was spent covering Asia, and he was known among journalists for his almost unrivaled knowledge of the region. He was also the author of ten books.

WILLIAM LAWRENCE SHIRER
1904–

William Shirer was born in Chicago and graduated from Coe College. While a student, he was a sports reporter on the *Cedar Rapids* (Iowa) *Republican.* After a summer of travel in Europe he was employed at the copy desk of the *Chicago Tribune*'s Paris edition. In 1927, Shirer became a European correspondent for the *Tribune.* From 1929 to 1932 he was chief of the *Tribune's* Central European Bureau, located in Vienna. In 1930 and 1931 he toured Afghanistan and India, and reported on Mahatma Gandhi's civil disobedience movement.

Shirer returned to Paris in 1934 to work on the Paris edition of the *New York Herald.* In the same year he became a correspondent in Berlin for the Universal News Service, a position that he retained until 1937, when Hearst discontinued the service. First from Vienna, then from Prague, and finally from Berlin, Shirer was a commentator for CBS News until 1947. From 1942 to 1948 he was a columnist for the *New York Herald Tribune* and the Herald Tribune Syndicate.

Toward the end of the war, Shirer returned to Germany to cover the Nuremberg war crimes trials. He was also in San Francisco for the organization of the United Nations in 1945.

Shirer resigned from CBS in 1947, and from 1947 to 1949 was a commentator for the Mutual Broadcasting System. Later he devoted himself mainly to the writing of history and fiction.

Shirer's first book, *Berlin Diary* (1941), became a best-seller. In 1960 he published *The Rise and Fall of the Third Reich: A History of Nazi Germany,* which was also a best-seller and won the National Book Award in 1961.

CHRISTOPHER LATHAM SHOLES
1819–1890

Christopher Sholes was born on a farm near Mooresburg, Pennsylvania. He was an apprentice for four years on the *Danville* (Pennsylvania) *Intelligence.* After his parents moved to Green Bay, Wisconsin, young Sholes became state printer. He then went to Madison to serve as editor of the *Wisconsin Enquirer,* in which his brother, Charles, had acquired an interest. In 1941, Sholes became editor of the *Southport Telegraph* for four years. He resigned when President Polk appointed him Southport postmaster. In 1860, Sholes returned to journalism as editor of the *Milwaukee News,* and later as editor of the *Milwaukee Sentinel,* a position that he gave up when President Lincoln appointed him Collector of the Port of Milwaukee.

WILLIAM WIRT SIKES
1836–1883

William Wirt Sikes was born in Watertown, New York, and learned the printing trade in the office of a local paper. In 1856 he was employed on the *Utica Morning Herald* and in 1863 worked on the *Chicago Evening Journal.* Over a period of several years, he contributed to the *Youth's Companion, Oliver Optic's Magazine, Harper's Magazine,* and the *New York Sun.* Starting about 1868, Sikes edited *City and Country* (Nyack, New York) and the Rockland County *Journal* (Piermont, New York), in both of which he had a financial interest. In 1876, he was appointed U.S. consul in Cardiff, Wales, and became well known for his research and writing on Welsh folklore.

JAMES WILLIAM SIMONTON
1823–1882

James Simonton was born in Columbia County, New York. At age twenty he was hired as a reporter on the *Morning Courier* and *New York Enquirer*. A year later his paper sent him to Washington as its congressional correspondent. He remained there until 1850, after which he went to San Francisco and joined the staff of the *California Daily Courier*. When the *New York Times* was established in 1851, Simonton returned to Washington to serve as correspondent for the *Times* and for papers in New Orleans, San Francisco, and Detroit.

In 1859, Simonton became part-owner of the *San Francisco Evening Bulletin* and afterwards of the *Morning Call*. In 1967, he went to New York as general agent of the Associated Press and remained in the position for fourteen years. During that period, Simonton played a key part in exposing some of the corruption in the Grant administration.

UPTON BEALL SINCLAIR
1878–1968

The palm for achieving foremost rank among modern American propagandist novelists is readily carried off by Sinclair. Simultaneously, he was one of the most prolific writers in the nation's literary history, and is probably the most widely read abroad of all American authors. According to a recent count, there are 772 translations of his books in forty-seven languages and in thirty-nine countries, with the totals continuing to mount.

Sinclair has been aptly compared to another great propagandist, Thomas Paine. Like Paine, he attacked with burning indignation and reckless courage every variety of social abuse and injustice. The appellations "a pamphleteer for righteousness" and "the last of the muckrackers" are apt descriptions of Sinclair's stormy literary career.

When Sinclair died in 1968, at the age of ninety, he could view in retrospect a lifetime devoted to crusades: smiting labor spies, the meat-packing industry, a corrupt press, Wall Street speculators, New York society, alcoholism, the murders of Sacco and Vanzetti, Tom Mooney's persecution, bourgeois morality, coal-mine conditions, popular evangelism, secondary and higher education, the oil industry, and evils of war.

Sinclair's first five novels (published from 1901 to 1906), produced very limited royalties. The turning point was *The Jungle* (1906), the most popular and most influential of all Sinclair's numerous novels. This savage indictment of labor and sanitary conditions in the Chicago stockyards first appeared serially in *The Appeal to Reason,* a socialist weekly, when the author was a mere twenty-seven.

The Appeal to Reason, with a circulation of half a million, mainly in working-class districts, offered Sinclair five hundred dollars for subsistence while he investigated the lives of the Packingtown workers. For seven weeks, Sinclair lived with the underprivileged, wretched aliens of the Chicago stockyards, and then returned to his home in New Jersey to write about what he had seen, heard, and smelled. According to the author, "*The Jungle* was written in a board cabin, eight feet by ten, set on a hillside north of Princeton, New Jersey," in a period of about nine months.

Among Sinclair's numerous later books were *The Profits of Religion* (1918), *The Brass Check* (1919), *The Goslings* (1924), and *Mammonart* (1925). In 1940, Sinclair published *World's End,* the first of eleven novels centering on Lanny Budd as hero. One of the series, *Dragon's Teeth* (1942), won a Pulitzer Prize. As a whole, the series presents a history of Europe and America in the period of the World Wars.

Sinclair was unquestionably a great journalist and his works are an important record of twentieth-century American culture.

GEORGE WASHBURN SMALLEY
1833–1916

George Smalley was born in Franklin, Massachusetts. In 1861, he arranged to do a series of articles on South Carolina black life and served as war correspondent for the *New York Times.* His was the earliest account of the battle of Antietam.

Smalley's distinguished career as a foreign correspondent began in 1866 when he was sent to Europe to report on the Austro-Prussian War. A second trip in 1867 was to organize a London bureau to receive and coordinate all European news. When the Franco-Prussian War broke out in 1870, Smalley formed the first international newspaper alliance with the *London Daily News.*

Smalley remained in charge of the *Tribune's* European correspondence until 1895. He returned to America to act as American correspondent of the *London Times,* a position that he held for ten years (1895–1905). Thereafter, he retired from journalism except for weekly letters to the *Tribune* and occasional reviews.

CHARLES EMORY SMITH
1842–1908

Charles E. Smith was born in Mansfield, Connecticut, but grew up in Albany, New York. He began his journalistic career while still in school, by writing for the *Albany Evening Transcript*. In 1865 he joined the staff of the *Albany Express,* for which he had previously been writing articles. Five years later Smith became associate editor and in 1865 editor of the *Albany Evening Journal,* the leading Republican paper.

Smith transferred to Philadelphia in 1880 to become editor of the *Philadelphia Press*. He reestablished the *Press* as the leading Republican paper of Philadelphia and Pennsylvania.

Smith's journalistic activities gained political influence. He served as minister to Russia (1890–92), and in 1898 President McKinley appointed him postmaster general.

CHARLES HENRY SMITH
1826–1903

Charles Henry Smith, popularly known as "Bill Arp," was born in Lawrenceville, Georgia. He served in the Confederate Army during the Civil War. The first use of the pen name "Bill Arp" was in several letters published in Rome, Georgia (1861–62). Later sketches transformed Bill Arp into an uneducated but wise, humorous, rustic philosopher, using the illiterate dialect favored by many early American humorists. Weekly letters were contributed by Smith over a twenty-five-year period to the *Atlanta Constitution,* and reprinted in other papers.

After the Civil War, Smith edited the *Rome Commercial* and produced a series of popular collections of Bill Arp pieces.

GEORGE HENRY SMITH
1873–1931

George Henry Smith was born in Knoxville, Tennessee, and graduated from Yale University. At seventeen he was a reporter on the *Knoxville*

Journal, and before entering college he was writing for the *Knoxville Sentinel* and the *Chattanooga News.*

Smith entered a special field of journalism by concocting droll bedtime stories for children. These stories first appeared in the *New York Globe,* were syndicated, and soon were found in newspapers throughout the country. Smith used two pen names: "Farmer Smith" and "Uncle Henry." Smith became the *Globe's* children's editor (1900–1915), and later held the same post with several other papers from 1915 to 1927. Three collections of his early stories were published in book form.

H. ALLEN SMITH
1906–1976

Harry Allen Smith was born in McLeansboro, Illinois. He was a master storyteller who first achieved fame with his best-selling book, *Low Man on a Totem Pole.* His family moved to Huntington, Indiana, and there he began his newspaper career, working for the *Huntington Press* as a proofreader. Soon he became a reporter and wrote a column called "Miss Ella Vator." The name "H. Allen Smith" was suggested by his mother to separate him from all the other Smiths. He was fired by the *Press* for writing a ribald, although unpublished piece, and then worked briefly for the *Jeffersonville* (Indiana) *Bulletin,* followed by jobs with the *Louisville* (Kentucky) *Post* and *Times* and the *Tampa* (Florida) *Telegraph.* At age nineteen he was editor of the *American,* a small daily in Sebring, Florida. When the *American* ceased publication in 1926, Smith was employed by the *Tulsa* (Oklahoma) *Tribune,* moving on to the *Morning Post* in Denver and an evening paper, the *Denver Post.*

In 1929, Smith went to New York and landed a job there with the United Press, with which he remained until 1934. In 1936, he joined the *New York World-Telegram* as a rewrite man and to contribute humorous articles. Smith became celebrated for his interviews with famous stage and movie personalities. Meanwhile, his books were establishing him as a popular and successful humorist. He left the *World-Telegram* in 1941 to devote full time to writing books, mainly humorous anecdotal works and several novels. There were also numerous shorter pieces published in various magazines. He signed with United Features Syndicate to do a daily column, "The Totem Pole," but canceled the contract after six months. He always thought of himself as more of a humorist than a journalist. His writing career covered half a century.

HAZEL BRANNON SMITH
1914-

Hazel Brannon Smith was born in Gadsden, Alabama. She is the first woman to win a Pulitzer Prize for editorial writing. Smith is the owner and editor of four weekly newspapers in rural Mississippi. She has been exposing political and social injustice in Mississippi for many years.

Smith began to build her small newspaper empire in 1935 when she bought a near-bankrupt weekly, *Durant News,* serving Holmes County, Mississippi. She was realistic enough to avoid competing with large daily newspapers, and instead concentrated on local news of particular interest to the citizens of Holmes County.

In 1943, Smith purchased a second newspaper, the *Lexington Advertiser,* an independent weekly published in the county seat. Two more weekly Mississippi newspapers were added later: the Banner County *Outlook* in 1955, and the *Northside Reporter* in 1956.

Smith has strongly supported the civil rights movement, a stand that has hurt advertising revenue, led to public harassment, acts of vandalism, and the firebombing of her editorial office in 1964, while she was attending the Democratic national convention. Her courage and determination, however, have remained steadfast, and she has received support and awards from many directions.

HEDRICK L. SMITH
1933-

Hedrick Smith was born in Scotland. From 1959 to 1962, he was with the United Press International in Minneapolis, Nashville, and Atlanta. Thereafter he joined the *New York Times,* that sent him first to Vietnam, and from 1964 to 1966 to the Middle East and Cairo.

Smith served two terms in Washington (1962–64 and 1966–71) as the *Times*'s diplomatic news correspondent, and then went to Moscow as bureau chief (1971–74). On returning to the United States, Smith was named deputy national editor in 1976 and soon moved to Washington to become bureau chief until 1979. After 1980, he was the *Times*'s chief Washington correspondent until he resigned in 1988 to join the Universal Press Syndicate.

He is the author of a best seller, *The Russians,* published in 1976 by

Quadrangle The New York Times Book Co. His second best-seller was *The Power Game* portraying the real workings of Washington, D.C.

Smith created a significant four part mini-series for Public Broadcasting entitled "Inside Gorbachev's U.S.S.R.," and he is a regular panelist on PBS "Washington Week in Review." His latest book is *The New Russians,* published in 1990 by Random House.

Smith won the Pulitzer Prize in 1974 for his international reporting. He was coauthor of the *Pentagon Papers,* which also won a Pulitzer Prize.

HOWARD KINGSBURY SMITH
1914–

Howard K. Smith, born in Ferriday, Louisiana, has been a journalist for more than forty years. After graduating from Tulane University and traveling in Europe, Smith went to work as a "leg reporter" for the *New Orleans Item-Tribune.* He was hired by United Press when World War II started in 1939, and was stationed first in its London and Copenhagen bureaus and then moved on to join the CBS Radio staff in Berlin. Forced to leave Germany because of his criticism of Nazism, Smith crossed over to Switzerland to report the progress of the war in Europe.

In 1946, Smith succeeded Edward Murrow and reported on Europe and the Middle East from his base in London. During the Suez crisis, he spent several weeks in Egypt.

After twenty years in Europe, Smith returned to the United States in 1957 to broadcast CBS News. In 1961, he resigned from CBS because of policy disagreements and joined ABC, youngest of the networks. In recognition of Smith's intimate knowledge of politics, he was given a regular assignment on Capitol Hill. The expanding war in Southeast Asia led him to spend a month in Vietnam in 1966 for first-hand observation. In 1969, he was placed in charge of the ABC network newscasts, but he resigned the top spot in 1975 to comment on "a world growing more complex."

LIZ SMITH
1923–

Liz Smith was born Mary Elizabeth Smith in Fort Worth, Texas, and graduated from the University of Texas in 1948. Between 1953 and the early

1960s, she assisted Mike Wallace, news commentator on CBS radio, and was an associate producer of NBC television's "Wide, Wide World," a ghost writer for the *New York Journal-American* gossip column, and staff writer for various magazines. In 1975 the *New York Daily News* offered Smith the job of writing a daily gossip column for the *News* and sixty-five other newspapers. During the course of the next twelve years she became America's most popular gossip columnist. In 1978 she began doing a twice-weekly news commentary on WNBC-TV in New York City.

RED SMITH
1905-1982

Walter Wellesley Smith, always known as "Red" Smith, was born in Green Bay, Wisconsin. For more than fifty years he wrote about sports. He began his journalistic career as a reporter for the *Milwaukee Sentinel* (1927–28), as a copyeditor and sportswriter on the *St. Louis Star* (1928–36), and with the *Philadelphia Record* (1936–45).

The sports editor of the *New York Herald-Tribune,* Stanley Woodward, admired Smith's writing and hired him in 1945 to produce six columns a week, forty-eight weeks a year. Smith stayed with the *Herald-Tribune* until 1966, worked for a year for the *World-Journal-Tribune,* and finally joined the *New York Times.* His syndicated column "Views of Sport" (later "Sports of the Times") appeared in more than five hundred newspapers.

Smith particularly enjoyed writing about the big spectator sports, baseball, football, boxing, and horse racing. He was less fond of basketball and hockey. He covered forty-five World Series games. Smith also traveled widely to many cities throughout the world.

In recognition of his writing, Smith won a number of awards: a Pulitzer Prize in 1976, the Grantland Rice Memorial Award, and other honors.

SAMUEL HARRISON SMITH
1772-1845

Philadelphia-born Samuel H. Smith began his journalistic career with the publication of a Jeffersonian newspaper, the *New World,* from 1796 to

1797. In September 1779, he bought the *Independent Gazetteer* and changed the title to *Universal Gazette.*

Upon Thomas Jefferson's invitation, Smith moved from Philadelphia to Washington, D.C., in 1800, where he continued to publish the *Universal Gazette* as a weekly. In the same year, Smith inaugurated a tri-weekly, the *National Intelligencer and Washington Advertiser.* The *Intelligencer* recorded congressional debates and carried news stories about the new national government. The reliability of its reports was increased by Smith's close friendship with Jefferson and closeness to his administration.

By the opening session of Congress in 1801, Smith had a large share of government printing contracts. His support of the Jefferson administration assured financial security for Smith while the Republican party was in office.

With Jefferson's retirement in 1809, Smith lost his principal reason for editing the *Intelligencer* and announced that the paper was for sale. On August 31, 1810, the *Intelligencer* was sold to Joseph Gales, Jr., who was joined two years later by his brother-in-law, William Winston Seaton. Under the leadership of the new team, the *Intelligencer* remained a leading American newspaper for half a century.

WILLIAM HENRY SMITH
1833–1896

William Henry Smith was born in Austerlitz, New York, and began his journalistic career by acting as correspondent for Cincinnati papers. He was on the staff of the *Cincinnati Gazette* and later edited the *Cincinnati Evening Chronicle.* In 1870, Smith took charge of the Western Associated Press, and in 1882, brought about a combination of the New York Associated Press and the Western Associated Press. Smith was chosen general manager of the joint organization and remained in that position for twenty-two years. During his tenure, a system of leased wires was established and typewriters were used to receive telegraphic news reports.

HENRY HUNT SNELLING
1817–1897

Henry Hunt Snelling, born in Plattsburg, New York, was a pioneer in photographic journalism. He began writing on the subject in 1849 with a book entitled *The History and Practice of the Art of Photography.* The following year he proposed a periodical devoted to photography and in 1851 the first number of the *Photographic Art Journal* was published. Soon after, the name was changed to *Photographic and Fine Arts Journal.*

Snelling was constantly experimenting with photographic processes. In 1851, he invented the enlarging camera and also a ray filter to eliminate yellow rays. He developed a color process, but apparently never perfected the idea.

Snelling moved to Newburgh, New York, and became editor of the *Cornwall Reflector* for eight years. Illness forced his retirement in 1887.

EDGAR PARKS SNOW
1905-1971

Edgar Parks Snow was born in Kansas City, Missouri. He was a newspaper correspondent in Asia, Europe, and Africa. He made a special study of Russia and China, aided by gaining the confidence of Chinese communist leaders. Snow's book, *Red Star over China,* was the first important report on Chinese communism. From 1943 to 1951, Snow was associate editor of the *Saturday Evening Post.* He began newspaper work with the *Kansas City Star;* was assistant editor of the *China Weekly Review* in Shanghai (1929–30); and special correspondent of the *New York Sun* (1934–37), and the *London Daily Herald* (1932–41).

GEORGE E. SOKOLSKY
1893-1962

George Sokolsky had a varied career, in America and abroad. The son of a rabbi, he was born in New York City and educated at Columbia University. After graduating from college, he went to Russia in 1917 and edited the *Daily News,* an English-language newspaper, in Petrograd. The following year, Sokolsky was assistant editor of the *North China Star* in Peking and in 1919 he served as a reporter on the *Shanghai Gazette,* operated by Sun Yat-Sen. From 1921 to 1924, he managed the *Shanghai Journal of Commerce.* For the next ten years, he covered the Far East for the *Philadelphia Public Ledger,* the *New York Evening Post,* and other papers. Sokolsky returned to the United States in 1933, where he wrote for the *New York Herald-Tribune* (1935–40); *New York Sun* (1940–44); and King Features (1944–62). He was noted for his highly conservative views. According to one critic, he was "a one-man intellectual front for conservative capital."

JAMES COCKE SOUTHALL
1828–1897

James Southall was born in Charlottesville, Virginia, and graduated from the University of Virginia. A few months before the start of the Civil War, Southall launched a newspaper, the *Charlottesville Review,* which became a casualty of the war about 1862. In 1865 he acquired the *Charlottesville Daily Chronicle* and conducted it until 1868, when he was made chief editor of the *Richmond Enquirer.* He resigned the editorship in 1874 and devoted himself mainly to the writing of several important books.

LARRY SPEAKES
1939–

Larry Speakes was born in Cleveland, Mississippi, and achieved some fame as principal deputy press secretary and later press secretary in the White House from 1980 until his resignation in 1987.

Prior to his White House appointment, Speakes had been news editor of the *Oxford* (Mississippi) *Eagle,* the local evening paper, and then news editor and managing editor of the *Bolivar Commercial* in Cleveland. From 1966 to 1968, he was general manager of Progress Publishers of Leland and editor of its four weekly newspapers: the *Leland Progress, Hollandale Herald, Bolivar County Democrat,* and *Sunflower County News.*

For six years, starting in 1968, Speakes was press secretary to Senator James Eastland, staff assistant in President Nixon's office, first assistant press secretary to President Ford, and after Reagan's victory in 1980 was hired by James Brady as deputy. In 1983, Speakes was named chief White House spokesman and assistant to the president.

After Speakes retired as press secretary in 1987, to become vice president of Merrill Lynch and Co., he wrote *Speaking Out: The Reagan Presidency from Inside the White House* (1988), a gossipy view of President Reagan and his associates.

SUSAN SPENCER
19XX–

Susan Spencer was born in Memphis, Tennessee, graduated from Michigan State University, and holds an M.A. degree in journalism from Columbia University. Her introduction to TV newscasting was in Louisville, Kentucky, and New York City (1970–71). She joined WCCO-TV in Minneapolis in 1972 and remained for five years as a reporter, coauthor, and producer. In 1977 she moved to the CBS Evening News Washington bureau. She has been a correspondent for CBS News, Washington, since 1978.

LAWRENCE E. SPIVAK
1906–

Lawrence Spivak was born in New York City. Before his broadcasting career began, he was associated with several magazines, including the *American Mercury,* for which he was first business manager and later publisher and editor.

Spivak is most widely known as the promoter and regular panelist of the Sunday interview program, "Meet the Press," which began with NBC in 1945. Over the years, the program has interviewed a host of celebrities under Spivak's direction. Since 1975, Spivak has been a consultant for NBC.

LESLEY R. STAHL
1941–

Lesley Stahl was born in Lynn, Massachusetts, and graduated from Wheaton College. She was a writer and researcher for the "Huntley–Brinkley Report" in London (1969); reporter and producer for WHDH-TV in Boston (1970–72); reporter (1972–74), and correspondent (since 1974) for CBS News Washington bureau. She has been moderator of the "Face the Nation" program since 1983.

FRANK L. STANTON
1857–1927

Frank Lebby Stanton was born in Charleston, South Carolina, the son of a printer. In 1892, the family moved to Savannah, Georgia, where he went to work for the *Savannah Morning News* as a copyboy and then as a printer's devil. There he became friends with Joel Chandler Harris. For ten years, Stanton was an itinerant printer, moving from town to town. He was offered a chance to write a column for the *Smithville News,* a southeast Georgia paper, and in 1887 he became owner and editor of the *News,* which he made into one of the state's leading weeklies. Stanton livened up the contents with lively tabloids, humor, verse and stories. There was a short sojourn as night editor of the *Rome* (Georgia) *Daily Tribune,* and then Stanton joined the *Atlanta Constitution* to do reportorial work, feature stories, write a column, and serve on the editorial staff, along with Harris. Two popular features by Stanton were "Just from Georgia" and "Briefs from Billville."

Stanton won enduring fame with his poetry and songs, usually sentimental in nature and based on Southern themes.

EDMUND CLARENCE STEDMAN
1833–1908

Edmund Stedman was born in Hartford, Connecticut. After attending Yale for two years, he edited newspapers in Connecticut and later was on the staff of the *New York Tribune.* During the Civil War, Stedman was a war correspondent for the *New York World,* covering the campaigns of 1861.

Stedman was not highly regarded as a poet, but was an influential literary critic and compiled several standard collections of poetry and general literature.

LINCOLN STEFFENS
1866–1936

Lincoln Steffens was born in San Francisco and graduated from the University of California in 1889. He traveled and studied in Germany and France before beginning a newspaper career in New York City, including four years a city editor of the *Commercial Advertiser* (1897–1901). In 1902,

Steffens joined the staff of *McClure's Magazine,* the leading journal of exposure and reform.

The first major exposures of the corruption existing behind the facade of representative government was the work of Lincoln Steffens, who was tagged, around the turn of the century, by Theodore Roosevelt, along with Ida Tarbell, Ray Stannard Baker, and others, as a "muckraker." Steffens himself claimed the honor of being "the first muckraker," because his series of articles revealing the sordid operations of crooked politicians in American cities began a month before Ida Tarbell's equally startling exposure of the iniquitous activities of John D. Rockefeller's Standard Oil Company.

Steffens's muckraking activities began more or less by accident. In 1892, he had been a newspaper reporter on the *New York Evening Post.* His reporting assignments included Wall Street, where he covered the Panic of 1893, and the police department, where he collected his first evidence of a police-criminal tie-up. The latter beat brought Steffens in touch with Theodore Roosevelt, new commissioner of police.

Steffens thus became part of a publishing revolution that was rapidly changing the reading habits and ideas of the American public. S. S. McClure's magazines were setting new styles in low prices, lively formats, and controversial content, and his stable of writers was among the nation's most widely read. Steffens's original appointment as managing editor, for which he showed slight talent, was soon superseded by a roving assignment—to go out and search for suitable material.

A series of articles by Steffens in *McClure's* exposed corruption in six major American cities (St. Louis, Minneapolis, Philadelphia, Chicago, Pittsburgh, and New York), culminating in a sensational book, *The Shame of the Cities.*

In each of the half-dozen cities he investigated, Steffens discovered the same pattern: an alliance between "respectable" businessmen and disreputable gang politicians to rob the taxpayers. For every dollar spent for public improvements, another went to the thieves. Slums, firetraps, and brothels continued to exist because law enforcement officers had been bribed, frequently by landlords who posed as churchmen and pillars of the community. The process of corruption, Steffens contended, was universal and uniform. Further, "no one class is at fault, nor any breed, nor any particular interest or group, or party. The misgovernment of the American people is misgovernment by the American people.... The people are corrupt in small ways as their leaders are in big ways."

The Shame of the Cities exerted a wide influence and resulted in an immense amount of cleaning up of the conditions that Steffens had described so vividly, in such minute detail, and with such startling skill. *The Shame of the Cities* constitutes a primary source on American city government.

Steffens's later years were spent in Carmel, California, where he edited the *Pacific Monthly* and contributed to the *Carmelite* and *Controversy.* He joined with other writers in the development of *American Magazine.* His admiration for the Soviet Union after a visit there in 1919 and adherence to communism alienated many of his American followers.

THOMAS L. STOKES, JR.
1898–1958

Thomas Lunsford Stokes, Jr., was born in Atlanta, Georgia. To support himself at the University of Georgia, he worked in the college library and was a sports and college news correspondent for the *Atlanta Constitution* and the *Atlanta Georgian.* After graduation, he was hired by the *Savannah Press* and *Macon News* for general assignments and sports events, and was city editor for the *Athens Herald,* all for brief periods.

In Washington, Stokes found a job with the United Press (1921–33), reporting on Congress, the White House, various federal departments, and presidential campaigns and conventions. In 1933, he joined Scripps–Howard's *New York World-Telegram* as Washington correspondent to cover general news about the Capitol. Three years later, Stokes was transferred to the Scripps-Howard Newspaper Alliance to report on general politics nationwide. The next move was to join United Feature Syndicate as a Washington political columnist. More than a hundred papers were publishing his commentaries. His coverage of Roosevelt's New Deal was especially thorough. *Time* magazine characterized Stokes as "one of the nation's shrewdest, most diligent, and forthright political reporters."

Stokes believed that legwork was an essential element in good reporting. Accordingly, he spent much time traveling around the country. Among a number of awards he received in recognition of his work were a Pulitzer Prize, the Raymond Clamper Award, and the Saturday Review of Literature Award.

ISIDOR FEINSTEIN STONE
1907–1989

I. F. Stone was born in Philadelphia and was a journalist from his teens. At age fourteen, he and a classmate printed a monthly newspaper, the *Progressive,* carrying advertising, poetry, and editorials, with five hundred subscribers. While still in high school, Stone was a reporter for the

Haddonfield (New Jersey) *Press,* and correspondent for the *Camden* (New Jersey) *Courier-Post.* As a student at the University of Pittsburgh, he served as a copyeditor and rewrite man for the *Philadelphia Inquirer.* After leaving the university, he returned to the *Courier-Post* for several years as a reporter and editor.

In 1933, Stone moved to New York to join the staff of the *New York Post,* working at the same time as a reporter and editorial writer for the *Philadelphia Record.* In 1940, he moved to Washington to become Washington editor of the *Nation,* a position that he held until 1946. In 1942, he also became a reporter and columnist for *PM,* the daily started in New York by Ralph Ingersoll.

Travels abroad in 1945 took Stone to Palestine to report on the Jewish struggle to establish a homeland. On a second trip to Palestine in 1948 he reported on the Israeli-Arab war.

Short-time appointments held by Stone later included the *New York Star* (1948–49), the *New York Post* (1949), and the *New York Daily Compass* (1949–52). Unable to find another newspaper job, Stone decided in 1953 to launch his own publication, *I. F. Stone's Weekly.* In 1967, the Weekly became *I. F. Stone's Bi-Weekly.* Its circulation increased to seventy thousand by 1971, but Stone ended the paper in 1972.

From his early days, Stone has been known for his leftist sympathies, supporting Norman Thomas for president, attacking U.S. foreign policies, exposing Department of Defense misinformation, and publishing similar muckraking stories.

MELVILLE ELIJAH STONE
1848-1929

Melville Stone was born in Hudson, Illinois. After attending public schools in Chicago he became a reporter on the *Chicago Republican.* In 1875, he joined with two partners to start a penny daily, the *Chicago Daily News.* A morning edition began in 1881. After that, Stone sold his interest in the paper and dropped out of newspaper work for some years.

After his return to journalism, Stone was managing editor for a short time of the *Inter-Ocean,* and then managing editor of the *Chicago Evening Mail* (later consolidated with the *Chicago Evening Post*), which sent him to Washington as its correspondent. He also corresponded for the *New York Herald* and *St. Louis Dispatch.* His greatest monument was the *Daily News,* which survived as a major Chicago newspaper for more than a century.

In 1893, Stone became general manager of the Associated Press of

Illinois. A court decision forced the Associated Press, the national organization, to reform and Stone became its general manager and secretary until he retired in 1921. In trips abroad, branches of the Associated Press were established in the principal European capitals.

Stone's greatest triumph as a journalist was in connection with the Russo-Japanese War of 1904–5. He was instrumental in presenting the failure of the peace negotiations between the combatants. President Theodore Roosevelt and Emperor Wilhelm II of Germany were induced to use their influence to persuade Japan and Russia to compromise and agree to peace.

LELAND STOWE
1899–

Leland Stowe was born in Southbury, Connecticut, and gained his first journalistic experience as a campus correspondent for the *Springfield* (Massachusetts) *Republican,* while a student at Wesleyan University. After graduation, he was a reporter with the *Worcester Telegram* (1921–22). Moving on to New York City, he was hired as a reporter by Frank Munsey's *New York Herald.* Stowe remained on the staff after the paper was sold by Munsey and became the *Herald-Tribune.* A few months later, he was appointed foreign editor of the Pathe News newsreel company. Stowe returned to the *Herald-Tribune* in 1926, was assigned to the paper's Paris bureau, and became chief of the bureau in 1927. In that position he covered the major news stories breaking in Europe until 1935.

When Stowe came back to the United States in 1935, he served as a roving Western Hemisphere correspondent for the *Herald-Tribune* until 1939. He also went to Spain to investigate the plight of children after the Spanish civil war. Several trips to Latin America covered Franklin Roosevelt's visits to Brazil and Argentina, the Inter-American Peace Conference in Buenos Aires, and the Pan-American Conference in Lima, Peru.

After the start of World War II, Stowe went to Europe to report for the *Chicago Daily News.* He did two long assignments for the *News* until the end of the war. By then "he had traveled with the armies of seven different nations, reporting in forty-four countries and colonies on four continents, and had been bombed by five different air forces," according to his biographer Jack Schnedler. He witnessed the Nazi takeover of Norway, the Russo-Finish War, and Mussolini's invasion of Greece. In 1941, Stowe went to the Far East, reporting from China on the Burma Road. He reached Moscow, by way of Burma, India, and Iran in 1942, in time to witness the German attacks on the Soviet Union.

Stowe left daily journalism after the war, to do freelance magazine writing, produce several books, lecture, edit, and teach. He was the recipient of a Pulitzer Prize and other awards for his notable achievements as a war reporter.

ANNA LOUISE STRONG
1885–1970

Anna Louise Strong was a graduate of the University of Chicago with a doctor's degree in 1908. She served as assistant director of the Russell Sage Foundation, with a particular interest in child welfare programs, there and later with the U.S. Children's Bureau in Washington. She began contributing to the socialist *Seattle Daily Call* and then was a feature editor of the *Seattle Union Record,* a labor paper. Strong traveled in Russia and China and became an internationally known propagandist for the Soviet Union and the People's Republic of China. In 1930 she founded the English-language *Moscow News.* She died in Peking in 1970 and was buried in Peking's National Memorial Cemetery.

RICHARD L. STROUT
1898–1990

Richard Strout was born in Cohoes, New York. After military service in World War I and graduating from Harvard, he began his journalistic career by working for a while on a British newspaper, the *Sheffield Independent,* a provincial daily. After returning to the United States, he worked briefly for the *Boston Post* and the *New York Sun.* The next year he joined the staff of the *Christian Science Monitor* as a desk editor and reporter, with an occasional assignment in Washington, D.C. In 1925, Strout was transferred to the *Monitor's* bureau in the nation's capital. Over the next twenty years, he covered the top news stories emanating from the national government.

In addition to his newspaper duties, Strout often contributed to popular magazines. In 1943, he took over the *New Republic's* weekly political column "TRB from Washington." The TRB columns became one of the most distinguished expressions of liberal political opinion in the nation. The Eisenhower, Kennedy, Johnson and Nixon administrations were closely followed and reported with keen understanding in Strout's TRB columns from 1944 until he retired in 1983.

FRANK SULLIVAN
1892–1976

Frank Sullivan was born in Saratoga Springs, New York, and graduated from Cornell University. As a columnist for the *New York World,*
essayist for the newspaper *PM* and the *New Yorker,* and author of a
number of popular books, Sullivan gained a reputation as a brilliant satirist
of the American life of his time. His satiric wit was applied to a variety of
subjects. Probably his favorite activity was the collecting of clichés found
in contemporary speech and writings.

Sullivan's numerous books include *Innocent Bystanding, A Pearl in
Every Oyster, Sullivan at Bay,* and the *Moose in the House.*

WALTER SULLIVAN
1918–

Walter Sullivan was born in New York City and graduated from Yale.
He joined the *New York Times* staff as a copyboy in 1940, spent ten years
as a foreign correspondent, and then turned to science reporting. In the last
area he has aimed to make technical subjects comprehensible to the
layperson.

Sullivan saw active service in the U.S. Navy, rising to the rank of
lieutenant commander. He returned to the *Times* and was given a chance
to cover Richard Byrd's fourth expedition to Antarctica. In his book, *Quest
for a Continent,* Sullivan described in vivid detail the breathtaking beauty
of Antarctica.

Starting in 1956, Sullivan was permanently assigned by the *Times* to
its science division. His reports on IGY (International Geophysical Year)
in 1957–58 were comprehensive. In 1961, Sullivan published *We Are Not
Alone,* subtitled *The Search for Intelligent Life on Other Worlds,* dealing
with the possibility of extraterrestrial life.

Over a period of many years, Sullivan contributed hundreds of articles
on an immense variety of scientific subjects to the *Times.* As science editor
of the *Times,* he heads a brilliant team of science writers, with various
specialties.

ARTHUR HAYS SULZBERGER
1891–1968

Arthur Hays Sulzberger was born in New York City and graduated
from Columbia University in 1913. He was in military service during World

War I. In 1917, he married the daughter of Adolph S. Ochs, who had been publisher of the *New York Times* from 1896. Sulzberger went to work for the *Times* in 1918, as first assistant to the general manager. He served as president of the New York Times Company from 1935 to 1957, and as chairman from 1957 until his death in 1968.

As publisher of the *New York Times,* Sulzberger expanded the paper's news coverage and pioneered in the transmission of photographs by wire. Under his direction, the daily circulation of the *Times* increased by 40 percent and the Sunday circulation doubled.

Sulzberger's son, Arthur Ochs Sulzberger (born in New York City in 1926), was assistant treasurer (1958–63), and president and publisher of the *Times,* starting in 1963.

JANE GREY SWISSHELM
1815-1884

Jane Grey Swisshelm had a long newspaper career during which she crusaded for two reforms: the abolition of slavery and women's rights. She was born in Pittsburgh. Her writing for publication began in 1842, under the pen name of "Jennie Dean," for two Philadelphia papers, the *Dollar Newspaper* and *Neal's Saturday Gazette.* Other papers, such as the *New York Tribune, Godey's,* and the *Home Journal* reprinted some of her work. Swisshelm also wrote for two abolitionist newspapers, the *Spirit of Liberty* and the *Albatross.*

Early in 1847, Swisshelm founded her own abolitionist paper, the *Pittsburgh Saturday Visitor,* whose subscribers soon rose to seven thousand across the country. During a visit to Washington in 1850 to hear congressional debates on slavery, Horace Greeley paid her five dollars per column for her Washington letters to the *Tribune.* She opened the press gallery to women despite objections by President Filmore.

Another turning point in Swisshelm's career came in 1857, when she moved from Pittsburgh to St. Cloud, Minnesota. The following year she founded another newspaper, the *Visitor,* which lasted only a short time because of legal and other problems. Immediately thereafter, she started the *St. Cloud Democrat,* which continued until 1863. In 1863, Swisshelm left St. Cloud, turned the management of the *Democrat* over to her nephew, and settled in Washington. A short-lived newspaper, the *Reconstructionist* was started. Her active newspaper career ended fifteen years before her death in 1884. Swisshelm's most important contribution as a journalist was her championship of the abolitionist cause, helping to establish the Republican party in Minnesota, and crusading for women's rights.

WILLIAM FRANKLIN SWITZLER
1819–1906

William F. Switzler was born on a farm in Fayette County, Kentucky. In 1841, he became editor of the oldest Missouri newspaper outside of St. Louis, the *Columbia Patriot*. The paper was renamed the *Missouri Statesman,* and strongly supported the Whig party. Switzler continued to edit the *Statesman* until 1885, when President Cleveland appointed him chief of the bureau of statistics in the Treasury Department.

For brief periods, Switzler edited newspapers in St. Joseph and Chillicothe, Missouri, and from 1893 to 1898, the *Missouri Democrat* at Boonville.

HERBERT BAYARD SWOPE
1882–1958

While still a teen-ager, Herbert Bayard Swope expressed a desire to become a journalist. He was given a cub reporter's job on the *St. Louis Post-Dispatch,* but was fired for spending too much time at the racetrack. He made a brief stop in Chicago, working for the daily *Inter-Ocean,* before going on to New York to be a reporter for the *New York Herald.* He was then age nineteen. At the *Herald,* and in all his other relationships, he was ever the rugged individualist – a brilliant reporter but a problem for his supervisors. In 1909, Swope joined the staff of the *New York World,* where he made a practice of being friends with politicians, gamblers, policemen – anyone who could aid him in collecting news. He shared a flat with John Barrymore, the actor, who was working as a cartoonist for the *Morning Telegraph* and later for the *Evening Journal.*

World War I brought special opportunities for Swope. He was the *World's* foreign correspondent in Germany in 1914, and sent exclusive dispatches on the sinking of three British warships by German submarines. In 1915, Swope was made city editor of the *World.* His reports on Germany won a Pulitzer Prize in 1917; he was the first reporter to receive that distinction. After the war, he was sent to Versailles by the *World* to cover the Paris Peace Conference. After his return from Versailles, Ralph Pulitzer named Swope executive editor, a title created specifically for him. He resigned from the *World* in 1929. In 1931, the *World* was sold to the Scripps–Howard chain to establish the *World-Telegram.*

Whether Swope deserved Lord Northcliffe's accolade as "the greatest reporter of his time" is debatable, but unquestionably he had a considerable impact upon the journalistic profession.

IDA M. TARBELL
1857-1944

Ida M. Tarbell was born in oil country, in Erie County, Pennsylvania, surrounded as she puts it, by "oil derricks, oil tanks, pipe lines, refineries, oil exchanges." The year of her birth, 1857, coincided with oil discoveries in the area. Franklin S. Tarbell, her father, had been one of the independent oil men who stood in the way of the Rockefeller juggernaut, had been run over, and thereby suffered financial ruin. Tarbell had previously demonstrated her ability as a biographer and editor. Her exceptional educational background included three years of study at the Sorbonne. Despite any personal animosity she may have felt, Tarbell approached her study of the Standard Oil Company with complete objectivity. A scholar by inclination and a research historian by training, she set out to write a factual, carefully documented account of the most gigantic of American business enterprises, carefully avoiding becoming a crusader for social justice.

Publication of *The History of the Standard Oil Company* (1904) brought Tarbell into the national limelight. Everybody was talking about trusts, and thus the Tarbell work was extremely topical. Reviewers were generally laudatory. An exception was an anonymous review in the *Nation,* which indicted the author on the grounds of sensationalism, ignorance, and misrepresentation — a striking contrast in editorial policy with that of the present-day *Nation.* The *Nation* review was reprinted by Standard Oil and distributed in hundreds of thousands of copies over the country, as was a brochure written by Elbert Hubbard in 1910, praising the company and attacking Tarbell's scholarship and manner of presentation. None of the criticisms altered a widespread public acceptance of the principal Tarbell thesis: that huge monopolistic trusts were inimical to the general welfare, their business practices were despicable, and for the good of the nation they should be dissolved.

From 1905 to 1915, Tarbell was one of the editors of *McClure's Magazine,* which she and her colleagues made into a leading muckraking journal. She was the author of a number of other books, including a standard biography of Abraham Lincoln.

BAYARD TAYLOR
1825-1878

Bayard Taylor was born in Kennett Square, Pennsylvania. At age seventeen he was apprenticed to a printer, but left two years later on a walking tour of Europe. His lively accounts of travel and colorful newspaper correspondence from foreign countries were highly popular. Arrangements were made with the *Saturday Evening Post* and the *United States Gazette* to finance Taylor's foreign travels in return for publication rights to letters describing his travels. His many books about his travels in Africa, Europe, and the Middle and Far East led him to be known as "the American Marco Polo." As a newspaper correspondent, he covered the California gold rush, Admiral Perry's voyage to Japan, and other exciting events. Taylor was secretary of the legation at St. Petersburg, Russia (1862–63), and for a time was chargé d'affaires there. In 1878, he was appointed minister to Germany but died in Berlin after serving only a few months.

BERT LESTON TAYLOR
1866–1921

Bert Leston Taylor was born in Goshen, Massachusetts. After attending college in New York, he was employed by several New England papers, the *Montpelier* (Vermont) *Argus and Patriot, Manchester* (New Hampshire) *Union,* and *Boston Traveler.* He was a reporter in 1896 for the *New York Herald,* where his father was in the advertising department.

Taylor won cash prizes from the *Chicago Journal* for contributions of jokes and other items and in 1899 he was hired by the *Journal* and given control of a regular column. In 1901, James Keeley offered Taylor a substantial increase in pay to transfer to the *Chicago Tribune.* From 1901 to 1921, except for a year with the *New York Telegraph* (1903–4), and serving as assistant editor of the humor magazine, *Puck,* Taylor contributed his immensely popular column, "A Line o'Type or Two" to the *Tribune.* Taylor remained with the *Tribune,* writing this column until his death in 1921. Comic poetry, literary satire, parodies, and letter filled much of the space. Franklin P. Adams, a lifelong friend, took over Taylor's column at the *Journal.*

CHARLES H. TAYLOR
1846–1921

Charles Henry Taylor was born in Charlestown, Massachusetts. At age fifteen he began work in a Boston printing office. Later steps in his journalistic career included setting type for the *Boston Daily Evening Traveller,* becoming a reporter for that paper, and serving as correspondent for the *New York Tribune.* In 1871, after being elected to the Massachusetts legislature, Taylor also began writing for the *Boston Sunday Times* and *Cincinnati Times.* In the summer of 1872, he began publication of *American Homes,* a ten-cent monthly magazine aimed at family reading. The following year, however, a fire destroyed the magazine's quarters and press, ending the publication.

Taylor accepted an offer to manage the *Boston Globe.* The *Globe* barely survived the 1873 panic. To keep the paper alive, Taylor cut the price to three cents, established an evening edition, and joined the Democratic party. Within a few years the two editions were selling fifty thousand copies. Factors in the paper's success were the use of sensational headlines, playing up crime news, and perhaps more important, providing thorough coverage of local and New England news. Another popular feature was serials by famous novelists. Taylor was succeeded in the management of the *Globe* by his sons. At the time of his death in 1921 he was the dean of American journalists.

FREDERICK WILLIAM THOMAS
1806–1866

Frederick William Thomas was a native of Providence, Rhode Island. For some years his father was editor of the *City Gazette.* In 1831, the son assisted his father in editing the *Cincinnati Commercial Daily Advertiser.* Frederick William edited the *Democratic Intelligencer* for a few months. In 1850, after some journalistic work in Kentucky, he became literary editor of the *Richmond Enquirer* and was later a member of the staff of the *Columbia South Carolinian.*

ISAIAH THOMAS
1750–1831

The great printer, publisher, and historian of printing, Isaiah Thomas, was born in Boston exactly in the middle of the eighteenth century and lived well into the nineteenth. His amazingly varied career included publishing a highly influential newspaper during the Revolutionary War, creating a nationwide publishing empire, writing the standard history of early American printing, and founding the American Antiquarian Society.

At the age of six, Thomas became an apprentice to Zechariah Fowle,

Boston printer, and served in that shop for eleven years. Following a disagreement with Fowle in 1766, Thomas went to Halifax, Nova Scotia, for six months to assist in printing the province's only newspaper, the *Halifax Gazette.* After leaving Halifax, Thomas had brief stays in Portsmouth, New Hampshire, where the *New Hampshire Gazette* was being published, and in Charleston, South Carolina, in Robert Wells's print shop. Patching up his quarrel with Fowle, Thomas returned to Boston and in 1770 the two founded the *Massachusetts Spy,* an anti–British journal destined to continue until 1904. Fowle withdrew from the partnership after three months and Thomas continued the *Spy* alone.

The *Spy* became an outspoken advocate of independence for the colonies—a stand that naturally incensed the Loyalists. To prevent a takeover by British troops as they approached Boston, Thomas moved his press and types to Worcester a few days before the Battle of Lexington.

From Worcester, Thomas began to create an extensive publishing business. In 1775, he began the *New England Almanac.* At Walpole, New Hampshire, he and a partner printed the *Farmer's Weekly Museum.* A bookstore was opened in Boston with branches in several parts of the United States. His early publications included the *Massachusetts Magazine* (1789–96); *Essex Journal* (1773–74); *Royal American Magazine* (1774–75); *Massachusetts Herald* (1783); *Worcester Magazine* (1786–88); *Worcester Intelligencer* (1794–95); and the *Albany* (New York) *Centinel* (1797–98). After the Revolution, Thomas became the leading American publisher, issuing more than nine hundred books, noted for their excellent format. His special interest was books for children. Another was music and medical publishing.

After his retirement, about 1802, Thomas spent two years writing *The History of Printing in America* (2 vols., 1810), based on his own records.

Another Thomas achievement was the founding of the American Antiquarian Society in 1812. To the society he bequeathed his large library, land, a building, and a generous endowment.

LOWELL THOMAS
1892–1981

Lowell Thomas was born in Woodingtown, Ohio. He grew up in Cripple Creek, Colorado, and began his career as a newspaper writer. From 1930 to 1976 his radio newscasts were broadcast over NBC.

Thomas was renowned as a globe-trotter. He was the author of more than fifty books, many about his foreign travels and adventures abroad. One of his achievements was the exclusive coverage of T. E. Lawrence's

Middle East campaign. While still in his early twenties, Thomas outfitted and led two expeditions into the sub–Arctic. At the end of World War I, he was the first reporter to enter Germany and bring back an eyewitness account of the German Revolution. From 1919 to 1922, Thomas made an extensive world tour. He traveled among the Pygmy tribes of the East, in the back country of Australia, and in the Himalayan area of Upper Burma. He was chief of a civilian mission sent to Europe by President Wilson to prepare a historical record of World War I.

NORMAN THOMAS
1884-1968

Norman Thomas was born in Marion, Ohio, and graduated from Princeton in 1905. As a journalist he founded and edited the *World Tomorrow,* was an editor of the *Nation* (1921–22), and was a regular contributor to the *Socialist New Leader.*

Thomas was six times the Socialist party candidate for president and ran unsuccessfully for other public offices. He was a founder of the American Civil Liberties Union and helped to organize the League for Industrial Democracy. Among the causes for which he fought were unemployment insurance and old age pensions.

DOROTHY THOMPSON
1893-1961

Dorothy Thompson was born in Lancaster, New York. For several years after graduation from Syracuse University she was active in the women's suffrage movement. In 1920 she went to Europe and freelanced for the *International News Service,* the *New York Post,* and the *Christian Science Monitor.* She also became a correspondent for the *Philadelphia Public Ledger.*

In 1922, she married the first of her three husbands. She and Sinclair Lewis, her second husband, were married in 1928 and divorced in 1942.

Thompson was a commentator on international affairs from 1936, when she wrote a column, "On the Record," for the *New York Herald-Tribune,* until 1958. At the peak of her popularity her reports were reaching an estimated eight million readers through two hundred newspapers. She was one of the most effective propagandists against Hitler, for which she was expelled from Germany in 1934.

In the postwar years, Thompson concentrated on the Middle East, especially on Zionism and the creation of a Jewish state. At first favorable to the Jewish cause, she changed her mind later, for complex reasons, ending up holding an anti-Zionist, pro-Arab position.

Starting in 1937, Thompson wrote a monthly column for the *Ladies' Home Journal* and continued for twenty-four years. She was dropped by the *Herald-Tribune* for her pro-Roosevelt views, after which she moved to the Bell Syndicate and her column appeared in the *New York Post* until March 1947.

In her late years, Thompson's influence and popularity declined, in part because of her stand on the Palestine problem and other controversial issues. Nevertheless, she made a strong impact on journalists and twentieth-century history, on the basis of which she was sometimes called "the first lady of journalism."

JAMES GROVER THURBER
1894-1961

James Thurber was born in Columbus, Ohio. He was ineligible for military service in World War I because of poor eyesight. He began his journalistic career as a reporter on the *Columbus Evening Dispatch* and correspondent for the *Christian Science Monitor.* He left Columbus in 1925 to go to Paris, where he wrote for the Paris and Riviera editions of the *Chicago Tribune.* After returning to the United States in 1926, Thurber worked for the *New York Evening Post.* The following year, Harold Ross, editor of the *New Yorker,* invited him to join the magazine's staff, the beginning of a long association. In the years that followed, Thurber established a reputation as a leading American humorist, cartoonist, and playwright. Thurber wrote a highly successful book for children, *Many Moons* (1943), combining fantasy with realistic details.

PETER TIMOTHY
CA. 1725-1782

Peter Timothy's father belonged to a group of French Huguenot refugees who came to America early in the eighteenth century. His father had been trained as a printer in Holland and Timothy practically grew up in the printing business. Shortly after arriving in America, Benjamin Franklin employed the elder Timothy as editor and translator for a new

German-language newspaper, the *Philadelphische Zeitung.* Later, learning that a printer was wanted in Charleston, South Carolina, Franklin sent Timothy there with all necessary equipment to organize a printing business. On February 2, 1734, the first weekly edition of the *South Carolina Gazette* was published. Timothy's father died in 1738 of an accident. The press was taken over by his widow, Elizabeth Timothy, who thereby became the first woman to publish a newspaper in the Southern colonies. She was assisted by her son, Peter, then about fourteen, and he assumed full control when he came of age about 1746.

Peter Timothy apparently had literary tastes. The *Gazette* reprinted the works of well-known English authors and contributions of essays, poems, and prologues to plays by Charleston writers.

Timothy became deeply involved in the Patriot cause as the movement for independence grew. When the British entered Charleston in 1780, he was arrested, on Cornwallis's order, imprisoned for a time in St. Augustine, Florida, and later sent to Philadelphia in a prisoner exchange. Timothy was lost in a shipwreck while headed for the West Indies in 1782.

Timothy's widow, Ann, returned to Charleston and resurrected the newspaper, now called *Gazette of the State of South Carolina,* in 1783, and continued its publication until her death in 1792. Her son, Benjamin Franklin Timothy, published the paper until 1802 when he left the printing business. In its time, the *Gazette* was the most effective Whig newspaper in the South.

SERENO EDWARDS TODD
1820–1898

Sereno Edwards Todd was born on a farm near Longingville, New York. After moving to Auburn, he began to contribute to the *Country Gentleman.* In 1865, he became associate editor of the *American Agriculturist,* in New York City. The following year he was placed in charge of the agricultural and livestock department of the *New York Times.* A variety of assignments came to him in the years ahead: editor of the home department of the *New York Observer,* editorial writer for *Hearth and Home,* and agricultural editor of the *New York Tribune,* under Horace Greeley. Todd also held a position on the *New York Herald* and edited the *Practical Farmer.* He was author of several books relating to agriculture.

GEORGE MAKEPEACE TOWLE
1841-1893

George M. Towle was born in Washington, D.C. He entered journalism in 1865 by becoming editor of the *Boston Post*. As U.S. consul in Nantes, France, he acquired proficiency in French, and translated the works of Jules Verne and other popular French writers. Later, as a commercial agent in England, he became a friend of Charles Dickens and contributed to Dickens's periodical, *All the Year Round.*

Towle returned to Boston in 1870 and acted as correspondent for the *London Athenaeum* and contributed American notes to the *London Graphic,* from 1871 to 1876. He also wrote for a variety of American publications, was associated with the *Youth's Companion,* and was a contributor or editor for most of the Boston papers. Todd was author of twenty or more books of a historical or literary nature.

BENJAMIN TOWNE
1740-1793

Benjamin Towne was born in Lincolnshire, England, and learned the art of printing before emigrating to Philadelphia in the 1760s. In 1769, he became a journeyman for William Goddard, publisher of the *Pennsylvania Chronicle.* When that job ended, Towne worked for other Philadelphia printers. With the backing of silent partners, he set up a printing house in 1774 and the following year inaugurated the *Pennsylvania Evening Post,* the first evening paper in Philadelphia. There was keen competition, however, from several other newspapers in the city.

Mott called Towne "a clever printer without any apparent principles." He frequently changed sides during the controversial period when Loyalists and Patriots were contending with each other. The *Evening Post* appeared loyal to the revolutionists until 1777. It had been the first newspaper to print the Declaration of Independence. When the British took Philadelphia and other newspapers were suspended, Towne changed his politics and the British allowed him to continue his paper. After the occupying forces evacuated the city and other newspapers returned, the *Evening Post* was accused of treason and found it impossible to win back its former following, although it announced its devotion for the Revolution.

In a final effort to enable his paper to survive, Towne published the *Evening Post* as a daily, in 1783, the nation's first daily newspaper. The last issue came off the press in October 1784. Thereafter, Towne is believed to have supported himself by working as a job printer.

GEORGE ALFRED TOWNSEND
1841–1914

George Townsend was born in Georgetown, Delaware. In 1855, the family settled in Philadelphia. After graduating from high school in 1860, Townsend began his newspaper career, first with the *Philadelphia Inquirer,* then with the *Philadelphia Press.* In 1861, he was employed by the *New York Herald,* first as Philadelphia agent and later as war correspondent. Trips abroad took him first to England in 1862 and then to report on the Austro-Prussian War in 1866. During the Civil War years, Townsend was war correspondent for the *New York World* and wrote memorable accounts of the early battles and of Lincoln's assassination.

In 1867, Townsend settled in Washington and spent the next forty years as a contributor to the *Chicago Tribune,* the *Cincinnati Daily Enquirer,* and many other newspapers. He came to be regarded as one of the most important journalists of the Reconstruction.

VANCE H. TRIMBLE
1913–

Vance Trimble was born in Harrison, Arkansas. While in high school in Okemah, Oklahoma, Trimble carried out small local reporting jobs for the *Daily Leader.* Later he was a cub reporter for the *Wewoka Times-Democrat.* In high school, he edited the school's paper, and after graduation was a full-time reporter for *Times-Democrat* for several months, before becoming news editor of the *Maud* (Oklahoma) *Daily Enterprise.* Over a period of several years he worked on several Oklahoma papers: *Seminole Producer, Seminole Reporter, Wewoka Morning News, Shawnee Morning News,* and *Muscogee Times-Democrat.* He served as news editor of the *Okmulgee Times* for a year, and financial writer on the *Tulsa Tribune.*

Trimble's next move was to Texas as a reporter and deskman for the *Beaumont Enterprise* in 1937, and copyeditor and later city editor of the *Houston Press,* a Scripps–Howard paper. After World War II, Trimble pioneered in radio and TV coverage of the news for the *Press,* and served as managing editor of the *Press* from 1950 to 1955. In 1955 he became news editor of the Washington, D.C., bureau of the Scripps–Howard newspaper alliance.

BENJAMIN CUMMINGS TRUMAN
1835-1916

Benjamin Truman was born in Providence, Rhode Island. He learned typesetting in Providence and from 1855 to 1859 was a compositor and proofreader on the *New York Times.* In 1859 he was employed by John Forney, publisher of the *Philadelphia Press,* and in 1861 went to Washington to work on Forney's *Sunday Morning Chronicle.* After the outbreak of the Civil War, he was sent to the front as a correspondent. In 1865 as President Johnson's confidential agent, Truman traveled through the South to investigate conditions and sent back perceptive letters for publication in the *New York Times.*

As special agent of the Post Office Department on the Pacific Coast, Truman visited China, Japan, and Hawaii. In 1869 he was in Washington as a correspondent of the *New York Times* and the *San Francisco Bulletin.* He was again in California in 1870 and became editor of the *Los Angeles Evening Express* in 1872. After various other ventures, Truman for some years edited the weekly *Western Graphic* in Los Angeles.

Besides his newspaper articles, Truman produced a number of books and pamphlets based on his varied experiences and interests.

GEORGE PUTNAM UPTON
1834-1919

George Putnam Upton was born in Roxbury, Massachusetts. He went to Chicago in 1855 for a position on the *Native Citizen.* Six months later he became city editor of the *Chicago Evening Journal.* There he began the first musical column to appear in a Chicago paper, reviewing the important musical events in the history of the city.

In 1862 Upton joined the staff of the *Chicago Tribune* and continued to serve that paper for fifty-seven years, as city editor and war correspondent (1862–63); music critic (1863–81); associate editor (1872–1905); and editorial writer (1870–1919). His writings as a music critic were published under the pen name of "Peregrine Pickle," and were highly influential in Chicago's cultural life.

CARR VAN ANDA
1864-1945

Carr Van Anda was born in Georgetown, Ohio. His long career as an outstanding journalist was spent (chiefly) with two New York newspapers:

reporter and night editor of the *New York Sun* (1888–1904), and managing editor of the *New York Times* (1904–32). Before his teens Van Anda was using a toy printing press to publish the *Boy's Gazette* and to do job printing for local businesses. While attending Ohio University, he was a correspondent for newspapers in Cleveland and Cincinnati. After his sophomore year he worked for the *Aylaize Republican*. Following his useful experience with the *Republican*, Van Anda was a typesetter for the *Cleveland Herald*, from which he was promoted to telegraph editor. When the *Herald* was sold to the *Cleveland Plain Dealer*, he remained for about a year and then joined the staff of the *Cleveland Evening Argus*. The *Argus* ceased publication in 1886, and Van Anda went east to become the night editor of the *Baltimore Sun*.

Lured by New York, Van Anda obtained a job as a combination reporter and copyeditor on the *New York Sun* in 1888. His sixteen years with the *Sun* included serving as night editor after January 1893.

The next important step in Van Anda's career came in 1904, when he was appointed managing editor of the *New York Times*. Adolph Ochs had bought the *Times* seven years previously and he gave Van Anda practically a free hand in developing a great newspaper.

In the years that followed, the *Times* became celebrated for its detailed coverage of national and international issues: World War I, submarine warfare, the first airplane flights, the sinking of the *Titanic*, the discovery of the South Pole, the Versailles Treaty, and discoveries in astronomy, physics, and other sciences.

An editorial eulogy for Van Anda at the time of his death in 1945 commented, "His signature is written large across *The Times* today."

ABIGAIL VAN BUREN
1918–

Abigail Van Buren, the pseudonym of Mrs. Morton Phillips, and universally known as "Dear Abby," was born in Sioux City, Iowa, the daughter of Russian immigrants, and the twin sister of another celebrated columnist, Ann Landers.

Van Buren started her "Dear Abby" column in the *San Francisco Chronicle* in 1956. Eventually, it was syndicated to more than five hundred newspapers by the McNaught Syndicate.

Van Buren has been described as a "jet-age sob sister," whose columns are filled with advice to the lovelorn, solutions for marital problems, and advice to teen-agers. Some three thousand letters a week are received and in certain instances Dear Abby sends personal replies. A staff of four secretaries are kept busy.

IRITA BRADFORD VAN DOREN
1891–1966

Irita Van Doren was born in Birmingham, Alabama, and graduated from Florida State University in 1908. As a doctoral candidate at Columbia University, she met and married Carl Van Doren.

In 1919, Van Doren joined the editorial staff of the *Nation* and became literary editor in 1923. The move that was to occupy her for the rest of her life occurred in 1924 when the *New York Herald Tribune* launched its *Book Review* as a Sunday supplement. In the beginning, she was assistant to the editor, Stuart Sherman, and after Sherman's death succeeded him as editor. A brilliant group of associates was assembled as contributors: Mark Van Doren, Joseph Wood Krutch, John Erskine, Stephen Vincent Benét, Carl Sandburg, John Gunther, and several English and French authors.

Under Van Doren's guidance for thirty-seven years the *Herald Tribune Book Review* was made "one of the liveliest, best balanced, best written, and most authoritative" of American literary publications.

ROBERT L. VANN
1879–1940

Robert Lee Vann was born near Ahoskie, North Carolina. He got his first contact with journalism while a student at Virginia Union University in Richmond. He contributed poetry and prose to the *University Journal.* In 1904 Vann won a scholarship to the University of Pittsburgh and began writing for the *Courant,* the university magazine. During his senior year he became editor-in-chief of the publication.

In 1907 a small newspaper called the *Courier* was started in Pittsburgh. Vann drew up papers of incorporation and was paid off in *Courier* stock. For the first few years, it was a question whether the paper would survive. In 1914 Ira F. Lewis was hired as sportswriter, shortly became business manager, and the *Courier* began to prosper. Vann's editorials stressed the cause of black improvement, better housing, better health care, educational reforms, and more jobs for blacks in business and industry. The *Courier* also urged a war on crime and better police protection in black communities.

In 1920 Vann launched a heavily illustrated monthly magazine, the *Competitor,* but it was too expensive for potential black readers and suspended publication after eighteen months.

Vann concentrated his efforts on building up the *Courier.* More national news was carried and stories were made more sensational. A number of talented writers were added to the staff. Feature articles on the Italian invasion of Ethiopia, the rise of heavyweight champion Joe Lewis, reports from the 1936 Olympics, and a column by W. E. B. Du Bois stimulated circulation. By 1937 the *Courier* was the leading black weekly in the nation, with a weekly circulation of 149,000.

In 1939 Vann formed the Interstate United Newspaper Company, the first black-owned newspaper advertising agency, a not very successful venture.

In 1960 the *Courier* was sold, after Vann's death, to the owner of the *Chicago Defender,* the *Courier*'s long-time rival.

HENRY VILLARD
1835–1900

Henry Villard was born in Germany and landed in New York in 1853, to begin a remarkable career as journalist, railway promoter, and financier. From New York he proceeded west to Cincinnati and Chicago, supporting himself along the way by peddling books, selling real estate, and editing a small town newspaper. In 1858 he reported the Lincoln–Douglas debates for the *New York Staats-Zeitung.* Hearing of the discovery of gold in the Pike's Peak area, Villard traveled across the plains and spent several months in the mining camps as a correspondent for the *Cincinnati Commercial.* For the same paper, he covered the Republican national convention in Chicago in 1860, and added the *Daily Missouri Democrat* of St. Louis and the *New York Tribune* to report on the ensuing campaign.

When the Civil War broke out, Villard became a war correspondent for the *New York Herald* and later for the *New York Tribune.* He was with the Army of the Potomac and gained fame covering Bull Run, the wilderness campaign, Missionary Ridge, Pittsburgh, Richmond, and other engagements. At the conclusion of the war, Villard served as a correspondent in Europe and the United States until 1868.

Villard's interest in journalism was revived in 1871, when he purchased the *New York Evening Post* and the weekly *Nation* and combined them. The *Nation* became the *Post*'s weekly supplement. Both were subsequently edited by his son Oswald Garrison Villard.

Villard was something of a business genius. He was president of the Oregon and California Railroad and the Oregon Steamship Company. In 1889 he headed the Edison General Electric Company, after giving financial aid to Thomas A. Edison. The corporation became the General Electric Company in 1893.

Villard was married in 1866 to Fanny Garrison, only daughter of William Lloyd Garrison, the famed abolitionist editor.

OSWALD GARRISON VILLARD
1872–1949

Oswald Garrison Villard was born in Wiesbaden, Germany, while his parents were on a European vacation. He was the son of Henry Villard and grandson of William Lloyd Garrison. Following his graduation from Harvard in 1896, he was a reporter for the *Philadelphia Press* (1896–97). After the death of his father in 1900, Villard became proprietor of both the *New York Evening Post* and the *Nation*. As editor of the *Post,* beginning in 1897, he crusaded for such liberal causes as free trade, women's suffrage, pacifism, and racial equality. He was a cofounder of the National Association for the Advancement of Colored People in 1910. His antiwar memo in World War I caused the *Post* to lose circulation and Villard was forced to sell the paper in 1918. The *Nation* became a leading liberal journal and Villard remained as its owner and editor until 1932. In 1907 he founded *Yachting Magazine.* The highlights of Villard's career are described in his autobiographical book, *Fighting Years; Memories of a Liberal Editor* (1939).

WILLIAM LIGHTFOOT VISSCHER
1842–1921

William L. Visscher, born in Owingsville, Kentucky, was introduced into the newspaper world in 1865 by serving as private secretary and amanuensis of George Dennison Prentice, editor of the *Louisville Daily Journal.* In the 1870s he went west and for the rest of his life was engaged in newspaper work. His first jobs were in Saint Joseph and Kansas City, Missouri. After that (until the 1890s), he was an editorial writer for the *San Francisco Daily Mail, Cheyenne Daily Sun, Denver Great West, Portland Morning Oregonian,* and *Tacoma Globe.* Beginning about 1895, Visscher lived in Chicago, where he became a special contributor to the *Herald* and other papers. He also wrote much verse for newspaper publication, plays, sketches, and novels, as well as lectured and acted.

ALEXANDER WALKER
1818–1893

Alexander Walker was born in Fredericksburg, Virginia. He opened a law office in New Orleans in 1840 and became one of the managers of the *Jeffersonian,* the chief Democratic organ of the state. During the Mexican

War he was associated with the *New Orleans Daily Delta.* From 1855 to 1857 he edited the *Cincinnati Enquirer,* then the leading Democratic paper in the west. After a short stay in Washington, D.C., in 1858 he returned to New Orleans and the *Daily Delta.* He edited the *New Orleans' Times* until it was suspended and then helped to establish the *Herald,* which was merged with the *Daily Picayune* in 1874. Walker edited the *Picayune* until 1875. He was no longer an editor after that date, but continued to be a frequent contributor to the daily press, especially on matters of local history and tradition.

MIKE WALLACE
1918–

Mike Wallace was born in Brookline, Massachusetts, and graduated from the University of Michigan in 1939. In 1940 he became a narrator, announcer, and actor on popular adventure stories. In 1941 he went on to Chicago to write and broadcast the news for the *Chicago Sun.* During World War II, Wallace was in the Navy. A series of television shows in Chicago and New York followed. In 1955 he began broadcasting the nightly news on WABD-TV. For a time Wallace headed the news staff of WNTA-TV, a local station serving New York and New Jersey, and then joined the independent Westinghouse Broadcasting Company in 1960 to do news, interviews, and variety shows. In 1963 CBS hired Wallace as a special correspondent and anchor for the "CBS Morning News." There were several overseas assignments, including a tour of Vietnam.

The program that was destined to establish Wallace's fame, "60 Minutes," began in September 1968, in collaboration with Don Hewitt, Harry Reasoner, and Morley Safer. The show was an immediate success and was scheduled for a full hour fifty-two weeks a year. Wallace is known for his unsurpassed skill as an interviewer.

ROBERT WALSH
1784–1859

Robert Walsh was born in Baltimore. As a youth he spent three years traveling and studying in France and England. After returning to America, he settled in Philadelphia and from 1809 to 1810 edited the *American Register.* In 1811 Walsh founded the first American quarterly, the *American Review of History and Politics,* which survived for only eight months.

Another short-lived journal, *American Register,* was founded in 1817 and lasted about a year. In 1820, Walsh and William Fry founded the *National Gazette and Literary Register.*

Barbara Walters
1931–

Barbara Walters was born in Boston. Her introduction to journalism came as an assistant to the publicity director of WRCA-TV, NBC's New York outlet. She soon was promoted to a position of producer and writer for WRIA-TV. Later she moved to WPIX-TV as women's program producer. With this background of experience, Walters was hired for the CBS Television network as a news and public affairs producer and writer. She joined the "Today Show" in 1961, and was a regular panel member (1963–74) and cohost (1974–76). In 1976, she became a newscaster on "ABC World News Tonight." One assignment while with the "Today Show" was to accompany Mrs. John F. Kennedy on a trip to India and Pakistan. Walters cohosted the ABC-TV news show "20/20" with Hugh Downs.

Ervin Wardman
1865–1923

Ervin Wardman was born in Salt Lake City, Utah, and graduated from Harvard in 1888. He joined the staff of the *New York Tribune* and was soon promoted to assistant city editor. In 1895 he left the *Tribune* to become managing editor of the *New York Press.* A year later he was made editor-in-chief and remained in that position until 1916. Under his editorship, the *Press* became an aggressive and influential organ of liberal Republicans.

In 1916, Frank A. Munsey bought the *New York Sun* and merged it with the *Press.* In another merger, Munsey bought the *Herald* in 1920 and combined it with the *Sun.* Wardman was named as publisher. He continued to contribute editorials to the paper, with particular attention to the field of labor economics.

Ben J. Wattenberg
1933–

Ben Wattenberg was born in New York City and graduated from Hobart College. He is author of such books as *The Real Majority, This*

USA, Against All Enemies, The Real America, and *The Good News Is the Bad News.* Earlier he had contributed articles to popular magazines like *Ladies' Home Journal* and the *Reporter.*

Wattenberg is generally seen as a spokesman for conservative viewpoints in politics and economics. Since 1977 he has been a senior fellow at the American Institute for Public Policy Research, a right-of-center think tank in Washington, D.C., and coeditor of its bimonthly magazine *Public Opinion.* Wattenberg is also a nationally syndicated newspaper columnist for United Features and a commentator for "Spectrum," a weekly show on the CBS Radio Network.

HENRY WATTERSON
1840–1921

For decades, Henry Watterson, a native of Washington, D.C., was the prime representative of Southern journalism. As the leader of the press for that section of the country he exerted unusual authority and influence and there was no one to challenge his preeminence. Watterson typified the opinion of the South in the minds of most Northern editors, for which reason his views were widely sought and quoted.

Watterson's journalistic and editorial career began before the Civil War and lasted until after World War I. Thirteen presidents occupied the White House during his active newspaper years and he knew all of them more or less intimately, from Lincoln to Harding. Only Lincoln won his wholehearted admiration. Most of the rest, Democrats and Republicans, he quarreled with, for a variety of reasons.

Watterson entered the newspaper field at age eighteen, in 1858, by way of a brief time spent as a reporter for the *New York Times,* after which he held a reportorial assignment with the *Daily States* of Washington.

Then came the outbreak of the Civil War. Although he was a strong Unionist opposed to secession, Watterson's sectional sympathies led him to become a secessionist and Confederate soldier. Apparently he saw little military action. Much of his time was spent working on a Southern propaganda newspaper in Nashville, Tennessee. After the fall of Nashville, he was appointed editor of a Chattanooga newspaper, which he named the *Rebel* and made the organ of the army.

With the war just over, Watterson held several short-term jobs: an editorial position with the *Cincinnati Evening Times* and appointments in Nashville. His great opportunity came in 1867, when he was offered two jobs in Louisville, Kentucky—editorships of the *Louisville Daily Journal* and the *Courier.* He joined the *Journal.* After six months, the two papers merged and the *Courier-Journal* came into existence.

Henry Garrison Villard, the great liberal editor, suggested that "probably Henry Watterson will be best remembered in the years to come by what he did to bring North and South together." Immediately after joining the *Courier-Journal,* Watterson began a campaign for the restoration of Southern home rule. He had always been opposed to slavery and he agitated for the complete bestowal of civil and legal rights upon blacks simultaneously with the end of Reconstruction rule. Even after emancipation, he realized that the nation could not exist half-slave and half-free.

Watterson backed the wrong horses in several presidential races. He supported Horace Greeley in 1872 and Governor Samuel J. Tilden of New York in 1876, both of whom came out on the losing end. Tilden was the ideal statesman in Watterson's view. Except for Lincoln, he was the editor's only public hero. During the Tilden–Hayes controversy growing out of the election, Watterson served in Congress for a short time and led the floor fight for Tilden. After the inauguration of Hayes, he never held public office or strongly supported any Democratic presidential nominee or president.

Ulysses S. Grant was an easy target for Watterson's diatribes. He was also highly critical of Grover Cleveland and bitterly opposed his third nomination. William Jennings Bryan he considered a menace to the nation. Theodore Roosevelt, said Watterson, was not merely dangerous, he was insane. Roosevelt, he wrote, was "as sweet a gentleman as ever scuttled a ship or cut a throat." Roosevelt's aim, he believed, was to run for office again and again until he became King Roosevelt. In 1909, Watterson bet the *New York World* a dinner that Roosevelt would quarrel with his chosen successor, Taft, and won the bet easily. In 1912, Watterson supported Champ Clark or Oscar Underwood for the Democratic nomination, but endorsed Woodrow Wilson in 1916. He rejected the idea of the League of Nations after the First World War and broke with Wilson over that issue. The nomination of Bryan as secretary of state in Wilson's cabinet had been deplored in 1913, and Watterson assailed him as an impractical dreamer when Bryan resigned over the war issue. He had been damning the Germans since the outbreak of the war in 1914.

The Haldeman family, which shared ownership of the *Courier-Journal* with Watterson, gave him complete editorial freedom, realizing that he was the paper's greatest asset and had won national fame for their newspaper. It was no longer purely local or sectional.

During Watterson's lifetime, he was temporary chairman of several national conventions and wrote the resolutions passed by four of them. He was in wide demand as a lecturer and public speaker.

In 1918, at age seventy-eight, Watterson transferred control of the *Courier-Journal* to Judge Robert Worth Bingham, retaining the title of editor emeritus for a short time. Two years earlier, he had written a two-volume autobiography, entitled *Marse Henry,* which one critic described as "rambling, discursive, without form." Watterson had the distinction of having been a top editor during a period when journalism was highly personal and when editorial opinions sometimes had quick and dynamic effect.

CHARLES HENRY WEBB
1834–1905

Charles Henry Webb, who wrote under the pseudonym "John Paul," was born in Rouses Point, New York. After a variety of occupations, including shipping aboard a whaler at age seventeen, he founded the *Californian* in 1864, in which early works by Mark Twain and Bret Harte were printed. Webb returned to New York in 1866 and the following year published Mark Twain's first book, *The Celebrated Jumping Frog of Calaveras County.* He is most famous for his *John Paul's Book* (1874), a collection of letters first written for the *New York Tribune.*

JAMES WATSON WEBB
1802–1884

James Watson Webb was born in Clarverack, New York. His youth was spent in military service. After resigning from the army, in 1827, he moved to New York and began a journalistic career, in the course of which he became one of the most influential editors of his time.

At the outset, Webb acquired a major share in the *Morning Courier,* a new mercantile daily, and became its editor and publisher in December 1827. Two years later he acquired the *New York Enquirer* and merged the two papers to form the *Morning Courier and New York Enquirer.* James Gordon Bennett and Henry Raymond were his assistants. Bennett went on to found the *New York Herald* and Raymond to establish the *New York Times.* Webb's chief rival was the *Journal of Commerce.* In the 1830s the competing papers sent schooners a hundred miles to sea in a race for news from abroad and used pony expresses to speed up news from Washington.

Webb was actively involved in politics, at first supporting Andrew Jackson and later was a chief voice for the Whigs. Controversies with rival editors brought on duels and affairs of honor with other journalists and prominent politicians. Webb sold the *Morning Courier and New York Enquirer* to the *World* in 1861. Later he had a distinguished career in the diplomatic service, as ambassador to Brazil for eight years.

NOAH WEBSTER
1758-1843

The American colonies' declaration of political independence from Great Britain was followed soon thereafter by a declaration of intellectual independence. The latter was proclaimed by a young Connecticut schoolteacher, Noah Webster. When the first of his efforts toward the creation of a separate American language appeared, the future great American lexicographer was a mere twenty-five years of age.

The versatility of Webster's career was on a par with Benjamin Franklin's. Beyond his prodigious labors on language, Webster wrote prolifically on political and economic matters, produced a two-volume *History of Epidemics,* edited two newspapers, and led the fight for national copyright legislation.

Webster's ambition, after being granted two degrees from Yale University, was to become a lawyer, but times were hard and money extremely scarce. Legal practice was found unremunerative. Public school teaching was the sole avenue immediately open to Webster for earning a living, and he turned to it. Thereby was saved one of the giants of American educational history.

Webster recognized the extreme inadequacies of the contemporary grammar schools, and he was dissatisfied with the textbooks and teaching methods currently in use. In particular, he objected to the use in the village schools of books that were saturated with English speech, spelling, and ideas.

Webster's dream of a national language for the United States began early. He recognized that as the new nation expanded over a vast territory and absorbed a people of diverse cultural elements, unity of language, both in written form and in speech, was essential. A uniform American language, Webster proclaimed, would make America "independent in literature as she is in politics."

As his own contribution to that end, Webster projected a tripartite work pompously entitled *A Grammatical Institute of the English Language, Comprising an Easy, Concise and Systematic Method of Education, Designed for the Use of English Schools in America. In Three Parts.* Part 1, the speller, was the first to be published, subsequently followed by a grammar in 1784, and *Lessons in Reading and Speaking* in 1785. About twenty years went by before Webster brought out his *Compendious Dictionary of the English Language,* and finally in 1828, his most monumental work, *The American Dictionary of the English Language.*

As he proceeded with his texts on spelling, grammar, and speaking, Webster had become increasingly aware of the need for an American dictionary. He was irked by the inclination of the English dictionaries to ignore the United States and the thousands of new words being added to the language. His exceptional qualifications for writing a new dictionary were well summarized by his chief biographer, Harry R. Warfel, who noted that Webster had literally universal interests and had written on a variety of subjects. In law, he had practiced in courts and served as judge and legislator; in medicine, he had studied the history of epidemic diseases and carried on scientific experiments; he was a student of economics and a theologian of some standing; and he was an experienced lecturer, schoolmaster, and editor.

In addition, Webster possessed an innate talent for defining words. He enjoyed research in the history of words, and he was a man of infinite patience, with a passion for perfection. In preparation for his monumental enterprise, by 1813 he had learned twenty languages, seven of which were Asiatic or dialects of the Assyrian. To these he later added Portuguese, Welsh, Gothic, and the early dialects of English and German. Extensive investigations into etymology, then practically a virgin field, were carried on by Webster as he studied and compared all languages in which dictionaries were available, attempting to trace the origins of the English word. Finally, to perfect the work and because of the inadequacies of American libraries, he spent a year in France and England, working in the Bibliothèque du Roi, Paris, and the Cambridge University Library.

The Americanization of the English language was accomplished by Webster in part by what he called "expunging the superfluous letter," such as the *u* in *honour, favour, labour,* and *colour,* and the *k* in *critick* and *musick.* He reversed the imitation French order of letters in words such as *theatre* and *centre.* American place-names and abbreviations replaced English lists, and there was a chronology of important American dates. Attacking the chaotic matter of syllabication, Webster established logical principles of dividing words to facilitate pronunciation and spelling — rules that are still in effect today. Standards of pronunciation were also developed, based upon "general custom," that is, current speech, especially prevailing New England modes. Footnotes sternly warned children against vulgar and colloquial pronunciations, examples of which were cited.

The disorganized, unsystematic, nonstandardized orthography of Webster's times is almost incredible — practices of which great statesmen were as guilty as the common people. Eighteenth-century Americans had few rules about how even ordinary words should be spelled.

The two-volume first edition of Webster's dictionary included 70,000 words — 12,000 more than were to be found in any previous dictionary. The work was based throughout on American usage in spelling and pronunciation, and it relied heavily upon prominent American authors and statesmen in citing authorities.

In historical perspective, certain aspects of Webster's contribution rank high in importance, while others have fallen by the wayside. Most significant, unquestionably is the vocabulary. Spelling reforms that Webster attempted to introduce have been accepted in part, while certain oversimplified and eccentric forms have been rejected. The same holds for pronunciation; some practices then current and recommended by Webster have changed with time. His definitions are generally excellent; furthermore, in range the *American Dictionary* far surpassed anything before its day. The weakest feature was the etymologies, for, in the light of later scholarship, many of his theories and concepts on the origins of words were proven to be invalid. Webster took particular pride in the moral and religious instruction offered by his books and their inculcation of patriotic sentiments in American youth.

In *The American Language,* H. L. Mencken claims that Americans speak more distinctly than Englishmen because their speech-ways were molded for four generations by Noah Webster's "Blue-backed Speller." "From 1783, when it was first published, until the beginning of the Twentieth Century," continues Mencken, "it was the most widely circulated book in the country, and the most influential."

Webster's leading biographer, Harry R. Warfel, concurs: "No other secular book has reached so many minds in America as *Webster's Spelling Book,* and none has played so shaping a part in our destiny.... He (Webster) became our greatest schoolmaster, not by pontificating from a chair in a great university; but by teaching simple fundamentals — in language, morals, economics, politics — to the masses." Because of Webster's teaching, Warfel concludes, a basic pattern of written and spoken English came to prevail in all the states of the Union, among millions of immigrants, as well as the population in general. The speller may justly rate as one of the great unifying forces in American culture.

Journalistically, Webster edited the daily *American Minerva,* founded in 1793. A publishing device was a weekly or semiweekly edition "for country readers," much of it reprinted from the daily *Minerva* and later from the *Commercial Advertiser,* a paper that lasted for more than a century.

THURLOW WEED
1797–1882

Thurlow Weed was born in Cairo, New York, and began learning the printer's trade at age twelve. After several years in various printers' shops in central New York he became foreman of the *Albany Register.* Several independent newspaper publishing ventures failed and Weed moved on to Rochester, where he found a position on the *Rochester Telegraph.* In 1825, he was able to buy the *Telegraph.*

Weed was active in the Anti-Masonic party and in 1826 gave up the *Telegraph* to publish the *Anti-Masonic Enquirer*. His paper, the *Albany Evening Journal,* founded in 1830 became a leading Whig organ and spokesman for the new party.

Secretary of State Seward sent Weed to England in 1861 as a special agent and in that role he successfully pleaded the American cause.

Tired and frustrated in his political ambitions, Weed gave up the *Evening Journal* in 1863 and moved to New York. He returned to journalism briefly in 1867 as editor of the *Commercial Advertiser*. Failing health forced his retirement from editorial work.

PHILIP HENRY WELCH
1849–1889

Philip Henry Welch was born in Angelica, New York. In 1882 he went to Rochester, New York, to write a column, "The Present Hour," in the *Post-Express*. From that point he devoted himself to journalistic humor. In 1883, Welch conducted a column entitled "Accidentally Overheard" in the *Philadelphia Call*. The following year, 1884, he joined the staff of the *New York Sun* and remained with that paper until the end of his life.

While preparing his weekly column for the *Sun,* Welch wrote humorous material for *Puck, Life, Judge, Epoch, Harper's Bazaar,* and other periodicals. A common occurrence, because of lack of copyright protection, was for Welch's jokes to be plagiarized by many different newspapers across the country.

WALTER WELLMAN
1858–1934

Walter Wellman was born in Mentor, Ohio, and achieved fame as a journalist, explorer, and aeronaut. At age fourteen he started a weekly newspaper at Sutton, Nebraska; at twenty-one he founded the *Cincinnati Post;* and from 1884 to 1911 he served as Washington correspondent of the *Chicago Herald* and its successor, the *Record-Herald*.

Wellman was a born explorer, first traveling to the Bahamas in 1891 to find what he claimed was Christopher Columbus's exact landing spot; journeying by boat and sledge in 1894 to a point northeast of Spitzbergen; and leading a similar expedition to Franz-Josef Land in 1898–99. Several unsuccessful attempts from 1906 to 1909 were made to reach the North Pole by air. Wellman's most ambitious undertaking, also a failure, was an attempt to cross the Atlantic by air in 1910. His airship, *America,* was in the air for seventy-two hours and traveled 1,008 miles setting a world record for the time.

IDA BELL WELLS-BARNETT
1862–1931

Ida Bell Wells-Barnett was born to slave parents; her mother was the child of a slave mother and an Indian father. She came from Holly Springs, Mississippi. In 1884 she moved to Memphis, Tennessee, and taught in a nearby rural school. When she wrote articles for some of the small black-owned newspapers critical of the inadequate schools available to black children, the Memphis school board did not renew her teaching contract.

Turning to journalism, Wells-Barnett bought an interest in the *Memphis Free Speech.* She used that forum to expose and denounce lynchings. In 1892, while she was on a visit to Philadelphia and New York, the offices of the paper were mobbed and destroyed. It was unsafe for her to return to Memphis.

Wells-Barnett served briefly as staff writer for the *New York Age.* In 1895 she married a black lawyer in Chicago who was founder and editor of the *Chicago Conservator.* She remained a militant opponent of lynching, founded the first black women's suffrage organization, worked with Jane Addams in a successful campaign to block separate schools for black children in Chicago, and was one of the founders of the Cook County League of Women's Clubs.

THOMPSON WESTCOTT
1820–1888

Thompson Westcott was born in Philadelphia. His interest in literature led him to write humorous stories for the *St. Louis Reveille,* the *New York Evening Mirror,* and the *Knickerbocker,* or *New York Monthly Magazine,* all under the pen name of "Joe Miller, Jr." From 1846 to 1851 Westcott was a law reporter for the *Philadelphia Public Ledger.* In 1848 he established and edited the *Sunday Dispatch.* In addition, from 1863 to 1869, he was an editorial writer for the *Philadelphia Inquirer.* During the period 1860–72 Westcott edited the *Old Franklin Almanac,* and the *Public Ledger Almanac* from 1870 until near his death in 1888.

ANDREW CARPENTER WHEELER
1835-1903

Andrew Carpenter Wheeler was born in New York City and entered journalism as a member of the *New York Times* staff. Traveling west, he became local editor of the *Milwaukee Sentinel,* a position that he held for three years. After returning to New York, Wheeler became drama critic for the *New York Leader,* next drama and music critic for the *World,* and finally for the *Sun.* His last contributions to a newspaper were a series of autobiographical letters sent to the *Evening Post.*

ELWYN BROOKS WHITE
1899-1985

E. B. White was born in Mount Vernon, New York, and graduated from Cornell in 1921. While at Cornell he was editor-in-chief of the *Cornell Daily Sun.* With a friend, White drove west and served for a year as a reporter for the *Seattle Times.* He then signed on as a newsboy on a ship making a trading voyage to the Aleutian Islands and the Arctic. After returning to New York, White worked for two years as a production assistant and copywriter in an advertising agency.

A major event in White's career was the appearance of the *New Yorker* magazine in 1925. He began to contribute sketches, poems, stories, and articles. In 1926, a founder and managing editor of the *New Yorker,* Harold Ross, invited White to join the magazine's staff. For twelve years White wrote the editorial essays in the *New Yorker's* "Notes and Comments" and contributed verse and other pieces. He became recognized as a supreme stylist and one of America's leading essayists.

In 1937, White moved to a farm from where he continued writing, including a column, "One Man's Meat," in *Harper's* (1938-43), and freelance pieces for the *New Yorker.* White was the author of a highly popular book for children, *Charlotte's Web* (1952).

HORACE WHITE
1834-1916

Horace White was born in Colebrook, New Hampshire, and entered journalism immediately after graduating from Beloit College. In 1854 he became city editor for the *Chicago Evening Journal.* The following year he was made Chicago editor of the New York Associated Press. After time out for political activities in Kansas, he returned to Chicago in 1857 where he was employed by the *Chicago Tribune*. One of White's assignments was to cover the Lincoln–Douglas debates, during which he formed friendships with Lincoln and Henry Villard, who was reporting for the *New York Staats-Zeitung*.

White was placed in charge of the *Tribune's* reporting staff and wrote editorials for the paper. When the Civil War began the *Tribune* appointed him its Washington correspondent. At the same time, he was clerk of the Senate committee on military affairs. With several other journalists, White formed a news agency to compete with the Associated Press to serve the *Tribune, Springfield Republican, Boston Advertiser, Cincinnati Commercial, Rochester Democrat,* and the *St. Louis Missouri Democrat.* At the end of the war, the syndicate was dissolved and White became editor-in-chief of the *Tribune.*

In 1874, White retired, at age forty, from the *Tribune,* partly because of the paper's financial problems and partly because of the destruction of its Chicago plant in the 1871 fire.

In 1881, White joined Henry Villard and Edwin L. Godkin in purchasing the *New York Evening Post* and the *Nation.* White took charge of the financial and economic policies of the two journals. When Godkin retired in 1899, White became editor-in-chief of the *Evening Post,* a position that he held until his retirement in 1903. As an editor, he once asserted that "a newspaper which merely inked over a certain amount of white paper each day might be a good collector of news, it might be successful as a business venture, but that it could leave no mark upon its time and could have no history."

RICHARD GRANT WHITE
1822–1885

Richard White was born in New York City and graduated from the University of the City of New York in 1839. He contributed musical criticisms to the *New York Courier and Enquirer,* of which he was coeditor in 1851–58, and became a member of the staff of the *New York World* when that paper was established in 1860. In 1853 he contributed anonymously to *Putnam's Magazine* some acute literary criticism. During the Civil War, White contributed to the *Spectator,* under the pseudonym of "A. Yankee," articles designed to influence English public opinion in favor of the North.

ROBERT MITCHELL WHITE II
1915–

Robert Mitchell White was born in Mexico, Missouri. His association with newspapers began before graduation from college. His grandfather owned and edited the Mexico *Evening Ledger,* established in 1855, until World War I, after which his father became editor and publisher. White served as school correspondent, sold advertisements, covered sports, and after traveling in Africa, South America, and Europe sent back reports for publication in the *Ledger.* In 1939 he joined the Kansas City bureau of the United Press. From 1940 to 1945, White saw active military service in World War II. During the period 1956–58, he was a consultant to Marshall Field, Jr., editor and publisher of the *Chicago Sun-Times.*

White's major opportunity came in 1959, when John Hay Whitney, its owner announced his appointment as president, editor, chief executive officer, and member of the board of directors of the *New York Herald Tribune.* The *Herald-Tribune* had many problems and Whitney was seeking a person to set the paper on the right course. White's chief competitors were the *New York Times* and the *New York Daily News.* Despite all White's reforms and valiant efforts, the *Herald-Tribune* ceased publication in 1966.

THEODORE H. WHITE
1915–1986

Theodore White was born in Boston and graduated from Harvard in 1938. On a round-the-world tour after college, he freelanced for the *Boston Globe* and the *Manchester Guardian.* He witnessed the bombing of Peking in 1939 and decided to become a war correspondent. For *Time* magazine he covered East Asia until 1945, and finally became chief of *Time's* China bureau. He filed many stories on the progress of the war up until the Japanese surrender.

White resigned from *Time* in 1946, and for six months in 1947 was a senior editor of the *New Republic.* For a time he contributed to the *Saturday Review of Literature, New York Times Magazine,* and *Harper's Magazine.* In 1948, White moved to Paris, where he reported for the Overseas News Agency and the *Reporter.*

White began gathering material for his celebrated book *The Making of the President 1960* in 1959 and published it in 1961. It was the beginning of a series covering the presidential campaigns of 1964, 1968, and 1972. As an end result, White came to be regarded as America's preeminent political journalist.

WILLIAM ALLEN WHITE
1868–1944

The editor and proprietor of a small Kansas newspaper for most of his life, William Allen White became nationally known for his editorials, for his advocacy of grass-roots political opinion, and for his progressive Republicanism. Although virtually a lifelong resident of Emporia, Kansas, he was prominent in national literary and journalistic circles and both the friend and advisor of several presidents. During his heyday, his editorials in the *Emporia Gazette* were widely quoted.

White was born on February 10, 1868, in Emporia. His parents were a country physician who also operated a pharmacy and a schoolmistress who had attended Knox College.

In the summer of 1885, White got a position on the staff of the *Eldorado Democrat* and thus joined the profession with which he would be associated for the rest of his life. He entered Kansas State University at Lawrence in 1886 and was a student sporadically there until 1890, but did not take a degree. The need for partial self-support, wide but sometimes irrelevant reading, and early successes in placing newspaper stories distracted his attention from scholarship. In 1891 White took a job with the *Kansas City Journal* and soon was allowed to write editorials. He temporarily was the newspaper's correspondent in Topeka but soon switched to the *Kansas City Star* in 1892 at a weekly salary of twenty-five dollars. During the three years that he remained there he became widely known to Kansas journalists and politicians as a specialist on his native state. On April 27, 1893, he married Sallie Lindsay and thus began a partnership that lasted many years. In 1895 he made a crucial professional decision. Having managed to borrow $3,000 from various sources, he bought a small newspaper, the *Emporia Gazette*. This was to be his forum for the next forty-nine years.

White's editorials enjoyed an amazing circulation, and two of them became journalism classics. One published August 15, 1896, was entitled "What's the Matter with Kansas?" beginning with a frank acknowledgment of Kansas's faults of limitations but concluding with the conviction that there was nothing fundamentally wrong with the commonwealth. The other, published May 17, 1921, was a personal tribute from a bereaved father to his only daughter, Mary, who died at the age of seventeen from an accident while riding horseback. But editorials and articles, even if widely copied in the press, never demanded all of White's time and energy.

He tried to write verse at an early age and published together with his friend Albert Bigelow Paine in 1893 a slight volume entitled *Rhymes by Two Friends.* He printed at least two tales which had been rejected by other editors in the *Gazette,* "Aqua Pura" and "The Court of Boyville," which eventually became part of a collection of Kansas stories published by the Chicago firm of Way & Williams in 1896 under the title *The Real Issue.* A later collection of stories called *In Our Town* appeared in 1906. By this time White had won the recognition of major Eastern magazines, and he contributed frequently to *Collier's, McClure's* and the *American Magazine.* George Horace Lorimer, the editor of the *Saturday Evening Post,* thought well enough of his work to pay him a thousand dollars a story. White also attempted longer fiction, and at least one novel, *A Certain Rich Man* (1909), won critical acclaim and some popularity. Set in a small Kansas town, it deals with a wealthy malefactor who after a series of palpable misdeeds sees the error of his ways but dies while striving to make amends. White's direct, journalistic style served him well at a time when realistic fiction was the national vogue.

White's later books reflected his interest in politics and topical events. He had become a close friend of Theodore Roosevelt, whom he followed in the progressive camp. Later he resumed his role of a fairly liberal Republican, although he was a steadfast supporter of national prohibition. His book *The Old Order Changeth* (1910), which dealt chiefly with trends in federal and state politics, gave him the opportunity to discuss leaders like Roosevelt, Bryan, and La Follette. *The Changing West* (1939) contained his observations on American society and politics just prior to his death. White also wrote *Puritan in Babylon: The Story of Calvin Coolidge* (1938), a well-received biography of the thirtieth president. White died in Emporia from inoperable cancer on January 29, 1944. Two of his more significant books were published posthumously. His *Autobiography,* which carried his story down to the mid-1920s, was published in 1946 and awarded a Pulitzer Prize. The next year saw the appearance of the *Selected Letters of William Allen White, 1899-1943,* edited by Walter Johnson.

White never held any elective office, but he was active in Republican politics for several decades. He was a friend of two Kansas governors, Henry Allen and Alfred Landon, and he met every American president from McKinley to Hoover. Various trips to New York and Washington familiarized him with literary and government circles, and he knew such writers as Lincoln Steffens, Ray Stannard Baker, and Edna Ferber. From 1903 to 1913 he served as a regent of Kansas State University and was a trustee of both the Rockefeller and Woodrow Wilson Foundations. In 1926 he was named a judge of the Book of the Month Club selection committee and retained that post for some time.

Essentially White was a small-town editor who lived happily in

Emporia, Kansas. Extraordinarily successful in expressing the views of the common man for national audiences, he combined clarity and vigor with an asperity of his own. To borrow the term used by a recent biography, White was a "maverick on Main Street."

CHARLES GOODRICH WHITING
1842–1922

Charles Goodrich was born in St. Albans, Vermont. At twenty-six he joined the staff of the *Springfield Republican,* edited by Samuel Bowles II. Except for a period of eighteen months, Whiting remained in Springfield for more than fifty years. For a short time he was assistant editor of the *Albany Evening Times,* and then was recalled to Springfield as head of the local department and from 1874 to 1910 as literary editor. In 1910 Whiting became associate editor of the *Republican* and continued in that position until his retirement in 1919.

WALT WHITMAN
1819–1892

The greatest and surely the most influential American poet, Walt Whitman supported himself for many years as a journalist and worked for a variety of newspapers. He began his career by writing news stories, editorials, and conventional verse. Although he wrote a good deal of prose, much of it collected and republished posthumously, he is essentially the author of one book of verse, the famous *Leaves of Grass,* originally a slim volume including only twelve poems and a preface, published in 1855 with the author's photograph but no name on the title page. In the next thirty-seven years he revised and steadily added to the book, retaining the original title but incorporating additional verse, much of which had been published separately. The first edition of *Leaves of Grass* attracted little attention, although Whitman himself reviewed it enthusiastically and Emerson wrote him a letter of praise about it. Whitman's fame grew slowly but by the time of his death the Good Gray Poet, as he became known, was widely recognized in the United States and had been favorably received by such writers as Symonds, Swinburne, and William Rossetti in England.

Whitman was born in West Hills, Long Island, on May 31, 1819, of English, Dutch and Welsh stock. His father was a carpenter and builder who inspired respect but little affection from his son; the boy's love was focused on his mother, a woman notable for her storytelling ability and for the comfort and support she habitually gave him. It has been argued that Whitman's failure to marry can be partially explained by his close relationship with his mother. Born into a large and rather impecunious family, Whitman had a limited formal education, which he supplemented by wide desultory reading throughout his life. In 1823 the family moved to Brooklyn, where the boy attended elementary school and in his free time roamed the community. At the age of twelve he was apprenticed to a printer and in 1831 and 1832 worked for two Long Island newspapers, the *Patriot* and the *Star*. But beginning in these years there were gaps in the Whitman story that biographers have not yet wholly resolved.

About the time that his mother became severely ill in 1833, the family moved back to the country. Whitman himself apparently lived briefly in New York City and probably worked as a compositor. But despite his lack of advanced education, he also taught in rural schools in Long Island between 1836 and 1841 and as Henry Seidel Canby pointed out got along without inflicting physical punishment and read poetry to his pupils rather than sermonizing. In 1839 Whitman wrote and published his own weekly newspaper, the *Long Islander,* in Huntington, Long Island, and when that collapsed taught school again and combined this employment with work for the *Long Island Democrat* in the town of Jamaica. Some of his early verse appeared here. For three years (1842–44), Whitman was associated with various New York periodicals, the *Aurora,* the *Tatler,* and the *Democrat.* He also contributed to such magazines as the *Democratic Review* and in 1842, he published his only novel, a temperance tract entitled *Franklin Evans: or, the Inebriate.* With this background at the age of twenty-four he was named editor of the *Brooklyn Eagle,* a liberal and influential newspaper that welcomed his support of the Free-Soil Democrats during the Mexican War. This position Whitman retained until January 1848, when he and his publisher no longer shared political views.

For about a year Whitman edited the *Freeman* in Brooklyn, again a Free-Soil journal, but gradually moved toward the new Republican party and contributed to the abolitionist *New York Tribune,* the *Evening Post,* and the *Brooklyn Advertiser.* Without a secure job in the early 1850s, Whitman helped his father with carpentry and building, lived at home, enjoyed musical and theatrical experiences in New York, and belonged to a Bohemian group of artists and writers who met regularly at Pfaff's Cellar on Bleecker Street. Later in the decade he returned to journalism, contributing articles to *Life Illustrated,* a weekly, and editing the *Brooklyn Times* (1857–59), but without expressing much concern about politics. After the initial edition of *Leaves of Grass* and especially after the second edition of 1856 with the famous salutation from Emerson's letter, "I greet you at the beginning of a great career," emblazoned on the cover without Emerson's permission, Whitman seemed free to pursue his great ambition, to write effective verse and to extend his magnum opus, *Leaves of Grass.*

THOMAS GREY WICKER
1926–

Tom Wicker was born in Hamlet, North Carolina, and graduated from the University of North Carolina in 1948. For eleven years of his journalistic career he was associated with North Carolina newspapers, the longest stretch of time with the *Winston-Salem Journal.* In 1960, Wicker became a staff member of the *New York Times* Washington bureau and from 1964 to 1968 served as chief of the bureau. In 1962 Wicker began a two-year tour of duty with the U.S. Naval Reserve and during the academic year 1957–58 attended Harvard University as a Nieman Fellow in journalism. In 1968, he was named associate editor for the *New York Times.*

JAMES RUSSELL WIGGINS
1903–

J. R. Wiggins was born in Luverne, Minnesota. After graduating from high school in 1922, he became a reporter for the *Rock County* (Minnesota) *Star,* and from 1925 to 1930 was publisher and editor of the *Star.* From 1930 to 1946 Wiggins was on the staff of the *St. Paul Dispatch-Pioneer Press:* editorial writer (1930–33), Washington correspondent (1933–38), and managing editor (1938–46).

After serving in World War II (1942–45), Wiggins became an assistant to the publisher of the *New York Times* (1946–47), and then was named managing editor of the *Washington Post.* Later he became editor and executive vice president of the *Post* after it had absorbed the *Washington Times Herald.*

GEORGE WILKES
1817–1885

George Wilkes was a native New Yorker. In 1857 he and an associate started the *National Police Gazette,* a robust, rowdy scandal sheet that was destroyed by gangsters on several occasions.

In 1853, Wilkes made his first trip to Europe. After his return he became associated with the sporting paper, *Spirit of the Times,* edited by William Trotter Porter. Wilkes bought the paper in 1856 and from 1859 to 1866 the publication was known as *Wilkes' Spirit of the Times.* The *Spirit* remained primarily a sporting paper, but Wilkes had a great interest in politics and the *Spirit's* political articles were influential.

Wilkes was present at the battle of Bull Run during the Civil War. He became war correspondent and reported the major engagements for his paper.

As a sportsman, Wilkes promoted prize fights and the Pari-Mutuel System of betting.

FRANC BANGS WILKIE
1832–1892

Franc Bangs Wilkie was born in West Charlton, New York. While a student at Union College he supported himself by writing and setting type for the *Schenectady Evening Star.* In 1856 he and a friend edited and published the *Daily Evening News* in Davenport, Iowa, a failed venture. In 1858 Wilkie was appointed city editor of the *Dubuque Daily Herald.* During the Civil War, he reported war news for the *Herald.* His reporting ability attracted the attention of Henry J. Raymond, editor of the *New York Times,* and he became the *Times's* chief war correspondent in the West until 1863, when Wilkes left the army.

In September 1863, Wilkes became assistant editor of the *Chicago Times* and remained with that paper for twenty-five years, chiefly as editorial writer. In 1877–78 and 1880–81, he was the *Times's* European correspondent.

Wilkie left the *Chicago Times* in 1888 and the next two years wrote for the *Chicago Globe* and *Chicago Herald.* Ill health forced his retirement in 1890.

ALLEN SINCLAIR WILL
1868–1934

Allen Sinclair Will was born in Antioch, Virginia. He entered newspaper work in 1888 as a reporter for the *Baltimore Morning Herald.* The following year he transferred to the *Baltimore Sun,* for which he was assistant editor (1893–96), telegraph editor (1896–1905), and city editor

(1905–12). Will left the *Sun* in 1912, after which he was associate editor and editorial writer of the *Baltimore News* (1912–14), and news editor of the *Philadelphia Public Ledger* (1914–16). From 1917 to 1924, Will wrote special articles for the *New York Times* and was assistant editor. He was recognized as an authority on American history and biography and wrote book reviews for the *Times* in that field. Starting in 1920, Will taught journalism at Columbia University and Rutgers University until his death in 1934.

GEORGE WILL
1941–

George Will was born in Champaign, Illinois, and educated at Union College, Oxford, and Princeton. His career included several years as a political science professor and a congressional aide to Senator Alcott of Colorado. Will began his *Washington Post* column on a regular basis in 1973 and it was soon appearing in several hundred newspapers. In 1976, he started a regular column in *Newsweek*. In 1972 he began to contribute articles to William F. Buckley's ultraconservative *National Review* and was Washington editor of the *Review* from 1973 to 1975. Will is a regular panelist on ABC's "This Week with David Brinkley."

Will has been described as "one of the youngest conservative columnists ever to gain national recognition," and has been lauded for the intellectual content of his writings. He won a Pulitzer Prize in 1977 for distinguished commentary. Will was awarded an honorary degree and delivered the commencement address at the University of Illinois in 1988.

TALCOTT WILLIAMS
1849–1928

Talcott Williams was born in Turkey, the son of a missionary. His brother Samuel was instrumental in establishing Roberts College in Constantinople, and the American College at Beirut. After graduating from Amherst College in 1873, Williams joined the staff of the *New York World,* where he progressed from Albany correspondent to assistant night editor to night editor. In 1877 Williams went on to Washington, where he served first as correspondent for the *World* and later for the *San Francisco Chronicle* and the *New York Sun.* He also became an editorial writer for the *Springfield Republican.*

In 1881, Williams left the *Republican* to write editorials for the

Philadelphia Press. He also wrote a weekly review of business conditions.

In 1910 Williams left the *Press* to organize and to become the first director of the Columbia University School of Journalism, from which he retired in 1919.

NATHANIEL PARKER WILLIS
1806–1867

Nathaniel Parker Willis, noted as journalist, poet, editor, and dramatist, was born in Portland, Maine. His first verses, written in his seventeenth year, appeared in his father's paper, the *Boston Recorder.* In 1829 he established the *American Monthly Magazine,* which lasted two and a half years. Going on to New York, Willis became associated with George Pope Morris, editor of the *New York Mirror.* He was sent abroad for five years, during which his observations were reported in a series of weekly letters aimed at American readers. He contributed articles to *Graham's, Godey's,* and other periodicals. He joined T. O. Porter in establishing the *Corsair,* a short-lived weekly (1839–42), devoted to copyright reform, and later formed a partnership with Edgar Morris in editing the *Evening Mirror.* In that position he and Edgar Allan Poe became lifelong friends. In 1846 he joined Morris again in the *National Press,* renamed the *Home Journal.*

EDMUND WILSON
1895–1972

Edmund Wilson was born in Red Bank, New Jersey, and graduated from Princeton in 1916. He worked as a reporter in New York City and served in the Army during World War I. In 1920–21 he was managing editor of *Vanity Fair.* In 1926, Wilson became book review editor of the *New Republic,* of which he was named associate editor in 1931. From 1944 to 1948 he was book reviewer for the *New Yorker.*

Wilson is most famous as a literary critic. He is the author of some thirty works of literary criticism, among which the most noted are *Axel's Castle,* a standard text on the analysis of the symbolist movement; *The Scrolls from the Dead Sea;* and *Patriotic Gore,* concerning American Civil War literature. His reviews helped to bring recognition to such authors as F. Scott Fitzgerald and Ernest Hemingway.

WALTER WINCHELL
1897–1972

Walter Winchell was born in New York City, the son of poor Russian Jewish immigrants. At age thirteen he became a vaudeville performer. He began to write for the *Vaudeville News* in 1920. In 1924 he joined the *New York Evening Graphic,* where he originated the gossip column. When the *Graphic* failed, Winchell went to the *New York Daily Mirror* in 1929. The Winchell column, "On Broadway," became nationally syndicated, and his exploitation of public interest in the private affairs of famous people was widely read and imitated, reaching an estimated 20 million readers and listeners through newspapers and radio and television programs. His style was a brash mixture of coined words, gossip, and tips on the stock market and it remained popular until near the end of his career. On radio, he used a breathless delivery, with what one critic described as "the staccato of a telegraph key between stories."

Eventually, Winchell's feuds with individuals, defamations of character, and accusations that he was more often wrong than right alienated his mass audience. His association with the *Mirror* ended in 1963.

GEORGE WISNER
1812–1849

George Wisner, called the first police reporter, was born in Springport, New York, and had a varied career in journalism. He began as an apprentice in printing the *Cayuga Patriot,* edited by Ulysses F. Doubleday, father of Abner Doubleday, generally regarded as founder of the game of baseball. A short time later, Wisner went to work for the *Republican Advocate* in Batavia, New York. In New York City he served as a compositor or typesetter on several newspapers, including the *Journal of Commerce.*

Wisner's most important opportunity came in 1833 when Benjamin Day started his famous penny paper, the *Sun.* Wisner joined the staff at once, bringing a new feature to the news, daily reports of police court cases of crimes and accidents. Most of his stories were concerned with drunkenness, assault, and petty theft, but they provided new insights into some sordid aspects of the community.

Because of personal differences, Wisner and Day separated in 1835. Wisner moved to Pontiac, Michigan, where he was editor for a year of a new Whig weekly, the *Pontiac Courier.* In 1848, Wisner and his family moved to Detroit, where he edited the *Detroit Daily Advertiser.*

Wisner died at age thirty-seven. His chief impact on journalism was a new approach to news reporting, covering police records and the everyday life of a large city, phases previously neglected by newspapers of the period.

THOMAS KENNERLY WOLFE, JR.
1931–

Tom Wolfe was born and grew up in Richmond, Virginia. He graduated from Washington and Lee University and received a Ph.D. in American studies from Yale University. In college he was sports editor of the campus newspaper and one of the founders of the literary quarterly *Shenandoah.*

After a short apprenticeship as a reporter for the *Springfield* (Massachusetts) *Union,* Wolfe joined the staff of the *Washington Post* in 1959, to report local and Latin American news. In 1962 he left the *Post* to become an artist-reporter for the *New York Herald-Tribune.* During a newspaper strike in 1963, Wolfe went to California to do an article for *Esquire* on new automobile styles. It was at that time, apparently, that Wolfe was inspired to adopt his unorthodox writing style. No longer bound by traditional journalistic form, he began to produce numerous impressionistic pieces for *Esquire, Harper's Bazaar,* and other magazines. Some of Wolfe's satiric pieces were brought together in book form in 1965 and in later works, with bizarre titles, the latest of which is *The Bonfire of the Vanities* (1987).

JUDY WOODRUFF
1946–

Judy Woodruff was born in Tulsa, Oklahoma, graduated from Duke University, and began her career toward becoming a nationally recognized broadcast journalist as a regional correspondent for NBC News, based in Atlanta. When Jimmy Carter became president in 1977, she was assigned to the network's White House press team. Woodruff remained at the White House for six years, covering the Carter and early years of the Reagan presidencies. In 1982 she was made Washington correspondent for NBC's "Today Show." As the daughter of an Army officer, she had moved from West Germany to Taiwan and other Army posts, and had learned to cope with a variety of situations.

Earlier, in 1975, Woodruff had joined the NBC Atlanta bureau as a general assignment reporter, traveling thousands of miles around the

Southeast covering "stories that ranged from statehouse politics to red-ant plagues." Among her top stories was covering Jimmy Carter in his campaign to win the presidential nomination in 1976. The most sensational story during her White House stay was the attempted assassination of President Reagan in 1981, which she witnessed.

In July 1983, Woodruff left NBC to become chief Washington correspondent of public television's "MacNeil/Lehrer News Hour," a national news and public affairs program. She is married to Albert R. Hunt, newspaper bureau chief with the *Wall Street Journal* in Washington, D.C.

Bob Woodward
1943–

Bob Woodward was born in Geneva, Illinois, and graduated from Yale in 1965. He had a four-year tour of duty in the U.S. Navy (1965–69). Afterward, the Navy assigned him to Washington for a year as a communications liaison officer between the Pentagon and the White House.

In 1970, Woodward applied for a job at the *Washington Post.* Rejected at first, he got a job as a cub reporter for the Montgomery County *Sentinel,* a Maryland weekly. In 1971 he was hired by the *Post.*

Nine months after starting with the *Post,* Woodward received the journalistic assignment of the century. He and Carl Bernstein, a fellow investigative reporter, covered the Watergate affair from the break-in of the Democratic National Committee's headquarters in 1972 to the resignation of President Nixon in 1974. The best-selling account of their coverage was *All the President's Men,* published in 1974 and winning a Pulitzer Prize for the *Washington Post. All the President's Men* was followed in 1976 with *The Final Days,* a detailed account of Richard Nixon's last months in office.

Samuel Woodworth
1784–1842

Samuel Woodworth was born in Scituate, Massachusetts. In 1880, in a desire to learn the printer's trade, he went to Boston and served an apprenticeship under Benjamin Russell until 1806. In 1805–6, he edited a juvenile paper called the *Fly* and in 1808 started a short-lived literary weekly, the *Belles-Lettres Repository* in New Haven. A miscellany of journalistic and literary activities followed: the *War* (1812–14); *Ladie's Literary Cabinet* (1819); *Woodworth's Literary Casket* (1821); editor of the *New York Mirror*

(1823); and the *Parthenon* (1827). Woodworth was an ardent Swedenborgian and from 1812 to 1824 published two Swedenborgian magazines.

In addition to his efforts as a magazine publisher, Woodworth had
literary ambitions and wrote poetry, plays and a novel.

ALEXANDER WOOLLCOTT
1887–1943

Alexander Woollcott was born in Phalanx, New Jersey. During a colorful career he became celebrated for his acid wit and chatty theater gossip.
While in high school in Philadelphia he wrote book reviews for the *Evening
Telegraph* and *Record*. As a student at Hamilton College, he edited the college literary magazine.

Woollcott was always fascinated by the stage. After repeated applica-
tions he was hired by the *New York Times,* but not as a theater critic. Instead, he was taken on as an obituary writer and court reporter. When the
Times critic married an actress and resigned, however, there was an opening for Woollcott. He wrote reviews as drama critic for the *Times* from 1914
to 1922, except for a period out for military service during World War I.
While in France he was a reporter for the AEF magazine, the *Stars and
Stripes.*

In 1922, Woolcott received an offer from the *New York Herald* to
become drama critic with a large increase in salary. That position lasted until 1925, when he moved to the *New York World* (1925–28). That was the
end of Woollcott's career as a drama critic.

Woollcott himself became the hero or the villain, depending upon the
point of view of a popular Broadway play, Kaufman and Hart's "The Man
Who Came to Dinner." He was the model of the major character and
played the role in the West Coast company for four months. He was also
the author or coauthor of several plays.

After sustaining heavy financial losses in the 1929 stock market crash,
Woollcott began his long connection with radio, becoming a national
celebrity for his "Town Crier" program. He reviewed books in another
radio show, "The Early Bookworm."

Woollcott was a member of the so-called Algonquin Club. Other
members were Heywood Broun, George S. Kaufman, Franklin P. Adams,
Dorothy Parker, Robert Sherwood, Harpo Marx, Robert Benchley,
Harold Ross, Ring Lardner, and Marc Connelly.

During his fifty-six years, Woollcott published fifteen books, wrote
thousands of theater reviews, was host for innumerable radio programs,
and wrote hundreds of magazine articles.

JOHN RUSSELL YOUNG
1840-1899

John Russell Young was born in Ireland and brought to America as an infant. He graduated from a New Orleans high school and then became a proofreader for a Philadelphia publisher and printer. In 1857, he was employed as a copyboy for the *Philadelphia Press,* and soon became a reporter for the *Press.* In 1861, Young was sent to the front as a war reporter. His account of the Battle of Bull Run made him famous, and led to his being made managing editor of two Philadelphia papers owned by John W. Forney.

In 1865, Young wrote articles for the *New York Tribune* and was invited by Horace Greeley to become a regular column writer. At age twenty-six, he was made managing editor of the *Tribune.* In 1872, Young accepted an editorial position on the *New York Herald* and spent several years in London and Paris. When former President Grant visited London on his tour around the world, Young was asked to accompany him. This was the beginning of Young's interest in the Far East, which led in 1882 to his appointment as minister to China by President McKinley. In 1885, Young resumed his editorial work on the *Herald.* In 1897, McKinley appointed him Librarian of Congress, an office that he filled until his death in 1899.

STARK YOUNG
1881-1963

Stark Young was born in Como, Mississippi, graduated from Columbia University, and taught English for twenty years. In 1921 he joined the editorial staffs of the *New Republic* and *Theatre Arts Monthly.* Later (1924-25), he served as drama critic for the *New York Times.* In these several posts, Young exerted a vital influence on the New York theater world.

During the period from 1926 to 1935, Young became prominent as a writer of historical fiction. One of the most popular of the Civil War novels was his *So Red the Rose* (1934). He was also identified with the Southern agrarian movement.

JOHN PETER ZENGER
1697-1746

John Peter Zenger was born in Germany and at age thirteen emigrated with his family to New York with a large company of Palatines. In 1711 he was indentured for a term of eight years to the pioneer printer William Bradford. Afterward he formed a brief partnership with Bradford.

The turning point in Zenger's life came in 1733 when a group of lawyers, merchants, and other opponents of the unpopular Governor William Cosby set up Zenger as editor of an antiadministration paper, the *New York Weekly Journal*. After the *Journal* published articles critical of acts by the governor, Zenger was arrested for libel and jailed when he was unable to meet the exorbitant bail. The *Journal* continued to be produced by Zenger's wife, who received instructions from her husband.

Zenger was brought to trial for criminal libel after ten months in prison. His defense was conducted by the eminent Philadelphia attorney Andrew Hamilton. Hamilton based his defense on the question of the truth or falsity of the libel. After brief deliberation, the jury brought in a verdict of not guilty, "to the acclaim of spectators and populace." It was the first major victory for the freedom of the press in the American colonies.

In reward for his services, Zenger was appointed public printer for the New York Colony in 1737 and to the same office in New Jersey the following year. After Zenger's death in 1746, the *Journal* was published by his widow until 1748, then taken over by his son John Zenger. It ceased publication in 1751.

SELECTED BIBLIOGRAPHY

Bailyn, Bernard, and John B. Hench, editors. *The Press and the Revolution.* Worcester, Mass.: American Antiquarian Society, 1980.

Bezanson, Randall P., Gilbert Chanberg, and John Solaski. *Libel Law and the Press.* New York: Free Press, 1987.

Blain, Gwenda. *Almost Golden: Jessica Savitch and the Selling of Television.* New York: Avon Books, 1989.

Boorstin, Daniel J. *The Americans: The Colonial Experience.* New York: Random House, 1958.

Brinkley, David. *Washington Goes to War.* New York: Alfred A. Knopf, 1988.

Brown, Charles H. *The Correspondents' War: Journalists in the Spanish American War.* New York: Scribner's, 1967.

Contemporary Authors: A Bio-bibliographical Guide to Current Authors and Their Works. Vol. 1- . Detroit: Gale, 1962- .

Crozier, Emmet. *Yankee Reporters, 1861–1865.* New York: Oxford University Press, 1956.

Current Biography. New York: H.W. Wilson, 1940- .

Dictionary of Literary Biography. Detroit: Gale, 1978- .

Donaldson, Sam. *Hold on, Mr. President.* New York: Random House, 1987.

Fang, Irving E. *Those Radio Commentators!* Ames: Iowa State University Press, 1977.

Fisher, Charles. *The Columnists.* New York: Howell Soskin, 1944.

Ford, Edwin H. *History of Journalism in the United States.* Minneapolis: Burgess Pub. Co., 1938.

James, Edward T., editor. *Notable American Women, 1607–1950.* 3 vols. Cambridge, Mass.: Belknap Press of Harvard University Press, 1971.

The Journalism Quarterly. Iowa City, 1924- .

Klever, Anita. *Women in Television.* Philadelphia: Westminster Press, 1975.

Kobre, Sidney. *The Development of the Colonial Newspaper.* Pittsburgh: Colonial Press, 1944.

Lee, Alfred M. *The Daily Newspaper in America: The Evolution of a Social Instrument.* New York: Macmillan, 1937.

Lee, James. *History of American Journalism,* rev. ed. Boston: Houghton Mifflin, 1923.

Lewis, Jerry D., editor. *The Great Columnists.* New York: Collier Books, 1965.

Mott, Frank L. *American Journalism,* 3rd ed. New York: Macmillan, 1962.

National Cyclopedia of American Biography. New York: White, 1892- .

Olasky, Marvin. *Central Ideas in the Development of American Journalism: A Narrative History.* Hillsdale, N.J.: Lawrence Erlbaum Associates, 1991.

Paneth, Donald. *The Encyclopedia of American Journalism.* New York: Facts on File, 1983.

Payne, George H. *History of Journalism in the United States.* New York: D. Appleton, 1920.

Regier, Cornelius C. *The Era of the Muckrakers.* Chapel Hill: University of North Carolina Press, 1932.

Rutland, Robert Allen. *The Newsmongers: Journalism in the Life of the Nation 1690–1972.* New York: Dial Press, 1973.

Sanders, Marlene, and Marcia Rock. *Waiting for Prime Time: The Women of Television News.* Urbana: University of Illinois Press, 1988.

Saturday Evening Post. *More Post Biographies.* Athens: University of Georgia Press, 1947.

Schmitt, Jo Ann. *Fighting Editors.* San Antonio: Naylor Co., 1958.

Schudson, Michael. *Discovering the News: A Social History of American Newspapers.* New York: Basic Books, 1978.

Sicherman, Barbara. *Notable American Women.* Cambridge, Mass.: Belknap Press of Harvard University Press, 1980.

Taft, William H. *Encyclopedia of Twentieth-Century Journalists.* New York: Garland, 1986.

Thomas, Isaiah. *History of Printing in America.* 2 vols. Worcester, Mass.: From the Press of Isaiah Thomas, Jun., 1810.

Wanniski, June, et al., editors. *MediaGuide.* Morristown, N.J.: Polyconomics, Inc., 1986– .

Washington Journalism Review. Washington, D.C., 1977– .

Weiner, Richard. *Syndicated Columnists,* 3rd ed. New York: Weiner, 1979.

Who Was Who in America. Chicago: Marquis, 1942– .

Who's Who in America. Chicago: Marquis, 1899– .

INDEX

Women's periodicals 50–51
Woodruff, Judy 11, 17, 184, 231, 370–371
Woodward, Robert 5, 44–45, 55, 371
Woodworth, Samuel 371–372
Woollcott, Alexander 372
Worcester Spy 37
Working Man's Advocate 15, 128, 129
World 94
World Federalists, United 94; World Association of 94
World Tomorrow 338
World War I 14–15, 110, 242, 333, 338
World War II 15, 63, 239, 244, 277, 312, 329

Y

Yankee A. *see* White, Richard Grant
"Yellow journalism" 63–64, 275
Young, John Russell 14, 284, 373
Young, Stark 373
Youth's Companion 265, 341

Z

Zenger, John Peter 2, 373–374